SAP Enable Now Development

Create high-quality training material and online help
using SAP Enable Now

Dirk Manuel

SAP Enable Now Development

Copyright © 2018 by Dirk Manuel

First published: December 2018
Release 1

Cover image © Gerry McGlamery 2018
`http://photography.mcglamery.com`

ISBN-13: 978-0-578-42638-9

About the Author

Dirk Manuel is a Senior Consultant at Stefanini. He specializes in change management for large-scale ERP systems, in particular training development and delivery activities. His job titles have included Technical Writer, Training Developer, Training Team Lead, Knowledge Management Consultant, and 'the UPK guy'.

Dirk is the author of three books on Oracle UPK, including the best-selling (in UPK circles) *Oracle UPK 12 Development*.

Dirk has a B.Sc. (Hons.) in Computer Science, and a City & Guilds in the Communication of Technical Information. He is a Fellow of the Institute of Scientific and Technical Communicators (ISTC).

Dirk can be contacted via LinkedIn:
`http://www.linkedin.com/in/dirkmanuel`

About the Reviewers

Joel Harris is a software services consultant from Toronto, Ontario, Canada specializing in the management of customer-facing education development and enablement services that drive organizational success stories. His professional specialties include learning and development, end-user training, software consulting, organizational readiness, and project management.

Vicki Hurt is a highly-skilled training instructor and developer, with extensive experience in integrating training products into an organization, and developing and implementing training standards and best practices. She is a certified Oracle UPK Administrator/Developer, and is also experienced in uPerform, Adobe Captivate, and Adobe Presenter.

Acknowledgments

I would like to thank the great team at SAP for the support they have given me in implementing Enable Now, and their speed and effectiveness in responding to my (sometimes self-inflicted) issues and many enhancement requests. In particular I would like to thank **Matthew Donovan** and **Jesse Bernal Jr.** for sharing their knowledge and expertise, and their patience in answering my many questions.

I would like to thank my long-standing client, Exxon Mobil, for taking me out of my UPK comfort zone and providing me with the opportunity to learn a new product. I'd also like to thank the many UPK developers I've worked with over the years, and for whom this book was really written.

Addenda

The SAP Enable Now product is being constantly developed and improved by SAP. There is a very good chance that additional functionality has been provided, or some of the existing functionality described in this book has changed, by the time you read this—especially in the cloud edition, for which quarterly updates are released.

■ Check for updates.

As the product changes, or new functionality is added, I will endeavor to provide updates on the Website, at http://EnableNowExpert.com/addenda.html. I will also post errata and corrigenda to the same place (and if you notice any typos, mis-statements, and so on, please let me know by e-mailing me at dirk@EnableNowExpert.com).

Additional support

- Website: EnableNowExpert.com
- Twitter: @EnableNowExpert
- YouTube: bit.ly/SENtube (case-sensitive)

Contents

Introduction

This book is an author's guide to SAP Enable Now (previously Workforce Performance Builder). It was written using Enable Now release 1811 (which was the latest release at the time of publication) as the guide system. Enable Now is a rapidly-evolving product, and it is highly likely that additional functionality has been added since the publication of this book, but the base functionality covered here is likely to remain the same. This book was written against the Cloud edition of Enable Now. Although there may be minor differences in the On Premises edition, specifically in how it is accessed and some client-server aspects, the same functionality is available in both editions.

This book covers all aspects of Enable Now's functionality, and—more importantly—explains how to get the most out of these features in order to build high-quality training content that will ensure the most effective knowledge transfer possible for your users.

This book is primarily aimed at new or intermediate Authors, focusing solely on the Producer component. It does not cover the installation or configuration of Enable Now. It also does not cover customization of Enable Now (which will likely be the subject of a separate book), but it does provide pointers to where this customization can be performed, to at least give Administrators a starting point. It includes tips on how to get the most out of Enable Now, suggested best practices for training material development with Enable Now, and advice on how to avoid some common mistakes.

What this book covers

This book provides a guided tour of SAP Enable Now. Each chapter focuses on a specific area of functionality within Enable Now, allowing you to focus on the components you currently use, and ignore those that you don't. Copious examples are used, for a number of common scenarios, so that you can immediately apply what you learn to your own work.

By chapter, this book contains the following information:

Chapter 1   **An Introduction to SAP Enable Now**
This chapter provides a high-level overview of what SAP Enable Now is, and describes the various deliverables that Enable Now can produce. You may want to read this chapter first, if you are new to Enable Now and want to learn about its capabilities before you start using it.

Chapter 2   **Navigating in Producer**
This chapter provides an introduction to the Producer component of Enable Now. It explains how to access Producer and synchronize your Workarea with the server. It explains the format of the Producer screen, the different views that are available, and how to filter views and search for content objects. It also explains the different types of objects that can be created within the Workarea, and the properties that can be maintained for these.

Chapter 2   **Recording a Simulation**
This chapter explains how to capture a recording using Producer. It explains how to record full-context-capture simulations, and also how to use 'quick recording' to generate simulations that can also be used to generate screencast videos. Finally, this chapter explains how to re-record simulations (for example, when the interface changes but not the steps).

Chapter 4   **Editing a Simulation**
This chapter is probably the most important chapter if you are developing training simulations. It explains how to take a recording and edit it to provide a full-featured, classroom-ready training simulation. It covers all of the key functionality of the *Project Editor*, through the use of several practical examples, and provides a wealth of hints and tips that should help novices and experts alike.

Chapter 5   **Workflow**
This chapter explains Enable Now's workflow capabilities. It describes the basic workflow concepts, and explains the (additional) steps that you need to perform when working with content objects to which a workflow process has been assigned. Using workflow is optional (you can use Enable Now perfectly well without workflow—you just lose some control), so you may choose to skip this entire chapter if you do not use workflow in your implementation.

Chapter 6   **Working with Instant Producer**

Instant Producer provides an easy way for SMEs and other occasional Enable Now users to capture recordings for use as simulations. There is nothing that you can do in Instant Producer that you cannot do in the 'full' Producer component, so you may want to skip this chapter if you are more than an 'occasional' user (which is likely the case if you have invested in this book). This chapter has been included simply in case you have SMEs capturing recordings for you, so that you can teach them how to use this functionality.

Chapter 7   **Publishing Your Content**

This chapter explains how to publish your training content so that it is accessible to your users. This includes publishing to a cloud *Trainer* or to a standalone website. This chapter also explains how to generate screencast videos and single-executable deliverables suitable for distribution (for example, for review).

Chapter 8   **Books and Book Pages**

This is another significant chapter. It explains how to use Books and Book Pages to create training presentations. It provides a comprehensive explanation of the functionality available in the *Book Page Editor*, including animation, and objects such as text, images, video, and links to other content. This chapter also covers how to use Book Pages in simulations and as index pages for content objects in the *Trainer*.

Chapter 9   **Creating Tests**

This chapter explains how you can use Enable Now to test your users. This includes using simulations in Test mode, and building quizzes. It explains all of the available Question types, providing examples of each of these. It also covers how to use Quiz Questions within a simulation project (for example, as a knowledge check).

Chapter 10   **The Desktop Assistant**

This chapter covers everything to do with the Desktop Assistant EPSS component of Enable Now. This includes recording Desktop Assistant content or converting simulation projects to Desktop Assistant Guided Tours or Context Help. It explains how to capture or edit context keys for content objects, and how to generate the Desktop Assistant itself. If you choose not to use the Desktop Assistant, you can skip this chapter.

Chapter 11   **The Web Assistant**

This chapter covers the Web Assistant EPSS component of Enable Now. This includes the types of content that can be provided via the Web Assistant, and how to create these. It also covers how to provide context-sensitive training content via the Learning Center, and how to adopt and edit SAP-provided training content. If you choose not to use the Web Assistant, you can skip this chapter.

Chapter 12   **Working with Documents**
This chapter covers all of the document output types that can be generated for simulation projects. It provides examples of all of these documents, and explains how to edit your simulation projects to generate them. It also covers all of the document macros you can add to simulations to support these document formats.

Chapter 13   **Additional Workarea Functions**
This chapter gathers together a few more 'advanced' topics, including how to import content and other files into your Workarea, and how to export training content from your Workarea—either to import into another Workarea, or as a backup. It also explains how to integrate simulations created using Instant Producer into your main Workarea structure.

Chapter 14   **Adding Audio to Your Content**
This chapter covers everything to do with using audio in your training content. This includes capturing audio during recording or editing, and how to use Enable Now's Text-to-Speech capabilities in simulations and Book Pages.

Chapter 15   **Localizing Your Content**
This chapter explains how to convert your recorded simulations into another language. This includes using local language texts, translating custom text, and replacing screenshots with localized versions.

Who this book is for

This book has been written with the following audiences in mind:

- New users of Enable Now, who want to understand the capabilities provided by Enable Now and learn how they can best utilize these to meet their training goals.

- Intermediate users of Enable Now who want to improve the quality of their training deliverables.

This book has not been written for installers and customizers of Enable Now (sorry!), simply because that would double the book's size, and the most pressing need is to get Authors up and running on Enable Now. However, I have endeavored to provide enough pointers via the 'advanced topics' side-notes to at least give Administrators a nudge in the right direction. If this book sells well, maybe a *SAP Enable Now Administration* book will follow.

Conventions used in this book

This book uses a number of typographic conventions to differentiate between different types of information, and uses specific terms to mean certain things. These are described below:

Formatting conventions

Certain typographic conventions are used to identify specific types of information in this book. The table below outlines these and provides examples of each.

Convention	Example
Words that you see on the Enable Now screen, in menus or dialog boxes for example, appear in bold navy. This includes all button names, field names, menu options, and property names.	Click on the **Start Recording** button.
Screen names (including dialog boxes, panes, sections, and tabbed pages) are shown in navy italics.	The *New Project* dialog box is displayed.
Macro names are shown in small caps	Use an EXPLANATION macro to provide additional information.
Values or options are shown in bold.	Here, you can choose from **Always**, **Never**, and **Ask**.

Additional information appears in the outer margins of the page. The following icons are used to differentiate between the various types of information provided:

● Additional information

■ Tips and Tricks

▲ Warnings

✚ Version difference

★ 'Advanced' knowledge or functionality for Administrators or Enable Now Power Users

● This is how a side-note appears.

Specific terminology

Enable Now-specific entities are identified by initial caps, to differentiate them from more general nouns. Examples are Book, Book Page, Highlight, and so on.

"The Database" is the database in which Enable Now content is stored. "The Workarea" is a view of the Database that shows (a portion of) the content of the Library, organized in folders.

The term "author" refers to a training developer (in Enable Now terms this may be an Author or a Master Author). The term "user" refers to the people who will use the training content that the author develops (sometimes referred to in Enable Now as a Consumer).

Piracy

Please don't make illegal copies of this book. The author is an independent consultant, not a faceless corporation (not that *that* would make it any less wrong…). What little I make from this book (and I have endeavored to keep the price low) is unlikely to even cover the cost of the hardware and software I have had to buy just so that I could write this book. If you *have* obtained an illegal copy of this book, you can offset some of your guilt by making a PayPal donation to **donations@technicalauthoring.com**.

1

An Introduction to SAP Enable Now

In this first chapter, we will take a quick look at what SAP Enable Now is, including a first look at the various deliverables that you can produce using SAP Enable Now.

In this chapter, you will learn:

- What deliverables Enable Now can provide
- What components are available in Enable Now—for both development and delivery of training content
- What you need to consider before starting your development

What is SAP Enable Now?

Very broadly, SAP Enable Now is a software application that facilitates the creation and delivery of training material and in-application help. The delivery of these two things is markedly different, but their development is, for the most part, very similar. However, the lines between the two are blurred somewhat in that training material can also be provided as in-application help. To understand this better, it is useful to look at the broad categories of deliverables that can be provided by Enable Now (we'll look at the individual deliverables a little later in this chapter).

The cornerstone of Enable Now is the **simulation**. A simulation is effectively a 'recording' of a task being performed in a software application. Users can then 'play back' this simulation—in a number of different modes, which we'll look into later—to learn how to perform the recorded task themselves.

Enable Now can also provide printable **documentation**. A document is generated directly from a recorded simulation and therefore describes how to perform the single specific task recorded in that simulation. A number of different formats of document can be generated in Enable Now, but they are all variations on the same information captured in the simulation on which the document is based.

Because simulations alone are rarely sufficient to provide comprehensive training, Enable Now also allows for the creation of training presentations, in the form of **Books and Book Pages**. Book Pages are conceptually similar to Microsoft PowerPoint slides, and a single Book Page provides a 'screenful' of information. Books are used to group multiple Book Pages together, and are therefore conceptually similar to PowerPoint presentations—although as we shall see in *Chapter 8, Books and Book Pages*, the functionality provided by Enable Now is significantly more advanced than that provided by PowerPoint.

For in-application help, Enable Now provides two options: the **Desktop Assistant**, which provides context-specific help on how to use a Windows application, and **Web Assistant**, which is designed for use with browser-based applications, and in particular SAP's own browser-based Fiori interface. Both of these overlay the help content directly onto the actual application screen.

● Strictly speaking, this is the **Fiori UX** (User Experience), and refers to a consistent set of design principles that provide a common interface.

These various components are best understood by way of example, so let's look at examples of each of the individual delivery options that Enable Now provides.

Enable Now Deliverables

Enable Now allows you to create and deliver several different types of training content and in-application help. Several of these are generated from the same source material, and many of them can be delivered in multiple ways.

In this section, we will look at the various deliverables and delivery formats, so that you can decide which ones you want to use. Don't worry if you don't understand all of the terminology used; that's what the rest of the book is for. This section is just to show you *what* you can deliver; *how* to do this is covered later.

Simulations

Traditionally, the most commonly-used deliverable of Enable Now is the **simulation**. A simulation is effectively a recording of an activity—typically a self-contained business task—being performed in a software application. (As we shall see later in this book, this is a gross over-simplification, but it is an adequate explanation for our current purposes.) Simulations are captured in the application for which the training content is being developed. This means that the simulations have the 'look and feel' of the actual system. When these simulations are executed, the user gets the impression that they are interacting with a real system whereas, in reality, they are working within the safe confines of a training tool—in this case, Enable Now.

Any given simulation can be 'played' in a variety of different *modes*. The modes that can be provided for a simulation are explained in the sub-sections below, although you (the author) can choose which modes to make available for an individual simulation. All modes are generated from the same, single recording, although you will need to edit the recording separately for Demo mode, Practice mode, and Test mode.

Simulations can be made available via the *Trainer*, or launched directly from a presentation or other location via a simulation/mode-specific URL. Simulations may also be made available via the Desktop Assistant, or via the Web Assistant (through the Learning Center).

Demo mode

Demo mode provides a 'hands-off' demonstration of the (recorded) task being performed. To the user, it looks as though they are watching a video of the task being executed in the application, and they will see the cursor being moved around the application screen, and text being entered into fields, without the user having to do anything. Informational bubbles may be displayed on top of the screen, to explain what is being done, or to provide additional information. If audio has been recorded for the simulation, then the user will also hear this.

A partial example of a Demo mode screen is shown below (note that this has been captured as a 'window' and not full-screen, to provide a larger example).

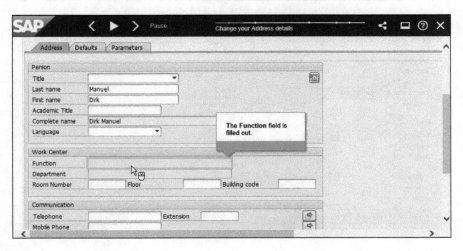

Things to note in this example:

- An information bubble is shown, explaining what is happening.
- A blue 'highlight' is shown around the object on the screen to which the bubble refers.
- A small 'mouse' icon is shown to the lower-right of the cursor. This indicates which mouse button is clicked (and how many times), during playback.
- There is a 'toolbar' displayed across the top of the screen (this is not part of the application screen), which includes navigation buttons and a progress bar.

Practice mode

Practice mode provides an interactive exercise so that users can carry out the task themselves. To the user it looks as though they are performing the task in the actual system, but they are really just interacting with Enable Now. Bubbles are displayed on the screen telling the user what they need to do, and the user needs to perform this exact action in order to progress to the next step. The down-side of this is that the user can only perform the actions that were captured in the original recording (there is no scope for 'poking around' or 'discovery') but often this is exactly what you want your training material to do—just teach them the correct way to perform a specific task.

A partial example of a simulation being played in Practice mode is shown below. You can compare this against the example for Demo mode, which is for the same step.

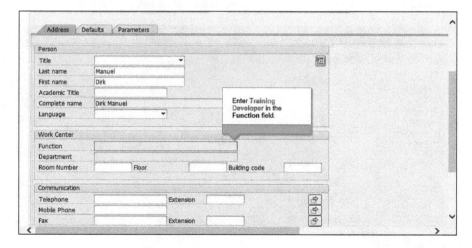

Things to note in this example:

- A bubble is displayed telling the user what they need to do. Note that the text is different to the text provided in Demo mode—this is an important point.
- There is (by default) no 'highlight' around the current screen object.
- There is no 'toolbar'.

Test mode

Test mode, as the name suggests, is designed to test the user on their ability to perform the recorded task in the application. It is very similar to Practice mode (in that the user has to perform the actions), but with much less in the way of instructions. No action-level bubbles are displayed, but instead a single set of instructions providing (by default) only the string input values to use is displayed throughout the test.

A partial example of a simulation being played in Test mode is shown below.

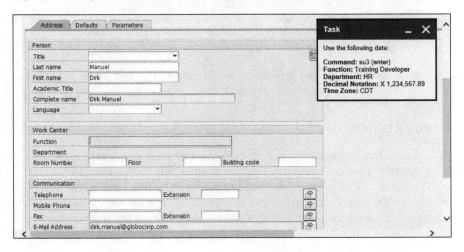

Things to note in this example:

- The only instructions available to the user are those provided in the text box in the upper-right corner of the screen.

Concurrent mode

Concurrent mode is designed to show the user how to do something as they are performing the same thing in the actual application at the same time (*concurrently*) as they are reviewing this content. For this reason, it is often made available in the Desktop Assistant. Playback appears almost identically to Demo mode, but the user has to manually advance each step. The playback window is 'always on top' of all other application windows, so the user can always see it while they are working in the application. It is movable and re-sizable, in case it is obscuring content on the actual application screen.

A partial example of a simulation being played back in Concurrent mode is shown below.

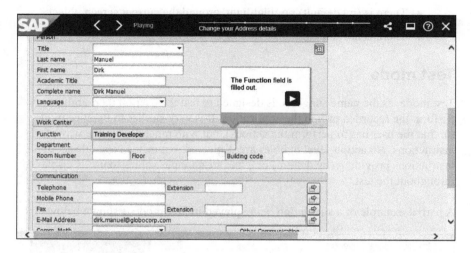

Things to note in this example:

- A 'continue' button is included in the bubble. The user needs to click on this button to progress to the next step.

Presentation mode

Presentation mode is designed to be used for simple classroom demonstrations. Each screen is shown without any bubbles or other help (so exactly as it appears in the system), and actions are performed automatically (the same as for Demo mode), but the user (or instructor) has to press the *ENTER* key on the keyboard to advance from one step to the next. For mouse-click actions, the user has to press *ENTER* once to show the cursor moving to the correct position, and then a second time to show the actual 'click' action.

Presentation mode can be thought of as 'Demo mode without bubbles'.

Free Presentation mode

Free Presentation mode is very similar to Presentation mode in that each application screen is shown without any bubbles or other help. However, the user (or instructor) is required to perform all actions themselves to progress through the simulation.

Free Presentation mode can be thought of as 'Practice mode without bubbles'.

Documents

'Printable' documents can be provided for individual simulations. Several different document formats can be generated, all from the same simulation recording, and can generally be generated in Microsoft Word. HTML, and/or PDF format. The PowerPoint document can (unsurprisingly) only be generated in PowerPoint format.

The following document types can be generated and provided to your users:

- *Audit and Compliance Document*: This document type includes all screenshots and texts, as well as additional information typically required to ensure compliance with various requirements (such as a full revision history).

- *BPP Document*: This document type includes all screenshots and texts, along with space to record additional information (Value and Description) for each action.

- *Hands-on Guide*: This document type provides a compressed format, with instructions and screenshots presented alongside each other in a two-column table, and with minimal use of headers.

- *HPQC Guide*: This document type is specifically designed to be used with HP Quality Center.

- *Job Help*: This is a concise document that includes only the step instructions, with no screenshots.

- *PowerPoint Document*: This generates PowerPoint presentation that contains one slide for each step, which shows the step instructions and a cropped screenshot.

- *Process Guide*: With this document type, details are provided in a three-column table, with columns for What to do (the instructions), What to see (the screenshots), and What to say (the contents of any Explanation bubbles entered into the simulation).

- *Standard Document*: This is the 'main' (and default) document type, and includes the most complete set of information, including instructions and screenshots, and screen call-outs identifying the exact screen object to which the action applies.

- *Test Sheet*: This document type is designed to be used for recording the results of manual tests of the application (for example, for regression testing). For each action, space is provided to record Input, Expected Results, and whether the test Passed or Failed.

- *Training Document*: This document type is designed to be used as a companion to (classroom) training—for example, as a handout. It includes all of the texts and screenshots in an easy-to-follow format.

- *Work Document*: This document type is possibly the longest of the document types, and includes a table of contents and a 'process flowchart', along with all screenshots and texts.

You would typically not want to provide *all* of these document types. Most of the time, you would choose one format to make available to users via the *Trainer*, and generate other types as required, for special purposes (for example, testing, classroom training, and so on).

In addition to these single-simulation documents, Enable Now also allows you to create a *Master Document*, which consolidates multiple simulations, and a *Compound Document*, which can include simulations, Book Pages, Quizzes, and additional content. These are more 'specialized' documents that would typically not be made available via the *Trainer*.

Examples of all of these documents are provided in *Chapter 8, Books and Book Pages*.

Books and Book Pages

Books and Book Pages are used to create training content other than simulations. Conceptually, they can be thought of as the equivalent of PowerPoint presentations and slides—although that comparison does an injustice to Book Pages.

Most of the time, you will organize your Book Pages into Books, although this is not strictly necessary—Book Pages can be used independently of Books, and can also be inserted into simulations, or used as the index page of a simulation in the *Trainer*. Books are displayed in the *Book Reader*, and can be launched either directly via their 'Start URL' or via the *Trainer*.

An example of a typical Book, as it appears in the *Book Reader*, is shown below.

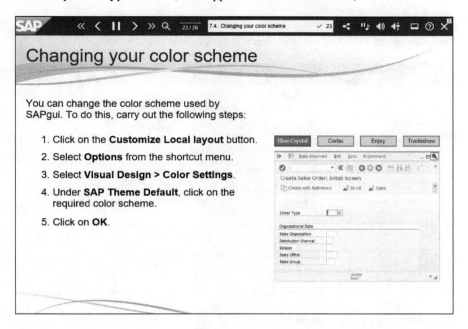

Things to note in this example:

- A single Book Page is displayed.

- The Book 'table of contents' is represented by a drop-down list (of Book Pages within the book) in the center of the toolbar.

- This particular Book Page includes audio (audio controls are shown on the right side of the toolbar).

- A small "2" is shown above the **Close** button on the far right of the toolbar. This indicates that this (Book) is the *second* object opened in this browser window. Closing the Book will return the user to the previous object—which is the object from which the Book was opened, and in this case is the *Trainer*.

The Trainer

The *Trainer* is effectively a website that provides access to all of your training content (or at least all of the training objects that you choose to include in the *Trainer*). This is typically all of your simulation projects and your Books and Book Pages. The *Trainer* may be located in the cloud or on a local server, and is accessed via a standard Internet browser.

The *Trainer* uses the same hierarchical structure as your Workarea to organize your content. You can include a Glossary in your *Trainer*, and users can save content to their 'favorites' (within the *Trainer*). Users can also share (links to) content with other users.

An example of a typical *Trainer* screen is shown below:

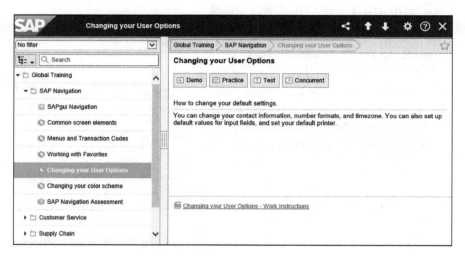

Things to note in this example:

- The outline structure on the left provides examples of (from top) organizational Groups, a Book, simulation projects, and a Quiz.
- For the selected object, buttons are shown for the available play modes.
- A document is listed at the bottom of the simulation details, on the right.
- 'Breadcrumbs' (the path to the current object) are shown above the object details.

In-application Help

● You can also provide simplified help via the use of a **Context Help** file, but this is more of a fall-back option, if you cannot use either of the two primary methods.

Enable Now provides two primary options for providing in-application help—otherwise known as an EPSS (Electronic Performance Support System). These are the Desktop Assistant and the Web Assistant, which are explained separately, below.

Help via the Desktop Assistant

The Desktop Assistant is the Electronic Performance Support System (EPSS) that provides in-application, context-sensitive help for Windows applications. This help can be either Guided Tours, which explain how to perform a specific task in the application, or Context Help, which provides help on a specific screen object.

The Desktop Assistant consists of a *Sidebar*, which indicates whether help is available and provides access to some other functions, a *Content Pane*, which lists the available content, and the help content itself, which is typically displayed via bubbles overlaid on the actual application screen.

An example of these three components is shown below. Note that this would not normally be the case—as soon as help content is displayed, the *Sidebar* and *Content Pane* are hidden; they have all been included in this example just for the sake of illustration.

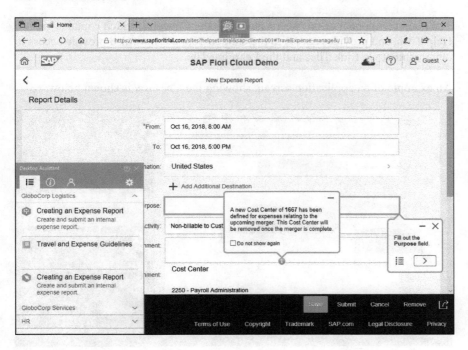

Things to note in this example:

- The *Sidebar* is shown at the top of the screen, in the center. The light bulb icon on the left is 'lit up', meaning that content is available for the current context.

- The *Content Pane* is shown along the leftmost edge of the application screen. This lists content available for the current context. For this example, this includes (from top to bottom) a Guided Tour, a Book Page, and a simulation in Concurrent mode.

- A Guided Tour Step bubble is shown. This is the bubble on the right, which points to the highlighted field.

- A Context Help bubble is also displayed. This is the leftmost bubble of the two, and is displayed when the user clicks on the icon to which it is currently pointing.

Help via the Web Assistant

The Web Assistant is the Electronic Performance Support System (EPSS) that provides in-application, context-sensitive help for browser-based applications. As with the Desktop Assistant, this can include Guided Tours, which provide step-by-step instructions on how to complete a task in the application. It can also include Context Help in the form of Tiles.

The main component of the Web Assistant is the *Carousel*, which contains the Help Tiles, and provides access to the Guided Tours. It may also provide access to other content via Link Tiles and the Learning Tile.

An example of an application screen, showing the *Carousel* is shown below.

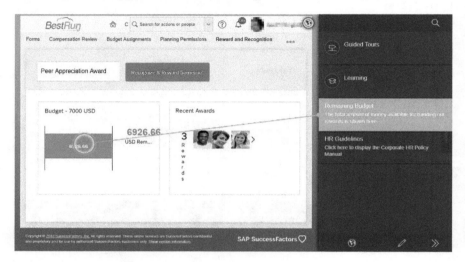

Things to note in this example:

- The *Carousel* is shown on the rightmost side of the screen,
- The *Carousel* provides (from top to bottom) access to Guided Tours, the Learning tile (which provides access to the Learning Library), a Context Help Tile along with a 'tether' pointing to the object to which it relates, and a Link Tile (which has no tether, but displays a pop-up bubble if clicked).
- A 'hotspot' is shown over the screen object to which the selected Help Tile applies. This is the circle at the end of the tether.

Cross-delivery of training content

Now that you have better understanding of the distinct deliverables offered by Enable Now, throw away any preconceptions you may have just formed about their independence or compartmentalization—because the lines between them are blurred. For example, you can link (full) simulations into your Desktop Assistant, or insert a Book Page into the middle of a simulation. You can even insert a Book into a Web Assistant Help Tile, then provide a link on a Book Page within that Book to launch a simulation, and include a further Book Page within that simulation that then directs the user to yet another simulation—but only if the simulation is played in a certain mode! Confused? Don't worry; this book is here to help you make sense of it all. Read on!

Deciding how you will use Enable Now

Although you *can* provide all of the deliverables outlined in the previous section, this does not necessarily mean that you *should*. In fact, providing *all* of them would likely be confusing to your users, and possibly disastrous to your overall knowledge transfer objectives. Instead, you will likely choose a specific subset of these deliverables, depending on your individual requirements.

Knowledge transfer is often provided in three principal ways: through classroom training, through self-study, and through in-application help. Enable Now can help in each of these, as we'll see in the following sections.

Instructor-led training

Traditionally, the vast majority of instructor-led training—whether this is in the classroom or through remote learning—has involved an instructor presenting some form of slide show (more often than not, via the ubiquitous PowerPoint, with it's much derided bullet-points). For training on software applications, the training also usually includes demonstrations and/or practice exercises.

Enable Now has extremely robust presentation capabilities through Books and Book Pages. Anything that you can do in PowerPoint you can do using Book Pages—and certainly, creating a 'page-flipper' that can be used in the classroom is easily done in Enable Now.

If your classroom session includes demonstrations, then you can use simulations in either Presentation mode or Free Presentation mode for this. Because neither of these modes provides anything in the way of visual cues on the screen, you will likely want to provide the instructor with one of the document formats— perhaps the Training Guide, or the Hands-on Guide, to guide them through the steps. The limitation of using a recording for a demonstration is that the instructor can only demonstrate what was captured in the recording—and can't branch off and show other things in response to questions. But the advantage of this is that the demonstration will work every time—there is no trying to find suitable data, or discovering that some setting has changed since you last demonstrated this functionality.

This brings us to classroom exercises. This is where the use of simulations really comes into its own. Historically, training exercises have been provided by allowing trainees into a 'live system'—whether this was a dedicated training client, a development or test system, or even the actual production system. This approach is fraught with potential problems, such as the need to set up data (unique to each trainee, and refreshed for each classroom conduct), trainee Userid access and authorization, system status uncertainty or instability, and so on.

Using a simulation in Practice mode solves these problems because the simulation is external to the application; once the simulation has been created, access to the application is no longer required. Trainees do not need to log onto the system, and it does not matter if the developers change anything in the meantime—or even remove the system from availability. Furthermore, any information that the trainee requires (such as data values) is built directly into the simulation, so there is no need for separate data sheets.

More importantly, every trainee can carry out the same simulation, at the same time, using the same data, and see the same result, which makes things much easier—and predictable—for the instructor. As with the use of simulations for demonstrations, the trainees can only see and do what was captured in the recording, but here this is a definite advantage—trainees can't take a wrong menu turn and get lost, or do something they shouldn't be doing in the system and possibly adversely impact something else; they can only do exactly what they *should* be doing.

Furthermore, a trainee can carry out a single simulation multiple times and see exactly the same result every time. This is important, as it means that the trainee can return to a simulation after the course conduct and see exactly what they saw during training, as a refresher.

A further advantage of using simulations instead of a training client is that training clients often have a finite life-span. They are usually made available for pre-implementation training as part of a project, and are taken away once training is complete, or at the end of the project. Simulations, by contrast, are potentially *always* available—for the life of the system—via the *Trainer*. This means that people who move into the position after the initial implementation will still be able to carry out the same exercises as the original trainees.

Self-Paced Learning

Self-Paced Learning is where users carry out (typically) Computer-Based Training (CBT) packages at a time and location that suits them, rather than having to be scheduled into a classroom conduct. You may find that you can provide training just as effectively via a well-crafted, robust CBT as you can via classroom training—and at a significant saving.

The same Enable Now capabilities that are used for instructor-led training can also be used for self-paced learning. Book Pages can easily provide the presentation component, and simulations in either Demo mode or (preferably) Practice mode can be launched directly from these Book Pages, providing a 'learning experience' comparable to full classroom training.

By making the training material available in the *Trainer*, or loading it into a Learning Management System, users can take training at a time that suits them best—and typically around their regular work. This also removes the burden on trainers and other logistical resources (such as classrooms, and potentially travel to and from these), providing further savings for the company.

However, it is important to understand that it is unlikely you can just re-purpose instructor-led training material for use in self-paced learning—or that you can follow a similar development model. In a classroom environment, the instructor is there to explain an exercise, point out interesting information on a slide, and provide additional business-specific information. They add *context* to the presentation's bullet-points, and to the mechanics of the key-strokes and mouse-clicks captured in the recording. If the instructor is not present to provide this information, then this information needs to be provided to the trainee through the course material itself. This problem is not unique to Enable Now, but Enable Now does not necessarily provide any unique solutions to it. That said, Enable Now does supports the development of engaging, robust, stand-alone training through the use of audio, pop-ups, and the ability to display additional information through actions and events on Book Pages. Just bear in mind that providing all of this can take significantly more of time and effort than building content solely for use in the classroom.

In-application help

In-application help is the provision of help or other training content while the user is working in the application for which help is being sought. Typically, this refers to an Electronic Performance Support System (EPSS), but in recent years has expanded to include 'just-in-time' training and 'microlearning' in addition to pure application help.

If you are using Windows-based applications, you may find it helpful to provide context-sensitive help by way of Desktop Assistant. You can use Guided Tours to guide users through tasks in the application, and provide Context Help for specific screen objects if required. You *can* convert all of your simulation projects into Desktop Assistant Guided Tours (or even Context Help Bubbles) but if you have multiple simulations for the same functionality (for example, to cover different scenarios) it is probably more effective to choose one or two key simulations to convert. Furthermore, don't feel that you have to stick to the 'one bubble per field' approach with Guided Tours—it may be clearer to cover multiple (related) fields in a single bubble.

Extending the help into true *information provision*, you can provide access to your simulations via the *Desktop Assistant Content Panel*. Here, although you can provide any and all playback modes, you may find it best to pick one playback mode to include—perhaps Concurrent mode. You can also include additional training material, such as Books or Book Pages, by tagging these with the correct context. However, be careful of providing too much content through Desktop Assistant, as it is easy to overwhelm users. It is better to choose a few essential quick references (or perhaps a single Book Page that consolidates links to other resources) rather than provide access to *everything* just because you can. Bear in mind that you can always allow your users to access the full *Trainer* via the **Extended Search** button on the *Desktop Assistant Sidebar*, so all of your training material is only a mouse-click or two away, anyway.

For web-based applications, you can provide the same level of help via Web Assistant. As a minimum you can provide Guided Tours to guide users through tasks, and Help Tiles to provide help on specific screen objects. The same caveats discussed for Desktop Assistant also apply to Web Assistant help: avoid providing blanket coverage of every single field—especially where these are relatively self-explanatory—as this can overwhelm the user. Ask yourself: Do you really need to tell the users 'Enter the customer number in the Customer Number field'? Instead, limit yourself to providing in-application help only on elements for which the users are likely to *need* help.

As with Desktop Assistant, you can provide additional training material to users of Web Assistant, in this case via the Learning Center. Again, you may want to be selective about what help you make available in this way—especially for the context-sensitive Recommended Learning panel.

The notion of applications being self-explanatory is an important point, especially as software applications begin to use more intuitive interfaces, and users become more technologically sophisticated through exposure to smart-phones and on-line systems. We are edging closer to a situation where it may not be necessary to provide formal training on applications (the *process* is perhaps another matter...), and can simply allow the users into the application and let them know that they can get help, if they need it, via Desktop Assistant or Web Assistant. This may sound extreme, but ask yourself: did you need to be trained before you placed your first order on Amazon.com? And is your procurement system really any more complicated?

Components of Enable Now

SAP Enable Now consists of a number of software components. For an on-premise solution these are installed on the user's PC—for both developers and consumers (users). For a cloud solution, all of these components are accessed via the browser. In either case, you may end up using all of the available components, or you may choose to use only specific ones. The components and their use are explained separately in the sub-sections below.

Manager

The Manager component, as the name suggests, is used for managing the development of training content. All of the Enable Now administration tasks are performed in Manager, including user administration, defining workflow processes and assigning workflow tasks to authors, assigning courses to users, and so on. Manager is therefore typically used by Training Team Leads and Administrators.

There is very little that an author can do in Manager that they cannot also do (and typically much more easily) in the Producer component, so in this book we largely avoid the Manager altogether (save for a small portion of Web Assistant development).

Producer

The Producer is the component of Enable Now in which authors will typically spend most of their time. Simulations are recorded and edited in Producer, as are Books and Book Pages. Desktop Assistant Guided Tours and Context Help Bubbles are also created in Producer. Finally, the Document output formats (including Word, PDF, HTML, and PowerPoint files) are also generated in Producer. Finally, training content is published to the *Trainer* from Producer.

Instant Producer

Instant Producer is a simple application that allows for the recording and basic editing of simulations. It requires very little training (although a quick demonstration would be wise), and is therefore ideally suited to use by Subject Matter Experts or other users who are not skilled in Enable Now. Simulations recorded via Instant Producer are accessible to authors in Producer (or Manager), but this is a one-way transfer: once a simulation has been edited in Producer, it can no longer be edited in Instant Producer.

Desktop Assistant

The Desktop Assistant is an application help *delivery* tool; content is not developed in Desktop Assistant. The Desktop Assistant provides context-sensitive help by monitoring what the user is doing on their PC, and then proffering applicable help whenever the user accesses a context for which help content is available. This means that Desktop Assistant must be running on the user's PC. Ideally, this should be configured to automatically start Desktop Assistant as soon as the user powers on their PC, but if you are only providing help for a specific application (for example, SAPgui) you could perhaps configure it so that Desktop Assistant is automatically started and closed with this application.

Web Assistant

Web Assistant is the component used to both develop and deliver in-application help for supported web applications. It is effectively a stand-alone component (in that all creation and editing of content can be done directly in Web Assistant), but content created in Web Assistant is also visible within Manager and Producer, and can be edited there if necessary. Web Assistant can also provide access to training content created within Producer.

The development process

Once you have decided which deliverables you will provide, and what components of Enable Now you will need to do this, you should define your development process: who will create the deliverables, when they will do so, and how long this is likely to take them.

Choosing a development model

As you plan your training development project, you should consider how the material will be developed. Unless you will only use Web Assistant (and have no plans to bolster this through links to simulations) it is recommended that you always start from a simulation project, as this gives you the most flexibility: you can use the simulation in any of the play modes, you can create document or video output for it, and you can convert it to a Desktop Assistant Guided Tour or Context Help.

In fact, even if you will use Web Assistant, you may find it more effective to first create a simulation project and then copy/paste this content into a Web Assistant project. This is because Web Assistant content is created outside of the Producer environment, and so workflow and (author) role-level controls are not available for Web Assistant content development. If these things are important to you, then you may want to create a simulation project, during which you can use this functionality, and then once the simulation has been reviewed and approved via your Producer processes, you can copy/paste the Bubble text from the simulation into Web Assistant. (And as an added bonus, you will also have a full simulation that you can provide access to in Web Assistant via the **Learning App**.) With this in mind, the following suggestions pertain largely to the development of simulations.

When developing simulations, the initial recording (of the actions in the target application) is the easy part. Adding all the bells and whistles, and turning this simulation into an effective training tool, is what takes time and effort. The former is best done by someone who knows the application being recorded (such as a Subject Matter Expert [SME]), and the latter is best done by someone who is skilled in Enable Now,

The ideal situation is for the Subject Matter Expert to be skilled in Enable Now (or vice versa), but this is not always possible. Your organization may not have a dedicated training development team, and may bring people onto a project specifically to help with training development. In this case, the training developers are unlikely to have business knowledge of the application being recorded. In other cases, you may have a new application that is currently only understood by the application developers or designers, who do not know Enable Now at all. Teaching them how to use Enable Now effectively may be more effort than your organization or project is willing to commit. It is also likely to be met with resistance (most application developers do not *want* to be training developers) and the results are likely to be less than optimal. (Of course, there are exceptions, but in this author's experience, these are very few and far between.)

An alternative is to have simulations *recorded* by an SME who is an expert in the application, and then *finessed* by a skilled Enable Now author who can use the full power of Enable Now to turn this basic recording into an effective training simulation. Luckily, Enable Now includes functionality to support this 'split development' model. The SME can use Instant Producer to record the simulation, without having to learn very much about Enable Now at all. This recording can then be handed off to a skilled Enable Now author, who can edit the recording in Producer, using the full functionality of this to create the finished, training-ready simulation, with all of the required bells and whistles.

When to record

It is important to decide upon the stage during the application development cycle at which you will capture your simulations. Ideally, your simulations should be captured in the final version of the system—although in an increasingly-agile world, this is not always possible.

The whole point of simulations is that they should have the 'look and feel' of the actual system. Specifically, they should match reality as closely as possible— there should be a willing suspension of disbelief on the part of the user that they are actually looking at static screenshots. This is a common fault with poor-quality simulation exercises: they do not allow for this suspension of disbelief because it is glaringly obvious that the user is not using an actual system. With a high-quality exercise, however, the user has the impression that they are using a 'live' system. One of the common complaints that users have with training conducted using simulations is that they would rather have a 'real' system to play with. The easiest way to avoid such comments is by providing simulations that are as close to reality as possible.

That said, it is often impractical to wait until development for the entire application is complete before developing your training. Often, training development and application development will run in parallel. Fortunately, development is often gradual, with different parts of the application being completed over time (as opposed to *nothing* being ready until the whole thing is ready). You should therefore work closely with your development team to ensure that the training developers are informed as and when different pieces of the functionality are finalized, so that you can start developing training for these pieces, while the development teams work on the next piece of functionality.

Enable Now has the ability to cope with late changes to the application, through the use of its re-record functionality. If the only thing that has changed is the interface, then re-capturing a simulation using this updated interface can be done largely automatically, with Enable Now performing the actions in the system and re-capturing the screenshots and object names and locations as it does so. Even if additional elements have been added to the application, re-recording allows you to easily insert these into the existing simulation during re-recording.

What to record

Although you might think that determining *what* to record is obvious—just record whatever the user will actually do—this is not necessarily the case. You should think about whether you will demonstrate a specific scenario, provide general (or generic) instructions, or show everything that the user *can* do in the application regardless of whether they actually *will* do this. Ask yourself: do you want to document "what the application does", or do you want to teach "how to use the application to complete an identified business task". This is an important distinction, especially when it comes to determining effort required, because if you take the latter approach, of documenting business tasks, you will likely end up with multiple recordings for some pieces of functionality (or transactions), where that functionality is used for multiple business purposes.

You should also decide whether you want to only the 'correct' way of doing something (sometimes referred to as the 'golden path'), or do you want to provide examples of common problems or mistakes, and how to identify and resolve them? Again, taking the latter approach will most likely result in more recordings (but a more complete suite of training material).

A useful technique when making these decisions is to produce a 'storyboard'—a simple flowchart of what screens you will use in the application, what you will do on each screen, and how you will get from one screen to the next. Having this information available beforehand will save you from having to decide these things during the recording itself, and potentially missing steps out. Storyboards are also useful if you have less-experienced developers who perhaps need some more guidance for their recordings.

Development time

How long it takes to develop training content using Enable Now will largely depend upon how much information you want to provide, and how much in the way of 'bells and whistles' you want to include. That said, there are some very rough guidelines that you may find useful when planning your initial development—you can then refine these based on your personal experience.

- For a simple **simulation project** with a linear step progression and around 15-20 steps, you should allow around two hours from initial recording to classroom-ready content. For a more complex simulation with around 40-50 steps, including some branching, merged steps or forms, and possibly narration, you should allow one workforce day.

- To create a new **Desktop Assistant Guided Tour** you should allow around the same amount of time as for recording a simulation. If you are converting a simulation project into a Desktop Assistant Guided Tour, allow at least 30 minutes for the conversion—most of which will likely be spent 'genericizing' the page keys.

- To create a **Web Assistant Guided Tour**, allow an hour. Web Assistant Help Tiles can be created in a matter of minutes.

- For **Book Pages**, allow slightly longer than you would expect to spend on a PowerPoint slide. This is because Enable Now is a little more complex. If you want to add interactions, triggers and events, it will likely take you significantly longer.

Summary

SAP Enable Now is a software application that allows for the creation and delivery of training content and in-application help. Enable Now can be used to create a variety of training deliverables, including simulations, help panels, documents, and presentations. You should decide which of these you want to provide, before starting development.

Enable Now consists of a number of separate components. The key one of these is the Producer, which provides the main development environment for authors (and is the primary focus of this book). Subject Matter Experts may use the Instant Producer, and Administrators and Team Leads may need to use the Manager. The Desktop Assistant and the Web Assistant can be deployed to provide in-application help, as required.

2

Navigating in Producer

In this chapter we will look at the Producer component of Enable Now—what it is, how to access it, and what you can do with it.

In this chapter, you will learn:

- How to open and close Enable Now Producer
- How to check out and check in objects
- How to synchronize your Workarea with the Server
- How to structure your Workarea(s)
- What properties are available for Enable Now content objects and how they are used

If you are impatient to get started, just read the section *Accessing the Producer* on page 29, and then skip forward to *Chapter 3, Recording a Simulation.* You can always come back to this chapter later.

Accessing the Producer

There are a number of ways of accessing Enable Now Producer, depending on your Enable Now implementation model (cloud or on-premise). In this book we are concentrating on the cloud edition, so we will look at the following two methods, which are applicable to the cloud:

- Via the Enable Now Manager component
- Via a direct URL

Accessing Producer via the Manager

The simplest way of accessing Enable Now Producer is via the Manager component of Enable Now. However, in this book we do not look at the Manager; there are no tasks that you, as an Author, can only do in Manager and not in Producer, so there is little need for you to use it.

If you *do* use the Manager component of Enable Now (perhaps you are a Team Lead or an Administrator) them you can access Producer by clicking on the **Open Producer** link in the Workarea header.

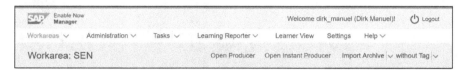

Note that the Producer is specific to a Workarea, so if you have multiple Workareas, you need to make sure that you are in the correct Workarea (which is specified in the upper-left corner of the screen) before clicking on this link.

Accessing Producer via a URL

Assuming that you are using a cloud implementation of Enable Now, you should have received a URL from your Administrator or Team Lead.

> If you are a Team Lead and need to provide your Authors with a link to the Producer, then the URL should be in the format:
>
> ```
> https://client.enable-now.cloud.sap/wa/
> workarea?download=1
> ```
>
> where `client` is your client identifier (given to you by SAP when your Enable Now client was instantiated), and `workarea` is the Workarea that you want to access. For example:
>
> ```
> https://globo.enable-now.cloud.sap/wa/
> GlobalTraining?download=1
> ```

Access Producer as follows:

1. Access the provided URL in your browser. (You may want to bookmark this.)

2. Depending on your version of Windows, you may see the following message:

Click **Keep**.

3. The specified file is downloaded. You should see an icon for it at the bottom of your browser window, as show below:

Click on this icon.

Alternatively, you may see a message asking you if you want to open or save the file, in which case you should click on **Open**.

4. You should see a Java panel, as shown below:

● Some of these messages can be prevented by adding `https://*.cloud.sap` to your browser's Trusted Sites.

5. This will be replaced by a dialog box indicating that resources are being downloaded and then extracted:

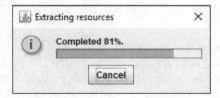

Once the resources have been downloaded, Producer will be opened in a new application window (not in the browser). If the browser page is left open, you can close it once the Producer window is opened.

The Producer screen

Regardless of the access method used, when you access Producer, you will be presented with the Producer main screen. An example of this screen is shown below. Note that this has been reduced for illustration purposes—more complete examples are provided later in this book.

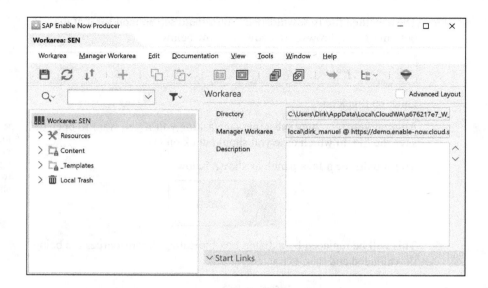

Initial set-up

When you first access the Producer, you will probably see only one entry, called **Content**, on the left. You need to synchronize your local Workarea with the server, to copy required files and other content in the central database. To do this, follow the steps shown below:

1. Click on the **Synchronize Workarea** button on the toolbar.

2. A new entry called **Unsorted** will be added to the hierarchy on the leftmost side of the screen. Expand this, and navigate to the **Root** group. (Your company's hierarchy may have been predefined and the high-level entry for your content may be called something else—check with your Team Lead.)

3. Right-click on the **Root** Group (or other entry point, as instructed by your Team Lead) and select **More | Set as Root** from the shortcut menu. This will move the selected Group structure to the 'main level' of your Workarea. This is the primary Group in which you will do most of your work.

You are now ready to work in Producer!

The (very) basics

We'll look at the various components of the Producer screen a little later in this chapter (in *The Producer screen* on page 43), but you're probably just eager to get started, so we'll first cover the absolute basics you need to know in order to start work, and then we'll come back to the details of the Producer screen after that.

The Structure of the Workarea

Once you have synchronized your Workarea to the server, your Workarea structure will probably look similar to the following example:

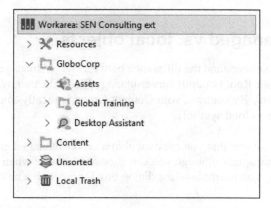

Each of the entries (or 'Groups' in Enable Now terminology) has a specific function. Let's look at each of these.

- The **Resources** Group contains files required by Enable Now to function, including templates, configuration files, scripts, and so on. You should not need to change any of these files (although your Administrator might), but you must have this Group in your Workarea.

● The **Resources** group is only displayed if you select menu option **View | Workarea Details | Show Resources**.

- You are likely to have at least one group that looks similar to the GloboCorp Group in the above example. This is the Group that you set as **Root** during the initial set-up (see above). All of your training content should be contained in this Group in order for users to be able to see it. Note that this Group has a blue 'cloud' symbol in the lower-right corner of its icon. This is important, and indicates that this Group is synchronized with the central content library on the server.

- The **Content** Group contains objects that only exist in your local storage and not on the server (note that the Group icon does not contain a cloud symbol). You can use this Group for practice, or for creating content that you do not want to save to the server.

■ You may want to rename this Group to something like "My local storage", to better reflect its use.

- The **Unsorted** Group. This contains content that exists on the server but is not currently part of the Root structure. Content that you import from a .dkp archive file (see *Importing content files* on page 551), recordings that you import from Instant Producer (see *Integrating simulations created in Instant Producer* on page 546), or projects created via Web Assistant (see *Chapter 11, The Web Assistant*) will initially be stored in the **Unsorted** group. You can also create content in this Group if you want it to be managed on the server, but don't want to include it in the Root structure just yet.

● The **Local Trash** group is only displayed if you select menu option **View | Workarea Details | Show Local Trash**.

- **Local Trash** contains all content objects that you have deleted. They will remain in here until you empty the trash.

You will almost certainly want to adjust your Workarea structure at some point (or your Administrator may do this for you). Refer to *Building your Workarea structure* on page 59 for more information on how to do this.

Server-managed vs. local objects

It is important to understand the difference between server-managed objects and local objects. Your Root Group is server-managed (as indicated by the blue cloud symbol in its icon). By contrast, your Content Group is locally-managed (its icon does not include a cloud symbol).

By default, any content that you create within a server-managed group will also be server-managed (although you can choose otherwise when you create the object). Here's an example of the dialog box for creating a new simulation project:

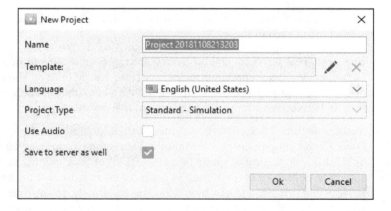

Don't worry about most of the information in this dialog box for now—the only thing you need to be aware of is the **Save to server as well** checkbox. If this checkbox is selected, then the created object will be server-managed. If you deselect this checkbox, then the object will only be created locally—even if it exists within a server-managed Group.

By contrast, if you create an object in your **Content** Group (or any other locally-managed Group) then the **Save to server as well** checkbox is simply not available in the *New Object* dialog box, and the object will be created as a locally-managed object. However, this is just an default setting. If you subsequently want a locally-managed object to be server-managed then you can click on the **Save to server** button at the top of the *Object Editor* pane, to change it to being server-managed. Alternatively, you can

Save to Server

drag the locally-managed object into the Root Group (or other server-managed Group), and you will be asked whether you want the object to be server-managed, or continue to manage it locally, as shown below.

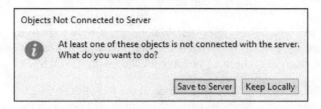

This means that you can have server-managed objects in a locally-managed Group, and you can have locally-managed objects in a server-managed group. The important thing is to pay attention to whether the object has a cloud symbol in its icon—if it does then it is server-managed; if not, then it is local only.

But what does it mean for an object to be server-managed? If an object is server-managed then it is stored in the central library on the server. This means that updates to it are controlled and tracked (and previous versions kept). It also means that a Workflow process can be used with the object. We'll explore server-management in more detail in the following sections.

Client-Server functionality

Enable Now is a client-server application. Content objects are stored in a database (the 'library') on a **server**—which is often in 'the cloud', but could be on your company's servers for an on-premises implementation of Enable Now. When you create or consume content objects you do so on a **client** machine (your PC). This is a common, and very effective, model as the content objects on the server can be accessed by multiple clients (users' PCs) as and when they are needed.

Your users will typically only display your content objects, and the server can provide read-only copies of the same object to many users at the same time, without issue. However, if you, as an Author, need to edit a content object, it is important that no-one else can edit it at the same time, as this would cause conflicts and instability. To resolve these problems, Enable Now effectively uses check-in/check-out functionality (also sometimes referred to as 'library functions'). When one Author needs to change a content object on the server, they 'check out' the object. This prevents any other Author from being able to change it (although other Authors can still see the latest version on the server). When the Author has finished editing the content object they 'check it in' to the server again.

Checking out a content object

Whenever you create an object, it is created as checked out to you. If you want to change an object that already exists on the server (and is checked in), you first

■ If you want to open an object but do not want to check it out, then right-click on the object and select **Open as Read Only** from the shortcut menu.

need to check it out. If you double-click on an object to open it for editing, or click on the **Edit** button at the top of the *Object Editor* pane, it is automatically checked out to you. All the time that you have an object checked out, no-one else can edit it.

Edit

If you want to check out an object but do not immediately want to edit it, then you can manually check it out. This is useful if you want to prevent another Author from changing it before you have finished with it. You have two options:

- Click on the **Start Editing** button at the top of the *Object Editor* pane. Despite its name, this button will not open the object in the relevant object editor—but it will make all of the object *properties* editable. The object will remain checked out to you until you check it back in (but be warned that by default when you close the Producer all objects that you have checked out will be checked in automatically—which brings us to the second check-out option, below).

Start Editing

Keep Object for Offline Editing

- Click on the **Keep Object for Offline Editing** button at the top of the *Object Editor* pane. This will check out the object to you, and will keep it checked out—even after you close the Producer—until you release it by clicking on the **Release for Online Editing** button.

Release for Online Editing

Checking in a content object

Once you have finished editing an object (whether this is the contents of the object or just its properties), you should check it back in to the server, so that it is available to other Authors, or users. The simplest way of doing this is to select the object in the *Object Navigation Pane*, and then click on the **Finish Editing** button at the top of the *Object Editor*. (You can also right-click on the object and select **Finish Editing** from the shortcut menu.) The *Finish Editing* dialog box is displayed.

Finish Editing

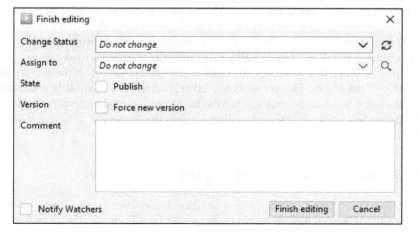

Complete the fields in this dialog box, as follows:

1. If you want to change the **Status** of the object, then select the required status in the **Change Status** field.

   Note that if a Workflow Process has been assigned to the content object, then the **Change Status** field is replaced by the **Workflow Action** field, and you can only select one of the (transition) actions possible for the object, based on its current state. The new state will then be set automatically based on the selected action. For more information on Workflow Processes and their actions, refer to *Chapter 5, Workflow*.

2. If you want to change the person (Author, SME, or other Enable Now user) to whom the object is assigned, then select the required person in the **Assign to** field.

3. If the object should be published (that is, made available to users), then select the **Publish** checkbox. Otherwise, make sure that this checkbox is not selected.

   Note that this is entirely independent of the **Status** of the object. Setting the **Status** to **Published** will not automatically make it available to users. Conversely, it is entirely possible to select the **Publish** checkbox for an object that has a **Status** of **Draft**. However, normally only selected Authors (Master Authors, Team Leads, and so on) will have authorization to set the **Publish** flag.

4. When you save your object back to the server, Enable Now will check to see if its content has been changed, and if it has will create a new version of the object on the server. (This is significant because you can revert to an earlier version if necessary.) If Enable Now determines that the object itself has not changed (perhaps you only changed its properties) then a new version will not be created (but your property changes will still be saved). You can override this logic by 'forcing' Enable Now to save a new version, regardless of whether it thinks any changes have been made to the object. To do this, select the **Force new version** checkbox. Otherwise, make sure that this checkbox is not selected.

   ★ Reverting to an earlier version is only possible in the Manager component. If you don't have access to the Manager, or don't know how to do this, ask your Administrator.

5. Optionally, you can enter a comment—for example, explaining what has changed—in the **Comment** field. This will be visible in the object's History (see *The Protocol category* on page 54), and may also be displayed in any notification sent to the Watcher or new Assignee.

6. If you want Watchers for this object to be notified via (automatic) email that the object has been checked in, then select the **Notify Watchers** checkbox. Otherwise, make sure that this checkbox is not selected.

   Watchers are really just 'people who are interested in the object, or need to know when it changes'. A Watcher can be manually assigned (in the Manager component), or may be automatically assigned based on Workflow settings.

7. Click on the **Finish editing** button. Your changes (to the object content and its properties) are saved to the server, and the object is checked in.

Deleting an object

If you determine that you no longer need an object that exists in your Workarea, then you can delete it as follows:

1. Click on the object in the Workarea to select it.

2. Press the *DELETE* key on the keyboard (you can also right-click on the object and select **Delete** from the shortcut menu.) The following confirmation dialog box is displayed:

3. If the object is server-managed, the **Delete on server** checkbox is displayed and selected. If you only want to delete the object from your local repository, but want to leave it on the server, then deselect this checkbox. If the object is not server-managed, then this checkbox will be disabled.

4. Click **Delete**. The object is deleted.

When you delete an object, it is moved to your Local Trash folder. From here, you can permanently delete the object or restore it, as explained in the following sections.

Permanently deleting an object

If you deleted an object from your Workarea, it will be moved to your Local Trash. Periodically, you should clear out your Local Trash, by permanently deleting any objects that you know you no longer need. To do this, carry out the following steps:

1. Open your Local Trash folder. (If this is not displayed, select menu option **View | Local Trash**.)

2. Select the object(s) that you want to permanently delete, and then click on the **Delete** button at the top of the *Object Editor* pane. The following confirmation message is displayed:

Delete

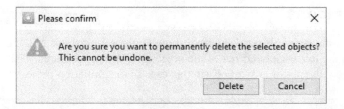

3. Click **Delete**. The object is permanently deleted.

Restoring an object

If you have deleted an object then realize that you still need it, you can restore it from your Local trash. To do this, carry out the following steps.

1. Open your Local Trash folder. (If this is not displayed, select menu option **View | Local Trash**.)

2. Select the object(s) that you want to restore, and then click on the **Restore** button at the top of the *Object Editor* pane.

Restore

The restored file will only exist in your local repository. If also deleted the server copy, and now want to restore the server version, then continue as follows:

3. Locate the restored object in your Workarea, and click on it to select it.

4. Click on the **Save to Server** button at the top of the *Object Editor* pane. A message is displayed advising you that a copy of the object is located in the server's trash.

Save to Server

5. Click on **Back Up and Restore**. The following message is displayed:

> • If you did not delete the server version, then when you try to save the restored version to the server then you will be informed that a version already exists on the server. Click **Use server object** to save your local version to your Unsorted folder and revert to the server version.

Create backup

At least one object may have local changes that are discarded with the following action. Do you want to create backup copies in "Unsorted" now?

☐ Do not show again

[Yes] [No]

6. Click **Yes**.

The copy of the object that you restored is moved to your Unsorted folder (this will not be server-managed), and the server version will be restored and copied back to your Workarea.

> • The **Duplication Source** property for this unsorted backup copy will list the original (restored) server version.;

Server icons

For server-managed objects, a symbol showing the server status of the object is shown in the lower-right corner of the object icon in the Workarea. The examples below show the possible symbols (in this case for a simulation project):

Icon	Meaning
	The object is server-managed, and is currently not checked out to *you*. It could be checked out to another user, but you can't tell from this icon. The only way you can tell if someone else has it checked out, and who that is, is by trying to check it out yourself, and reviewing the error message that is displayed.
	You currently have the object checked out for editing.
	You currently have the object checked out for editing, and want to keep it checked out even when you close the Producer.
	You currently have the object checked out, and you have changed the object but not yet saved these changes to the server. You can save the changes to the server by clicking on the **Save to Server** button and completing the **Save to Server** dialog box (which is exactly the same as the *Finish Editing* dialog box above). Note that your changes will not be visible to other Authors until you check in the object.

Synchronizing with the server

Regardless of whether you are working in a cloud implementation or an on-premise installation, the single master copy of all content is housed in a database on the server. Content objects that you are editing and any common files flagged as **Must Have** (see *The Protocol category* on page 54) are copied to your local repository on your PC.

When you log on to Producer, Enable Now will automatically synchronize your local repository with the server. Enable Now checks the contents of your local repository against the server copy, and downloads any new or updated objects available on the server (including copies of any **Must Have** objects—you will be prompted with a message of 'new content is available' if this is the case).

Similarly, when you log off, Enable Now will check for any changed objects in your local repository, and save these to the server, before shutting down. If these locally-changed objects are currently checked out to you, Enable Now will also check them back in as part of the synchronization process (unless you specifically tell it not to—see *Logging off from Producer* on page 42).

In addition to these two points of automatic synchronization, you can synchronize your local repository at any time by clicking on the **Synchronize** button on the *Producer Toolbar*. This will perform a

Synchronize

two-way synchronization: any new or updated server copies will be downloaded to your local repository, and any new or updated local copies will be uploaded to the server.

Refreshing content objects

Because the Workarea is typically quite large, synchronizing may take a while. Instead of synchronizing your entire Workarea, you can download the latest server version of an individual object to your local repository by selecting it in the Workarea, and then clicking on the **Update from Server** button at the top of the *Object Editor* pane. (You can also right-click on the object and select **Update from Server** from the shortcut menu.)

Update from Server

Note that this only refreshes the specific object that you select; if you select a Group, only the Group itself will be refreshed and not any of its contents. If you want to refresh multiple objects in a group, then you can do so by carrying out the following steps:

1. Click on the Group within the Workarea whose contents you want to refresh.

2. Click on the **Show Tree Operations** button at the top of the *Object Editor* pane, and then select **Update All Objects from Server**. This will display a list of the selected Group and all of its contents—as available **on the server**—in the update *All Objects from Server* dialog box. An example of this dialog box is shown below.

Show Tree Operations

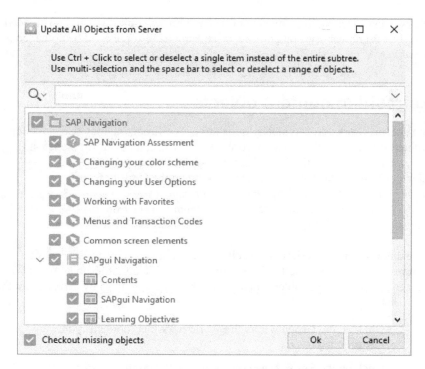

3. By default, all objects will be selected to be refreshed (that is, re-downloaded to your local repository). If there are any objects in this list that you do not want to be refreshed, deselect the checkbox to the left of those objects.

4. Click **Ok**. The selected objects are refreshed.

Logging off from Producer

When you have finished working in Producer, you can log off by selecting menu option **Workarea | Exit** (or just close the Producer window). The *Shutting down Producer* dialog box will be displayed.

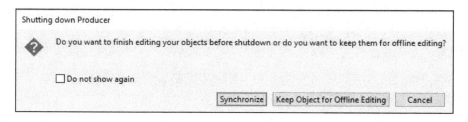

Here, you have the following choices:

- Click **Synchronize** to check in any objects that you currently have checked out **except for** those that you checked out using the **Keep for**

Offline Editing option, and synchronize your local repository with the content on the server.

- Click **Keep Object for Offline Editing** to shut down the Producer without checking in any objects that you have currently checked out (regardless of whether or not these were checked out using the **Keep for Offline Editing** option), and synchronize your local repository with the content on the server.

The Producer screen

Now that we've covered the basics, let's go back and look at the Producer screen in a little more detail—what the screen shows us, and what functionality it provides.

An example of a typical Producer screen is shown below.

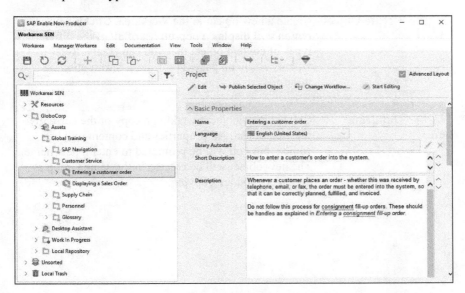

The Producer screen consists of three main components. These are identified in the graphic on the right, and explained below.

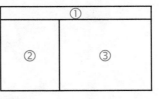

1. The menu and *Producer Toolbar*, across the top of the screen

2. The *Object Navigation Pane*, on the left of the screen

3. The *Object Editor*, on the right of the screen

We will look briefly at the contents of each of these components in the subsections below. Instructions on the use of these components are provided later in this chapter.

● The *Object Navigation Pane* is sometimes referred to in the SAP documentation as the *Project Explorer*, but as not everything in it is a project, the term *Object Navigation Pane* is used consistently throughout this book.

The Producer Toolbar

The *Producer Toolbar* is shown across the top of the *Producer* screen (immediately below the menu bar). This is actually a composite of eight separate toolbars, which can be selectively displayed or hidden via the **View | Toolbars** menu option. The toolbars, buttons, and their purposes, are shown in the table below.

Icon	Name	Purpose
Workarea Commands Toolbar		
	Save	Save the currently-select object to the server. Note that this will not check in the object.
	Synchronize	Retrieve the latest versions of all 'managed' objects from the server (including their details and their contents).
New Objects Toolbar		
	Create Object	Create a new object in the Workarea. Clicking on this button will display a pop-up list of all of the different types of content object that you can create. Refer to *Web Assistant* on page 24 for more information on these.
Clipboard Commands Toolbar		
	Duplicate	Create a new object by taking a copy of the currently-selected object. All properties and content will be copied, but you will be prompted to enter a new name. The new object will be created in the same Group as the object you are copying.

Icon	Name	Purpose
	Cut/Copy/ Paste/Delete	Display a drop-down menu that contains the following options: • **Delete**: Delete the currently-selected object from the Workarea. You will be prompted to confirm that this is what you want to do, and will have the option to also delete it on the server (versus just deleting it from your local repository). • **Cut**: Remove the currently-selected object and place it on the clipboard. • **Copy**: Take a copy of the existing object and place it on the clipboard. • **Paste**: Paste the object currently on the clipboard to the selected location. You will be given a choice of **As Duplicate** (a new copy of the original object will be taken) or **As Reference** (a reference to the original will be inserted; there will still be only one copy of the object but now it will appear in multiple places—see *The Object Reference Tree View* on page 64 for more information on object references).

Library Preview Toolbar

Icon	Name	Purpose
	Preview Library from Selected Group	Select a Group in the *Object Navigation Pane* and then click on this button to generate a temporary version of the *Trainer* that starts with the selected Group and includes everything under it. See *The Trainer* on page 17 for information on the *Trainer*.
	Preview Library	Preview the entire *Library*, from the **Root** (the highest-level Group under the Workarea) down.

Workarea Toolbar

Icon	Name	Purpose
	Generate Compound Document	Create a single document that contains multiple selected content objects, possibly including projects, Books and Book Pages, and text units. Refer to *Generating a Compound Document* on page 530 for additional information on this functionality.
	Generate Master Document	Create a single document that contains one or more simulation projects. Refer to *Generating a Master Document* on page 523 for additional information on this functionality.

● The terms "Library" and "Trainer" are used interchangeably in Enable Now (possibly one was a WPB term and the other a Datango term). This book uses *Trainer*, consistently.

Icon	Name	Purpose
Publishing Toolbar		
→	**Publish Selected Object**	Publish the selected object (and its 'owning' Group if it is not a Group itself), along with everything under it, to a local *Trainer*. Refer to *Publishing to outside of Enable Now* on page 219 for more information on publishing locally.
Workarea View Toolbar		
⊟˅	**Change Workarea View**	Use this button to change the way in which the *Object Navigation Pane* appears. Refer to *Workarea Views* on page 61 for more information on views.
Help Toolbar		
▼	**Info Center**	Display the SAP Enable Now Info Center, where you can find additional information on Enable Now, including the official documentation and release notes.

The Object Navigation Pane

The *Object Navigation Pane* occupies the leftmost side of the Producer screen, and shows all of the objects in your Workarea, organized into a single hierarchy. An example of a typical *Object Navigation Pane* is shown below.

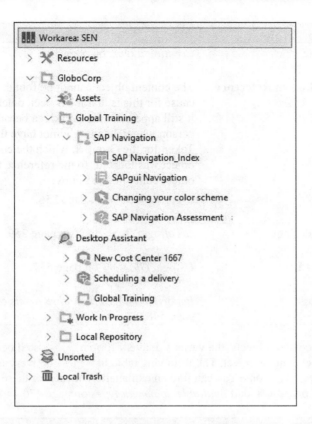

For information on how to set up your Workarea hierarchy and organize your content within this, refer to *Building your Workarea structure* on page 59.

Within the Workarea structure, each object is represented by its name, and an icon indicating the type of object. The full list of object types, and a reference to where you can find more information on them, is shown below.

Icon	Object Type	See
	Group	*Building your Workarea structure* on page 59.
	Simulation Project	*Recording a Simulation* on page 77.
	Desktop Assistant Guided Tour	*Recording a Guided Tour* on page 371.
	Desktop Assistant Context Help	*Recording Context Help* on page 396
	Web Assistant Guided Tour	*Creating a Guided Tour* on page 427
	Web Assistant Context Help	*Creating a Help Tile* on page 436.

Icon	Object Type	See
	Quiz	*Creating a Quiz* on page 325.
	Unknown Reference	The content object cannot be found. The likely cause for this is that it has been deleted, but it still appears in the Workarea because the person who deleted it did not have the Write Token for the Group in which the content object was located, so the reference to the object could not be removed.
	Book	*Creating a Book* on page 256.
	Book Page	*Creating a Book Page* on page 259.
	Text Unit	*Using a Glossary* on page 537.
	Image	*Importing images and other assets* on page 548.

● You can choose to show or hide **Unknown Reference** objects via menu option **View | Workarea Details | Show Unknown References**.

For Project content objects, the various delivery formats are nested below the actual Project content object. The following table lists these delivery formats and identifies their icons. You can find an explanation of each of these modes in *Simulations* on page 8, and *Available document types* on page 470.

Simulation Formats	
Icon	**Delivery format**
	Demo mode
	Practice mode
	Test mode
	Concurrent mode
	Guided Presentation mode
	Free Presentation mode

Documentation formats			
Doc	**PDF**	**html**	
			Standard Document
			Training Document

Icon			Format
🗎	🗎	🗎	**Work Document**
🗎	🗎	🗎	**Job Help**
🗎	🗎	🗎	**Test Sheet**
🗎	🗎	🗎	**Process Guide**
🗎	🗎	🗎	**BPP Document**
🗎	🗎	🗎	**Audit and Compliance Document**
🗎	-	-	**HPQC Document**
🗎	🗎	🗎	**Hands-on Guide**

Presentation formats

Icon	Delivery format
🗎	**Presentation (.pptx)**

For additional information on the various views that are available for displaying your Workarea, and the options you have for configuring these views, refer to *Workarea Views* on page 61.

The Object Editor

The *Object Editor* is where you can see and edit all of the properties (sometimes referred to as attributes) of the objects in your workarea. The properties displayed are those of the object that is currently selected in the *Object Navigation Pane*. Properties are grouped by expandable/collapsible categories. We will look at each of these separately, below. Note that in an attempt to simplify the interface, only the most commonly-used or most important properties are displayed on the Producer screen by default. Select the **Advanced Layout** checkbox in the upper-right corner of the *Object Editor* pane to display all available properties.

● Enable Now uses the terms "properties" and "attributes" interchangeably (and within programming circles there is debate as to whether there is even a difference). This book uses the term "properties" consistently.

At the top of the *Object Navigation Pane* (immediately below the identification of the type of object), there may be one or more action buttons. The buttons available will depend upon the type of object selected, so you should refer to the relevant object-specific section of this book for details of these buttons.

The Basic Properties category

The *Basic Properties* category contains general properties that are common to almost all object types. An example of this category is shown below.

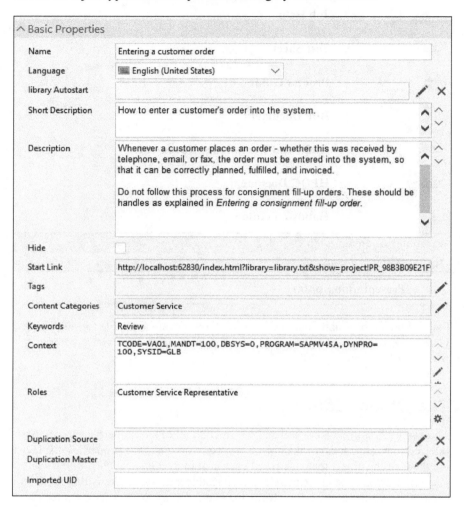

The table below describes the purpose of each of the properties found in the *Basic Properties* category.

Property	Purpose
Name	The display name of the object. This can be changed at any time without breaking any links, as objects are referenced internally via their **UID** (Unique Identifier), which never changes.

Property	Purpose
Language	The language of an object determines the spell-checker used for the object, and may also be used to filter content for a user, based on the user's selected language.
library Autostart	You can choose to have a Book Page (or other content object) displayed as the 'index page' for an object (in the rightmost pane of the *Trainer*) instead of the default display of **Short Description**, **Description**, and play mode buttons. This property specifies the **Name** of the 'index' object (if one is used). Refer to *Using a Book Page as an object index* on page 317 for details of how to do this.
Short Description	A one- or two-sentence description of the object. This is used both in the published *Trainer* (where it appears immediately below the 'play mode' buttons) and also (by default) in the Desktop Assistant (see *The Desktop Assistant Content Panel* on page 363).
Description	A longer-format description of the object. This typically takes up the largest portion of the rightmost side of the *Trainer* screen, and is therefore often used for providing context, concepts, or additional information about the object. For Books and simulations, this should provide enough contextual information to let the user know if they want to open the Book or play the simulation.
Hide	If this checkbox is selected, then the object is not listed in the hierarchical navigation tree of the *Trainer*, although the content is still available within the *Trainer* if it is linked to from another object. This is usually done for objects used as the 'index' of other objects, or for objects that users will not access directly from the navigation tree.
Tags	A tag is simply a word or character string that can be associated with a content object. Typically, Tags are used to conceptually group content objects together, but they can also be used in a filter within the Workarea. You can enter any number of Tags (separated by commas), but you should strive for consistency and agree on a common list before you start any development. Tags are internal to the Workarea (they are not visible to users), and are purely for the convenience of Authors.

★ The Desktop Assistant can be set to use either the **Short Description** or the **Description**, via **Settings | Desktop Assistant: Playback Settings | Desktop Assistant | Desktop Assistant - Content and Behavior | Use Text From**.

★ The Administrator can predefine common 'master tags' via menu option **Tools | Edit Master Tags**.

Property	Purpose
Content Categories	Categories are similar to Tags (see above) in that they are text strings that can be used to group content objects. However, whereas Tags are internal to the Workarea, Categories are visible to users in the Desktop Assistant (see *Using Content Categories* on page 364).
Keywords	Use Keywords to associate a specific text string that does not appear anywhere in the actual 'content' of the content object (such as in a simulation's bubble text, or a Book Page's text) with a content object. This allows users to locate this content object by searching on the Keyword.
Context	For simulation projects, context information is captured automatically during recording. The exact information captured will vary depending upon the application; for SAP ECC 6.0 systems this includes the system ID, transaction code, program, and screen. This information is published in the Context File, which can be used for providing context-sensitive help if Web Assistant or Desktop Assistant are not used (see *Electronic Performance Support* on page 239). You should not need to change this information.
Roles	Users can apply a filter to the Desktop Assistant, or to the Learning Center (via the Web Assistant), so that only content for a specific role is displayed. These roles are specified in this property. Note that this is a simple text field; there is no validation against or selection from a master list, so you should be careful to specify the exact role name.
Duplication Source	If this object was created by duplicating another object, then this property contains the UID of the source object from which this object was copied.
Duplication Master	If this object was created by duplicating another object that was itself created by duplicating yet another object, then this property contains the UID of the original source object.
Imported UID	If this object was imported from another implementation of Enable Now, or another Workarea, then this property contains the UID of the imported object as defined in the original workarea (*this* object will have been assigned its own UID, unique to this Workarea, when it was imported).
Subtype	Used for Groups and Projects only, this identifies the specific type of the object.

★ The Administrator can predefine Categories via menu option **Tools | Edit Content Categories**.

● Typically, you would use Keywords to associate synonyms with content—for example, specifying a Keyword of "localization" for a content object that describes "translation", but you could just as easily use *hashtags* to group related content objects—such as using a Keyword of **#2018UPDATE** to allow users to locate training material specific to the 2018 system update.

The Start Links category

The *Start Links* category contains a number of pre-built links that you can use for launching your content objects directly. This is most useful where you want to link to a specific simulation (or play mode) from outside of Enable Now (for example, on a website, from a PowerPoint presentation, or in an email), but you can also link to a Group at any level of the Workarea hierarchy, to provide a link that opens a Trainer starting from that specific Group.

➕ The *Start Links* category was introduced in the 1811 release. Prior to this, a single property of **Start Link** (which was effectively the **Authoring Preview** link) was available in the *Basic Properties* category, and the (equivalent of the) **Published View** link had to be manually constructed by adding `/~tag/ published` after the Workarea identifier.

An example of the *Start Links* category of properties, for a simulation project, is shown below.

∨ Start Links	
Local Preview	http://localhost:59794/index.html?library=library.txt&show=project!PR_564FD4523FBC1888
Authoring Preview	https://globo.enable-now.cloud.sap/wa/ConsEnable/index.html?library=library.txt&show=p
Published View	https://globo.enable-now.cloud.sap/pub/ConsEnable/index.html?library=library.txt&show=
Custom Location	http://globocorp.com/training/index.html?library=library.txt&show=project!PR_564FD4523F

The following table lists the properties available in the *Start Links* category, and describes their purpose.

Property	Purpose
Local Preview	Provides a link for launching the content object from your local repository.
Authoring Preview	Provides a link for launching the content object from the server Workarea, regardless of whether or not it has been published.
Published View	Provides a link for launching the content object from the publishing location (for example, from the cloud). This link is only available if the content has been published.
Custom Location	Provides a link for launching the content object from a location outside of Enable Now to which the content is published. This link is only available if a custom location prefix has been defined (see *Providing links to Enable Now content* on page 217).

To the right of each link field are two buttons. The first of these, **Copy Link**, copies the link to the clipboard so that you can paste it elsewhere. The second, **Play Content**, allows you to launch the content object via this URL, directly. For more information on how to use these links, refer to *Providing links to Enable Now content* on page 217.

The Protocol category

The *Protocol* category of properties in the *Object Editor* contains properties that relate to interactions with the server. This category is also present for Unmanaged objects, but most of the properties in it are irrelevant for Unmanaged objects. An example of this category is shown below.

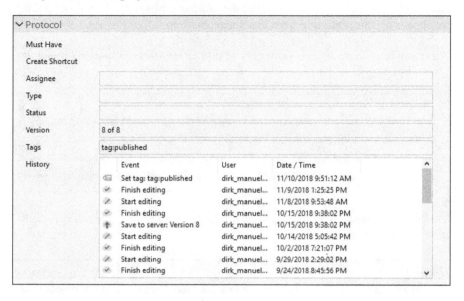

The following table lists the properties available in the *Protocol* category, and describes their purpose.

<table>
<tr><td>➕ If you're looking for the **Synchronization Behavior** and **Recommended Synchronization Behavior** properties, these were discontinued in the 1811 release. For backwards compatibility, some information on these has been retained in *Using a Glossary* on page 537.</td></tr>
</table>

Property	Purpose
Must Have	By default, when an Author logs in to Enable Now and starts working, certain required objects (such as templates, styles, and so on) are downloaded to the user's local repository automatically, so that they are available to the Author. If you select this option for an object, then this object will also be downloaded automatically. (The Author 'must have' it in their local repository.)
Create Shortcut	If you select this option, then a shortcut to this object (effectively, a *reference copy*) is instantly created in the high-level (root) Group for the Workarea (for all Authors). This also makes the Group available as a 'source' in some standard 'open' and 'insert' dialog boxes.
Assignee	This property identifies the Enable Now user to whom this content object has been assigned (if any).

▲ Deselecting the **Create Shortcut** checkbox will not automatically remove the shortcut. To do this, you need to manually delete it in the Workarea..

Property	Purpose
Type	If development types have been defined by your Administrator, this field specifies the development type currently assigned to this content object. Types are typically used to differentiate between different types of development effort (for example, initial development versus updates versus translations) for project management purposes.
Status	This property identifies the current development status of the object. Possible Status values are defined by the Administrator, and may be controlled by a workflow process.
Version	This property identifies the number of times that the object has been saved to the server, and the current version number. These will normally be the same, unless you have reverted to a previous version.
Tags	These Tags are different from the Tags that you can assign yourself in the *Basic Properties*. Tags here are set by Enable Now itself and provide additional information about the object. The most common use is the **published** Tag, which is (unsurprisingly) assigned when the object is published.
History	The History table provides a summary of every server-related interaction that has taken place for the (server-managed) object. For more information on the object history, refer to *Object History*, below.

Object History

For objects synchronized with the server, the History property provides a complete list of every server-related event that has taken place for the object, from the time that it was created to present. The following information is captured for each of these events:

Column	Description
-	An icon representing the type of event.
Event	A short text description of the event. This may contain additional information, depending upon the type of event captured—for example, a **Save to server** event will indicate the version number that was saved; a change in Status will show the old and new Status values.
User	The Userid and name of the user who triggered the event.

Column	Description
Date / Time	The date and time at which the event occurred (in your local time; allow for timezone differences when dealing with users in other locations).

Most of the events are fairly obvious, and you will likely know what caused them. However, the **Save to server** event may be captured in response to a number of different actions (for example, manually clicking on the **Save to Server** button or closing Producer and selecting **Synchronize**), and there is no way to tell the difference between these events.

You can display the details of any event by double-clicking on it in the **History** list. This will display a dialog box similar to the one shown below.

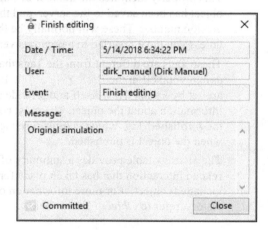

Most of the information shown is the same as that provided in the **History** table, but there are two additional pieces of information that are available.

The first of these is the **Message** field, which is shown only for **Finish editing** events. This provides any text that the Author entered in the *Finish Editing* dialog box (see *Checking in a content object* on page 36).

The other is the **Committed** checkbox, which is available for all events. This indicates whether or not the change was 'committed' (that is, saved and confirmed) to the server. It should always show as selected, to indicate that the event was successfully performed on the server.

History for local objects

Because server events are not captured for objects that only exist in your local repository (these objects are considered 'unmanaged'), the **History** table will normally be empty. Sometimes you still want to know what has been done for an object, so some type of history would be useful. Enable Now provides this by way of **Comments**.

To enter a comment for your local (unmanaged) content object, carry out the steps shown below.

1. Select menu option **Server Workarea | Add Comment**. The *Add Comment* dialog box is displayed.

2. Enter a short title for the comment in the **Title** field. This will be used in place of the **Event** name in the **History** list.

3. Enter your comment in the **Comment** field.

4. Click **Save**.

■ You can use the **History** button to the right of the Title and Comment fields to select from a list of recently-used entries.

This creates an en try in the **History** table, as shown below. Note that you need to double-click on the entry to display the actual comment.

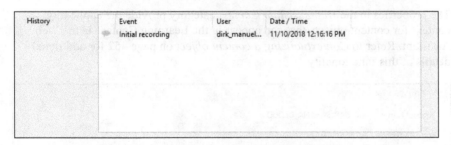

By judicious use of this feature, you can effectively log the key events that have taken place for unmanaged objects—such as when they were created, edited, approved, and so on.

If you change an unmanaged object into a server-managed object all comments are retained, although the event icon for the most recent comment is changed to the 'save' icon, to represent the 'save to server' that took place when the synchronization behavior was changed.

The Changes category

The properties in the *Changes* category contains information on who created the object and who last changed it, along with the dates and times at which this

✚ The *Changes* category was renamed from the *Modifications* category in the 1811 release.

happened. Note that 'change' details are (obviously) only shown if the object has been changed since its first creation.

∧ Modifications	
Created by	Dirk Manuel
Creation Time	5/17/2018 8:58:06 PM
Modified by	Dirk Manuel
Modification Time	10/27/2018 11:03:42 PM

Property	Purpose
Created by	The Userid of the person who initially created this content object.
Creation Time	The date and time at which this object was initially created.
Modified by	The Userid of the last person who changed this object (saved it to the server).
Modification Time	The date and time at which the object was last changed.

The Web Assistant Context category

The properties in the *Web Assistant Context* category provide the application context for content objects that can appear in the Learning Center via the Web Assistant. Refer to *Contextualizing a content object* on page 452 for additional details of this functionality.

∧ Web Assistant Context	
Product Name	SAP_S4HANA_CLOUD
Product Version	1811.500
System	

The table below describes the purpose of these properties.

Property	Purpose
Product	Identifier of the product (application) for which the project was created.
Product Version	Version of the product to which the help applies.
System	System in which the help was captured (if relevant).

The LMS Category

The *LMS* category contains two fields that are used for defining the total possible score and score required for passing (or completing) a content object that is loaded into a Learning Management System.

The following table explains the purpose of the properties available in the *LMS* category.

Property	Purpose
Maximum Score	If the simulation is loaded into a Learning Management System (LMS) then specify the maximum score that can be awarded to the trainee if they complete the required mode (typically Test mode, for simulations) without error.
Required Score	Enter the minimum score (based on the **Maximum Score**) that a trainee must get in order to have passed (or 'completed') this learning object.

Building your Workarea structure

Objects in the Workarea are organized into a hierarchical structure, primarily by using Groups. However, Groups are objects themselves, and have properties that can be set for them and actions that can be performed against them.

There are a few Groups that have specific purposes and their own dedicated icon. These are shown in the following table.

Icon	Object Type	About
	Resources	This is a controlled Group that contains all of the master objects and settings that Enable Now needs to operate. Your Administrator may customize these.
	Toolbox	This is a specific type of group that is used to hold all of your templates, graphics, and other common objects that are used by all Authors. Typically, this will be maintained by your Administrator and set to **Must Have** so that its contents are always available to all Authors.

● Although organizational elements in Enable Now use a 'folder' icon, Enable Now assiduously refers to them as 'Groups' (as does this book, capitalizing the term to be clear we are talking about a specific object type). *Folders* are something different; you can display the underlying folder for an object by right-clicking on it and selecting **Open Folder** from the shortcut menu, and you'll see that it does not contain the same thing as the Group (but this is getting into technicalities that you will likely never need).

■ You may find it useful to create shortcuts to your main template and assets Groups within your **Toolbox** Group. This will create a link to the Group immediately below the **Root** level, but will also make these Groups available as selectable sources in various dialog boxes in Enable Now. To do this, right-click on the Group, ands select **New Shortcut** from the shortcut menu.

Icon	Object Type	About
	Desktop Assistant	This icon denotes a Group that is used for generating your Desktop Assistant. See *Chapter 10, The Desktop Assistant* for more information on the Desktop Assistant.
	Unsorted	This folder contains all content objects that are not currently located in the 'Root' structure, but are nevertheless managed on the server.
	Local Trash	All content objects that you delete are initially moved to the **Local Trash** Group, and will remain there until you empty the trash (see *Permanently deleting an object* on page 38).

How you organize your Workarea into Groups is largely up to you or your Administrator or Team Lead. In fact, looking more broadly, you can organize your content into multiple Workareas. Let's quickly look at why you would want to do this.

Determining how many Workareas you need

★ The ability to control access at the individual Group level *may* be added to a future release of Enable Now, but as of the 1811 release, this functionality is not yet available.

Permission levels are set at the Workarea level. This means that Administrators can provide Authors with access to one Workarea but not another. This could be useful if, for example, your organization has multiple projects, to make sure that Authors are only able to change content for their specific project.

Much of the customization that can be performed in Enable Now—including Text Styles, Style Resources, and basically everything in the **Adaptable Resources** Group—is done at the Workarea level. This means that if you want to be able to provide different styles and standards for each project or organization, you need to have a separate Workarea for each project or organization.

However, the reverse is a good argument for having a single Workarea. If you want to have consistent styles and standards across all projects or organizations, then this will be easiest to achieve if every project or organization is using the same single copy within a single Workarea.

● You publish content at the Group level and not the Workarea level, so you can still provide separate *Trainers* even if all content is within the same Workarea.

This then suggests another good reason for using a single Workarea. If you want to be able to (re)use content objects across multiple projects or organizations, then you will find it much easier to have all of the projects and organizations in a single Workarea (but probably separated into their own Groups). For example, say you have a single, generic *SAP Navigation* course, and want all projects to use the same course. You can create this within one project's Group (or even a 'Common Content' group, and then simply insert references to this single course in the *Trainer* structure for the other projects.

There is one further consideration when it comes to choosing your Workareas. If you are implementing Web Assistant, then all of your Web Assistant projects should be in their own, dedicated Workarea. This is necessary as you need to point the application within which you are providing help via Web Assistant at a specific Workarea, and do not want all of your non-Web Assistant content cluttering this up.

■ You only need to do this for help content created within Web Assistant. You can still have other training content that you want to provide via the Learning Center located within a non-Web Assistant-specific Workarea.

Using Groups to organize your content

When determining your Workarea structure, the most important thing to bear in mind is that (assuming your are providing your users with access to a *Trainer*) the structure you see in the Workarea is exactly the same structure that your users will see in the *Library*—at least from the Group you select for publishing. You should therefore choose a structure that is logical to your users. This could be organized around system functionality, or job responsibilities, or any other hierarchical categorization that works for you and your users.

That said, you should also be aware that it is possible to provide users with a link to any Group in the hierarchy, and this will open in the browser as a self-contained *Trainer*. This means that if you organize your content into Groups by organization, you could effectively provide each organization with its own *Trainer*, by distributing Group-specific URLs (**Start Links**). Or you could do the same thing for roles—whatever is easiest for your users.

If you feel that your Authors would find another arrangement easier (for example, you want to organize content by Author, or you are adding content to an existing body of training material, and want your Authors to see only the new content, without it being buried in the middle of the existing content) then there is another possibility. You can create a 'development' Group structure, outside of your main structure, and populate this with *references* to the content in the main publishing Group structure. Functionally (and visually), there is no difference between the 'original' copy of an object and a reference to it, so Authors will be able to work in the development structure, and their work will be immediately reflected in the production structure. References are explained further in *Workarea Views* on page 61.

■ If you need to make significant changes to your Workarea structure, then you may find this easiest to do by exporting the structure to Excel, changing it there, and then importing the updated structure. How to do this is explained in *Using a Glossary* on page 537.

Workarea Views

By default, the *Object Navigation Pane*, on the left of the Producer screen, shows all of the content in your Workarea organized into a single, hierarchical (tree) view. There are actually three possible arrangements for this pane. These can be selected via the **Change Workarea View** button. The following options are available:

Change Workarea View

- **Single Tree View**
- **Double Tree View**

- **Single List View**

These views are explained separately in the sections below.

The Single Tree View

The default view for the *Object Navigation Pane* is the *Single Tree View*. In this view, all of the content in the Library is organized into a single hierarchical 'tree'. An example of this is shown below.

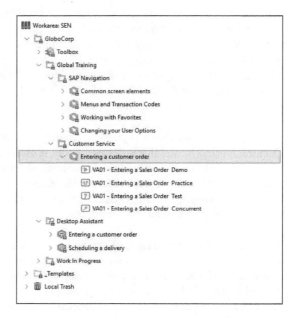

In this view, you can create content objects—including Groups for organizing your content—and drag and drop objects between Groups in the hierarchy to reposition them.

You can also show additional information for each of the objects listed (as explained in *Displaying additional object information* on page 67) and filter the hierarchy to show only specific objects (as explained in *Using Filters* on page 68).

The Double Tree View

The *Double Tree View* is similar to the *Single Tree View*, except that two views of the tree hierarchy are shown. These can be navigated independently, so you can have separate groups open in each tree. This is very useful for (re)organizing your Workarea, as you can drag and drop content objects between the two views to move the objects. An example of this view is shown below.

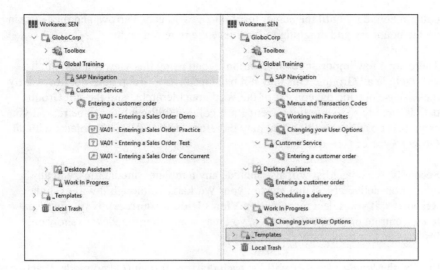

Prior to the 1808 release, the *Object Editor* would show the properties for the content object selected in the *rightmost* tree. As of release 1808, the properties shown are for the currently-selected object (the one with the border around the selection highlight— (which happens to be the rightmost one in this example), regardless of which tree this is in.

The Single List View

In the *Single List View*, all of the content objects (including their generated delivery formats) are displayed in a single, tabular list (that is, not in a hierarchical tree). An example of this is shown below.

By default, only two columns are shown: the object **Name** (including any of the additional optional information, as explained in *The Object Navigation Pane* on page 46) and the **Parent Path**, which shows the full path within the Workarea hierarchy at which this object is located (and if the object is located in multiple places within the Workarea hierarchy it will be listed multiple times in the view). You can include additional columns via the **View | Show...** menu options.

You can sort the object list on any of the displayed columns (except **Parent Path**), by clicking on a column header to toggle between **Ascending** and **Descending**. You can also resize the columns by hovering the cursor over the column boundary until the cursor turns into a two-headed arrow, and then clicking on the boundary and dragging to it achieve the required width.

There are a few important considerations when using this view. Firstly, the list will include all Groups. This may not be helpful, as a Group does not necessarily make sense outside the context of the Workarea hierarchy, and the full Group path is already shown in the **Parent Path** column (although for some reason you cannot sort or filter on this). You may therefore want to filter out objects with an **Object Type** of **Group**.

Secondly, the object list will also include any templates, media files, and any other 'non-deliverables' that exist in your Workarea (although it will exclude Resources, if you select menu option **View | Hide Resources**). If you just want to concentrate on your deliverables, you may want filter the view to show only Projects and/or Books and Book Pages.

Finally, the *Single List View* will list each delivery format (Demo mode, Practice Mode, document types, and so on) separately. Unfortunately, there is no easy way to filter these out. Even if you filter on an **Object Type** of **Project**, this will still include all delivery modes—even though these are listed in the view as having an **Object Type** of **Mode** or **Document**.

The Object Reference Tree View

The *Object Reference Tree View* displays a second tree hierarchy to the right of the object tree hierarchy (similar to the *Double Tree View*), but this second tree shows only the object selected in the tree on the left, along with all objects (including Groups) that contain, or link to, this object. An example of this view is shown below:

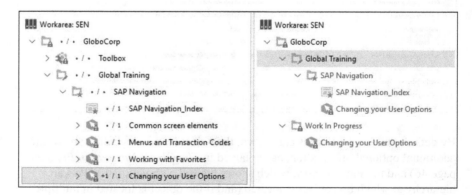

In this example, the object **Changing your User Options** is selected in the object tree on the left. This object is linked into two places in the overall Workarea hierarchy, as you can see in the reference tree on the right: the Group **SAP Navigation** and the Group **Work In Progress**.

Note in this example that the Book Page **SAP Navigation_Index** is also listed in the reference tree. This is because this Book Page *links to* the selected object. There is some additional information displayed in the **Referenced by** field at the top of the *Object Editor* pane (described further below) that supports this.

You may also have noticed that there are (possibly) two numbers, separated by a slash, shown to the right of the object name in the object hierarchy. For the selected object above, this is "**+1 / 1**". The first of these numbers (**+1**) is the **Structure Reference Counter**, and shows the number of *additional* times that the selected object is linked into the Workarea structure (that is, in addition to where the currently-selected instance appears). In our example, the number is +1, indicating that the selected object appears where it is currently shown (in the Group **SAP Navigation**) and *one additional time* (in the Group **Work In progress**). If the only place the object appears in the Workarea structure is in the currently-selected position, then this number is shown as a bullet (small circle), indicating that there are no additional references.

The second of these numbers (**1**) is the **Content Reference Counter**. This is the number of times that another object *links to* the selected object. In this example, the selected object is linked to from one other object (the Book Page **SAP Navigation_Index**). If there are no other objects that link to this one, then this number is shown as a bullet (small circle).

It is worth checking both the **Structure Reference Counter** and the **Content Reference Counter** before deleting an object to see if (a) there are any reference links that should also be deleted, and (b) if there are any links that need to be removed or revised.

The other place where you can see information related to the reference counters is at the top of the *Object Editor* pane. When you choose either the *Object Reference Tree* view or the *Object Reference List* view, the **Referenced by** field is shown. An example of the *Object Editor* pane including this field is shown below.

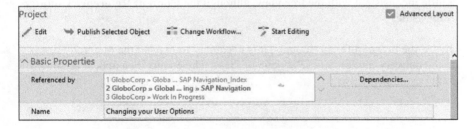

Here, you can see a list of all of the objects (Groups or content objects) that link to the selected object. In our example, there are three linking objects: the two Groups (as per the "+1" **Structure Reference Counter**) and the Book Page (as per the "1" **Content Reference Counter**). Structure references are shown in dark blue (with the current reference shown in bold). Content references are shown in light blue.

You can jump directly to any of these objects in the overall object hierarchy by clicking on them in the **Referenced by** field. This will make the object that you clicked on the 'focus' object, so the *Object Reference Tree* view and the **Referenced by** field will be updated to show references for *this* (focus) object.

Both of these counters—and the associated **Referenced by** field—can be displayed in any view, by selecting **Show Structure Reference Counter** and/or **Show Content Reference Counter** (as required) from the **View** menu.

The Object Reference List view

The *Object Reference List* view is similar to the *Object Reference Tree* view, in that it includes a second pane that identifies all of the Groups that contain the selected object, and other content objects that link to this object. But where the *Object Reference Tree* view provides the linking objects in a tree hierarchy, the *Object Reference List* view provides (as you'd expect from the name) a flat list of these objects. An example of this view is shown below.

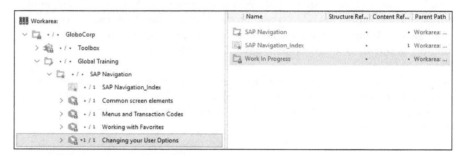

Note that the rightmost pane shows the **Structure Reference Counter** and the **Content Reference Counter** as columns in the list. In the above example, the **Structure Reference Counter** for each of the objects shows as a bullet, which is a little inconsistent with the tree view, although the **Content Reference Counter** is the same.

To see the *actual* reference counts, it is necessary to expand the hierarchy down to the delivery modes, and select one of these. The counts then appear as shown in the example below:

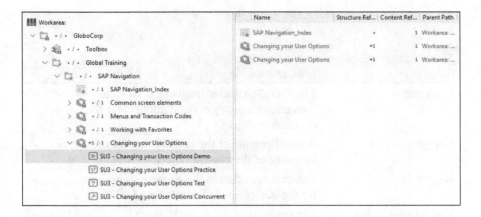

Here, we can see that the Demo mode for this simulation appears in two places in the Workarea structure - under both instances of the simulation. This play mode is also linked to directly from the **SAP Navigation_Index** Book Page.

As with the *Object Reference Tree* view, the *Object Reference List* view also results in the **Referenced by** field being shown in the *Object Editor* pane. For information on this, and an explanation of the reference counters, see *The Object Reference Tree View* on page 64.

Displaying additional object information

In addition to the basic object information shown by default in the various views, the following information can also be shown for objects, via the **View | Workarea Details | Show...** menu options. The two columns on the right show which properties are available in which types of views.

Menu option (Show...)	Information displayed	Tree Views	List Views
Unknown References	No idea.	✓	✓
Type	The object type. This can be **Group, Project, Mode, Documentation, Text Unit, Book, Book Page**, or **Image**.		✓
Modification Date	The date and time at which the object was last changed (saved to the server).		✓
UID	The unique identifier of the object. Note that this does not apply to delivery formats (Type **Mode** or **Documentation**) as these technically share a **UID** with the Project from which they were created, and use a common identifier.	✓	✓

Menu option (Show...)	Information displayed	Tree Views	List Views
Language	The ISO 2-character language code (plus 2-character country code, if applicable) for the content object.	✓	✓
Language Icon	A small graphic of the country flag for the language of the content object.	✓	✓
Keywords	Any text specified in the **Keywords** property for the object (excluding play modes).		✓
Short Description	The contents of the object's **Short Description** property.		✓
Context	The contents of the object's **Context** property.		✓
Desktop Assistant Context	The contents of the object's **Context Information** property, if captured during recording.		✓
Roles	The contents of the object's **Roles** property.		✓
Author	The name of the Enable Now user who last changed the object.		✓
Structure Reference Counter	This is a count of the number of *additional* times the object is linked in to the Workplace structure (via reference links).	✓	✓
Content Reference Counter	This is a count of the number of other content objects that link to this content object.	✓	✓

Using Filters

Regardless of the Workarea view used, you can use **filters** to limit the objects displayed in the view.

You can also use filters in other ways. For example, when publishing your content locally (that is, not making it available via the cloud) you can use a predefined filter to select the content that is to be published. Refer to *Chapter 7, Publishing Your Content*, for additional information.

Creating a new filter

To create a new filter, follow the steps shown below:

1. Click on the **Filter** button, and select **Edit Filters** from the drop-down menu. The *Edit Filter* dialog box is displayed.

Filter

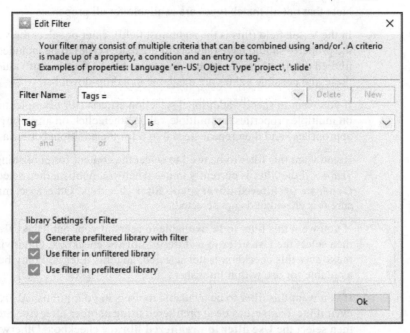

2. If filters have already been defined, then this dialog box will initially show the details of one of these filters. Click on **New** to define a new filter.

3. If you want to enter a specific name for your filter, then enter this into the **Filter Name** field. If you do not enter a name yourself, one will be generated automatically, based on the criteria you specify.

4. Select the object property on which you want to filter the Workarea from the **Property** drop-down list (this is the field on the left). You can filter on the following properties:

- Tag
- Name
- Language
- Description
- Short Description
- Context
- Context: Desktop Assistant
- Roles
- Keywords
- UID
- Duplication Master

- Duplication source
- Object Type
- Creation Time
- Modification Time
- Site
- Country
- Responsible
- Logical Component Group
- Activity
- Process Availability
- Document Type

5. Select the match type from the **Match** drop-down list (this is the middle field). Valid options are:

- is
- is not
- contains
- does not contain
- begins with
- ends with
- is higher
- is lower
- is between
- is not between

Note that not all match types are available for all properties.

6. In the **Value** field (this is the rightmost field), enter or select the value the property should have (subject to the match type) to be included in the filtered display. Note that some properties have a finite set of values; for these, the possible values are available in a drop-down list.

7. If you want to specify additional selection criteria (for example, to filter on multiple properties, or multiple values) then click on **and** or **or** (as appropriate) and then repeat steps 4 to 6 for the additional criteria.

8. If you want this filter to be used to select the content for publishing your *Trainer* if the filter is currently in use when you publish, then select the **Generate prefiltered library with filter** checkbox. Otherwise, make sure this checkbox is not selected.

9. If you want this filter to be available to users in your published *Trainer* then select the **Use filter in unfiltered library** checkbox. Otherwise, make sure this checkbox is not selected, and this filter will only be available for use within Publisher.

10. If you want this filter to be available to users in your published *Trainer* even if the *Trainer* has been prefiltered using another filter (see Step 8), then select the **Use filter in prefiltered library** checkbox. Otherwise, make sure this checkbox is not selected.

11. Click **Ok** to save your filter and close the dialog box.

Note that your filter will not automatically be applied. To apply your filter, refer to *Applying a filter* on page 71.

Editing a filter

To edit an existing filter, carry out the steps shown below.

1. Click on the **Filter** button, and then select **Edit Filters** from the drop-down menu. The *Edit Filter* dialog box is displayed (see page 69 for an example of this).

2. Use the drop-down list for the **Filter name** field to select the filter that you want to change.

3. Change the filter as necessary (see the instructions under *Creating a new filter* on page 69).

4. Click **Ok** to save your changes and close the dialog box.

Applying a filter

To apply a predefined filter to the Workarea, click on the **Filter** button and select the relevant filter from the drop-down menu. The *Object Navigation* pane is filtered according to the selected filter definition. The **Filter** button is colored blue to indicate that a filter is in effect.

Note that if you are displaying a 'tree view', the Groups containing the filtered objects will still be displayed (along with *their* containing Groups, all the way up to the Root). If you are displaying the *Single List View*, then you will just see a flat list of the matching objects.

There are actually two ways in which the *Object Navigation Pane* can display the 'filtered' content objects. The first is to display only content objects that meet the filter criteria. This is the more traditional way of working. However, Enable Now also allows you to display *all* content objects, but *highlight* the objects that meet the filter criteria. The partial screenshots below show examples of both of these methods, with the same filter applied.

Filter Results

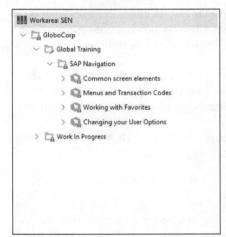

Highlight Results

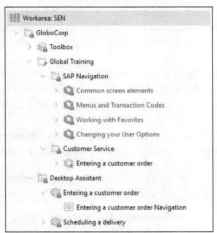

To select a filter method, click on the **Filter** button and select either **Filter Results** or **Highlight Results**, as required, from the drop-down menu. If you click on the **Filter** button again, you will see that the filter name has a check-mark alongside its name, to indicate that it is currently being used. To remove the filter, select it again from the **Filter** drop-down menu (which will also remove the selection check-mark).

All filters that you create are saved in the **Resources** Group, under the **Filters** category. This means that they are available to all users. You can also apply filters directly from here, by selecting a filter and then clicking on the **Apply Filter** button (although you can only remove a filter via the **Filter** button on the *Producer Toolbar*). The currently-active filter is shown in bold.

Searching for objects in the workarea

Enable Now provides a fairly robust search function for locating objects in the Workarea. To search for an object, simply type the text you want to search for into the **Search** field, and press *ENTER*. The *Object Navigation Pane* is filtered to show only those objects that match the search criteria.

Search

Note that if you have applied a filter to your Workarea (as explained in *Displaying additional object information* on page 67) only those objects selected by the filter will be searched. You should also bear in mind that the search function will only search object *properties*, and not the actual text within a project.

On the rightmost side of the **Search** field there are three buttons. These allow you to locate the next instance of the found text, cancel the search and clear the results, and select from a list of recently-used search terms (respectively, from left to right).

So far so simple, but the search function provides a lot of control over what is searched and how the results are displayed. This is done via the drop-down menu for the **Search** button (which is located to the left of the **Search** field).

Firstly, you can make the search case-sensitive by selecting **Match Case** in the drop-down menu, and/or match whole words only (so if you search for "test" it will not match "testing" or "tester") by selecting **Match Whole Words Only**.

You can also choose exactly *what* is searched, via the **Search Mode** option on the **Filter** drop-down menu. The choices are:

- **Search Name Only**: Select this option to limit the search to only the object names.

- **Search in Visible Attributes**: Select this option to search all of the attributes that are currently displayed in the *Object Navigation Pane*. This is of most use in conjunction with the *Single List View* (see *The Single List View* on page 63), in which you have the ability to display the most properties.

- **Search Custom Selection of Attributes**: Select this option to search only in those attributes that you specifically select for searching, via the **Select Search Attributes** option (see *Selecting search attributes* on page 73).

- **Search All Attributes**: Select this option to search through all object properties, regardless of whether they are currently visible.

Your search mode selection will be remembered and used in all future searches, until you change it again.

Selecting search attributes

If you choose a search option of **Search Custom Selection of Attributes**, you need to select the specific set of attributes that you want to search. To do this, carry out the steps shown below.

1. Click on the **Search** button and select **Select Search Attributes** from the drop-down menu. The search options pane will be displayed immediately below the **Search** field, as shown in the partial screenshot below.

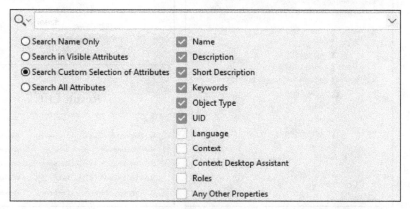

2. In the rightmost column, make sure all (and only) the properties that you want to be searched are selected.

3. To hide the search options pane, click on the **Search** button again, and deselect the **Select Search Attributes** option by clicking on it again in the drop-down menu.

Your selections will be remembered and used every time you search using the **Search Custom Selection of Attributes** option, until you change them.

Choosing the search results display format

When you search for objects, Enable Now can present the results of this search in a number of different ways. The method used is selected from the **Search** button's drop-down menu, where you have the following options:

*   **Highlight Results**: The entire contents of the Workarea are listed, but non-matching objects are grayed out, leaving only matching objects in the more prominent black.

*   **Filter Results**: Only objects matching the search criteria are displayed (but still within the Group structure).

*   **Result List**: Only objects matching the search criteria are displayed, in a flat list (that is, not within the Group structure).

If the search term is found in the object name, then this is highlighted in orange, regardless of the format in which the results are displayed.

The partial screenshots below provide examples of each of the possible display formats for the search results.

Highlight Results

Filter Results

Result List

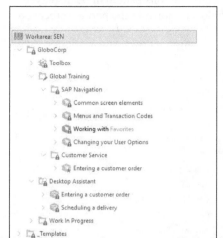

Note that you can search against a Workarea that has already been filtered, and the search results will be constrained to only those objects that have been (pre-)selected by the filter. If you chose the **Highlight Results** option for both the filter and the search you will see two levels of highlighting—a light blue for the filtered content, and then a darker blue for the search results (and then orange on top of this for the search term).

Keyboard Hotkeys

Enable Now comes with a full set of customizable keyboard hotkeys (sometimes referred to as keyboard shortcuts) that you can use to perform many tasks. Because they are customizable, you will not find these showing up on the menus or Tooltips. Instead, to display or change the currently-defined hotkeys, select menu option **Tools | Keyboard Settings**, and the *Keys* dialog box will be displayed. An example of this is shown below:

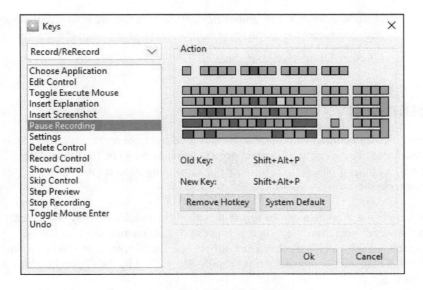

The *Keys* dialog box contains two primary areas:

- On the left is a list of actions to which you can assign a hotkey. These are grouped by category, which you can select via the drop-down field above the list. Click on an action in this list to show its current hotkey (if any)on the right.

- On the right is a diagram of a typical 102-key keyboard, and below this are listed the current hotkey assigned to the selected action, the new hotkey assigned by you, and buttons to remove the hotkey or reset it to the default. The following color-coding is used in the diagram:

    ♦ **Gray**: Available key modifiers (that must be used in conjunction with a character or function key). These are the *SHIFT*, *CTRL*, and *ALT* keys.

    ♦ **Blue**: A key modifier currently selected for the action.

    ♦ **Yellow**: The currently-assigned hotkey for the action.

    ♦ **Green**: A key that is available to be assigned as a hotkey for the action.

    ♦ **Red**: A key that cannot be selected as a hotkey for the action because it is already assigned to another action.

    ♦ **White**: A key that cannot be selected.

To assign a hotkey to an action, carry out the steps shown below:

1. Select the action to which you want to assign a hotkey from the list on the left.

2. On the keyboard diagram (not on your physical keyboard), click on the key or key combination that you want to assign to the action. You should

select the *SHIFT*, *CTRL*, and/or *ALT* keys first if you are going to use them, and then select the character or function key.

3. Click on **Ok** to save your changes.

Summary

The Producer component of Enable Now is used to create and manage objects in a Workarea. These could be content objects (such as projects, Books, and Book Pages), organizational objects (Groups) or supporting objects (such as templates or other assets).

Objects in the Workarea can be server-managed (in which case they are stored on the server, and controlled via check-in/check-out functionality), or can be unmanaged (in which case they exist only in your local repository). Whether an object is managed or unmanaged is initially determined by the Group in which it is created.

Content objects that are made available to your users (via the *Trainer*, Desktop Assistant, or direct link) should be present in your **Root** Group. Objects that are not in this Group are stored in a Group called **Unmanaged**, and will not be visible to your users.

You can control the objects displayed on the Producer screen, and the information shown for them, through views, filters, and the search function.

3

Recording a Simulation

Simulations are perhaps the most widely-used of Enable Now's deliverables, and are often the first thing to be created. This is probably because they can be used in a multitude of ways. A single simulation recording can be 'consumed' by users as a hands-off demonstration, as an interactive exercise, or as a knowledge verification test. Any of these forms can be used as part of classroom training or incorporated into self-paced training. Simulations can also be used to generate printable documentation, or to provide in-application help—including being converted into Desktop Assistant Guided Tours.

In this chapter, you will learn how to:

- Record a simulation project via Producer
- Re-record a simulation project
- Replace the entire contents of one recording with another

● Recording via Instant Producer is described in *Chapter 6, Working with Instant Producer.*

Planning your recording

Although the mechanics of recording a simulation are relatively straightforward, the actual recording is only one step in the process of creating an effective training simulation. It is worth remembering the term PREP:

- **Plan**
- **Record**
- **Edit**
- **Publish**

Firstly—and most importantly—you should always plan exactly what you want to record. This will save you from having to insert missing screenshots later, or having to re-record the simulation because you forgot to capture a part of the task. Consider mapping out the screens that you want to include, the actions you want to perform on these screens, and how you intend to navigate from one screen to the next (especially in SAP systems where there may be several ways of doing this). An example of a simple plan for recording SAP ECC 6.0 transaction SU3 is shown below:

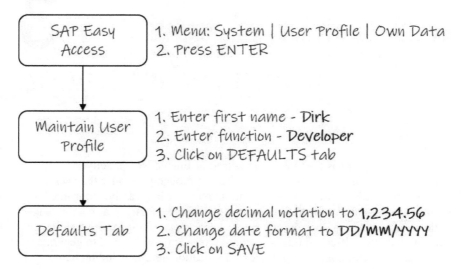

You should also make sure that any required data is available in the system before you start recording—that you know which customers, products, plants, and so you will use, and have checked that nothing is blocked or otherwise unusable. Bear in mind that the simulation should match reality as far as possible. This means that the screens captured in the simulation should look exactly the way the screens in the actual application will look when the user sees them for the first time—with no 'history' retained, no fields already filled in, and so on. As an example, if we will enter a first name of "Dirk" in our exercise we are planning above, we need to make sure the field doesn't already contain this name.

Preparing for recording

Before recording a simulation, there are a number of things you should do to prepare, or at least be aware of. Some of the things to watch out for are listed below:

- **Set your display to 100%:** Make sure your Windows display scale is set to 100%. Enable Now will not be able to record your application if the scaling is set to anything else. How you set this will depend upon your version of Windows, but it will be somewhere in the **Display Settings**, most likely under **Scale and layout** (as it is for Windows 10).

- **Use Internet Explorer as the browser:** If you are recording web-based applications, you should always record against Microsoft Internet Explorer, as this has more robust object recognition profiles.

- **Remove any personalization:** Make sure you are not using personalized display profiles or color settings. If the application that you are recording allows users to change (for example) their color profile, make sure you record using the default color profile. If users access an application for the first time and see a color scheme different than the one they saw in training, they may become confused and/or concerned (really, I've seen it happen). If a user has customized their own profile, then the chances are that they are knowledgeable enough to realize that this explains the difference between what they saw in training and what they see in the actual application.

- **Watch out for session data:** When recording a simulation, try to capture screens as data-neutral as possible. Some applications will remember the last values used, and automatically use these for subsequent tasks (similar to session cookies in the browser). Remove any data that will not be auto-populated for a user the first time they carry out the task in the 'live' system. Similarly, remove all personal favorites, parameter defaults, and so on. Always ask yourself: "What would the user see if they were doing this for the first time?". This may necessitate closing and then restarting the application before every recording.

■ For applications that provide a 'dynamic search' feature for input fields—where possible matches are displayed in a drop-down list below the field as the user types, narrowing the selection with each keystroke—it is recommended that you always type the full value, and do not select from the drop-down list.

- **Record the complete task:** Related to this last point, endeavor to record simulations from a neutral starting point, for example, the initial screen of an application (although it would probably be excessive to require the user to log on to the application every time). Unless you are providing something such as advanced troubleshooting exercises that start from the premise of "If you see this…", you should not just drop the user into the middle of a task—always explain to them how to get there. Similarly, at the end of the task, always return to the same neutral screen, leaving the user ready to start the next task. There is nothing more annoying than being told how to navigate deep into an application's screens, and then just being left there.

- **Watch out for the cursor position:** When performing the actual recording, make sure you pay attention to where the mouse pointer is located. Although Enable Now will automatically hide the pointer itself, it will not automatically hide any ToolTip text that may be displayed. If you have screen objects that change appearance when you hover over them, make sure the cursor is not hovering over them when you capture the screen print—especially if this is the object they will be clicking on, as this would give users too much of a clue to the action.

- **Maintain data continuity:** If you record your simulation in more than one go, or if (when!) you have to re-capture screenshots, watch out for continuity of screen data throughout the simulation. For example, if you record a simulation on one day, and then replace a few screens the next day, make sure that any timestamps shown on the screens are consistent, that any data used is consistent throughout, and so on. If anything is inconsistent, then this will be evident during playback—it may only be a quick flash as the user navigates from one screenshot to the next, but it could cause the user to question what they saw, and wonder whether they did something wrong, or worse, whether the system or training is incorrect.

- **Use realistic data:** Your simulations should look as close to the actual, live system as possible. This means that the data used in the simulations should, to the greatest extent possible, be realistic data. Avoid using customers called "Test Customer", products called "Dummy", and so on. Try to use valid number ranges, document types, and so on. This will better facilitate the trainees transitioning their knowledge to the actual system. However, you should also make sure that you do not use any sensitive or confidential data (use realistic data, not necessarily real data), such as actual customer names and addresses (unless, of course, you are recording a simulation on how to handle a specific customer). Although it may take longer to prepare before starting your recording, it is worthwhile setting up (or having the data team set up for you) your own set of data (such as products, customers, and suppliers) that is only used in training development.

- **Perform a test run before recording:** Finally, consider testing the activity before you record it. Make sure the application works as expected, and that you can perform the activities that you need to capture. But when doing this, be careful not to 'consume' data that you will need for the actual recording.

Recording a simulation

In this section you will see how to record a simulation via Enable Now Producer. This is a good first skill to master, as you can create a variety of outputs from a simulation—including a Desktop Assistant Guided Tour project or Context Help project. Simulation projects are also the most feature-rich projects, so once you have mastered these, everything else will be easy.

Step 1: Create a new project

Simulations are always created as *projects* in Enable Now, so the first step in recording a simulation is to create a project for it.

To create a new simulation project, carry out the steps shown below.

1. Click on the Group within which you want to create the project. Ideally, you should check this Group out for editing, but if you do not, it will be checked out to you when you create the recording. Alternatively, you

may want to create the recording in the **Unassigned** Group, and then move it to the correct final group when you have finished it.

2. Click on the **New Object** button on the *Producer Toolbar*, to display the *New Object* panel.

New Object

3. In the *Process Tutorials and Documentation* **category** in the *New Object* panel, select **Simulation**. The *New Project* dialog box is displayed.

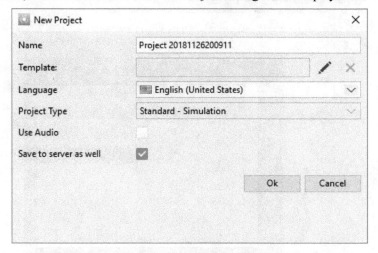

4. Enter a suitable name for your new simulation in the **Name** field.

5. If you have a template (or another, existing project) that you want to use for the project, then use the **Change** button (pencil) on the right of the **Template** field to navigate to and select this. If a template is defaulted into this field and you do not want to use it, then click the **Cancel** button on the far right of the field.

★ The Administrator can set the default template via menu option **Tools | Settings | Producer | Templates**.

6. If you want the simulation to be created in a language other than the default one, change the **Language** field as appropriate. This will determine the language in which the default bubble texts are generated.

● If you select a template in Step 5 then the **Project type**, **Use Audio**, and **Save to server as well** fields are hidden, and their values taken from the template.

7. The **Project Type** field defaults to **Standard - Simulation** (because this is what you selected in Step 3). You cannot change this.

8. If you want your project to include audio (*narrative* audio, published in the final simulation), then select the **Use Audio** checkbox. This will result in another two fields being added to the dialog box. These fields, and the use of audio in general, are discussed in *Chapter 14, Adding Audio to Your Content*.

9. If you are creating the simulation in a server-managed folder, then the **Save to server as well** checkbox will be selected and the simulation will also be created as server-managed. If you only want the simulation to be saved locally (for example, to your **Content** Group) then deselect this checkbox. (Refer to *Server-managed vs. local objects* on page 34 for more information on this if necessary.)

10. Click **Ok**.

11. The project is created, and opened in the *Project Editor*, as a separate tab within *Producer*.

Do not worry about the content and functionality of the *Project Editor* for now; we will look at it in detail in *Chapter 4, Editing a Simulation*.

Step 2: Select the application

Now that you have a project, you can record your simulation within this. To do this, you need to select the application that you want to record, and set the recording properties. Do this by following the steps below:

1. If your new project contains any Steps—copied from the selected Template (for example, a standard 'Start Step')—then click on the existing Step after which the recording should be inserted.

2. Click on the **Record** button on the *Editor Toolbar*. The first step of the recording wizard is displayed: *Select Window and Profile*.

● This would be the same approach you would take if you wanted to add additional Steps to an existing simulation.

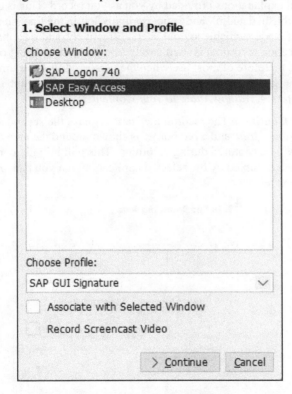

3. The *Choose Window* section of the dialog box lists all of the applications that are currently running on your PC. Click on the application that you want to record in this list.

4. The **Choose Profile** field automatically defaults to the most appropriate profile for the application that you select in Step 1. The profile controls the context and object recognition, and you should not normally need to change this from the default selection. However, in some circumstances—such as for new, unknown applications—you may experience problems with the default selection, and can chose another profile (or the 'catch-all' **Standard** profile) if necessary.

● The **Record Screencast Video** option is only available if you select a profile of **Quick Recording**.

5. If you also want to capture the information required to generate a full-motion video of your simulation (without any bubbles) then select the **Record Screencast Video** checkbox. Screencast videos are explained in *Generating a video file* on page 244.

6. If you always want the specified profile to be used for the selected application, then select the **Associate with Selected Window** checkbox. This should only be necessary if you have changed the default profile selection.

7. If you want audio to be captured when you record the application, select the **Record Audio** checkbox. Note that refers to microphone-captured verbal explanations provided by you as you record. This is not the same as 'published audio', and is not normally left in the final simulation that is made available to your users. Effectively, audio captured during application recording is used purely as input to the editing process, and is therefore of most use when the person editing the simulation is not the same person who recorded it. Audio is discussed in detail in *Chapter 14, Adding Audio to Your Content*.

8. Click **Continue**. The recording wizard displays the second step, *Define Recording Area*, and a red border is shown around the area of the screen that will be captured during recording. This will initially correspond to the area occupied by the selected application, but you can change this in the next few steps.

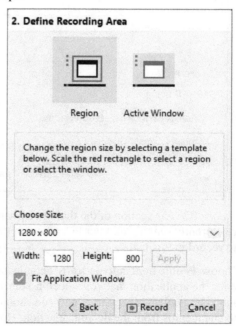

9. In the upper part of the dialog box, you can choose exactly what you want to capture during recording. The options are:

◆   Click on **Region** to capture a specific area on the screen. This is the area bounded by the red recording marquee; you can change this area by dragging the marquee to a new location, or by dragging its borders to select a different area of the screen (but note that the your selection in the Choose Size field will set this for you).

◆   Click on **Active Window** to capture the active window—regardless of where this window appears on the screen or whether it dynamically resizes itself (for example, in response to changes in screen content).

10. In the **Choose Size** field, select the screen dimensions that you want to capture. You can either select one of the predefined sizes, or you can use the **Width** and **Height** fields to specify exact dimensions. Most standard screen dimensions are available as predefined selections, but there are a few other options that are worth looking at in a bit more detail:

◆   **Full Screen without Taskbar**: This will select the full (primary monitor) screen area, but exclude the Window Taskbar. Typically, you would not want to include the Taskbar unless you are specifically recording its use.

◆   **Full Screen with Taskbar**: This will select the full (primary monitor) screen area, including the Windows Taskbar.

◆   **Apple iPad Landscape**: This will set the recording area to the same ratio as that used by an Apple iPad in landscape mode (actually just 1024x724).

◆   **Browser Client Area**: This option is only available when you select a browser as the application. It selects the application area within the browser window, and excludes the Titlebar, menus, tabs, address bar, favorites bar, status bar (at the bottom) and so on. This is very useful if you are recording a web application, and only want to capture the actual application itself.

◆   **Custom**: Any non-preset selection. You will need to drag the selection marquee to the required area yourself. This option is automatically selected if you click on Region in Step 9.

11. If you selected **Region** in Step 9, and selected a recording size and shape that is different from the current application size and shape, then you can click on the **Fit Application Window**, and the application will be resized to fit the recording marquee.

12. Click on the **Record** button. The *Recording Bar* is shown across the top of the screen. You are now ready to record your application, as explained in *Step 3: Record the application* on page 86, below.

Step 3: Record the application

To record the application, simply perform the actions you want to include in your recording, and Enable Now will automatically capture them. Work slowly and methodically, taking care to perform the exact, correct actions. This will save you from unnecessary editing later.

Whenever Enable Now is busy capturing an action for you, the *Recording Bar* will turn red. Wait for it to turn green again before performing the next action. For more information on the *Recording Bar*, and the things you can do with it, refer to *Working with the Recording Bar* on page 86.

Other things you may find useful to do while you are recording are:

- Insert an explanation bubble: See *Adding an Explanation* on page 88.
- Insert an additional screenshot: See *Adding a screenshot* on page 91.
- Switch applications: See *Step 2: Select the application* on page 83.
- Pause: See *Pausing during recording* on page 91.

Once you have finished recording, click the **Stop** button to stop recording. The *Recording Bar* will close, and you will be returned to the *Project Editor*. You can then edit your project, as explained in *Chapter 4, Editing a Simulation*.

Working with the Recording Bar

The *Recording Bar* is displayed across the top of your primary screen all the time that you are recording. The color of the recording bar identifies the current status of recording, as follows:

- **Green**

Enable Now is waiting for you to perform an action. The last action captured is shown in the text (in the example above, Enable Now had captured the user clicking on the **Minimize** button).

- **Red**

Enable Now is busy capturing the last action that you performed. Wait until the *Recording Bar* changes back to green before performing your next action.

- **Yellow**

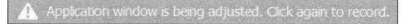

Enable Now is not yet ready to record. This may be because you have clicked in an application other than the one you initially selected. Click back in the original application, or if you need to change application, do so as explained in *Step 2: Select the application* on page 83.

- **Gray**

| **II** | Pause (Active Area) |

You have paused recording. Enable Now will not capture any further actions until you resume recording.

The following table shows the options that are on the (rightmost side of the) *Recording Bar* and explains their purpose. Note that the availability of individual options will depend upon the status of the *Recording Bar*.

Button	Name	Purpose
II	Pause	Temporarily pause recording. Any actions you perform while recording is paused are not captured. Everything that you have captured so far will be copied into the project.
⊙	Record	Re-start recording after you have previously paused it.
■	Stop	Stop recording. Everything captured will be inserted into the project, and you will be returned to the *Project Editor*.
↩	Undo	Cancel the last action captured.
Insert menu		
▭	Insert Explanation	Insert an EXPLANATION macro. For instructions on this functionality, refer to *Adding an Explanation* on page 88.
▢	Insert Screenshot	Insert a screenshot without an associated action. For instructions on this functionality, refer to *Adding a screenshot* on page 91.
Tools menu		
↖	Execute Mouse Actions	You record your simulation by performing the actions in the actual application. If you want an action to be captured, but do not want to actually perform the action in the application, then (de)select this option. The action will still be captured, along with its full context, but the action will not be executed in the application. This is very useful if you do not want to 'consume' the data used in the recording. Select this option again to return to performing the actions in the application.

Button	Name	Purpose
	Choose Application	When you first start recording, you need to choose the application that you are recording against, so that Enable Now can correctly capture the context. If you need to switch to another application during recording, then you can use this menu option to display the *Select Window and Profile* dialog box and choose the new application.
	Settings	Selecting this option will display the *Settings* dialog box, showing only those Enable Now settings directly related to recording. You can then adjust these settings as required. Note that any changes you make will apply to all subsequent recordings, so you should remember to change them back after you have finished the recording, if necessary.
	Minimize	Hide the *Recording Bar*. A single icon will be visible in the System Tray, instead. This will be one of: • **Pause** • **Record** • **Stop** These have the same function as the buttons of the same name on the full *Recording Bar* (see *Working with the Recording Bar* on page 86.)
	Close	Close the *Recording Bar* and return to the *Project Editor*. This is effectively an alternative to the **Stop** button, which seems to do the same thing.

Adding an Explanation

An Explanation is a bubble that is overlaid on the application screen which does not have an associated action. Explanation bubbles are therefore not tied to a specific object, and by default are not displayed with a bubble pointer. EXPLANATION macros can be added during editing, but you can also add one during recording, as explained below.

To add an Explanation bubble to your recording, carry out the steps shown below:

▲ If you are capturing audio as you record, then this will be captured all the time that you are adding and formatting your Explanation. There is no 'pause' option.

1. While you are positioned on the screen for which you want to provide an Explanation, select menu option **Insert | Insert Explanation** on the *Recording Bar*. The cursor changes to a 'cross-hairs'.

2. Click on the application screen at the point at which you want the center of the explanation bubble to be positioned (or the point at which the tip of the bubble pointer will be, if you will add a pointer to the bubble—see step 10). You can change the position of the bubble (and its pointer)

later, if necessary. The *Explanation* dialog box is displayed, as shown below.

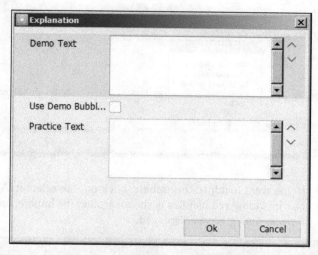

3. Click in the **Demo Text** field. The *Text Entry* dialog box is displayed.

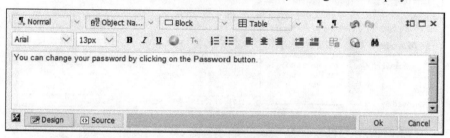

4. Enter the text that you want to appear in the Explanation bubble in Demo mode into the text box. You can use all of the formatting options available, including using styles, inserting tables and other objects, and applying text formatting. All of these options are explained more fully in *Adjusting Bubble text* on page 111. Once you have finished, click on **Ok**.

5. If you want exactly the same text to be displayed in Practice mode, then select the **Use Demo Mode Bubble or Practice mode** checkbox. Otherwise, click in the **Practice Text** field and enter the required Practice mode text as explained in Step 4.

6. Click the **OK** button. The Explanation bubble is displayed over the application screen, as shown in the partial screenshot below.

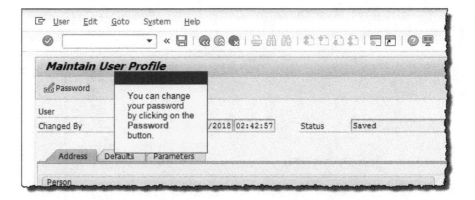

7. If you want to adjust this bubble, click on it to select it. A bounding box including red handles is shown around the bubble, and the *Bubble Format* dialog box is displayed.

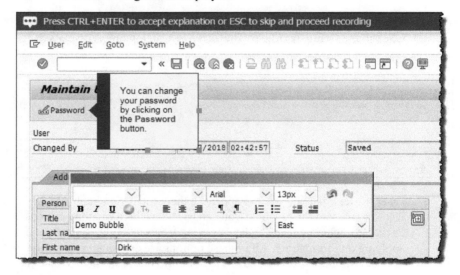

8. To change whether the Demo text or the Practice text is currently displayed on the screen, use the drop-down list field in the lower-left of the *Bubble Format* dialog box to select the required mode.

9. To move the bubble to a new position on the screen, click on it and drag it to the new location. To resize the bubble, drag the handles on the bounding box as required.

10. To add a pointer to the bubble, use the drop-down list field in the lower-right of the *Bubble Format* dialog box to select the position of the bubble relative to the tip of the pointer. In the example above, the position is set to **East**, so the bubble appears due East of the pointer.

11. Once you are happy with the content, format, and position of your Explanation bubble, press *CTRL+ENTER* on the keyboard. This is stated

in the *Recording Bar* at the top of the screen—it is important that you do not miss this, as you will not be able to return to recording the application until you have done so.

12. You can then continue recording your application as required.

Adding a screenshot

Enable Now will automatically capture applicable screenshots as you record in your application. You should therefore not normally need to capture screenshots yourself. However, there are circumstances under which you may want to capture additional screenshots that are not directly related to an action that you perform. For example, you may want to capture an intermediate screenshot that shows the current status of a progress bar, or you may want to show some other form of automatic screen transition.

To capture a screenshot in your recording that is independent of an action, carry out the steps shown below.

1. While you are positioned on the screen that you want to capture, select menu option **Insert | Insert Screenshot** on the *Recording Bar*.

2. A screenshot is taken and inserted into the project as a new Step. Note that there is no visual indication of this (the recording bar does not turn red, and no message is displayed).

3. You can now continue recording your application as required.

Note that the Step containing the screenshot will contain only a single SCREEN macro containing the screenshot. You will need to add further macros (such as an EXPLANATION macro) to this step during editing, so that the screen is displayed during playback.

■ You may find it useful to add a screenshot immediately before the end of recording (as the last thing you do before clicking **Stop**) to show the result of the last action you performed—otherwise the simulation may seem to end abruptly. [Tip courtesy of Joel Harris.]

▲ Steps and macros are explained in *Chapter 4, Editing a Simulation.*

Pausing during recording

There may be times when you need to pause recording—for example, if you need to drag a pop-up box within the recording marquee, or if you need to check something or perform some action that you do not want to be captured in your recording. You can do this as follows:

1. Click on the **Pause** button on the *Recording Bar*. The *Recording Bar* turns gray, and everything that you have captured so far is saved to the project (you may see this if your Producer screen is also visible).

2. Do what you need to do. Enable Now will not capture any actions you perform. If you are recording audio, this will also be paused.

3. When you are ready to continue recording, click on the **Record** button on the *Recording Bar*.

Re-recording a simulation

If you need to re-capture all of the screens in a recording, and/or if some of the controls have changed, then you can re-record all or some of the simulation as explained in this section.

When you created an initial recording (as explained earlier in this chapter), Enable Now captures the context of everything you did. This includes the technical identifier of the objects that you interacted with (the fields you entered text into, the buttons that you clicked on, and so on). This information is stored in the *Rerecord* category of properties for the interaction macros, which means that it can be re-used during the re-recording process. Enable Now can even use this information to re-perform these actions itself, capturing new screenshots as it goes. So if the only thing that has changed is the screenshots, re-recording can be done almost automatically by Enable Now, with little involvement by you, the Author.

To re-record a simulation, carry out the steps shown below.

1. Open the simulation in the *Project Editor*.

2. Choose to re-record the entire simulation, or specific steps, as follows:

   ♦ To re-record the entire simulation, click on the **Rerecord Application** button, and then select **Rerecord Project** from the drop-down panel.

   ♦ To re-record only specific Steps, first select the required Steps in the *Step View*, then click on the **Rerecord Application** button and select **Rerecord Selected Steps** from the drop-down panel.

   ♦ To re-record everything from a specific Step onward (or until you stop re-recording), click on the first Step that you want to re-record in the *Step View*, and then click on the **Rerecord Application** button and select **Rerecord From Current Step** from the drop-down panel.

   The *Rerecord Project* dialog box is displayed.

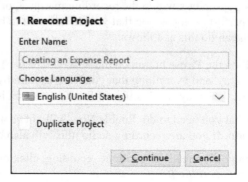

3. Under **Enter Name**, check the proposed name for the project, and change this if necessary (typically, only if you want to create a new project (see Step 5 below).

4. If you are going to create a new project, and want this to use a different language, then select the required language under **Choose Language**.

5. If you want your re-recording to be saved as a new project (and leave th original recording unchanged) then select the **Duplicate Project** checkbox. Otherwise, make sure that this checkbox is not selected.

6. Click **Continue**. The *Select Window and Profile* dialog box is displayed.

7. In the **Choose Window** list, select the window for the application you want to record.

8. Under **Choose Profile**, check that the correct recording profile has been selected, and change this if it has not.

9. If you always want the selected profile to be used for the selected application, then select the **Associate with Selected Window** checkbox. This should only be necessary if you have changed the default profile selection.

10. If you want your new recording to use exactly the same input text values as were used in the original recording, then deselect the **Revise Input Values** checkbox. Otherwise, leave this checkbox selected, and you will have the option to adjust the input values before starting the recording (see step 13).

11. By default, Enable Now will attempt to progress through the recording automatically, performing each action captured in the original recording itself before moving on to the next step. If you want to check and confirm each action yourself, then make sure that the **Interactive Mode** checkbox is selected. Otherwise, deselect this checkbox. Normally, you would want the recording to progress automatically, unless you know there have been significant changes to the interface.

12. Click **Rerecord**.

● Even if you choose to re-record 'automatically'. Enable Now will stop and ask you to manually capture or confirm any interaction for which the **Interactive** property is set in the *Rerecord* properties of the simulation project.

13. If you chose **Revise Input Values** (in step 10) then the *Revise Input Values* dialog box is displayed.

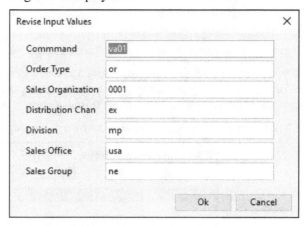

The *Revise Input Values* dialog box contains an input field for each INPUT TEXT macro in the original recording, showing the values used in the original recording. Make any necessary adjustments to these fields, and then click on the **Ok** button.

14. You are passed into the application, and the *Rerecording Bar* is displayed at the top of the screen.

You can now rerecord the simulation as explained in the subsections below.

The Rerecording Bar

The following table shows the options that are on the *Rerecording Bar* and explains their purpose.

Button	Name	Purpose
	Accept Control	Accept the currently-displayed control and/or bubble (either as identified, or after adjustment). See Step 7 of *Interactive rerecording* on page 96.
	Show Control	Re-select the screen object (and replace the currently-identified one). See Option (a) under *Capturing an unrecognized control* on page 98.
	Step Preview	Display the *Step Preview* dialog box, which shows the currently-recorded screen, control, and bubble text. See the example in *Capturing an unrecognized control* on page 98.

Button	Name	Purpose
▮▮	Pause	Temporarily pause rerecording. Any actions that you perform while rerecording is paused will not be captured. Everything that you have captured so far will be applied to the project.
↻	Rerecord	Re-start rerecording after you have previously paused it.

Insert menu

Button	Name	Purpose
⦿	Record Control	Record additional steps not present in the original recording. See Option (a) under *Capturing an unrecognized control* on page 98.
⊕	Insert Explanation	Insert a new EXPLANATION macro.

Tools menu

Button	Name	Purpose
🗑	Delete Control	Delete the current (interaction or EXPLANATION) macro from the recording. See Option (b) under *Capturing an unrecognized control* on page 98.
▶▶	Skip Control	Leave the current interaction macro unchanged, and continue to the next step.
⏏	Choose Application	When you first start recording, you need to choose the application that you are recording against, so that Enable Now can correctly capture the context. If you need to switch to another application during recording, then pause the rerecording and then select this option to return to the *Select Window and Profile* dialog box and choose the new application.
⚙	Settings	Selecting this option will display the *Settings* dialog box, showing only those settings directly related to recording. You can then adjust these settings as required. This option is only available when rerecording is paused. Note that any changes you make to your settings will apply to all subsequent recordings, so you should remember to change them back after you have finished the recording, if necessary.
▬	Minimize	Hide the *Recording Bar*. A single icon will be visible in the System Tray, instead. This will be one of: • Pause • Record • Stop Clicking on any of these will re-instate the full *Rerecording Bar*.

Button	Name	Purpose
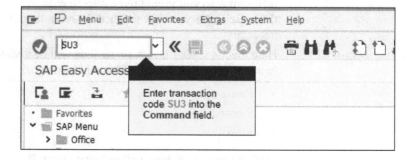	Close	Close the *Recording Bar* and return to the *Project Editor*.

Automatic rerecording

If you did not select **Interactive Mode** then Enable Now will attempt to carry out the originally-recorded task in the application, by performing each step in the recording, as it is currently recorded. You will see Enable Now performing each action in the application; you do not need to do anything at this stage—just let Enable Now do its thing.

Execution will progress, with Enable Now re-capturing the screenshots and object images, until one of the following happens:

- Enable Now reaches an EXPLANATION macro—continue with *Re-recording Explanations* on page 99.

- Enable Now reaches the last step and finishes—continue with *Finishing the rerecording* on page 100.

- Enable Now reaches an interaction macro for which the **Interactive** property (in the *Rerecord* category) is selected—continue with *Interactive rerecording* on page 96.

- Enable Now reaches an interaction for which it cannot identify the correct control on the current application screen—continue with *Capturing an unrecognized control* on page 98.

Interactive rerecording

With interactive rerecording, Enable Now will progress through the current recording, overlaying the currently-recorded action area and bubble onto the actual application window, as shown in the example below.

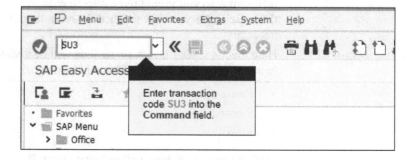

To confirm that the correct object has been identified, and assuming that you do not want to change the bubble text, confirm this action by clicking on the

Confirm button on the *Recording Bar*. (In theory, you can also press ENTER on the keyboard, but in practice I have found that this does not always work.)

If you want to change the bubble, then you can do so as follows:

1. Click in the bubble itself. You are passed into edit mode in the bubble, and the *Text Format* dialog box is displayed, as shown below:

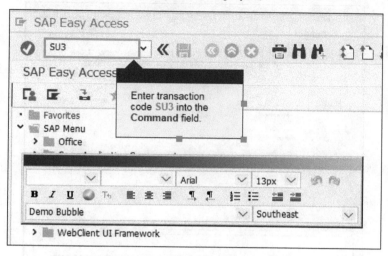

2. Select whether you are changing the Demo Text or the Practice Text via the drop-down list button in the lower-left of the *Text Format* dialog box.

3. Edit the bubble text as required, directly in the bubble itself. The *Text Format* dialog box provides you with common options for formatting the text.

4. If you want to change the size of the bubble, use the handles on its border to drag the bubble box to the required shape and size.

5. If you want to change the location of the bubble pointer (and therefore, the position of the bubble relative to the object), select the required bubble position from the drop-down list in the lower-right corner of the *Text Format* dialog box.

6. If you want to move the bubble to a new position, click on the bubble and drag it to the required position. You should not normally do this for interaction bubbles, as it will break the link between the object and the bubble, which can reduce the effectiveness of a Desktop Assistant project if one is created from this simulation project.

7. Once you have made all required changes to the bubble (including its text, pointer, and position, click on the **Confirm** button on the *Recording Bar*.

8. Processing continues with the next step. Continue as appropriate (by either returning to automatic recording, or by repeating the above steps for interactive recording).

Capturing an unrecognized control

If Enable Now cannot locate a previously-captured control on the current application screen, the *Step Preview* dialog box is displayed, as shown below. You can also display this dialog box at any time by clicking on the **Step Preview** button on the *Recording Toolbar*.

The current screenshot for the simulation is shown, along with the position of the control on this (you can click on this image to zoom in, if necessary). The current bubble text is shown in the lower portion of the dialog box. You cannot change this text here, but you will have the opportunity to change it (as explained in *Interactive rerecording* on page 96) after you have selected the control.

You have four options available to you from the *Step Preview* dialog box. These are:

a.   To select the correct control on the current screen, click on the (misleadingly-named) **Show Control** button. The cursor changes into a cross-hair cursor. On the application screen, click on the correct control to select it. Your recording is amended to use this control (the control's name, image, and position are (re-)captured).

b.   To delete the macro for this control from your simulation, click on the **Delete Control** button. This is useful if the control no longer exists on the application screen, and this step is therefore no longer required in the simulation.

c.   To skip recapture for this control, click on the **Skip** button. The original macro for this control will be retained in your simulation project. This is useful for optional controls or dialog boxes that for some reason are not displayed during the re-recording.

d.   To insert additional steps into your recording, click on the **Record Control** button. The full simulation recorder functionality will then be available to you, just as if you were creating a brand new recording. Refer to *Step 3: Record the application* on page 86 for full details of this functionality. Once you have recorded the last (new) step, press the *Esc* key on the keyboard to stop recording and return to the rerecord function.

Tip:
If you need to perform additional steps in the application to get to the correct control (for example, clearing a message box) but do not want these steps to be captured as part of the re-recording process, then hold down the *Esc* key while performing these steps.

Re-recording Explanations

Regardless of whether you are rerecording interactively or automatically, Enable Now will stop at an EXPLANATION macro, and display the bubble for this on top of the application.

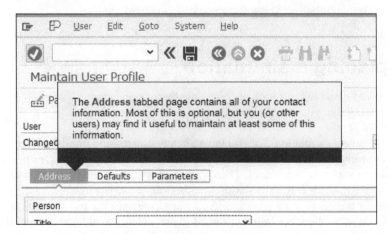

Process the Explanation bubble as follows:

1.   Always check the positioning of the bubble, in case the object being described (and possibly pointed to) is now at a different position on the screen.

     If you need to move the bubble, just click on it and drag it to the new location. If you need to change the relative position of the pointer, click on the bubble to display the pointer tip (represented by a blue square), and drag this pointer tip to the required position.

2. You can change the text in the bubble by clicking in the bubble and editing the text directly (and/or using the displayed *Format Text* dialog box to format the text - see the example under *Interactive rerecording* on page 96).

3. Once you are happy with the Explanation bubble, click on the **Confirm** button on the *Recording Bar*.

Finishing the rerecording

Once you reach the end of the rerecording—whether this is automatic or interactive, or for all Steps or selected Steps, the following confirmation message is displayed:

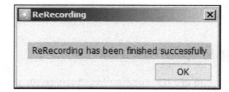

At this point, just click on the **OK** button and you are passed back into the *Project Editor*. Your simulation is now fully updated, and ready to use!

Replacing a simulation

Before we finish with our look at recording, there is one more piece of functionality that you may find useful.

Say you have a simulation that you have already created and published—and quite possibly embedded into training presentations, AICC packages, or otherwise linked into various other places. Then, somehow, you find you have a newer, better version of the same simulation, but this version exists as a separate simulation project in your Workarea. You want to replace the old simulation with this new version, but you don't want to just delete the old one and publish this new one, as all the existing links will break. Fortunately, Enable Now has a solution to this: **Replace Contents**.

The Replace Contents function allows you to effectively replace the entire content (all Steps, macros, screenshots, and so on) of one simulation project with the content of another. This allows you to effectively keep the existing links, but use the new version of the simulation.

Note that there are no 'checks' on this functionality. The two simulations do not have to have the same number of Steps, or even be recordings of the same application. Enable Now simply guts the old one and then inserts the contents of the new one into it. (Yes, you could manually do this, but then you'd also need to copy over all of the project properties, as well.)

To replace the contents of one simulation project with another, carry out the following steps:

1. In the Workarea, click on the simulation whose contents you want to replace (that is, the 'old' version).

2. Select menu path **Edit | Replace Contents**. The *Replace Contents* dialog box is displayed.

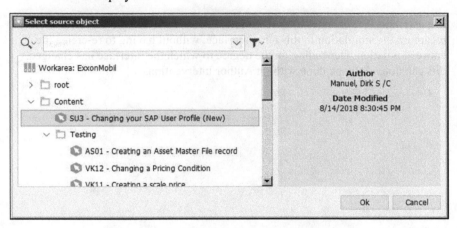

3. Navigate to and select the simulation project that contains the contents you want to use (that is, the 'new' version). You can use the search and filter features at the top of the dialog box to locate this project, if necessary.

4. Click **Ok**. A warning message is displayed, stating:

   ```
   Are you sure you want to replace the content of
   <old> with the content of <new>? There is no
   undo and the original content will be lost.
   ```

5. Click **Ok** in the message dialog box.

The entire content of the original simulation is replaced with the content of the new simulation. This includes all Steps, macros, and screens, as well as all of the project's properties. Effectively, the only thing that is kept is the UID, so that any existing links still work.

The simulation that you copied (the 'old' version) is still retained, so if you don't need this any more, you can delete it.

Summary

The cornerstone of SAP Enable Now training content is the simulation. Simulations can be played by users in a number of ways, and can also be re-purposed in several different formats, from printed documentation to in-application help.

Recording a simulation is as easy as performing the task you want to capture in the application itself. Recording is automatic, and Enable Now provides a selection of profiles that support effective context capture for a number of different applications and user interfaces.

If a user interface changes after recording, Enable Now has the ability to recapture the simulation in this new interface, without having to re-create the entire simulation. Depending on the degree to which the interface has changed, this can potentially be done without Author intervention.

4
Editing a Simulation

Most of the work in creating effective simulations is in the editing of the recording. Conceivably, you could spend ten times as long on the editing of a project versus recording it. Enable Now provides a vast amount of functionality for precisely controlling the look and feel of the simulation and making it classroom-ready. Some of this functionality may seem overly-detailed, and some of it could well be considered 'optional', and you may not need to use all of the available functionality in every simulation. However, over time you will find that you do use it all, and you will appreciate the level of control that it affords you. The extensive editing capabilities of SAP Enable Now allow you to create training simulations that truly shine.

In this chapter, we will focus on the functionality available via the *Project Editor* within Producer. You will learn:

- How to maintain the meta-data (properties) for a project
- How to change the size, position, type, and content of bubbles
- How to control user interactions
- How to merge screens
- How to use decisions and branches

Opening the simulation for editing

Before you start editing a simulation project, you should check it out for editing. The easiest way to do this is to simply double-click on it in the Workarea. This will open the simulation in the *Project Editor*. Refer to *Checking out a content object* on page 35 for additional details if necessary.

Once you have finished editing the simulation, save it, close the *Project Editor* and check in the project as explained in *Checking in a content object* on page 36.

The Project Editor

When you edit a simulation, it is opened in the *Project Editor*, in a separate tab within the Producer. An example of the *Project Editor* screen is shown below.

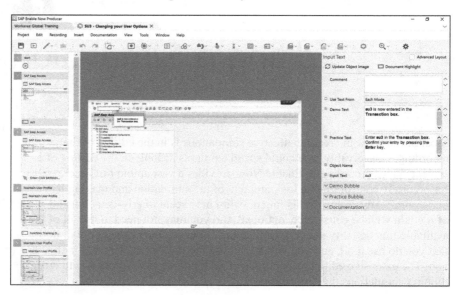

The *Project Editor* screen consists of four main components. These are identified in the graphic on the right, and explained below.

1. The *Project Editor Toolbar*.

2. The *Step View*, in which you can see small thumbnails of all of the screens in the simulation (along with some additional information we will cover later). In the example above, this is in the leftmost section of the screen.

● WYSIWYG stands for What You See Is What You Get, and here refers to the fact that content appears in this pane (more-or-less) exactly the way it will appear to users during playback.

3. The *WYSIWYG Editor*, which shows a single screenshot. In the example above, this is in the largest, center section of the screen.

4. The *Macro Editor*, which contains the properties available for the currently-selected macro (we will cover what a macro is, below). In the example above, this is in the rightmost section of the screen.

You can change the exact arrangement of these elements (for example, if you prefer to have the *Step View* across the top of the screen instead of down the side) by selecting menu option **View | Layout** and then selecting the required arrangement. The example above uses the **Vertical** layout.

You can also choose to have any of the three main panes 'undocked' from the edges of the screen so that they appear in a separate window that 'floats' above the Producer window, by selecting menu option **View | Floating Windows** and then selecting the pane that you want to float. This is extremely useful if you are using multiple monitors, as you can move one or more panes to your secondary monitor, providing more space for the remaining pane(s) on your primary monitor. To return to a 'docked' view, either select a docked layout as described above, or simply close the floating window, and the view will be reset to the last-used layout.

Now, let's look at each of these sections in a little more detail.

The Step View

The *Step View* shows all of the Steps in the project. Each Step typically consists of a screenshot and one or more **macros**. A macro defines an element that is to be displayed in the simulation, or an action that is to be performed, and so on. The order of the macros within a step is significant. You can think of them as being 'layered' on the screen in the order in which they are shown in the *Step View*, from top to bottom. So a macro element listed at the bottom will appear over the top of any macro element listed immediately above it, and so on. You can reorder these elements by dragging them into the required order.

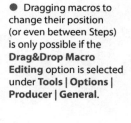

● Dragging macros to change their position (or even between Steps) is only possible if the **Drag&Drop Macro Editing** option is selected under **Tools | Options | Producer | General**.

The names shown on the elements in the *Step View* are taken from the element properties, which are shown in the *Macro Editor*. The *Macro Editor* is explained separately below, but it is worth looking at these names, and their use, now. Let's do this by examining one of the Steps from our sample recording.

When you create a recording, a separate Step is created for each action that you perform. This Step contains a screenshot, and a macro for the action that you performed (in the example above, we have combined multiple actions into the same step for the purposes of illustration—how to do this is explained later in this chapter). Each of these elements (Step, SCREEN, and interaction macros) has its own name, which is shown in title bar for that element.

The Step name is taken from the screen name. The Step name is used in Demo mode, where it appears in the *Progress Bar* (see *Advanced Editing* on page 159), and also in several of the Document outputs (see *Chapter 12, Working with Documents*), so you may want to change this to something meaningful.

You can also change the SCREEN name, if necessary, via the SCREEN macro's **Title** property. The SCREEN name/**Title** can also appear in some of the Document outputs (depending on the **Use Title as Heading** property), so again you may want to change it to something more descriptive than the default value.

Information on the macro bar

The 'bar' for each macro in the *Step View* contains (from left to right) an icon indicating the macro type, a very short macro description, and possibly one or more additional icons on the far right indicating additional properties that apply to the macro.

For interaction macros, the macro description is initially comprised of the **Object Name** property followed by the **Demo Text** (regardless of which mode is currently displayed). The same is true of EXPLANATION macros—although typically there is no **Object Name** for EXPLANATION macros.

For all macros, you can influence the macro description via the macro's **Comment** property. This property is really designed to allow you (the Author) to record some internal (Author-only) information about the macro, but any text you enter in this property will automatically replace the macro description in the *Step View*. You can further influence this as follows:

- Prefix the **Comment** with a plus sign (+) and the text will be appended to the end of the default macro description.

- Prefix the **Comment** with a minus sign (-) and the text will be added to the front of the default macro description.

- Prefix the **Comment** with a slash (/) and the macro description will be unchanged.

The WYSIWYG Editor

The *WYSIWYG Editor* takes up the largest part of the screen. It contains the screenshot for the Step, along with all of the elements that are displayed on top of this screen (such as Bubbles, text boxes, shapes, and so on).

You can adjust the scale of the screenshot via the drop-down for the **Zoom** button on the *Project Editor Toolbar*.

By default, the *WYSIWYG Editor* shows all of the macro elements in the Step at the same time, even though during playback they are more likely to be displayed one at a time (at least for interaction macros), and with the currently-selected macro element on top. To allow you to focus on one element at a time, you may find it useful to use the **Show Bubbles** button to toggle from **Show Bubbles for Step** to **Show Bubbles for Macro**. Then, the screen will show only the macro element selected in the *Step View* normally, and will 'fade out' all of the other macro elements on the screen. This is illustrated in the examples below:

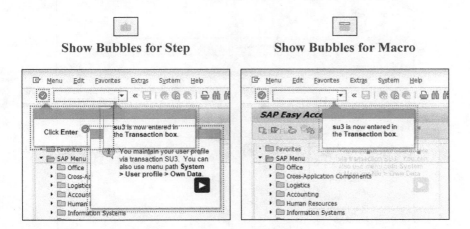

Show Bubbles for Step   **Show Bubbles for Macro**

The Macro Editor

The *Macro Editor* pane displays the properties of the currently-selected object (Step, Screen, or macro element). The object can be selected either in the *Step View* or in the *WYSIWYG Editor*. The type of object selected is shown in the upper-left corner of the pane header.

At the top of the *Macro Editor* is a toolbar, which may contain buttons for key actions that you can perform for the macro element. The object properties are listed below this. Aside from a few general properties listed at the top of the *Macro Editor* pane, most of these are grouped into expandable/collapsible categories based on their function.

There are typically a *lot* of properties for an element (reflecting the large degree of control Enable Now affords over elements). To simplify the display, and avoid overwhelming new or occasional Authors, the *Macro Editor* initially shows only the most important or commonly-used properties. To display *all* properties, select the **Advanced Layout** checkbox in the upper-right corner of the pane.

Rather than provide an exhaustive list of all of the properties for every type of macro element here, we will describe the various macros as we use them (but if

■ This book assumes that you are always using the Advanced Layout. If you do not see a property mentioned in the book on your screen, check that you have the **Advanced Layout** checkbox selected.

you need to locate a specific property, you can look it up in this book's index). However, there are a few things worth knowing about property definitions and how to change them, before you delve into using trying to use them. Let's look at these things by way of an example. The partial screenshot below shows the *Macro Editor* for a MOUSE ACTION interaction macro. Here, the **Advanced Layout** option has been deselected, and all categories collapsed, for the sake of simplicity.

■ You can change the width of the *Macro Editor* pane by hovering the cursor over the leftmost border (assuming it is docked on the rightmost side of the screen) until the cursor changes to a two-headed arrow, then clicking and dragging the divider to the required position. You can also change the width of the property label area by hovering the cursor over the area slightly to the left of the value fields and doing the same thing.

To the left of most properties is an **Active** indicator. If a property is available for editing, the **Active** indicator shows as a green square (as is the case for the **Use Text From** property in the example above). If a property is not available for editing, then this indicator shows as a gray square (as is the case for the **Hotkey** property in the example above), and the property's value is taken from the default settings.

Where are the default property settings defined?

The default values for macro properties are defined in **Tools | Settings | Playback Settings | Macro Fallback Settings**. However, the *initial* settings are defined in **Tools | Settings | Authoring Settings | Macro Initialization**. When you record a simulation, the values specified in the **Authoring Settings** are used. If you deselect the **Active** indicator for a property, then its value is set to the **Macro Fallback Settings** value.

Just because a property shows as inactive does not mean that you cannot change it. You just need to click on the **Active** indicator to activate the property first, and then it will be available for editing. In this way, the **Active** indicator can be thought of as being like a 'safety cover' on a physical switch—it is there to make sure you don't *accidentally* change the property value from the default value. It also has the advantage that if you decide you don't want to keep your changes to a property you can just deselect its **Active** indicator, and the property will be reset to the default value.

At the bottom of the *Macro Editor* pane is a yellow help panel. This provides some basic help for the selected property (the selected property is highlighted in blue, as is shown for the **Use Text From** property in the example above). However, this help can be very hit-and-miss, and you are advised to test your settings to confirm that they do indeed work the way described.

How you change the value of a property will depend on the property that you are changing, but most fall into the categories shown below.

For properties that provide a **text box** (regardless of whether this a single line, or multiple lines) type the required value into the text box. For some properties (typically those that can include a lot of text) you may be passed into the full *Text Editor* to edit the text.

● The *Text Editor* is described starting on *page 111*.

For properties with a **drop-down field** (indicated by a downward-pointing arrow inside the rightmost edge of the field), select the required value from the drop-down list.

For properties with a **checkbox** for a value, simply click on the checkbox to select or deselect it, as required.

For properties that provide an **Edit** icon (a pencil) in the value column, click on the **Edit** icon to open a dialog box into which you can enter or select the required value(s). There may be multiple values, and these are typically summarized in a non-editable field on the main Macro Editor pane. Some properties will also include **Copy** and **Paste** buttons that you can use to copy the values to similar properties within the same macro (or to the same property for other macros).

For properties that have an **image** as a value, click on the **Replace Image** button and then select the relevant option from the drop-down context menu. This menu will typically provide options for editing the image, or capturing or loading a new image.

Editing simulation objects

The properties available for a given object within the simulation will depend upon the type of object. In the next few sections of this chapter, we'll look at how to edit the properties for different object types, by performing some of the more common changes you will want to make to a simulation project. You may not need to use all of these features every time, but you should at least be aware of what features are available, and how to use them.

Working with Bubbles

Most likely, the first thing you will want to do when editing a new simulation is adjust the Bubble. The Bubble is the rectangular pop-up box that (for interactions) points to the screen object against which the interaction was performed during recording. An example of a typical Bubble is shown below.

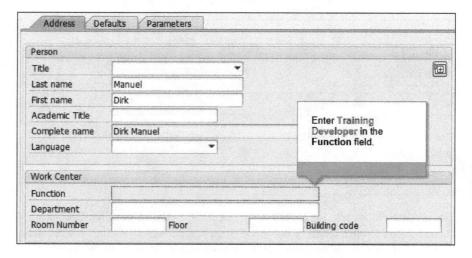

In the sub-sections below, we'll look at the various things you can do to influence the Bubble—from editing the text in it, to its appearance and its position on the screen.

Adjusting Bubble text

When you capture a recording, Enable Now will automatically determine the most appropriate instructional text to insert in the Bubble, based on the action performed and the screen object against which this was done. If necessary, you can adjust this text, or include additional information, as explained in this section.

Before you decide to change the default Bubble text you should consider any localization you may do into other languages. Enable Now provides translations of the Recording Dictionary texts into a number of other languages, which means that translation of the default Bubble text into one of these languages is as simple as changing the language code of the simulation project to the target language, and Enable Now will automatically use the Recording Dictionary texts for that language instead. If you change the Bubble text to use your own texts, then these texts will have to be manually translated.

There are effectively two texts that can be maintained for a Bubble: **Demo Text** and **Practice Text**. All playback modes, documentation formats, and Desktop Assistant projects created from the simulation project use one or other of these texts. If you do not need to make a distinction between these two modes, you can maintain only one of them by selecting the relevant option as follows:

- For interaction macros, the **Use Text From** property allows you to choose whether all modes should use the **Demo Text**, all modes should use the **Practice Text**, or both texts should be used as appropriate.

- For EXPLANATION macros, you can select the **Use Demo Bubble for Practice** checkbox to use the **Demo Text** in all modes, or deselect this checkbox to maintain the two texts separately. EXPLANATION macros are described in *Inserting Explanation Bubbles* on page 126.

Regardless of which texts you choose to use and/or change, the way in which you change the texts is exactly the same.

To edit a category of Bubble text, either double-click on the Bubble in the *WYSIWYG Editor*, or select the macro in the *Step View* (or single click on the Bubble in the *WYSIWYG Editor*) and then click in either the **Demo Text** field, or the **Practice Text** field in the *Macro Editor*, as appropriate. Regardless of the method used, the result is that the *Text Editor* dialog box is displayed.

★ The default text is taken from the **Recording Dictionary**, which is maintained in **Resources | Recording Dictionaries**.

● Localization and translation is covered in *Chapter 15, Localizing Your Content*.

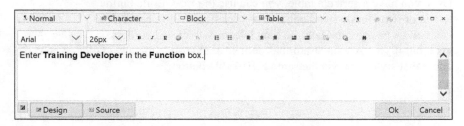

You can change the default text (or replace it with your own) by simply editing the existing text in the large text area. Whatever you enter in here will be included in the relevant Bubble. This is very intuitive, so isn't described here.

You can format this text using the buttons and controls at the top of the dialog box. Most of these are standard and will be familiar to anyone who has used any modern application that allows text formatting (such as Word, PowerPoint, Google Docs, and so on, so we won't describe them here. However, there are a few controls that warrant further explanation. These are described in the sections below.

Predefined text styles

The first three drop-down fields across the top of the *Text Editor* dialog box allow you to select pre-defined text styles for paragraphs, characters, and text blocks (from left to right, respectively).

It is always advisable to use predefined styles (instead of applying direct formatting), because if the style to be used for a specific text element changes later, these changes are automatically reflected in all of your texts as soon as the Administrator changes the Text Style definition.

One additional option is worth noting in relation to this. This is the **Remove Formatting** button . If you select a portion of the text and then click on this button, it will remove *all* formatting that has been applied to the text. This is extremely useful if you have copied and

Remove Formatting

pasted the text in from another source (especially Microsoft Word, which has an annoying habit of applying all kinds of [sometimes hidden] styles to text), and want to remove all of the source formatting before applying your own styles.

Using Tables

You can insert tables into a Bubble—either to provide tabular information, or just to better control the layout of the text in the bubble. To insert a table, use the **Table** drop-down and select either **Border**, to insert a table with borders, or **Borderless** to insert a table without borders.

Once you have inserted a table, you can use the **Edit Table** button to add or remove rows and columns, or delete the entire table. You can't add a background color to the table, or set colored borders

Edit Table

here, but if your Administrator has defined a table style that uses colors, you can apply that style here, via the same **Edit Table** button.

Inserting Objects

In addition to tables, there are a number of other things that you can insert into a bubble, via the **Insert Object** button. You can insert the following objects:

Insert Object

- Link
- Step link
- Placeholder
- Screenshot of window
- Screenshot of object
- Screenshot of area
- Image file
- Image from workarea

Each of these options has its own peculiarities, so we will look at them separately, below.

Inserting a link

Links allow you to jump to another location, or display content that exists at a certain location. Enable Now also allows you to trigger selected actions via a text link in a Bubble.

To insert a link, select the text or object that the user will click on, and then click on the **Insert Object** button and select **Insert link** from the drop-down list. The *Insert link* dialog box is displayed, as shown below:

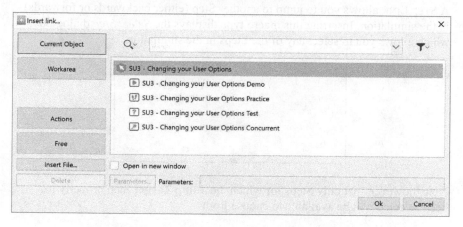

■ There may be other options available to you in the list on the left, if shortcuts to key Groups have been defined. See *Building your Workarea structure* on page 59 for more information.

Here, you have the following options:

- **Current Object**: Use this option to insert a link to an 'asset' for the current object. Click on the asset in the displayed list to link to it. Generally, assets are the various play modes and document formats available for the simulation, but you can use the **Insert File** button to insert other files from your workstation into this list, and then link to that file.

- **Workarea**: Use this option to insert a link to any object (simulation, simulation mode, Book, Book Page, and so on) that exists in the Workarea.

- **Actions**: Use this option to trigger a specific Enable Now playback or navigation action. Which actions are relevant will depend on where you are providing the link, but possibilities include **Next Step**, **Previous Step**, **Pause Simulation**, **Pause/Play Audio**, and so on.

- **Free**: Free links allow you to link to anything for which you have a URL (other content on the Internet, your intranet, and so on). Select this option and then enter the target URL in the **Link** field.

Regardless of which option you use (what you link to), you also have the option to open this content in a new browser window (instead of replacing the current window) by selecting the **Open in new window** checkbox. This will then make the **Parameters** button available, which you can use to set the properties of this new window (for example, should the menu bar, toolbar, scrollbars, and so on be shown or suppressed). The **Parameters** field to the right of the button summarizes the options that have been selected.

Inserting a Step Link

A STEP LINK allows you to jump to another Step (either backwards or forwards) in the simulation. Inserting this macro type displays the *Select Step* dialog box, which allows you to select any of the Steps in the simulation.

Note, however, that only Steps for which the **Jump Target** Step property has been selected will be available to choose from.

STEP LINK macros are useful when you want to give the user the option of continuing with a different part of the simulation and this decision is not triggered by an action that the user performs in the application (in that case you would use a BRANCH macro [see *Using a Branch* on page 164]).

Inserting a Placeholder

Placeholders provide an incredibly useful piece of functionality. They allow you to insert another piece of predefined content related to the macro, simulation, or other related object into the displayed bubble. The most useful of these—and the ones most used by Enable Now itself, when creating the default bubble text—are the ones that apply to properties of the current interaction macro, namely:

- **Object Name**
- **Object Image**
- **Input Text** (INPUT TEXT macros only)
- **Hotkey** (MOUSE ACTION macros only)

In addition to these four, you can also insert the name, short description or description of the simulation project. Other options allow you to insert the same information from a containing Book, Book Page, or Text Unit, if you are editing text within one of these types of object.

For an example of this in action, you can simply look at any of the Bubbles generated automatically by Enable Now during recording. The following partial screenshot is taken from a recording where the user is required to click on the **Enter** button.

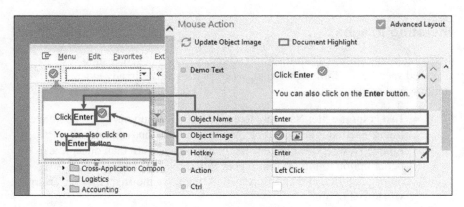

The two texts of "Enter" (one for the button name and one for the keyboard shortcut) and the image of the button are actually *placeholders* for the corresponding properties. You could change any of these in the relevant properties for the Step, and the contents of the Bubble would automatically be adjusted to reflect this.

● Which placeholders are included in the bubble text by default is controlled by the setting in the **Recording Dictionary** for the type of action/type of object combination.

Inserting screenshots

On the **Insert Object** button's drop-down menu, there are three separate options for inserting a 'screenshot'—although it should be understood here that the term *screenshot* really refers to 'information that you want to capture from a screen'. The options are:

- **Insert screenshot of window**: This allows you to capture and insert the entire contents of an application window.

- **Insert screenshot of object**: This allows you to capture and insert an image of a particular object on the application screen. This uses the same object recognition as is used during recording to identify individual objects on the screen, although here no context is captured, only the image.

- **Insert screenshot of area**: This allows you to capture and insert an image of a specific area of the screen (you will drag a marquee over the area to be captured).

For each of these options you should make sure that the application screen that you want to capture is displayed on your primary monitor, and then switch back to the Enable Now Producer. When you select the capture option, Producer will be minimized to reveal the last application that you used (which should be the one that you want to capture), and a red marquee will be shown around the capture area. Move this to the correct location and click to capture the image. (For an area, the cursor is changed to a cross-hair and you need to drag a marquee around the required area.

Inserting images

Inserting images differs from inserting screenshots in that screenshots are captured specifically for the insertion, whereas files must already exist. The options are:

- **Insert image file**: Navigate to and select a file on your PC. The image file is inserted into the bubble, but is otherwise unavailable within Enable Now. If this image is likely to be used more than once, it is a better option to import it into your Workarea (see *Importing an asset* on page 550), and then insert it from there, via the **Insert image from workarea** option.

- **Insert image from workarea**: Navigate to and select a file that already exists in your Workarea.

Editing the source HTML

Bubble text is ultimately saved within Enable Now in HTML format, as this provides the most flexibility for converting it into other forms of output.

Sometimes it is useful to be able to see—and optionally edit—this underlying HTML. Fortunately, Enable Now provides a feature for doing exactly that.

To switch to HTML mode, simply click on the **Source** button in the *Text Editor*. The dialog box then appears like the example shown below (which is for the same bubble used in the screenshot at the start of this section).

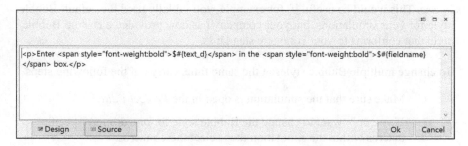

```
<p>Enter <span style="font-weight:bold">$#{text_d}</span> in the <span style="font-weight:bold">$#{fieldname}
</span> box.</p>
```

Obviously you need to have a working knowledge of HTML to make sense of this view, but if you do, it is helpful for being able to troubleshoot formatting issues or force specific formatting.

● All common HTML tags are supported, but not all tag *attributes* are, so be careful with these.

Click on the **Design** button to return to the regular view.

Adjusting the bubble appearance

There are a number of things you can do to change the way that the Bubble appears on the screen during playback. This includes changing the Bubble style, the Bubble size and position, and the bubble pointer. All of these things are explained in the sub-sections below.

Changing the Bubble style

The overall appearance of a Bubble is governed by its **Style** property. The default Bubble style is the **Edge bar** style, which is shown in the examples, and displays the Bubble as a rectangle with a thick blue bar along one edge, and a short, triangular pointer extending from this. If you don't like this default style, you can use the drop-down for the **Style** property field to select any of the other available Bubble styles (Enable Now ships with several pre-defined Bubble styles, with additional styles sometimes being added with new releases).

● At least that was the default when work on this book started; the default Bubble Style changed during a release upgrade, and may change again.

● The default Bubble style is defined via **Tools | Settings | Authoring Settings | Macro Initialization**.

You can change the **Style** property of individual Bubbles (it is not a global setting, or even a simulation-specific setting. Furthermore, the Bubble style for a given macro is set separately for the Demo Bubble and the Practice Bubble, so you could feasibly have one Bubble style in Demo mode, and another in Practice mode, or you could use a unique Style for EXPLANATION macros (or even for every type of interaction macro). You could even have a different Bubble style

● Administrators can define new Bubble styles via menu option **Tools | Customization | Edit Style Resources**.

on different Steps, if you wanted. However, it is strongly recommended that you strive for consistency—both across Steps and across simulations.

Replacing all Bubble styles in a simulation

If necessary, you can change the style of Bubbles throughout a simulations *en masse*. This would be useful if, for example, you initially used the default Bubble style for your simulations, but your company has now provided a custom Bubble style that conforms to your company standards.

To change multiple Bubble styles at the same time, carry out the following steps.

1. Make sure that the simulation is open in the *Project Editor*.

2. If you only want to change the Bubble style for one or more specific macros within the simulation then select these macros.

3. Select menu option **Tools | Replace Bubble Styles**. The *Replace Bubble Styles* dialog box is displayed.

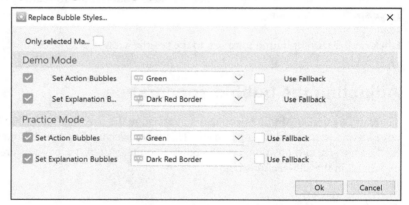

4. If you selected specific macros in Step 2, select the **Only Selected Macros** checkbox.

5. For each type of Bubble that you want to change (Demo vs. Practice, and Action Bubble vs. Explanation Bubble) select the checkbox to the left of the option, and select the required new Bubble style from the drop-down list.

    Alternatively, if you want to reset the Bubble style to the default style then select the **Use Fallback** checkbox. This will ignore any style selected in the drop-down, and deselect the **Active** indicator for the Style property of the macro(s)—which effectively resets the property to the default. Note that choosing this option will ignore any specific Bubble style you select here.

6. Click on the **OK** button.

★ The default settings for macros—including the default Bubble style—can be checked via menu option **Tools | Settings | Authoring Settings | Macro Fallback Defaults**.

The changes will be made throughout the simulation (or to the selected macros, if you chose this option). You may see a message of **No replacements performed**. Do not be concerned by this; it is only saying that there were no *more* Bubbles to change, once it has finished.

Changing the Bubble size

Bubbles in Enable Now are automatically sized during editing to accommodate all of the Bubble text. However, although the Bubble will always be adequately sized to accommodate all of the bubble text, the Bubble proportions are not always idea, sometimes resulting in a tall, thin Bubble—especially when there is a lot of text. In some cases you may find that the Bubble obscures some information on the screen that you want the user to see. In these cases (and others—maybe just for aesthetic reasons) you can resize the Bubble.

As with Bubble text, there are effectively two Bubbles that can be maintained for a simulation: the Demo Bubble and the Practice Bubble. Each of these has its own category in the *Macro Editor*, but the properties available are almost the same in both cases. An example of the properties for the Demo Bubble is shown in the partial screenshot below.

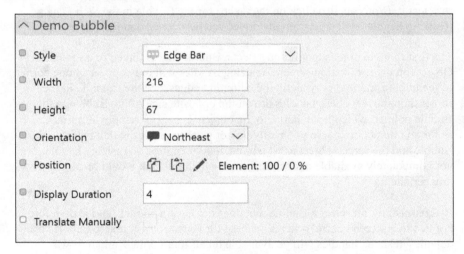

● The only difference between the properties for the Demo Bubble and the properties for the Practice Bubble is that the Practice Bubble does not have a **Display Duration** property for interaction macros (but it still has one for Explanation macros).

Note that the *WYSIWYG Editor* can only display Bubbles for one mode at a time. To determine which of these should be shown, use the **Macro Modes** button to select either **Edit Demo Mode**, or **Edit Practice Mode**, as appropriate. For more information on this, refer to *The WYSIWYG Editor* on page 106.

In the following sections, we will use the Demo Bubble from a recording of transaction VA01. An example of this, showing the default layout determined during recording, is shown below.

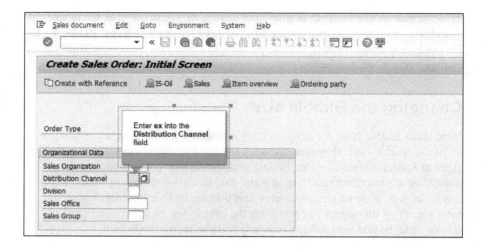

Assume we would like to limit the height of the Bubble to only two lines of text, to reduce the white space in the Bubble, and then move the Bubble so it is not obscuring any of the other fields on the screen. Let's look at how to do this.

To change the size of a Bubble, first click on the Bubble in the *WYSIWYG Editor*, to select it. (You can also click on the macro for the Bubble in the *Step View*.) Resizing handles will appear on the dotted red border surrounding the Bubble.

The first thing to note is that if you select a Bubble that is linked to a specific Object (on the application screen), resizing handles will only appear in one corner of the bubble and mid-way along the adjoining edges (see the example in the screenshot above). These handles are on the opposite side of the Bubble to the Bubble pointer, which is anchored to the object. This is extremely important, as for an interaction macro you really do not want to break the link between the Bubble and the screen object to which that macro applies, so resizing handles are not immediately available at positions from which this link would break if you dragged them.

By contrast, if you select a Bubble that does not have a pointer (and is therefore not tied to a screen control)—as is the case for EXPLANATION macro bubbles by default—resizing handles will be available on all four corners, and mid-way along each edge.

To resize a Bubble, click on a resizing handle, and drag it to the new location. Depending on the direction in which you drag it (horizontally or vertically, or diagonally from the corner) Enable Now will adjust the other dimension to ensure that the Bubble is never too small to accommodate its contents, leaving the Bubble pointer in the same place. Alternatively, for greater control, you can specify the exact size of the Bubble (in pixels) in the **Width** and **Height** properties in the relevant Bubble category in the *Macro Editor*.

In our example, we dragged the handle on the upper-right corner down and to the right. Our Bubble now appears as follows:

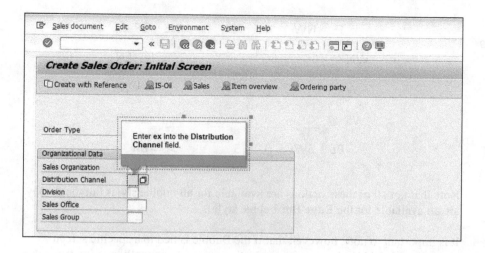

Changing the Bubble orientation

All Bubbles have a pointer (although for EXPLANATION macros this is initially 'hidden'). For Bubbles for interaction macros this points to the screen object to which the Bubble is linked, and is therefore typically aligned to one of the edges of the object. The location of the Bubble is then specified in relation to the tip of this pointer. This is defined in the **Orientation** property for the Bubble, which can have one of the values shown in the graphic below:

Northwest	North	Northeast
West	Center	East
Southwest	South	Southeast

Note that an **Orientation** of **Center** indicates that the Bubble is centered on the pointer, which means that it cannot be seen. You would not normally use this setting with a Bubble that is 'tied' to a screen object (which is all Bubbles for interaction macros, by default) as it would result in the Bubble over-laying the screen object.

To change the orientation of the Bubble pointer, you can just click on the Bubble's anchor point (the small blue square located at the tip of the pointer or in the center of the Bubble) and drag it to the new location. When you do this, there are actually more orientation points than the nine listed above—and, confusingly, the 'name' of the orientation point reflects the position from which the pointer extends from the bubble, and not the position of the bubble relative to the screen control. The composite diagram below shows all of the available pointer positions, and their identifiers. (These identifiers are shown in the center of the object as you drag the anchor point to the new position; it disappears when you release the mouse button).

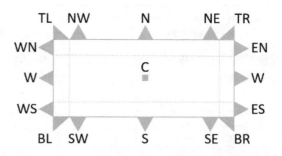

■ Not all of these 17 points have corresponding values on the **Orientation** property, which means that the only way to select some of them is by manually dragging the Bubble anchor point— which then breaks the object link. Luckily you can then re-instate this link by manually editing the **Position** property for the Bubble to re-set the orientation as relative to the **Element** (see *Inserting Explanation Bubbles* on page 126).

Note that not all of these options are available for all bubble styles (although they are all available for the **Edge Bar** bubble style).

It is important to note, however, that if the Bubble is tied to a specific screen control (as should be the case for interaction macros), manually moving the anchor point will break the link to the screen object. Instead, you should use the Bubble's **Orientation** property to select the required orientation.

In our example, we'll change the **Orientation** to **East**, so that the bubble is not overlapping the other fields on the screen.

Changing the Bubble orientation will only change the location of the Bubble relative to the anchor point. If the anchor point is currently tied to the upper-right (Northeast) corner of the object, and you change the orientation to Southwest, the Bubble will be moved so that it extends to the Southwest from the same point— which is still the upper-right corner of the object. This is shown in the following screenshot:

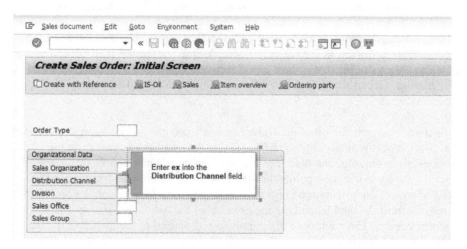

This clearly isn't exactly what we were aiming for. What we now need to do is change the point at which the Bubble extends from the screen object. This is governed by the location of the Bubble pointer, so we need to change the Bubble anchor point, relative to the object. How to do this is explained in the next section.

Moving the Bubble anchor point

When you change the orientation of an interaction macro Bubble (as explained in the previous section), you are really changing the location of the Bubble relative to the tip of the Bubble pointer (the 'anchor point'—the point at which it is anchored to the object or screen). Usually, if you change the Bubble orientation, you will also need to change the Bubble anchor point.

To change the position of the anchor point (the tip of the Bubble pointer), click on the **Edit** button for the **Position** property. The *Edit Position* dialog box is displayed, as shown below.

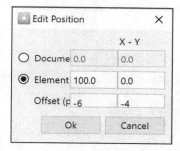

The *Edit Position* dialog box allows you to specify the exact position of the anchor point for the selected Bubble—which then, in conjunction with the **Orientation** property, controls the position of the Bubble itself. This dialog box may seem complicated at first, but is actually very concise once you understand what it is doing.

The Bubble anchor point is specified in terms of X and Y co-ordinates. Starting from the upper-left corner of whatever this is in relation to (see below), X is the position along the horizontal axis (from left to right), and Y is the position down the vertical axis (from top to bottom),

The **Document** and **Element** option buttons are used to select what the anchor point is specified in relation to. This is an either/or selection, and which option is selected determines which of the remaining input fields in the dialog box are available for editing.

● The term *Element* here refers to the screen Object. This book uses the term *Object* consistently to refer to an item (button, input field, or text) on the screen that is contextually-recognized during recording or editing.

If the Bubble is *not* tied to a screen Object (which, by default, includes all EXPLANATION macro Bubbles) then **Document** should be selected. This means that the Bubble anchor point is relative to the overall screenshot on which it is placed. The **X** and **Y** values to the right of this option then specify the *percentage* of the way along the axis that the anchor point should be located. For example, if the X and Y values are specified as 50.0 and 25.0 respectively, then the tip of the pointer will appear 50% of the way along the horizontal axis from the left edge and 25% of the way down from the top edge.

If the Bubble is tied to a screen object (which is normally the case for all interaction macros) then **Element** should be selected. In this case there are two sets of values. The first set—the percentages to the right of the **Element** option— work the same way as the percentages for the **Document** option, and specify the percentage of the way along the *screen object* (starting form the upper-left corner) that the anchor point should be located. The **Offset** fields then specify any adjustment to this position. These offsets are specified as a number of pixels, and can be positive (which will move the pointer tip to the right (**X**) or down (**Y**)), or negative (which will move the pointer tip to the left (**X**) or up (**Y**)).

Looking at our ongoing example, if we look at both the Bubble and the *Edit Position* dialog box at the same time (and assuming an **Orientation** property of **East**, as we left it at the end of the last section), we see:

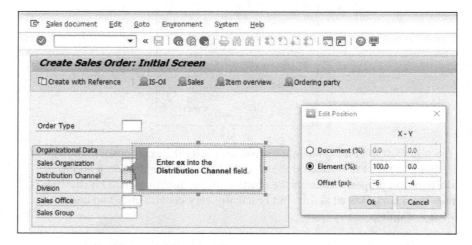

Here, the anchor point is specified relative to the **Element**, which in this case is the **Distribution Channel** input field. The X-axis values are 100% and -6 pixels. This is 100% of the way along the length of the screen object (which will position it on the rightmost edge of the object) and then 6 pixels *back* (it is a *negative* number) from this position. The Y-axis values are 0% and 4 pixels. This is 0% of the way down the height of the element (which will position it on the top edge of the control) and then 4 pixels *up* (it is a *negative* number) from this position.

This example uses the default settings determined by Enable Now during recording. So why are the offset values **-4** and **-6** used? A value of 4 or -4 is often used because the **Highlight** (the flashing blue border around the screen control) has a default width of 4 pixels, so using an offset of 4 or -4 makes sure that the bubble pointer does not overlap with this. An additional 2px may be added or subtracted from this just to pull the bubble pointer tip in slightly from the absolute corner, just to cater for cases where two screen objects are directly adjacent to each other, to make it clear which object is being pointed to.

★ The width of the Highlight is specified in **Tools | Settings | Playback Settings | General | Highlights | Border**.

If you need to change the position of the Bubble (and not just the orientation) then you will almost certainly need to manually change these values—and certainly if the Bubble is tied to a screen object and you want to retain this connection. This may seem overly-picky, but it's very easy to get used to. Most of the time you will use X and Y values of 0%, 50% or 100%, and an offset of 0, 4 or -4.

In summary, to change the position of a Bubble's anchor point via the *Edit Position* dialog box, you would therefore carry out the following steps:

1. Select either **Document** or **Element** as appropriate.

2. Enter the percentage of the way along the X and Y axes at which the anchor point should be located in the associated **X** and **Y** fields.

3. For Bubbles positioned relative to a screen object, enter any offset to the overall position in the **X** and **Y Offset** fields.

4. Click **OK**.

For our ongoing example, assume that we set the Bubble **Orientation** to East, and set the **X** coordinates to **100%** with a **+4px** offset, and the **Y** coordinates to **50%** with a **0px** offset. Our bubble now appears as follows (in the editor):

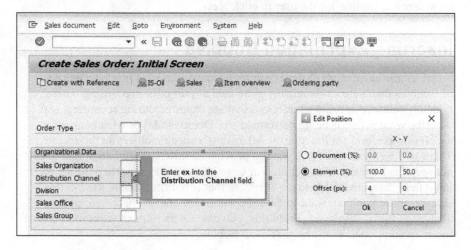

So now we have our Bubble positioned exactly where we want it. It's not obscuring any other fields on the screen, It took a little but of work, but it was worth it! But bear in mind that there are two Bubbles—one for Demo mode and one for Practice mode—and you've probably only changed one of these. Luckily, assuming you want to use exactly the same Bubble positioning in both modes, there is a quick way of copying the **Position** properties from one mode to another: click on the **Copy** button (⧉) for the **Position** property on the Bubble for one mode, and then click on the **Paste** (⧉) button for the **Position** property for the other—your values will be copied over, and you don't even need to re-open the *Edit Position* dialog box!

Changing the Bubble display duration

There is one more property that is worth looking at for Bubbles. This is the **Display Duration** property.

⭐ The default **Display Duration** property values can be defined in **Tools | Settings | Authoring Settings | Macro Initialization | Interactions** for the relevant macros.

In Demo mode, this property determines for how long a given Bubble will be displayed on the screen, before the interaction is performed. It defaults to **4** seconds, but you will likely need to adjust this, to make sure that users have the time to read the text in the Bubble, before watching the interaction being performed. In Practice mode, the user themselves performs the actions, and can therefore choose when to advance. Therefore, this property only exists in the *Demo Bubble* category, and not in the *Practice Bubble* category.

The exception to this is for Explanation Bubbles (described in the next section), where the **Display Duration** property is available for both the Demo mode Bubble and the Practice mode Bubble. Here, the duration defaults to **-1**, which effectively means "forever".—because there is no associated interaction, so the user is expected to advance at their own convenience. However, if you want your Demo mode to be truly 'hands off', you should change the *Demo Mode* **Display Duration** to be a positive number—otherwise, the demonstration will just sit there forever, waiting for the user to click **Next**.

Inserting Explanation Bubbles

So far in this chapter, all of the examples we have looked at involved editing of Bubbles that were automatically generated as part of our recording. These typically relate to specific interactions that are captured during recording, and describe what action is being performed (for Demo mode) or what action the user has to perform (in Practice mode) against a specific object on the screen. There will be times when you want to provide additional information that does not specifically relate to an action. For example, you may want to describe an input field that is available to the users but that is not specifically used in this simulation, or you may want to describe some element on the screen, such as a message that is displayed. To do this, you can use an EXPLANATION macro to insert an additional, 'non-object-related' Bubble.

To insert an Explanation Bubble, carry out the steps shown below.

1. In the *Step View*, locate the Step for the screen to which you want to add an Explanation Bubble, and then click on the existing macro after which the new Explanation Bubble should appear.

2. On the *Project Editor Toolbar*, click on the **Insert Macro** button, and select **Explanation** from the drop-down panel. (You can also select menu option **Insert | Insert Interaction | Explanation**.)

Insert Macro

3. A new EXPLANATION macro is inserted into the Step. This will result in a new Bubble being visible in the *WYSIWYG Editor*. This Bubble will be

positioned in the center of the screenshot, and without a Bubble pointer. The Bubble will also contain an icon, and a 'Continue' button that the user can click on to advance to the next macro.

Noe that Explanation Bubbles are displayed as a separate Step or action during playback. It is not possible to have an Explanation Bubble displayed at the same time as another (interaction macro) Bubble.

An example of an Explanation Bubble is shown below.

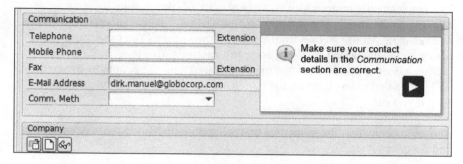

You can now edit the contents and appearance of this Bubble exactly the way you would any other bubble. Most of this is already explained above, but there is one property that is unique to Bubbles for EXPLANATION macros. This is the **Icon** property, which is described in the table below.

Property	Use
Icon	Select the type of icon (if any) that is to be displayed in the upper-left corner of the Bubble. This can be one of: **Remark** **Tip** **Info** **Warning** Alternatively, you can select **None** if you do not want to use an icon at all.

Working with interactions

During recording, every action that you perform in the application will be captured by way of an interaction macro that is inserted into your project. These interactions could be mouse-clicks, keystrokes on the keyboard, or the use of input fields—including input fields, checkboxes, radio buttons, and drop-down lists. The macros for each of these distinct types of interaction are unique, having different properties and unique capabilities. Therefore, we'll look at each of them separately, in the sub-sections below.

Working with Mouse Action macros

Mouse actions are captured every time you do something with the mouse during recording. This includes clicking or double-clicking with the left, center, or right mouse buttons, dragging or dropping with either the left or right mouse buttons, or using the scroll wheel to scroll up or down. Interestingly, there is also an option (during editing) to set a mouse action of **Mouse Enter**, which relates to the mouse moving over the screen object.

You can manually insert a MOUSE ACTION macro during editing by clicking on the **Insert Action** button on the *Project Editor Toolbar*, and selecting **Mouse Action** from the drop-down panel. (You can also select menu option **Insert | Insert Interaction | Mouse Action**.) Bear in mind that if you manually insert a mouse action the macro action will not be tied to an object on the screen, so you are better off recording a new Step if you can.

Insert Action

The table below lists the properties that are specific to MOUSE ACTION macros, and describes their purpose.

Property	Use
General	
Hotkey	Specifies the keyboard shortcut for the mouse action. This is typically captured automatically for single-click mouse actions, but can also be specified manually (as explained for KEY-STROKE macros— see *Key-Stroke actions* on page 142).
Ctrl **Alt** **Shift**	If one or more of the *CTRL*, *ALT*, or *SHIFT* keys were held down when the mouse action was performed (for example, a *CTRL*+click action was performed) then the relevant checkboxes here will be selected. You can adjust these manually if necessary.
Control	
Cursor Hand	Select this checkbox if you want the standard 'pointer' cursor to change to a 'hand' when the cursor moves over the object. You would only normally want to do this if that's how the application behaves.
Button	If the control should behave like a traditional button when it is clicked, then select this checkbox. The control will then appear to respond to the click by being pressed in (although in practice the object image is simply shifted slightly down and to the right). This is useful for adding a degree of 'realism' to your recordings.

Property	Use
Tooltip	Specifies the ToolTip text that is displayed in a small text pop-up displayed at the cursor point when the cursor moves over the object. This is typically captured automatically, but you should be wary of using it as it can provide too much of a 'hint' in Test mode, as only the correct control will have a ToolTip displayed.

Working with Input Text macros

When you record a simulation project, Enable Now will automatically identify instances where you enter a value into an input field, and will create an INPUT TEXT macro for you. Enable Now identifies the field that the value was entered into, and the value that was entered. This is normally sufficient, but there are situations in which you will need to provide additional information. In this section, we look at the options that are available in the *Macro Editor* for INPUT TEXT macros, by way of a few common scenarios.

Validating user input

A user carrying out a recorded simulation will be required to enter exactly the same text that was captured during recording. This is normally what you want, and in fact is usually necessary to ensure that the next step in the simulation appears correctly (that is, showing the text entered during recording). However, there are circumstances where this may not be ideal. Consider the following extract from ECC 6.0 transaction VK11 (Create Price Condition):

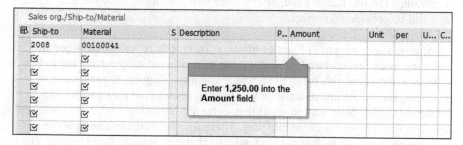

In this example, as per the initial recording, the user is required to enter **1,250.00** in the Amount field. If they enter exactly "1,250.00" then they can proceed to the next step. But if they enter "1250.00" or 1,250 this will be considered incorrect. This is particularly a problem in Test mode, where the user will be marked incorrect, and possibly 'fail' the test, even though they have performed an action that would be 100% valid in the actual system. Sure, you could explicitly state "Enter 1,250.00 into the Amount field" in the Test mode instructions (see *Editing a simulation for Test mode* on page 322) but then it is really little more than a reading/typing test.

Fortunately, Enable Now has a solution in the form of **Regular Expressions**. A Regular Expression allows you to validate a user's input against a predefined 'rule', as opposed to requiring them to enter exactly what was captured during recording.

You specify the Regular Expression in the appropriately-named **Regular Expression** property in the *Macro Editor* for the INPUT TEXT macro.

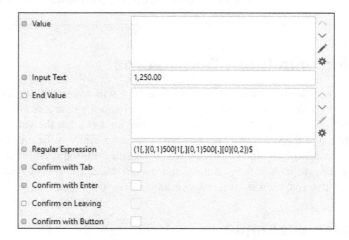

■ regex101.com is a great website for validating Regular Expressions. Just be careful as Enable Now does not appear to support all of the properties that this site does.

Regular Expressions can be fairly complex (depending upon the level of validation that you want to perform) and are really beyond the scope of this book (an entire book could be devoted just to Regular Expressions), but let's at least look at a solution to our current predicament.

The Regular Expression coded in the example above allows the user to enter **1,250.00**, **1250.00**, **1,250**, **1250**, or any other string with the same numeric value, and still be considered correct.

Normally, a user's input in Practice mode or Test mode is 'validated' when they enter the exact text required, with playback then automatically advancing to the next step. However, this is not as simple if you use a Regular Expression. For example, should the above input be validated as soon as the user enters "1250", or should Enable Now wait to see if they enter the following ".00"? This is where the 'confirm' properties come into play. These four fields determine how the user has to 'confirm' their input—effectively, that they have finished typing. The available options are shown as the last four properties in the partial screenshot above, and are explained in the table below.

Property	Use
Confirm with Tab	If selected, the user can press the *TAB* key on the keyboard to confirm their entry and proceed to the next macro.

Property	Use
Confirm with Enter	If selected, the user can press the *ENTER* key on the keyboard to confirm their entry and proceed to the next macro.
Confirm on Leaving	If selected, the user's input is validated as soon as they leave the input field (by pressing *TAB*, or clicking on anywhere on the screen outside of the current object)
Confirm with Button	If this option is selected, then the user will be required to click on a specific 'button' on the screen to validate their input and continue. When you first select this option, a new 'action area' will be added to the Step, and you need to move this to be over the appropriate control (you cannot use an existing MOUSE ACTION macro).

Note that these options are not specific to the use of Regular Expressions, and apply to all INPUT TEXT macros. However, you are most likely to need to adjust them where you are using a Regular Expression.

Now, let's suppose that we have our Regular Expression in place to allow the user to enter (amongst other things) "1250". But we still entered "1,250.00" in our recording, and this is what the user will see when they progress to the next step (and the next screenshot in the simulation is displayed). To make this more seamless, you can enter the 'final value' of the field into the **End Value** property. Then, regardless of what (valid input) the user enters, the field will show this value once the input has been validated.

Finally, let's look at how Enable Now handles changes to fields (as opposed to entering a value into an empty field). When you record an action for an input field, Enable Now automatically captures any value currently specified in the field, and stores this in the **Value** property for the INPUT TEXT macro. During playback, the input field is then pre-populated with this value. Here's an example of the same field as the previous example, but for transaction VK12, where the user is asked to change the value from 1,250.00 to 1,500.00:

Ship-to	Material	S	Description	P..	Amount	Unit	per	U...	C..
2008	100041		Air Conditioner ACJ/RC 2...		1,250.00	USD	1	EA	C
☑	☑								
☑	☑								
☑	☑			Enter **1,500.00** into the **Amount** field.					
☑	☑								
☑	☑								
☑	☑								

The advantage of this approach is that the user can use full edit field functionality, including clicking anywhere in this value, using cursor keys to navigate through it, and changing only the required characters within the string. The full, final value of this field is then validated (as above), regardless of the actual keystrokes used to enter it.

There is one problem with the above example that isn't immediately apparent, but will be glaringly obvious during playback when continuing to the next macro. The problem is that in the simulation, the typed text is left-aligned, whereas in the actual system it is right-aligned. In the next section we'll look at how to fix this, and a few other things we can do to modify the field's appearance.

Controlling the appearance of input text fields

Enable Now provides a large number of properties for controlling the appearance of the field control for INPUT TEXT macros. These are available in the *Control* category, as shown below:

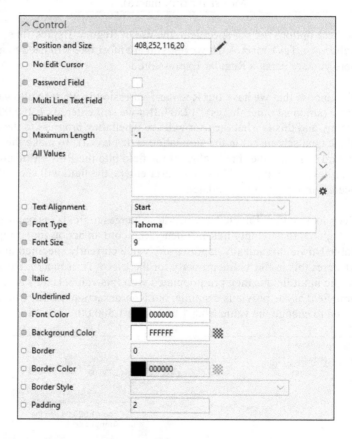

The following table lists all of these properties, and explains how to use them to influence the appearance and operation of the input field.

Property	Use
Position and Size	Specifies the size and location relative to the screenshot of the input field (actually, of the interactive text box that Enable Now overlays onto the screenshot to simulate the effect of an actual input field in the application). You should not need to change this, but can via the **Edit** button to the right of the field if necessary.
No Edit Cursor	By default, a cursor (typically, a horizontal bar) is displayed in the input field, to show the position of the cursor. If you do not want this cursor to be shown (for example, because it gives the users too much of a clue as to which field to use in Test mode), select this checkbox.
Password Field	If the string input is a password field, select this checkbox, and the user's input will be automatically masked, as shown in the example below: 

Property	Use
Multi Line Text Field	By default, an input field is a single line, and if the user types more text than can be visibly seen in the text box, the text scrolls horizontally. If the field is actually a 'text box' where multiple lines of text can be entered, then select this checkbox and the user's input will wrap within the text field. Note the input field must be large enough to accommodate multiple lines. A scrollbar will be used if the user's input exceeds the total height. An example of this is shown below: 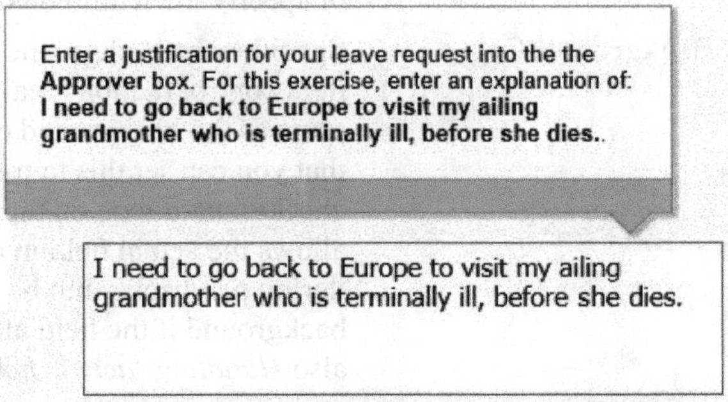

Property	Use
Disabled	If this checkbox is selected then the field is not available for input. This effectively makes it impossible to complete the action in Practice mode, so you would not normally select this.
Maximum Length	Specifies the maximum number of characters (including spaces) that the user cant enter in the field. A value of **-1** means that there is no limit.
All Values	If the input field has a drop-down list of possible values then these values are captured during recording and saved in this property. Note that this property does not affect the INPUT TEXT macro, but is useful if you replace this INPUT TEXT macro with a SELECT SINGLE macro (see *Simulating drop-down lists* on page 136).
Text Alignment	Select the alignment of the text within the field. Options are **Left**, **Start** (both of which seem to do the same thing—maybe it's to support right-to-left languages?), **Center**, **Right**, and **End** (again, both of which also seem to do the same thing).
Font Type	This should default correctly to the font used in the system, but can be changed if necessary. This is a free-text field (not a drop-down list of installed fonts) so enter your choice carefully.
Font Size	The font size for the input field. Again, this should default correctly during recording.
Bold	
Italic	Select any typographical emphases that should be applied to the input field.
Underlined	
Font Color	This property specifies the color of the text entered into the input field. If you need to change this, either enter the hexadecimal RGB code for the color in the input field, or click on the color chooser and select or specify the required color.
Background Color	Specifies the background (fill) color of the input field control (action area). This should be exactly the same as the background color in the system. Note that you can set this to transparent by clicking on the checkerboard icon on the far right of the field. This allows the actual field in the system to show through, during playback—but be careful using a transparent background if the field already contains a value. See also *Handling 'active' fields in SAP* on page 135.

Property	Use
Border	If the field control should be shown with a border,
Border Color	then select the thickness, color, and style of this
Border Style	border. This is useful if 'active' fields have a specific border, and you have multiple input fields within a single step, and therefore do not have individual screenshots showing each field as 'active'.
Padding	Specifies the number of pixels of space that should be left on the inside of the field's border, around the text.

Handling 'active' fields in SAP

In some applications, and most notably in the SAP R/3 and ECC 6.0 systems, the (one) 'active' field on a screen—the field that any typing on the keyboard will apply to—is shaded with a colored background (versus a white background for all 'inactive' fields). This can be a problem in Steps that contain multiple fields or Form structures, as multiple fields are effectively shown as 'active'. You can see an example of a Form structure showing this on page 144.

This is a problem even with single-field Steps, as the field to be completed in the Step is already highlighted when the screenshot for the Step is displayed. This may not necessarily be a bad thing in Demo mode or Practice mode where you specifically want to draw the user's attention to the field, but in Test mode it basically provides a huge clue to the user as to which field they have to complete next, making Test mode a fairly ineffective 'test'.

To provide a 'true to life' simulation you would need to require the user to explicitly click in each field to make it the active field, before entering the text. By default, Enable Now will not capture 'click-in' actions for input fields. If you *do* want these to be captured, then you can go to **Tools | Settings | Producer | Authoring Settings | Recording**, and select the **Generate Macros for Inactive Edit Fields** checkbox. Note that this is a global setting, so once changed it will apply to all recordings, and for all Authors.

A downside to this approach is that you effectively have to have a separate Step for every 'click in' action and for every Input Text action. You will not be able to merge screens, and you will not be able to use a Form structure (see *Using a Form structure* on page 142) because the screen will look different after every action—every 'click-in' Mouse Action and every String Input.

Handling Drop-down Lists

With a drop-down list field, the user is required to select a value from a drop-down list of available options. When you interact with a drop-down list control during recording, Enable Now will *usually* recognize this, and insert a

SELECT SINGLE macro that covers both the click on the field and the selection from the drop-down list.

The SELECT SINGLE macro fully simulates a drop-down list control in that during playback the user can move through the list (via the scrollbar, by using the mouse scroll-wheel, or by using the cursor keys) and select an entry by either clicking on it, or by pressing *ENTER* when the required value is highlighted.

Sometimes, however, Enable Now doesn't correctly identify the control and instead inserts two MOUSE ACTION macros: one for the click on the field, and one for selecting a value from the drop-down list. This is not necessarily a problem, unless you want to merge Steps including the Steps for this control (see *Merging screens* on page 145). In this case (or if you just want to tidy things up) you can create the drop-down list yourself as explained in *Simulating drop-down lists* on page 136.

The following table lists the properties that are unique to drop-down list controls, and explains their use.

Property	Use
General	
Selected Index	This identifies the position in the drop-down list of the value that was selected during recording (with **0** being the first entry, **1** being the second, and so on).
Selected Value	This contains the actual value selected during recording. This is necessary (in addition to the **Selected Index** property) to correctly insert the value into the Bubble.
Control	
Cursor Hand	Select this checkbox if you want the standard 'pointer' cursor to change to a 'hand' when the cursor moves over the object. You would only normally want to do this if that's how the application behaves.
All Values	This field contains all of the values in the drop-down list (one per line). The currently-selected value (before the action is performed) is preceded by {*}. You can edit this list, if required.

Simulating drop-down lists

If Enable Now does not correctly identify a control as being a drop-down list, you can recreate the control yourself, as explained in this section. Let's look at how to do this by way of a real-life example. During our recording of transaction SU3 in *Chapter 3, Recording a Simulation*, we interacted with a drop-down list, where we select the decimal notation format. In our project this was captured as two distinct MOUSE ACTION macros: one for clicking in the input field to display the list of available options, and one for clicking on the required option. These two steps—as they appear during playback in Practice mode—are shown below:

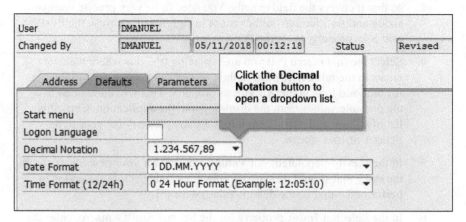

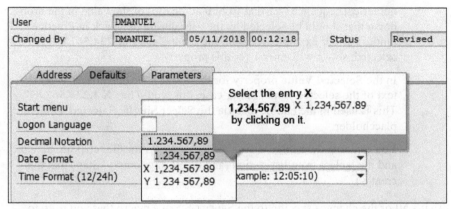

To replace these two captured MOUSE ACTION macros with a single SELECT SINGLE macro, carry out the steps shown below:

1. Click on the macro (or screen) before the first of the macros that you want to replace.

2. Select menu option **Insert | Insert Interaction | Select Single**.

3. A new control (which looks just like a drop-down list box) is added to your screenshot, along with a bubble. An example of this control, isolated from the screenshot for clarity, is shown below:

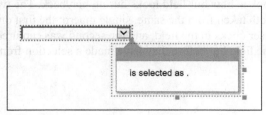

This is initially positioned in the upper-left corner of the screenshot. Drag it to the location of the actual field on the screenshot, and resize it so that it covers the field exactly. You need to be very precise with your sizing and positioning—either zoom in significantly, or use the **Position and Size** property to define these exactly.

■ Enable Now usually manages to capture the **All Values** property even if it doesn't create a SELECT SINGLE macro; if it does not, you will need to manually enter the values in the **All Values** property for your new SELECT SINGLE macro.

4. Select the first macro that you are replacing (the one where the user clicks in the input field). Go to the *Control* category of properties for this, and look at the **All Values** property. This will contain all of the possible values from the drop-down in the application. Copy this list of values, and paste them into the same property for your new SELECT SINGLE macro.

5. In the (newly-populated) **All Values** property for your new macro, prefix the entry that should be shown in the input field (before the action is performed—that is, the default value) with {*}.

6. In the **Selected Index** property for the SELECT SINGLE macro, enter the numerical sequence (starting from **0** at the top) of the value in the drop-down that should be selected by the user during playback in Practice mode. For our example, we want the *second* entry (**1,234,567.89**) to be selected, so we will enter **1** for this property.

■ For more information on placeholders, refer to *Inserting a Placeholder* on page 115.

7. In the **Selected Value** property for the SELECT SINGLE macro, enter the text of the selected value. In our case, this would be "**X 1,234,567.89**". This is used in the bubble text via the **Select Single: Selected Value** placeholder.

8. You can now delete the MOUSE ACTION macros for the 'click in' action and the 'select from list' action (and delete any 'empty' Steps that this creates).

That's all of the changes specific to the SELECT SINGLE macro that you need to make, but there are still several other things that you will need to fix. These all use standard functionality described elsewhere in this chapter, but in brief, you may need to do the following for your new SELECT SINGLE macro:

- Specify the **Object Name** and (if required) capture the **Object Image**

- Specify the **Demo Text** and **Practice Text**

- Adjust the position of the Practice Bubble and Demo Bubble

- Adjust the control's **Font Type** and **Font Size** properties

Now let's look at how our field looks during playback. The two screenshots below are both taken from the same, single macro; the first one was captured before the user clicks in the field, and the second was captured after they have clicked in the field but before they have made a selection from the drop-down.

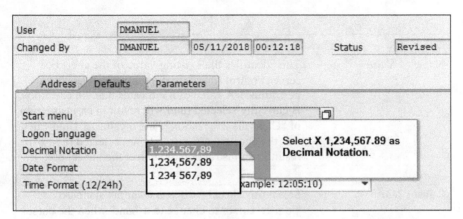

Comparing these with the screenshots of the original recording on page 137, we can see that this is pretty close to the original (although the bubble has been moved to the side, for clarity). The big advantage of this is not immediately obvious in print, but this is a fully-functioning drop-down list. The user can use the cursor keys on the keyboard (or the scroll wheel) to navigate through the list (even to values not currently shown), and then press *ENTER* to select the highlighted entry. This is much closer to how the application itself works.

Handling checkboxes

When you click on a checkbox control during recording, Enable Now correctly identifies this (as being distinct from a click on a button or other screen control) and inserts a RADIO/CHECKBOX macro. Enable Now does not capture an image for this screen object (the **Object Image** property will indicate "No image selected"), and will instead overlay a checkbox control onto the screen during playback (and in documentation).

You can manually insert a checkbox control (for example, if Enable Now does not correctly identify the control as a checkbox during

Insert Action

▲ In this author's experience, Enable Now does not always identify checkbox screen controls correctly (often just capturing a standard Mouse Action), and even if it does recognize the object correctly, does not always identify cases where the checkbox was already selected and is being cleared, incorrectly recording an action of "Select the...".

recording) by clicking on the **Insert Action** button on the *Project Editor Toolbar*, and selecting **Checkbox** from the drop-down panel. (You can also select menu option **Insert | Insert Interaction | Checkbox**.)

This checkbox responds correctly during playback in Practice mode and Test mode, and will be selected/cleared (as appropriate) in response to the user's action. This is extremely useful in that it does not require an additional screenshot to be captured of the 'post-action' state of the screen, which can reduce the number of screenshots needed in your simulation, and facilitates screen merging (see *Merging screens* on page 145).

The following table lists the properties that are unique to checkbox controls, and explains their use.

Property	Use
General	
Selected Value	This identifies the existing value of the checkbox screen control (that is, before the action has been performed). A value of **0** indicates that the checkbox is currently selected (and will result in an instruction of "Clear the...checkbox") and a value of **1** indicates that the checkbox is currently not selected (and will result in an instruction of "Select the...checkbox").
Control	
Cursor Hand	Select this checkbox if you want the standard 'pointer' cursor to change to a 'hand' when the cursor moves over the object. You would only normally want to do this if that's how the application behaves.
Radio Button	Should be deselected for checkboxes.
Radio Button Group Name	Ignore for checkboxes

Handling radio buttons

Radio buttons (or, more accurately, option buttons) are a group of (at least two) buttons, where the selection of one button in the group deselects all of the other buttons in the group. During recording, Enable Now correctly identifies such radio button controls, and inserts a RADIO/CHECKBOX macro into the recording. As with checkboxes, Enable Now does not capture an image for this screen object, and will instead overlay a radio button control onto the screen during playback and in the generated document outputs. This works exactly as intended, and will show as selected when the user clicks on it in Practice mode or Test mode.

You can manually insert a radio button control by clicking on the **Insert Action** button on the *Project Editor Toolbar*, and selecting

Insert Action

Radiobutton from the drop-down panel. (You can also select menu option Insert
| Insert Interaction | Radiobutton.)

The following table lists the properties that are unique to radio button controls,
and explains their use.

Property	Use
General	
Selected Value	This indicates whether or not the radio button (against which the action was performed) is selected before the action is performed. A value of **0** indicates that the control is currently selected and a value of **1** indicates that the control is currently not selected. As captured during recording, this should be 1 (otherwise there would be no need to click on it).
Control	
Cursor Hand	Select this checkbox if you want the standard 'pointer' cursor to change to a 'hand' when the cursor moves over the object. You would only normally want to do this if that's how the application behaves.
Radio Button	Should always be selected for checkboxes.
Radio Button Group Name	This property is used to group radio buttons together—so that when you select one radio button in this group, all other radio buttons are deselected. To group radio buttons, just enter exactly the same identifier in this property for all the buttons.

▲ The **Radio Button
Group Name** property is
effectively worthless as
you cannot really use it for
reasons explained below
the table.

Although radio buttons are (usually) captured correctly during recording, and act
as expected during playback, there is a significant caveat to their use. If you use
a radio button, do not merge the Step containing the radio button with the next
Step in the simulation (see *Merging screens* on page 145). If you do, then when
playback reaches the next macro (but still on the same screen), you will see the
radio button for the recorded control selected (as expected) *along with* whichever
option in the application's radio button group was already selected—which clearly
isn't correct!

You could be forgiven for thinking that a solution to this would be to insert
RADIO/CHECKBOX macros for *all* of the options, and group them in the recording
via the **Radio Button Group Name** property. This would work correctly in that
when you selected the required option, the radio button for any currently-selected
option would be deselected. However, you will then have an *interaction macro*
for *every* option, and the user will have to perform every interaction during
playback by clicking on each radio button in turn!

So if you have a radio button captured in your recording, make sure that
the RADIO/CHECKBOX macro is the last macro in the Step, so that when the

user performs this action playback continues with the next Step, with a fresh
screenshot that shows this option (and no other) selected.

Key-Stroke actions

Enable Now will capture a key-stroke action when you press a key or key
combination during recording, and the cursor is not in an input field (if it is, an
Input Text action is captured instead). This has a single unique property, **Hotkey**,
which is explained in Steps 3-5 below.

You can also manually insert a key-stroke action into your simulation by
following the steps shown below.

1. In the *Step View*, locate the Step for the screen to which you want to add
    the key-stroke action, and then click on the existing macro after which
    the new action should appear.

2. On the *Project Editor Toolbar*, click on the **Insert Action**
    button, and select **Key-stroke** from the drop-down panel.
    (You can also select menu option **Insert | Insert
    Interaction | Key-stroke**.)

    Insert Action

3. A KEY-STROKE macro is inserted into the Step. Make sure that the
    Hotkey property for this macro is enabled, and then click on the **Edit**
    button to the right of this property. The *Hotkey* dialog box is displayed
    (although this does not seem to have a title).

    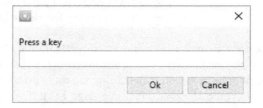

4. Press the key (or key combination) that should be used for this action.
    This is the key (combination) that the user will have to press in Practice
    mode. Once you have done this, the key (combination) will be listed in
    the **Press a key** field. You can use this to confirm that you pressed the
    correct key (combination).

5. Click **Ok** to confirm your key assignment.

Using a Form structure

If you have multiple input fields within a single Step (because you have merged
the screenshots, as explained in *Merging screens* on page 145), a further option
that is available to you is a **Form**. Normally, when a user completes a string input
interaction in Practice mode, their input is immediately validated to check if it
is correct, and if it is not, the user cannot proceed. With a Form, multiple string

input interactions (on a single screen, and in a single Step) are 'grouped' (into the Form) and all fields are validated at once, after the user has completed all of the fields in the form. To facilitate this, the last interaction in the Form must be a MOUSE ACTION macro, which triggers the validation.

The main advantage of this approach is that the user can complete the fields in any order, which is closer to how the actual application screen works. However, there are some significant disadvantages, as we shall see in the following example.

For this example, we will use our recording of VA01, where we have multiple input fields on a single screen. Assume that we have already merged these macros into a single Step (as explained in *Merging screens* on page 145). Our Step then appears as shown below.

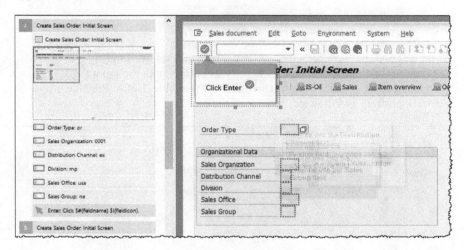

We will combine the six input fields and the final mouse-click on the **Enter** button into a Form.

To combine multiple interactions into a Form, carry out the steps shown below:

1. In the *Step View*, locate the Step containing the macros you want to combine, and *CTRL*+click on each macro to be included on the form.

2. Select menu **Insert | Special Macro | Create Form Structure**. A FORM BEGIN macro and a FORM END macro are added to the Step, with the selected macros being placed between these.

Our sample Step now looks as follows:

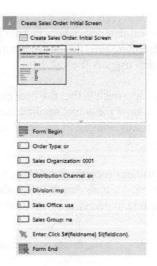

So far so good, but now let's look at how this manifests itself during playback. For Demo mode, playback appears exactly as before, with the input fields being completed one at a time, each with its own bubble. But in Practice mode, playback appears as follows:

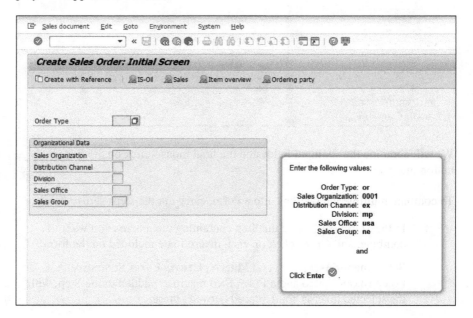

Here, a single Bubble is displayed for all of the input fields, instead of there being one Bubble per field. This is perhaps understandable, as the user can complete the fields in any order. However, all that is provided for each STRING INPUT macro is the field name and the input value; any additional explanation text that may have been specified in the **Practice Text** property is simply omitted! This may be acceptable, but if you are in the habit of providing additional explanations or business context in your bubbles (and you should!), this may be a significant limitation. You should therefore use Form structures with caution.

Removing a Form structure

If you have inserted a Form structure into a Step, and then decide that you do not want it (and want to revert back to a one-bubble-per-field approach), right-click on either the FORM BEGIN macro or the FORM END macro, and select **Remove Form Structure** from the shortcut menu.

Steps and screens

As you will have no doubt noticed by now, a simulation consists of a number of Steps. Each Step (with the exception of the Start Step and the End Step) will contain a SCREEN macro, and an interaction macro. Although the hard work in a simulation is performed by the macros, the Steps and the SCREEN macros are critical in determining the overall structure of the simulation and the possible paths through it. In this section, we'll look at what we can do with these elements.

Merging screens

When you record a simulation, Enable Now will capture each action that you perform, and take a copy of the screen as it appeared *before* you performed that interaction. These two things are saved in a Step within the project. This means that your project will initially contain a series of Steps, each of which contains exactly one screenshot and one interaction macro - you can see this in the *Step View*.

For STRING INPUT macros, Enable Now also captures an image of the Object (the input field) *after* you have performed the action. This has an interesting implication. It means that although Enable Now effectively does capture a full 'after' screenshot—as the 'before' screenshot for the *next* action—it does not really *need* this because it can effectively build this screenshot by taking the 'before' screenshot, and overlaying the 'after' object image on top of this, at the appropriate position.

Of course, each Step requires its own screenshot so you can't just delete these 'unnecessary' screenshots. But—crucially—each macro does not need to be in its own Step with its own screenshot. You can include multiple action macros in the same Step, along with a single screenshot that applies to all of them. This is possible because, again, Enable Now can build the 'missing' screenshots given the 'before' screenshot (before any of the actions in the Step are performed) and the 'after' Object image for each action macro (which is, conveniently, stored with the macro itself). This has some interesting benefits:

- You can save disk space by reducing the number of screenshots you need to save.

- Because you are not loading an entire screenshot after every interaction, load time will be improved, leading to a smoother, faster playback of the simulation.

- Your documentation will be shorter, as 'unnecessary' screenshots are omitted and multiple interactions are listed under the same screenshot.

- You can treat multiple input fields on the same screen as a related set of input fields, allowing them to be completed in any order, and validated as a whole.

So let's look at how we an do this; how to combine multiple interaction macros into a single Step and remove unnecessary screens. There are actually a number of ways that this can be done. These are explained separately in next four sections.

Automatic screen merging during recording

If the **Auto Merge** option is selected (in **Tools | Setting | Authoring Settings | Recording | Simulation/Documentation**) then Enable Now will attempt to merge screens automatically where it can, as soon as you save the simulation after recording it.

To do this, Enable Now checks each screenshot with the one before it, and if the two screenshots are different by less than the tolerance specified in the **Merge Screens Tolerance** setting (again, under **Tools | Setting | Authoring Settings | Recording | Simulation/Documentation**) then Enable Now will merge the steps, keeping the screenshot from the *first* step. The tolerance is set as the percentage of pixels that can be different between the two screenshots, and defaults to 0.4%. Mathematically, this means that with screenshots that are 1280x800 pixels, an area of up to 128x32 pixels (or other ratio totaling 4,096 pixels) can be different and the screenshots will be merged.

Because Enable Now does not care what is in this 0.4% of pixels that are different (whether it is just the input field, or something else which could be significant) this feature should be used with extreme caution (which is why it is disabled by default).

Full-project screen merging during editing

Even if the Workarea-level **Auto Merge** option is not selected, you can still merge all screens for an entire project, during editing. Simply open the simulation in the *Project Editor* and select menu option **Tools | Bulk Changes | Merge Screens**. Enable Now will check all of screens in the project, using the same **Merge Screens Tolerance** setting that it uses for automatic screen merging (see above), merging them where it can.

■ This is done by using a **Form**—see *Using a Form structure* on page 142.

● Note that Enable Now does not actually *merge* the screenshots in the sense of combining selected parts of all of them, or somehow determining a 'common' image. Instead, it simply takes one screenshot (usually the first) and places the macros for all of the other screenshots it determines are 'close enough in content' into the Step for this single retained screenshot.

Again, the same caution should be applied when using this feature as for automatic merging.

Merging individual screens

As an alternative to allowing Enable Now to check an entire project for screen merge opportunities, you can choose to manually merge specific screens within the project. To do this, select all of the Steps that contain the screenshots that you want to merge into a single step (either *CTRL*+click on them, or click on the first Step in the sequence and then *SHIFT*+click the last Step in the sequence) and then select menu option **Tools | Bulk Changes | Merge Selected Screens**.

This approach is different from a 'full-project' merge in that Enable Now effectively does not check that the screens are similar (within tolerance). Instead, the assumption is that you know what you are doing, and have already visually checked the screenshots yourself to determine their suitability for merging. Enable Now will simply retain the first screenshot in the sequence, merge all macros for the selected Steps into this first Step (in the sequence) and then delete the remaining initially-selected Steps and their screenshots. It will do this no matter how different the screens are—they could even be for separate applications; Enable Now does not care.

Manually merging screens

If you have control issues, and don't like the idea of just letting Enable Now do it's thing, you can effectively merge screens yourself, manually. This gives you absolute control, but will take a little more effort.

To manually merge multiple Steps, so that you have a single Step with one screen and multiple macros that apply to it, carry out the following steps:

1. Locate the sequence of Steps that you want to merge.

2. Go to the *second* Step in this sequence, and select the macro(s).

3. Drag these macros and drop them in the first Step in the sequence, after the existing macro(s).

4. Delete the second Step (which should now only contain a screenshot, and no macros).

5. Repeat Steps 2 to 4 for all additional Steps in the sequence that you want to merge, until you are left with a single Step (which now contains all of the macros from the deleted Steps).

Although this may seem like an easier method, especially if you only have a few screens to merge, there are a couple of compelling reasons for using the built-in functionality. These are:

- If you let Enable Now merge the screens for the entire project it will check that the selected screens are similar enough to make merging them feasible.

- When you merge screens that include multiple object actions, then Enable Now will re-determine the documentation screenshot crop size, to make sure that all relevant screen objects are included in the documentation.

You should therefore be certain that the benefits of a 'quick merge' outweigh the benefits of having Enable Now do it for you.

Merging screens: An example

So much for the theory. Now let's look at a practical example of merging screens. Consider the following screen, which is taken from ECC 6.0 transaction VA01 (Enter Sales Order):

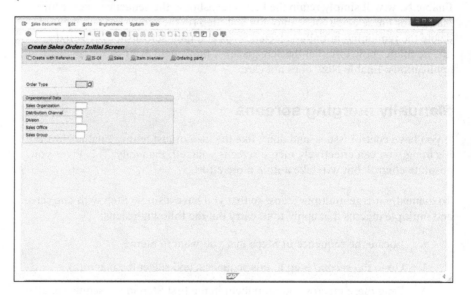

This screen requires the user to fill in (up to) six input fields, and then click a button to validate these and progress to the next screen. Looking at the *Step View* for the recording of this, you can see that Enable Now has captured seven different Steps, each of which contains one screenshot and one interaction macro.

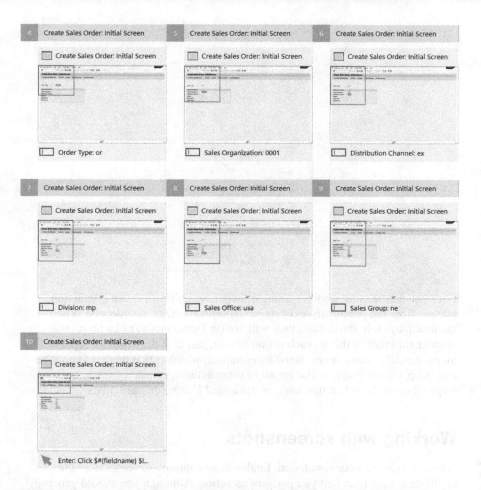

Each of these Steps is for the same screen of the application, which makes them candidates for merging.

Lets assume that we select these seven Steps, and then merge these screens by selecting menu option **Tools | Bulk Changes | Merge Selected Screens**. After doing this, the *Step View* shows the following single Step, in place of the previous seven Steps:

● There are additional things you can do once you have all fields in a single Step. These are described in *Using a Form structure* on page 142.

▲ Additional care should be taken if you will be providing audio for your simulation. Audio is provided at the Step level (not macro level) so you need to record audio for all of the merged macros in a single audio recording.

Here you can see that we have a single Step, containing all seven interaction macros from the previously-existing seven separate steps. So success! When the user plays this simulation, they will see (in Demo mode) or be prompted to enter (in Practice mode) each action in turn, just as if they were in separate Steps. Actually, there is one user-facing impact, which is that there will only be one 'stop' on the Progress Bar for all of these actions, instead of seven separate stops—but we'll look at that later, in *Advanced Editing* on page 159.

Working with screenshots

When you record your simulation, Enable Now captures screenshots of the application each time that you perform an action. Although you should generally strive for realism in your simulations, there may be situations in which you need to change these screenshots. Enable Now does not provide a lot of features for editing screenshots, but what features it does provide are enough to cover most requirements.

Most of these features are accessed via the (misleadingly-named) **Replace Image** button, which is located to the right of the thumbnail image of the screenshot in the *Page* property of the SCREEN macro.

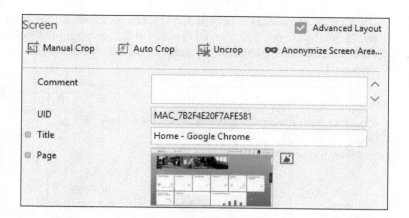

The table below shows the options that are available via this button, and explains their purpose.

Option	Use
External Editor	Open the screenshot image in the default/ defined image editing application, so that you can 'photoshop' it. See *Editing a screenshot image* on page 151.
Copy Image	Copy the screenshot image to the clipboard. This feature is provided so that you can then replace the screenshot for another Step with the screenshot for this one, via the **Replace with Image from Clipboard** option (see below).
Replace with Image from Clipboard	Replace the screenshot image with the image currently on the clipboard. Although it is expected that this is an image copied from another Step via the **Copy Image** option, this option is useful for quick screen replacements (without re-recording)— just capture the new image via *PRINTSCREEN*, SnagIt, or other image capture software, save it to the clipboard, and then use this option to copy it into your simulation project.

▲ It is important to make sure that the screenshot captured to the clipboard is exactly the same size as the image you are replacing.

Editing a screenshot image

There are times when you will need to directly edit a screenshot image—for example, to remove extraneous information that you did not mean to capture, or to change some data for consistency or for a better example. You can do this using whatever image editor you like, although the default option of Microsoft Paint is adequate for most purposes.

To edit a screenshot image, carry out the following steps.

1. Click on the **Replace Image** button, and select **External Editor** from the drop-down menu. The image is opened in the (currently-defined) default image editing application, and the *Edit External* dialog box is displayed.

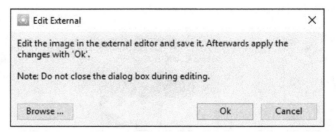

2. If you want to change your image editing application then click on the Browse button, and navigate to and select the `.exe` file for the required application. (Of course, this will only take effect from the *next* time you edit a screenshot—as the current screenshot has already been opened in the previously-defined default application—but you can always cancel that and then re-open it in the new application.)

3. Switch to the image editing application, and make the required changes to the screenshot image. Once you are done, save the image from within that application, and then close the image editor again.

4. Back in the *Project Editor*, click on the **Ok** button in the *Edit External* dialog box. Note that your changes will not be effective until you do this.

Replacing a screenshot

If you need to replace a single screenshot in your simulation with a new screenshot, the easiest way to do this is as follows:

1. In the application for which the recording was created, navigate to the screen that you want to use in your recording.

2. Make sure that the application screen is at exactly the same resolution as the original recording. This may take a bit of trial and error, especially if the application is windowed/

3. Press *PRTSCR* (or *ALT+PRTSCR* if the application is windowed) to capture the screen to the clipboard. Alternatively, you can use Techsmith's SnagIt (or similar screen capture application) to capture the screenshot, and then copy it to the clipboard from there).

4. Switch back to Enable Now Producer, and click on the macro for the screenshot that you want to replace.

5. In the *Macro Editor* panel, click on the **Replace Image** icon on the right of the screenshot for the **Page** property, and then select **Replace with Image from Clipboard**. The screenshot is replaced.

■ If you typically capture less than the full application window during recording (for example, you capture only the client area of a browser window), recapturing the screenshot at the correct size may be tricky. A solution to this is to resize your monitor to the exact size of your recording, press *F11* to display the application (or browser client area) in full-screen, and then press *PRTSCR* to capture the replacement screenshot. [Tip courtesy of Joel Harris.]

Anonymizing an area of a screenshot

If you are capturing your simulation recordings in a Production system (or in a copy of a Production system), you may find that a screenshot contains sensitive data, such as customer information, pricing, or personnel data. In this case, you might want to consider 'blurring out' this information on the screenshot, so that it is not readable.

For example, say we have a project that explains how to display the *Compensation Dashboard* in SuccessFactors. On one of the screens, the salary information of an employee is visible.

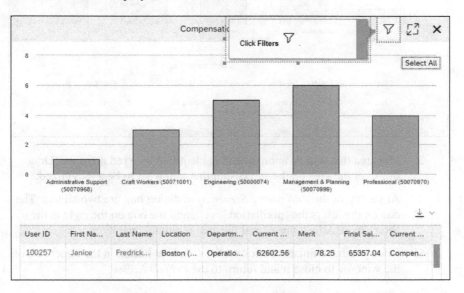

Clearly we don't want this information to be displayed to every trainee that carries out this simulation! We can anonymize this information as follows:

1. Click on the screen in the *Step View*, to select it.

2. At the top of the *Macro Editor* pane for the screen, click on the **Anonymize Screen Area** button. The *Anonymize Screen Area* window is displayed.

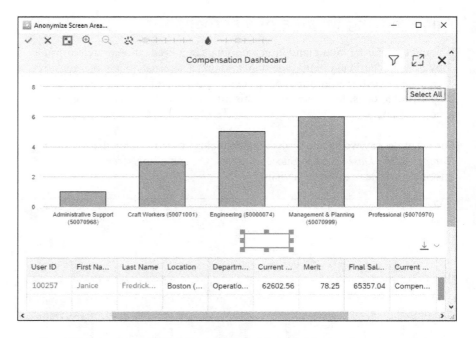

3. The area that will be anonymized is identified by a red marquee. Drag this over the area on the screenshot that you want to be anonymized.

4. At the top of the *Anonymize Screen Area* dialog box are two sliders. The one on the left is the 'pixillation level', and the one on the right is the 'blur' level. Adjust these until the area is suitably anonymized.

5. Once you have finished, click on the **Confirm** button in the upper-left of the window to close it and return to the *Project Editor*.

Now let's have a look at how the anonymized screen looks.

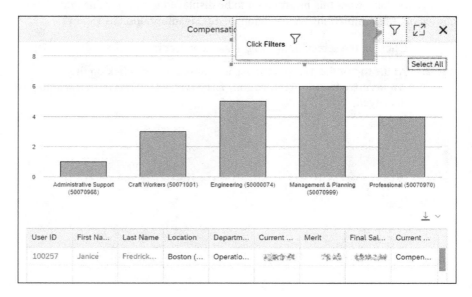

Now, it is impossible to read the actual data, but we can see that there is data there (just removing the data could be confusing as it might look as though there is no data there).

There are a couple of caveats with this function. Firstly, any anonymization is permanent; there is no way to return to the pre-anonymized version of the screenshot image (apart from using the **Undo** function before you save your changes). Secondly, you can only anonymize one area at a time; if you want to anonymize multiple areas on a single screenshot, you will need to carry out the above steps multiple times—once for each area.

Working with the 'after' object image

As we noted at the start of this section, when Enable Now captures a string input action, it effectively captures three things:

1. A screenshot of the full screen before the text is entered into the field. This is effectively the 'after screenshot' from the previous action.

2. The action itself: the text that was entered, the field it was entered into, and so on.

3. An image of the *input field* (only—not the entire screen) after the text has been entered into it.

The latter two of these are stored *in the macro* for that action, which means that if the screenshot is deleted (by merging the Steps, as explained above), Enable Now can still 're-construct' the screenshot by taking the 'after' screenshot from the previous macro and layering the 'after' image of the Object (the input field) on top of this. So if multiple String Input actions have been combined into a single step with a single 'before' screenshot), Enable Now still show the progression of the fields being completed one at a time, by layering successive 'after' Object images on the one screenshot that is available, as it progresses through the STRING INPUT macros.

This 'after' image is also used in the generated document output types (see *Chapter 12, Working with Documents*). Screenshots in documents always show the 'post-action' state of the screens, and again this is achieved by layering the 'after' image(s) over the 'before' screenshot.

As always with Enable Now, all of this is completely visible to the Author, and readily editable. You can find the relevant fields in the *Macro Editor,* under the *Documentation* category. An extract of this, for one of the input fields in our VA01 example, is shown below:

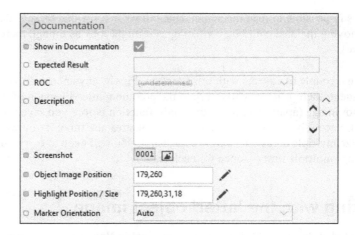

Don't worry about most of the properties in this category—we will look at them in detail in *Chapter 12, Working with Documents*. Instead, we'll look at the two specific properties that impact the 'after' screenshot. These are explained in the table below:

Property	Use
Screenshot	This is the actual image of the input field after the text has been entered into it. To the right of this field is a **Replace Image** button that opens a drop-down with a number of options for editing or replacing this image. These are discussed more fully in *Working with screenshots* on page 150.
Object Image Position	This property specifies the position on the 'full-screen' screenshot at which the 'after' Object image (from the **Screenshot** property) should be placed to produce the 'after' screenshot.

■ If you hover the cursor over the **Screenshot** property image, the size of the screenshot is shown in a ToolTip. Normally, the **Object Image Position** property values (X,Y) will match the first two numbers in the **Highlight Position / Size** property (X,Y), and the screenshot size will match the last two numbers of the **Highlight Position / Size property** (W,H).

You should not need to change either of these properties, but it's useful to know that you can. For example, if entry of text in a screenshot resulted in additional information being displayed alongside the input field (outside of the actual object area), you could re-capture the **Screenshot** to include this, and generate a more realistic simulation.

Controlling the Progress Bar

When you play back a simulation in Demo mode, a *Progress Bar* is displayed at the top of the screen. As the name suggests, this shows the user's progress through the simulation. An example of the *Progress Bar*, for our sample SU3 simulation, is shown below:

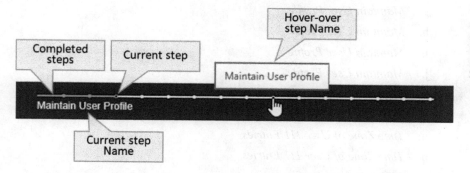

Completed steps

Current step

Hover-over step Name

Maintain User Profile

Maintain User Profile

Current step Name

★ This example uses the default settings for the *Progress Bar*. These can be configured via **Tools | Settings | Playback Settings | trainer - Global | Control bar**.

The *Progress Bar* effectively consists of a single horizontal line, with circular 'points' on it. Each point represents a Step within the simulation. Steps that have been completed are highlighted in blue, and the current step is identified by a black dot in the middle of the step circle. The name of the current Step is shown to the left, below the line, and if you hover the cursor over any Step, the name of that step is shown in a tooltip above the line. The user can click on a Step point to jump directly to that Step in the playback of the simulation.

All of this is default behavior, but there are a few things that we can do (and will normally *want* to do) to influence this.

Firstly, each Step's name is (unsurprisingly) taken from the **Name** property of the actual Step. Normally, this will default to the screen title in the application:

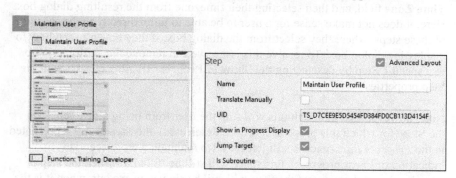

Often this will not be ideal, as the screen title may be the same throughout the entire transaction. In our sample SU3 simulation, the captured Steps have the following Names:

a. *Start*

b. *SAP Easy Access*

c. *Maintain User Profile*

d. *Maintain User Profile*

e. *Maintain User Profile*

f. *Maintain User Profile*

g.   *Maintain User Profile*

h.   *Maintain User Profile*

i.   *Maintain User Profile*

j.   *Maintain User Profile*

k.   *Maintain User Profile*

l.   *Maintain User Profile*

m.   *Time Zone of User 111 Entries*

n.   *Time Zone of User 111 Entries*

o.   *Maintain User Profile*

p.   *SAP Easy Access*

This is not particularly helpful as it is almost impossible for users to identify a specific point within the simulation that they may want to jump to. So the first thing we want to do is provide a unique, meaningful name for each Step. To do this, simply click on the Step in the *Thumbnails Pane*, to display the properties for the Step, and then enter the required name into the **Name** field.

As noted above, during playback, a user can click on any Step in the *Progress Bar* to jump directly to that step. This is useful if the user just needs to get help on a specific section of the transaction. However, there may be circumstances under which you don't *want* the user to be able to jump to a specific step. For example, in our SU3 simulation, the user selects their timezone by clicking in the **Time Zone** field, and then selecting their timezone from the resulting dialog box. Here, it does not make sense for a user to be able to jump directly to the second of these steps, where they select from the dialog box, if they haven't seen how to display the dialog box. To resolve this issue, we can remove the ability to jump to a specific Step by deselecting the **Show in Progress Display** checkbox in the Step properties.

Note, however, that although this will stop the user from being able to click on the Step (for which this property has been deselected), the Step is still represented in the *Progress Bar*: space is still left for it (to maintain a more accurate indication of linear progress), this space will still be 'filled in' when the step is completed, and the name of the Step will still be shown on the left, when it is the 'current' step. This situation is shown in the following image:

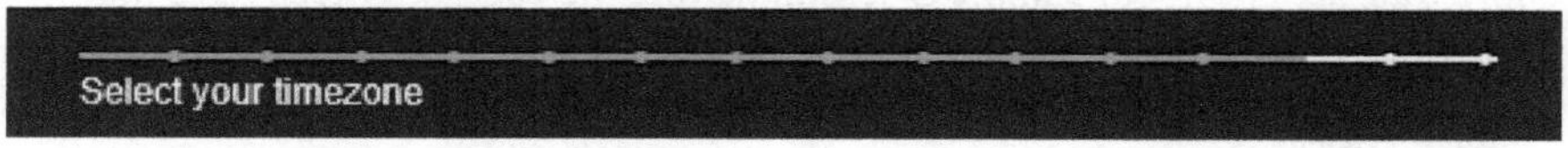

Here, you can see that for the current step, which is at the point where the blue 'progress' line ends (this is the step where the user selects their timezone from the dialog box), there is no Step 'point'; the user cannot hover over this point, or select this Step, but they can still see exactly how far they have progressed in the simulation. In this example we have also changed the **Name** property for this Step, which is shown on the left, to "Select your timezone"—and note that this is the name of the step for which we deselected the **Show In Progress Display** property, and not the name of the last Step with an actual 'point', as you might expect.

There is a further consideration with Step **Name** properties. They are also used (by default) in the Document deliverables, where the 'uniqueness' of the Step **Name** properties is even more important. This is discussed in *Chapter 12, Working with Documents*.

Advanced Editing

So far in this chapter we have looked at edits that you might expect to make to your simulations reasonably regularly, In this section, we will look at some other changes that you can make, but probably won't need to make as often. For this reason, you may want to skip this chapter until you have a bit more experience in Enable Now, but should at least read the headings so you know what is covered, so that if you do come across one of these situations, you know where to find help.

Inserting other content objects

Enable Now is very flexible in terms of the types of content objects that you can insert into a simulation project—over and above screenshots and interaction macros. Many of the object types that you can include in a Book Page you can also include in a simulation. You can also include a Book Page in a simulation. All of these things are covered elsewhere in this book (typically, where we describe Book Pages) so will not be repeated here. However, just for reference, they are:

- **Shapes**: See *Inserting shapes* on page 286.
- **Links** to other content: See *Inserting links* on page 290.
- **Book Pages**: See *Using a Book Page in a simulation project* on page 319.
- **Quiz items**: See *Using Questions outside of a Quiz* on page 353.
- **Documentation macros**: See *Documentation macros* on page 493.

Handling drag-and-drop actions

Drag-and-drop actions in an application are slightly tricky, and warrant a little more discussion. We'll look at this by way of a simple example. On the *SAP Easy Access* screen of an ECC 6.0 system, we will drag a transaction from the SAP Menu and drop it onto our Favorites folder.

With a drag-and-drop action, there are effectively two events: the click on the screen object that is being dragged, and the release of the mouse button at a certain point on the screen. These two events result in two macros being created within a single step. This is in contrast to all other interactions, where each Step contains a single macro (unless you have merged the screens—see *Working with the 'after' object image* on page 155). The partial screenshot below shows the Step and the two macros created for our sample exercise (of dragging a transaction to our Favorites), as they appear in the *Step View*.

Both of these macros are MOUSE ACTION macros, as you would expect. The first has an **Action** property of **Drag**, and the second has an **Action** property of **Drop**.

Before delving into the details, and to give Enable Now credit for its implementation of this functionality (versus some other simulation capture applications), it's worth noting that during playback this works very well. During recording, Enable Now captures an image of the Object that you click on (this is stored in the **Object Image** property), and during playback this image is moved across the screen as the user moves the cursor to the drop position—so it looks exactly like it does in the application. Furthermore, because Enable Now only captures the start point and the end point, the user can drag the cursor (with the object image attached to it) all around the screen, just as long as they finish up at the identified drop location. (Some capture applications require that the user drags the cursor along exactly the same path as was captured during recording!) Again, this is exactly how the application itself operates.

Now, with that in mind, let's take a closer look at the captured actions in our simulation. The *WYSIWYG Editor* (editing for Demo mode, although it appears exactly the same in Practice mode) shows these two interactions as follows:

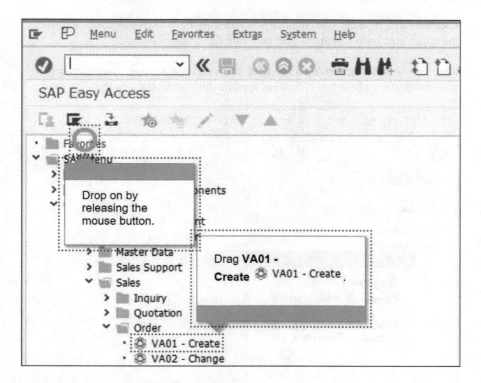

The first thing to notice here is that although there is an action area for the drag activity—this is around the object that we clicked on and dragged—the drop activity does not seem to have the usual rectangular action area. Instead, it has a **hotspot**. This is a circle that is centered on the exact point where the tip of the cursor was when we released the mouse button, during recording. Enable Now creates a hotspot because it does not know what screen element we dropped our dragged object onto.

During playback, the user is required to release the cursor when it is somewhere inside the hotspot circle. This isn't necessarily a problem in Demo mode, but in Practice mode, where the highlight (in this case the circle) isn't visible (by default), this can be tricky - especially if the actual underlying object is significantly larger than this hotspot. Fortunately, there is something we can do about this.

If you look at the **Position and Size** property for the drop activity, you will see that the size values are **0,0**.

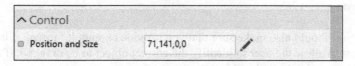

If you edit this property, and change the size values to be something larger (for example, 20,100), the hotspot will be changed to a rectangular action area of the

★ There is an option in **Tools | Settings | Authoring Settings | Recording | Recording of Controls** called **Object analysis on drag&drop** which attempts to identify the object, but this is disabled by default as it can take a while for Enable Now to identify the object (it has to scan most of the screen), and the results are sometimes hit-and-miss.

specified size. You can then manually resize it in the *WYSIWYG Editor* to cover the entire area onto which the user can drop the dragged object.

Now let's look at another anomaly with drag and drop actions. The following screenshot shows how this recording appears during playback in Practice mode.

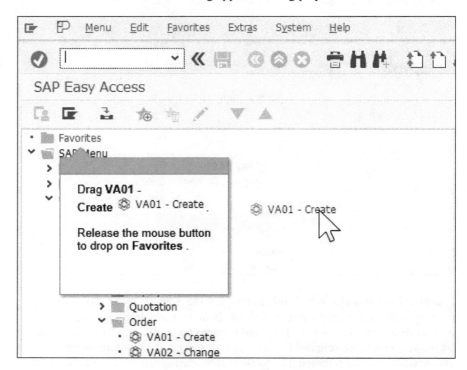

● In this example, you can also see the cursor dragging the object, to the right of the bubble. Note that this is way off to the side of a direct line between the drag and drop locations—showing that you can move the cursor anywhere around the screen before releasing the mouse button.

If you compare this with the same information in the *WYSIWYG Editor*, you will note that the bubbles for both macros have been combined, and the pointer points only at the drop location and not the start. (Note that this is specific to Practice mode - it does not work this way for Demo mode.)

Again, this may not necessarily be a problem, but you should be aware that if your drag and drop locations are very close, one of them may be obscured by the bubble itself. Furthermore, because the bubble is overlaid on top the screenshot, if you drag the object into the area covered by the bubble, the object will be behind the bubble and not visible. You may therefore need to reposition the Practice bubble to ensure that it is not obscuring the drag location, the drop location, or a reasonable drag path between these two locations (see *Inserting Explanation Bubbles* on page 126).

Finally, you should also make sure that you provide enough information in the 'drag' text to allow the user to identify the correct object to be dragged, if the bubble is not pointing to the object.

Decisions and Branches

Sometimes in an application, the user may to be able to perform one of a number of possible actions. For example, if the user is entering an invoice, they can either post the invoice, or park it. Our simulations will be much more realistic if they can mimic this choice.

Let's look at how we can do this, via a simple example. Here, we will look at a simulation for processing a travel request. Once the user has displayed the request, they have the option to approve the request or reject it. We will build both of these options into our simulation.

To capture this simulation, we need to record both options in the same simulation, so that the user can then choose between them. This is sometimes tricky to do, because if you record one method you have likely 'consumed' the data, so it is not available for recording the second method. However, with some judicious pauses during recording, along with deselecting the **Execute Mouse Actions** option (see *page 87*) at the end of the first option, it is possible to capture everything you need in a single project.

For the purposes of this example, assume that we have managed to do this, and have recorded the 'accept' method, immediately followed by the 'reject' method. (This example happens to have been captured in a Fiori-based system, but that's unimportant to this activity.) Our initial recording is then effectively structured as follows:

■ If you cannot capture both options in a single project (or you recorded them separately and then realized it would be better to have them both in a single simulation), you can always merge the two projects by copying and pasting Steps from one project into the other. Just be careful with data continuity on the screenshots.

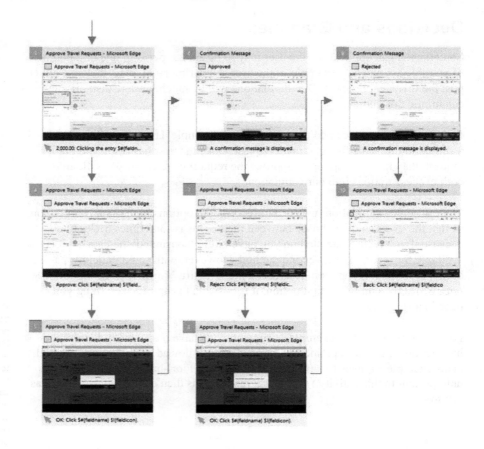

Note that in this example we have added EXPLANATION macros at Step 6 and Step 9 to describe the confirmation message that is displayed in each case (Accept and Reject, respectively).

Using a Branch

In the scenario outlined above, what we really want is for the user to be able to choose either Accept or Reject after Step 3 and complete only the relevant steps for the chosen action (Steps 4-6 for Accept, and 7-9 for Reject). The last step (Step 10) of returning to the main screen is the same in either case and should be carried out regardless of the choice. So let's look at how to do this.

The first thing we need to do is have a decision at Step 4. To do this, we need to combine Step 4 (where the user clicks on **Accept**) and Step 7 (where the user clicks on **Reject**) into a single step. How to merge steps is explained in *Working with the 'after' object image* on page 155, but in brief, the steps to perform are:

1. Click on Step 4 to select it.

2. *CTRL*+click on Step 7 to select it as well. (Important: Do not *SHIFT*+click!)

3. Select menu option **Tools | Bulk Changes | Merge Selected Screens**.

4. Delete the now-empty Step 7.

■ Don't overlook the significance of what this is doing: merging two non-contiguous Steps!

Once these two actions are in a single step, we can turn them into a branch. To do this, perform the following actions.

1. Within the step that now contains two interaction macros, select both macros (in our example, this is this is our new Step 4 with one macro for clicking **Accept**, and one for clicking **Reject**).

2. Select menu option **Insert | Insert Special Macro | Create Branch**. The *Edit Branch* dialog box is displayed.

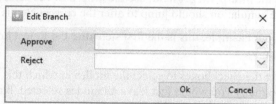

The dialog box contains one entry for each macro that we selected in Step 1. Each is named after the screen object used by the macro.

3. For each entry in the *Edit Branch* dialog box, use the drop-down box to select the Step (in our recording) to which the user should jump if they perform this action.

   For our example, if the user clicks on **Accept**, we want them to jump to the next step, which is Step 4. If they click on **Reject**, then we want them to jump to (new) Step 7 (this was Step 8 before we merged the steps).

4. Click **OK**. A BRANCH BEGIN macro and a BRANCH END macro are inserted into the Step.

Success! We now have a branch, and the user can click on either of the two options, and will be directed to the relevant next step. The only problem is that at the end of the Accept branch (Step 6) the simulation will just continue with the next sequential step (Step 7) which is the first step of our Reject branch. To fix this, we need to 'jump over' the Reject branch, after we have completed the Accept branch. We can do this by using a JUMP TO STEP macro, as shown below:

1. Click on the last macro for the Accept path. This is the EXPLANATION macro in Step 6.

2. Select menu option **Insert | Insert Special Macro | Jump to Step**. The *Jump to Step* dialog box is displayed.

■ All action macros have a **Jump Target** property (in the *Advanced* category, right at the bottom of the *Macro Editor* pane). You can use this to specify what Step to jump to after completing this macro, as an alternative to using a separate JUMP STEP macro.

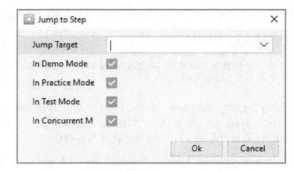

3. In the **Jump Target** field, use the drop-down to select the next step that the simulation should jump to after the current step is completed.

   In our example, this is the first step after the Reject branch, which is Step 9).

4. Use the checkboxes to select the modes in which this jump applies. Normally you would just leave all modes selected, but these options are useful if you want to skip only part of a simulation in certain modes.

5. Click **Ok**.

We now have two separate branches in our simulation, and the user will see only the steps that are relevant to the option they choose (Accept or Reject). Our simulation structure is now as shown in the following diagram. Note that the blue lines in this diagram are just to show the logical flow. The *Step View* will still show the steps in a single column, in Step number order. The only indication that they may be presented anything other than sequentially during playback is the small, orange 'jump' icons (🔲) shown on the right of the macros description bars. Note that you can hover over this icon to see the name of the target Step as a ToolTip.

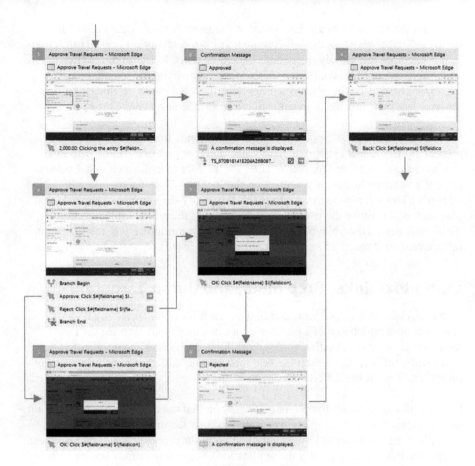

■ Note that the name of the JUMP TO STEP macro shows as a seemingly-random text (starting with **TS_**). This is the **UID** of the target step (the macro's **Jump Target**). You can change this to something more meaningful via the macro's Comment property (see *Information on the macro bar* on page 106).

Now let's look at how our branch looks during playback.

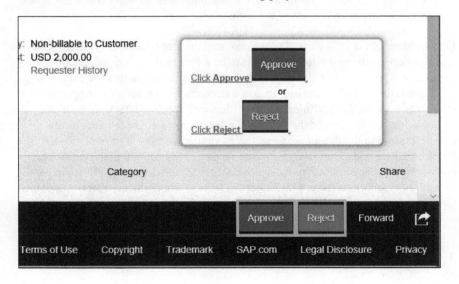

● The bubble style used is the one specified in the BRANCH END macro.

Note that the two options are now listed in the same bubble, separated by the word "or". Note also that the full Bubble text from each option is used (although in this example this is only the default generated text). In Demo mode (from which this example is taken), both of the options are hyperlinks, and the user clicks on one of these options to see the steps for that branch. In Practice mode the user just performs the relevant action to continue down the relevant branch.

If you want your Demo mode to be completely 'hands free' this is a problem (especially if you want to run them in kiosk mode as part of a rolling display), as playback will sit there forever waiting for the user to make a choice. Luckily, there is a solution to this. If you click on the BRANCH END macro, you will see a **Display Duration** property. Change this to specify the number of seconds that playback will wait for the user to make a choice. If they do not make a choice within this period then playback will automatically continue along the first branch (effectively, as if they had selected the first option listed).

➕ I *think* the **Display Duration** property was added to the BRANCH END macro in the 1808 release.

Using text links, Step links, and Jump Targets

In the previous section we looked at how to use a BRANCH macro to allow the user to choose which one of a number of options they wanted to see (in Demo mode) or perform (in Practice mode). Let's look at a similar scenario, but solve it in a different way. In doing this, we'll look at three different ways of providing jumps, and review the differences between them

Let's say that there is some optional information that the user may find interesting or useful, but that isn't completely essential to their learning. By way of an example, we'll continue to look at our simulation for processing a Travel Request. In an actual Travel Request (in the application), there may or may not be notes included in the request, and the user may or may not choose to review these. We'll add a 'detour' to our simulation, to explain to users how to review any notes, before continuing with the rest of the simulation.

Let's assume that during recording we captured the steps for displaying the Travel Request notes, but we do not want them to be a part of the main process flow. Instead, we'll provide our 'detour' via an EXPLANATION macro that we currently have immediately before the user makes a decision as to whether to Approve or Reject the request. For technical reasons (that we'll explain later), we need the 'optional' detour steps to be the next Step after the Step where the user has the option to jump to the detour. To keep things simple (and not interfere with the Branch that we added in *Using a Branch* on page 164) we will place the Bubble containing the decision before these optional steps, and then have the 'main path' (where they choose to Accept or Reject the request) immediately following these. Our recording therefore looks like the following diagram:

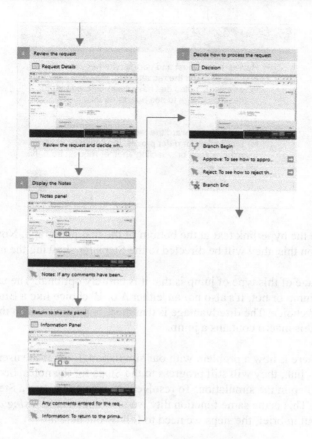

First, we'll create a **text link** in our EXPLANATION macro Bubble to jump to the steps that explain how to display the notes. Text links are explained in detail in *Inserting a link* on page 113, but in brief, the steps we need to carry out here are as follows:

1. Open the Bubble into which you want to insert the link, in the *Text Editor*. (In our example, this is the EXPLANATION macro in Step 6.)

2. Select the text that the user will click on to jump to the detour.

3. Click on the **Insert Object** button and select **Insert link** from the drop-down list. The *Insert link* dialog box is displayed. Select **Actions** from the link type list, and then select **Next Step** from the **Actions** drop-down on the right. (This is why we need the optional Steps to be the next Step—because there is no 'jump to step x' option on the **Actions** drop-down.)

4. Click **Ok** to confirm the link, and then close the *Text Editor*.

Our EXPLANATION macro Bubble now looks like this:

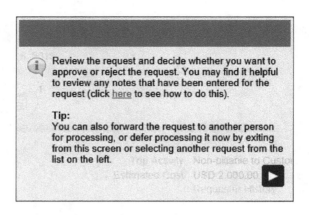

You can see the hyperlink text at the bottom of the first paragraph. Now, if the user clicks on this, they will be directed to the Steps for showing the notes.

The advantage of this type of jump is that it is entirely optional. The user can choose the jump or not. It's also not an 'either A or B' choice like a Branch is—it's an 'A or not' choice. The disadvantage is that there is no indicator in the macro bar to indicate this macro contains a jump.

However, there is now a problem with our simulation. Even if the user does not click on this link, they will still progress to the Steps for the notes, because that is the next Step in the simulation. To resolve this, we need to use a Step jump to bypass this. This is the same functionality we just looked at in *Using a Branch* on page 164, but in brief, the steps we need to follow out here are:

1. Click on the last macro before you want to make the jump. In our example, this is the EXPLANATION macro in Step 3.

2. Select menu option **Insert | Insert Special Macro | Jump to Step** to display the *Jump to Step* dialog box.

3. In the **Jump Target** field, use the drop-down to select the first Step after our 'detour'. In our example, this is Step 6.

4. Click **OK** to close the *Jump to Step* dialog box.

The main advantage of this type of jump is that it is entirely transparent to the user. They do not have to make a decision; they don't even know that they are being directed along a non-linear path through the simulation. It also has the advantage that you can enable or disable it in specific modes—which makes it very useful for bypassing content that you don't want to cover in some modes.

There's one last thing that we will do to our simulation to make sure that our detour is a *true* detour. Currently, if the user chooses to see the Steps on displaying notes (by clicking on the text link we provided) once they have completed these steps they will pass directly to the next Step in the simulation, which is the Step where they choose to Accept or Reject the request. What we really want to do is send them back to the same Step from which they launched the detour—this is our Step 3, which includes the Bubble that contains the text link that they clicked on. We want to do this in case there is other information in that Bubble that they want to re-check, or maybe another few macros following the EXPLANATION macro that they need to see. We could do this by using another JUMP TO STEP macro as the last macro in our detour Steps (exactly as we just did for branching around these steps), but just for the fun of it, and to learn something new, we'll use a different method: the **Jump Target** property.

The **Jump Target** property is available on all 'action' macros (it is not available on EXPLANATION macros, which is why we couldn't use it above), and effectively says, "After completing this macro, I want to jump to *here*". So let's use this in our example simulation, to push the user back to the Explanation Step after reviewing the notes. We can do this by following the steps below:

1. Select the last action macro in the 'detour'. In our example, this is the MOUSE ACTION macro where the user clicks on the **Info** button to return to the main view.

2. Scroll down to the bottom of the *Macro Editor* pane, and expand the *Advanced* category of properties.

3. Enable the **Jump Target** property (if it is not already activated), and select the Step to which playback should jump (after completing this macro) from the property's drop-down list. Note that only steps with their **Jump Target** property selected will be available in this list.

Now, when the user clicks on the **Info** button they are automatically taken back to the bubble from which they launched the detour, and can carry on as normal. Our simulation structure is now as shown in the following diagram.

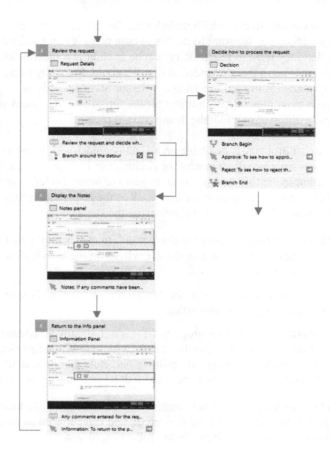

The main advantage of this type of jump is that it keeps our simulations 'tidier', by removing the need for additional JUMP TO STEP macros. In fact, if you look at the Branch macros used earlier in this chapter, they use exactly the same functionality: the **Jump Target** property on the action macros.

Alternative Actions

So far in this section on branches we have looked at ways to direct the user to a different Step, depending upon which action they perform on a screen. What if we want the user to be able to perform two different actions on a screen and still be directed to the same, single next Step? Why would we want to do this? Consider the final action in our simulation for processing a travel request. Here is how this appears during playback in Demo mode:

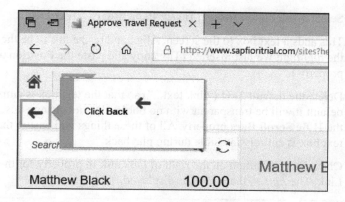

In reality, the user can either click on the **Back** button or they can click on the **Home** button. If we want our simulation to match reality—which should always be our goal—then we need to allow the user to do either of these things during playback. This may seem like a small thing in Demo and Practice mode, where we specifically tell the user that they should click on the **Back** button, but consider Test mode, where there is no bubble, and the only help provided (by default) is the input field values. If we leave the simulation as-is, and the user clicks on the **Home** button they will be marked wrong (and fail, if the passing score mark is set to 100%), even though they performed an action that is technically correct, and would have worked in the actual application. This seems a little unfair. So how can we resolve this?

Enable Now does not allow two interaction macros to be active at the same time; macros are executed one at a time, in the order in which they appear within the Step. However, we can add a **page macro**, which will be available throughout the entire Step—including when other macros are executed. For our scenario, we want to use a combination of a HIGHLIGHT macro and a TEXT LINK macro.

To add an additional highlight to a Step, carry out the following steps:

1. Select the Screen macro for the step to which you want to add the highlight for the alternative action. By positioning this before any interaction macros or EXPLANATION macros, we ensure that the highlight is always displayed for as long as the user is in the current step.

2. Select menu option **Insert | Insert Page Macro | Highlight**.

3. Our new highlight is added to the Step in the upper-left corner of the screen. Drag this to the required location, and resize it as appropriate. For our example, this will be over the **Home** button.

4. In the *Simulation* category for the highlight's properties, deselect the **In Practice Mode** property. This will keep the highlight consistent with other action highlights in the simulation.

Unfortunately, this highlight is purely visual—there is no 'action' associated with it. So to make this 'clickable', we need to add another page macro. So we continue as follows:

■ If you don't care about having a visible highlight (for example, you just want the user to be able to perform the alternative action in Test mode, where highlights aren't visible anyway), you can skip Steps 1-4 here, and just add the text box in Steps 5-8.

5. Select menu option **Insert | Insert Page Macro | Text Link**.

6. This adds a text box to the screen. Align and resize this to be the same as the highlight we just inserted (Tip: copy and paste the **Position and Size** property.)

7. Delete the default **Text** ("link text...") so that the text box is empty. By default it will be transparent with no border. Do not change this. Select the **Hide Scroll Bars** property. All of these things will ensure that the text box is entirely invisible during playback.

8. Click the **Edit** button on the right of the **Link to** property for the Text Link. The *Link to* dialog box is displayed.

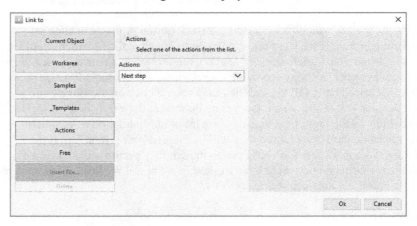

9. Select a category of **Actions** on the left, and then in the **Actions** field, select **Next step**.

10. Click **Ok** to save your selection and close the dialog box.

11. Adjust the bubble text for the original action to mention the alternative action. You may also want to remove the pointer, and position it so that it is not pointing directly to either option.

Now let's look at how this appears during playback. Again, this example is taken from Demo mode.

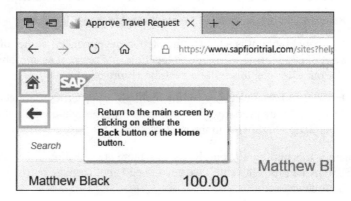

So there we have it. Two fully-functioning action areas. The user can click on either one, and will progress to the next Step in either case.

Switching modes

One incredibly useful feature of Enable Now is the ability to change from one play mode to another during playback. For example, if there is a step that is particularly difficult to perform correctly in Test mode (for example, because it involves a precise drag-and-drop action) then you could set the simulation to switch to Demo mode for that action, so that the user *sees* the action but is not required to perform the action themselves.

Let's look at how to use this functionality by way of another use case. Suppose we have recorded a simulation for the creation of a scaled pricing condition using ECC6.0 transaction VK11. Say we record the entry of six scale lines. The final screenshot for this will look like the following:

Scales								
Scale Type	Scale quantity	U...	Amount		Unit	per	UoM	
From		1 BBL		65.00	USD	1	BBL	^ v
	1000			64.00				
	5000			63.00				
	10000			62.00				
	20000			61.00				
	50000			60.00				

This screen requires twelve TEXT INPUT interaction macros to complete—one for each scale start volume (in the **Scale quantity** column) and one for each price (in the **Amount** column). In Practice mode, we could make the user perform all of these actions, but realistically, once they have entered one scale line, they pretty much know how to enter any number of scale lines—they are not going to learn anything more through doing exactly the same thing a further five times. So what we will do in our simulation is have them complete the first scale line, and then we'll complete the remaining scale lines for them, by switching into Demo mode.

The first thing we need to do is make sure that all of the macros that we want to carry out in a different mode are in the same, single Step. For our simulation, we

● An alternative to this would be to just delete the steps for the subsequent scale lines, and just jump to a final screenshot of "here is the completed screen", but that is less realistic, and could be seen as implying that some things just get done by magic, and we should always aim for realism (albeit tempered with a little pragmatism) in our simulations.

want the user to have to complete the first scale line themselves, and then have the remaining five scale lines completed automatically, so we only really need to merge the last 10 STRING INPUT macros into the same Step. However, for clarity, we'll just go ahead and merge all 12 of the macros into a single Step. How to merge Steps is explained in *Working with the 'after' object image* on page 155, so we won't repeat it here.

Once all macros are in the same Step, you can insert the mode switch into this Step by carrying out the steps shown below.

1. In the *Thumbnails Pane*, click on the macro immediately before the point at which you want to effect the switch (so that the macro immediately following the selected macro is the first macro executed in the new playback mode), to select it.

    In our example, we want the user to have to complete the first scale line themselves, so we will click on the macro for entering an **Amount** of **66.00**.

2. Select menu option **Insert | Insert Special Macro | Mode Change Begin**. The macro is inserted and selected. Its properties will appear as follows:

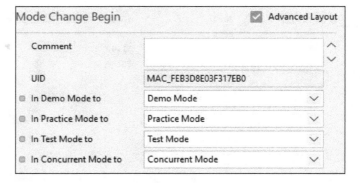

3. For each play mode for which you want to switch modes, select the mode into which you want to switch, from the drop-down list for that mode.

    For our example, we only want to switch if we are currently in Practice mode, and for this mode we want to switch to Demo mode. To do this, we select **Demo Mode** in the **In Practice Mode to** field.

4. Back in the *Thumbnails Pane*, click on the last macro that should be executed in the switched mode (so that the macro immediately following it is executed in the original mode), to select it.

    In our example, we want to switch back to Practice mode after entering **60.00** in the **Amount** field.

5. Select menu option **Insert | Insert Special Macro | Mode Change End**. The macro is inserted. There are no properties for this macro (you do

not need to tell Enable Now which mode to switch back to—it always switches back to the mode that it originally switched out of).

Our Step now appears as follows:

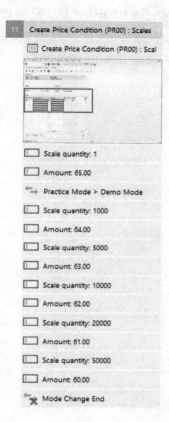

Now, if a user is playing the simulation in Practice mode, once the they complete the first scale line, the remaining five scale lines will be completed automatically for them. Note that the user will not receive any indication that this is what is happening, so you may want to add an EXPLANATION macro in Practice mode only to state something like "The remaining scale lines will be completed automatically for you", and maybe another EXPLANATION macro after the mode switch back, to tell them to "Continue the exercise as normal".

Summary

SAP Enable Now provides a wealth of features for editing training simulations. You can change the instructions provided in simulations, control the flow of progress through a simulation, and influence how the simulation appears in the various play modes.

You can also add a variety of additional content to simulations, from explanation texts, to images, to links to other content objects, graphics, and so on. Further options for enhancing your simulations are described in the following sections:

- *Using a Book Page in a simulation project* on page 319.
- *Using Questions in simulation projects* on page 357
- *Using audio with simulations* on page 567.

5
Workflow

In any large development project, it becomes necessary to *control* this development - especially if there are multiple parties involved (for example, authors, reviewers, approvers, and so on). Enable Now provides fairly robust workflow capabilities, which can facilitate this control. By using workflow, you can control the stages through which a content object must progress, and who can progress the object from one stage to the next.

Using workflow in Enable Now is not *necessary*; you can still set the Status of content objects, and assign them to people without using workflow—you just won't have as much control over this, in that any Author will be able to set any Status and assign content objects to any other Author.

In this chapter, you will learn:

- How workflow is implemented in Enable Now
- How to complete a workflow task assigned to you
- How to review your workflow tasks

This chapter does not cover how to set up a workflow process in Enable Now. That is something that should be done by the Administrator, and this book concentrates purely on Author activities.

■ Setting the **Publish** flag still requires specific authorization, regardless of whether or not workflow is used,

■ If you really need to set up a workflow process yourself, go to the Manager component of Enable Now, select **Administration | Workflow**, and there is enough information in this slim chapter to get you started.

Workflow process basics

When you create training content object (whether this is a simulation, a presentation, or other material) the content object typically progresses through a number of stages, from initial creation through to final publishing. A **workflow process** makes sure that development does indeed progress through these stages.

Typically, there is approval required at certain points (most commonly when moving from one stage to the next), and the workflow process ensures that this approval is obtained—by making sure that only an authorized approver can progress the content object to the next stage.

Suppose we have a simplified process for the creation of training simulations which sees the work go through the following steps:

A typical development process will usually include many more steps, and also allow for 'loops back'—for example, if the result of the review is that the object is rejected—but this over-simplified example is sufficient for our purposes.

If we accept that each task changes the status of the object—from what it was at the beginning of the task to what it is at the end of the task—we can identify the following possible statuses:

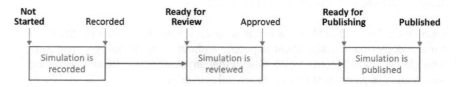

As no activity takes place *between* tasks (that is, 'on the line' in the flowchart), we only need to record a single status for these points. For example **Recorded** and **Ready for Review** are effectively the same state, so we only need one of these as a status. Which one you use is arbitrary but I personally prefer to use the 'input status' for a task, because it is conceptually easier for the executor of a given task to check for the status *going into* their task rather than the status coming out of another task (especially if there could be multiple paths into their task). For example, the Reviewer can just look for "anything that is Ready for Review" to identify their work. This means that we only need the statuses identified in **bold** in the diagram above.

● Statuses are defined by the Administrator in the Manager, via menu path **Administration | Status**.

These stages (**Not Started, Ready for Review, Ready for Publishing**, and **Published**) are what would be used for the possible **Status** property values for our content objects. We can then define a workflow process that requires a content object to go through these four Statuses, in this order.

The next thing the workflow process needs to do is control who can set the status to each of these values. This is achieved by defining *transitions*. A transition is the action that is performed on a content object that has one status, to move it to the next status. Handily, the transitions are the steps that we initially identified in our simplified process flowchart above, so we just need to identify who performs each step. This then gives us the following, final process flow:

In Enable now, a workflow simply codifies this, as follows:

Linked Status	Transition	Destination	Permission
Not Started	Simulation recorded	Ready for Review	Author
Ready for Review	Simulation reviewed	Ready for Publishing	Business Approver
Ready for Publishing	Simulation Published	Published	Team Lead

● Workflow processes are defined by the Administrators in the Manager, via menu path **Administration | Workflow**.

The column headings in the table above reflect the terminology used by Enable Now itself for workflow definitions. The table entries can be read as: "If the current status of the object is {Linked Status} then the {Permission} performs the task {Transition} which will result in the object having a new status of {Destination}". It is important to note that the emphasis is on the 'role performing the task', and not on the 'role changing the status'. This perspective, and the specific terminology used here for the transitions, comes into play later, as we shall see.

Assigning a workflow process to an object

If your Administrator has assigned a workflow process at the Workarea or Group level, this workflow process should automatically be assigned when you create a new object within the Workarea or Group (as appropriate). If a workflow process is *not* automatically assigned to an object, you can manually assign one at any time by carrying out the steps shown below:

1. Click on the content object in the Workarea, to select it.

2. Click on the **Change Workflow** button at the top of the *Object Editor* pane. The *Change Workflow* dialog box is displayed.

Change Workflow

3. In the **Set Workflow** field, select the workflow process that should be used for this content object.

4. As soon as you select a Workflow for the object, the **Change Status** field is disabled from editing. The Status of the object will automatically be set to the first status in the workflow process (this would be **Not Started** in our example workflow on page 181).

5. If you want to assign the workflow task (that will be created as a result of assigning the Workflow process to the object) to a specific person, then select this person from the **Assign to** drop-down list. This person will receive an email notification that the task has been assigned to them.

6. If you want to assign (or change) the task type currently applied to this object, then select the appropriate task type in the **Change type** field.

★ Change types are maintained in the Manager component, via menu option **Administration | Types**.

The **Change type** can be used to differentiate between different types of work task, typically for identifying and managing workload (because different task types will have different effort requirements). For example, tasks could be categorized as **Initial Creation**, **Update**, **Translation**, and so on. These types can then be included in progress reports generated via the Manager component.

▲ In this Author's experience, this feature does not work, and these (*Protocol* category) **Tags** cannot be set or cleared manually.

7. If necessary, you can add or remove tags assigned to the object in the **Set/clear tags** field. These are the **Tags** defined in the *Protocol* category (see page 55), and not the **Tags** in the *Basic Properties* category (see page 51). They are therefore normally only set by Enable Now itself.)

8. Enter any necessary comments in the **Comment** field. For example, if you are assigning the object to another user, you may want to explain why you are doing this and what you expect from them. This comment will appear in the email notification sent to the Assignee and any Watchers.

★ Notification emails are only sent out if the relevant **Notification** server settings are activated.

9. If you want anyone watching this object to be notified of the change, then make sure that the **Notify Watchers** checkbox is selected, and the 'watchers' will receive an email notification. Otherwise, make sure that it is deselected. (Whether it is selected or deselected when this dialog box is displayed will depend on the settings in the Workflow process.)

10. Click on **Save to server**.

Completing a workflow task

When you click **Finish Editing** on the *Content Editor* taskbar for a content object, the *Finish Editing* dialog box is displayed (this is covered in *Checking in a content object* on page 36). If a workflow process has been assigned to the content object, the *Finish Editing* dialog box looks slightly different (from the example shown on page 36), containing the **Workflow Action** field instead of the **Change Status** field (all other fields are identical). An example of the workflow-specific *Finish Editing* dialog box is shown below:

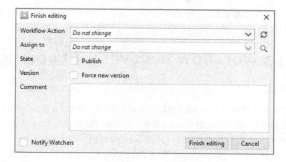

Complete this dialog box as follows:

1. In the **Workflow Action** field, select the task (*transition*) that you have just completed for the object.

   The values in the drop-down will depend upon the current Status of the object and the workflow process definition. For example, in our simple workflow process outlined on page 181, if the current status of the object is **Not Started**, the only possible transition is **Simulation recorded**, so the **Workflow Action** field will have only the following values in the drop-down:

   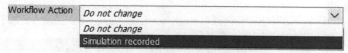

   This is why using a transition name structured as 'what has been done' makes sense—because this is exactly what you select here.

   Furthermore, there is no **Change Status** field in this dialog box because Enable Now *knows* what the next Status will be, based on the selected **Workflow Action**. Again, this is explicit *control*—you can't *not* follow the process. Here, because our workflow process states that if a **Workflow Action** of **Simulation recorded** is selected, then the next Status must be **Ready for Review**, so this is what Enable Now will set it to.

■ If the object is not yet ready to be transitioned to the next stage, you can leave the **Workflow Action** as **Do not change**. This is useful if, for example, you want to pass a content object to another Author for editing or peer-review— just leave the **Workflow Action** unchanged, and set the **Assign to** field to that Author

2. If you want to assign this content object to another user, then select this user in the **Assign To** field. This person will receive an email notification that the task has been assigned to them.

   Note that, unlike the **Workflow Action** field, there is no 'logic' applied to the values available in the **Assign To** field—you can effectively select any user, even if this user does not have the permissions to execute the transformation necessary to advance the content object out of the Status that it will be placed in based on the **Workflow Action** that you select in this dialog box. It is hoped that a future enhancement will address this.

3. Complete any other fields as necessary (see the instructions in *Assigning a workflow process to an object* on page 181 for details).

4. Click on **Finish editing**.

Changing a workflow task without editing the object

Even if you have not checked out and (optionally) edited a content object, you can still change the workflow settings for it—for example, to assign it to a specific user, or to record a transition. This is useful, for example, if you are a reviewer and just need to record the fact that you have reviewed the object (and you have not *changed* the object), or if you are an Author and want to pass it to another Author for additional work (or peer review) before submitting it for review.

To change the workflow task settings for an object, carry out the following steps:

1. In the Workarea, click on the object to select it.

2. Click on the **Change Workflow** button. The *Change Workflow* dialog box is displayed.

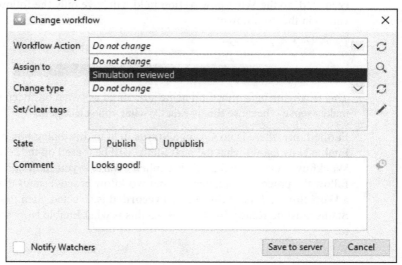

3. If you want to record completion of an action for the object, then select the appropriate transition in the **Workflow Action** field.

   In the example above, the current Status of the object is **Ready for Review**, and according to our simple workflow process, the only transition that can be selected for an object with this Status is **Simulation reviewed**. Therefore, this is the only choice available in the **Workflow Action** drop-down (other than **Do not change**, obviously...).

4. If you want to assign this object to another user, then select this user in the **Assign to** field.

5. If the (current version of the) object is *not* published, and you want to publish it now, then select the **Publish** checkbox in the **State** field. If the object is currently published, and you want to revoke this (and return the object seen by users to the previous published version), then select the **Unpublish** checkbox in the **State** field.

   Note that you can only publish or unpublish an object if you are assigned a role that has this authorization.

6. Complete any other fields as necessary (see the instructions in *Assigning a workflow process to an object* on page 181 for details).

7. Click on **Save to server**.

● Note that 'unpublishing' an object will not revert the version of the content object in the Workarea to the previous version—it will simply remove the currently-published version from the user's view. If a previous version had been published then that version will be visible instead; if no previous version has been published, then the object will no longer be visible to users.

Checking workflow information for objects

You can check a number of key workflow-related values for an object in the *Object Editor* pane, in the *Protocol* category. An example of this is shown below:

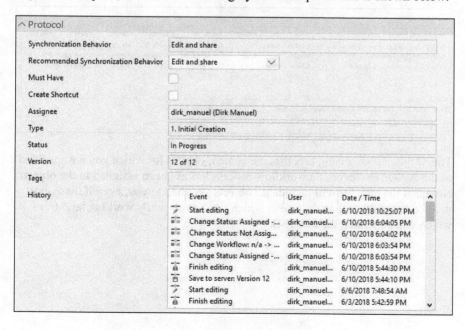

The workflow-related properties in the *Protocol* category are explained in the table below.

Property	Description
Assignee	The Userid and name of the Author to whom the object (or the current workflow task for the object) is currently assigned.
Type	The type of activity being performed by this workflow task (for example, **Initial Creation**, **Update**, or **Translation**). (See additional comments under Change Type on page 182.)
Status	The current Status of the object.

All other properties in the *Protocol* category are not specific to workflow, and are explained in *The Protocol category* on page 54.

Reviewing your workflow tasks

● A task cannot exist without an associated object—although an object can exist without a workflow task associated to it—so the "task" list is really an "object list".

To track all of the workflow tasks you need to complete, you can display a list of all of the *objects* that are currently assigned to you. You can also use the same functionality to review *all* tasks (for all Authors), according to a number of different criteria,as we shall see later in this section.

To list all of the tasks that are currently assigned to you, select menu option **Manager Workarea | Manage Tasks**. The *Manage tasks* dialog box is displayed.

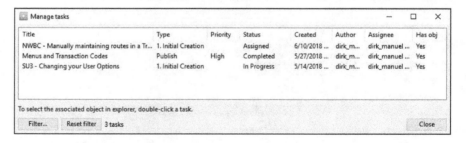

The *Manage tasks* dialog box lists the content objects for which you are specified as the **Assignee**—even if a workflow process has not been assigned to the object. Note that the task list will include *all* objects assigned to you, even if these exist in a workarea other than the one in which you are currently working (and from which you generated the task list).

The table below lists all of the information that is shown for each object (from left to right):

Column	Description
Title	The **Name** of the content object.
Description	Any description that has been entered for the task. Descriptions can only be entered in the Manager component, and are therefore only typically entered by the Administrator (or Team Lead).
Type	The type of task. Types are defined by the Administrator, and indicate the type of work to be performed (for example, **Initial Creation**, **Update**, or **Translation**). This designation is purely informational, and does not drive any processing in Enable Now (although your Administrator may choose to use different workflow processes for each task type).
Priority	The priority of this task. Priorities are defined by the Administrator, and assigned to tasks in the Manager. This is purely informational.
Status	The current Status of the task/object.
Workflow	The name of the workflow process assigned to the object.
Milestone	The milestone that this task is working toward. Milestones are defined by the Administrator, and assigned to tasks via the Manager. Typical milestones could be **Phase 1 Training**, **Go-live**, and so on. This field is purely informational.
Created	The date on which the content object was initially created.
Due	The date by which the task should be complete. Due dates are specified in the Manager.
Author	The Userid and name of the person who initially created the object.
Assignee	The Userid and name of the person to whom the task/object is currently assigned. By default, this will be you (otherwise it wouldn't appear in your task list).
Workarea	The Workarea in which the task/object exists.
Has obj	If a content object exists for the task, then this field will specify **Yes**. If the task has been created without an object (for example, because it is a placeholder and it is expected that the assignee creates the object) then this field will specify **No**.

■ If you only want to list your *tasks*, and not objects without a workflow process assigned to them that just happen to specify you as the **Assignee**, then you can filter the Workflow column to show only records with a value in this field.

● The **Has obj** property is only really useful if you (or your Team Lead) are in the habit of creating empty 'placeholders'—for example, for required simulation projects that SMEs will create in Instant Producer.

Although you cannot open any of the listed content objects by clicking on them, you can 'jump' to an object in the Workarea hierarchy by double-clicking on the object in the task list (assuming that the **Has obj** field specifies **Yes**—otherwise there is no object to jump to). The *Manage tasks* dialog box will remain open, allowing you to jump to additional objects, if required, without having to re-open it. Note that if the selected object appears in multiple places in the hierarchy, you will jump to the first instance of the object.

Changing the filter criteria

Although the primary purpose of the *Manage tasks* dialog box is to list all of *your* active tasks, you can change the list filter to show tasks that are assigned to other Authors, or only tasks meeting other specific criteria.

To change the task list filter criteria, carry out the following steps:

1. Click on the **Filter** button at the bottom of the *Manage tasks* dialog box. The *Filter tasks* dialog box is displayed.

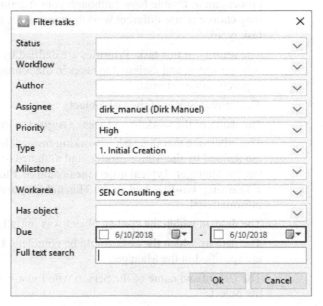

2. Specify the required filter criteria by selecting the appropriate value in the available fields (refer to the table in page 186 for an explanation of each of these fields).

3. To filter on all objects that contain a specific text within the object **Short Description** or **Description**, or within the *task* **Description**, enter this text string into the **Full text search** field.

4. Click **Ok**.

The *Manage tasks* dialog box is filtered based on your criteria. To revert to the default filter (of listing all/only your tasks), click on the **Reset filter** button.

Summary

Workflow can be used to control the development process for content objects. A workflow process effectively defines the Statuses through which a content object can progress, who can progress a content object from one Status to the next, and the task that they must complete to effect this progression.

The use of workflow is effectively optional. If workflow is not used, object Statuses and Assignees can still be set, but they can be set by any Author, in any order. Workflow is therefore highly recommended if you want to exert (verifiable, auditable) control over your development process.

6

Working with Instant Producer

Instant Producer is a component of Enable Now that provides a 'scaled-down' version of the functionality available via the 'full functionality' Producer. Instant Producer can be used to record simulation Projects and perform basic editing of them. Instant Producer does not allow you to organize content into Groups, create or edit Books and Book Pages, or perform any form of publishing. All of these things can only be done using Producer.

In this chapter, we cover everything to do with Instant Producer. You will learn:

- How to record a simulation project via Instant Producer
- How to create a printable document and a standalone video for a simulation
- How to work with the Instant Producer Workspace

If you (or your SMEs) are not using Instant Producer, then you can probably skip this chapter.

Who would use Instant Producer?

Because Instant Producer has limited functionality (when compared to Producer) it is much easier and quicker to learn, and is therefore ideally suited to use by Subject Matter Experts (SMEs) or other 'infrequent' users of Enable Now, or by recorders who do not have the time (or inclination) to learn all about Producer with all its details and intricacies.

Instant Producer lends itself very well to a 'split development' model of training content development. In a split development model, the basic recording of a simulation is performed by one resource (typically a SME), and this recording is then passed to another resource (most commonly a skilled Training Developer) who then edits it, performing all of the hard work to complete the simulation and prepare it for publishing. Applying this to Enable Now, the SME captures the recording in Instant Producer, and the Author edits it using the full functionality provided by Producer.

Enable Now can further facilitate this model by providing workflow functionality. A task to record a simulation can be assigned to a SME (typically as an empty 'placeholder' project). Once the SME has completed this task, they can reassign the task to a Training Developer. Judicious use of Statuses and authorizations can make sure that SMEs cannot progress a recording to publishing, and that this can only be done after the Training Developer has performed the editing steps. For more information on using workflow, refer to *Chapter 5, Workflow*.

Accessing Instant Producer

How you access Instant Producer depends upon whether you are working in an on-premise implementation or a cloud implementation,

- For an on-premise implementation, the Instant Producer (and, normally, the Producer, and Manager as well) will be installed on your PC, and will be accessible via the Windows **Start** menu.

- For a cloud implementation, no software is installed, and Instant Producer is launched via a URL. This will typically be provided to you by your Enable Now Administrator. The URL will be similar in format to:

  https://_client_**.enable-now.cloud.sap/wa/**_workarea_**/**
  .ipro?download=1

  where _client_ is your client identifier, and _workarea_ is the identifier of the Workarea into which content recorded via the Instant Producer will be stored.

▲ If you do not see either of these messages, or see a message asking Do you want to open or save ipro.ipro (and not ipro.jnlp) which does nothing when you open it, then check that you have Java installed.

Regardless of which method you use, when you launch Instant Producer, you may see one or more of system messages, depending on your version of Windows and your company's security settings and trusted Sites:

- This type of file can harm your computer. Do you want to keep ipro.jnlp anyway? (Select **Keep**, then click on the downloaded file.)

- Do you want to open or save ipro.jnlp? (Select **Open**.)

Once you get through any system messages, the following dialog box will be displayed:

Here, you have three options:

- **Record New Project**: Click on this option to immediately start recording a new simulation. Recording a simulation is described in *Recording a simulation project via Instant Producer* on page 198.

- **Display the Producer Workspace**: Click on this option to display the *Producer Workspace*, from where you can edit an existing recording that is assigned to you, or create a new recording. Refer to *The Instant Producer Workspace* on page 193 for further details of this.

- **Quick Guide**: Select this option to display some help information on using Instant Producer.

The Instant Producer Workspace

The image below shows an example of the *Instant Producer Workspace*. This provides access to all of the simulations that are assigned to you (including placeholders).

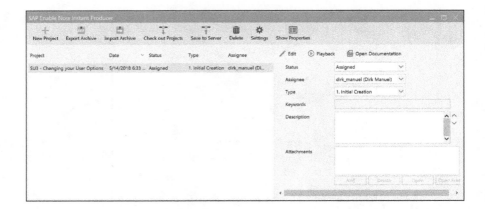

The *Instant Producer Workspace* consists of two main panes, and a toolbar. These are identified in the graphic on the right, and explained below.

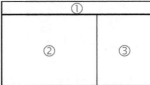

1. The *Workspace Toolbar*.

2. The *Project Manager*, in which you can see all of the projects that have been assigned to you.

3. The *Properties Pane*, which shows the properties of the selected project. Note that you can toggle between showing and hiding the *Properties Pane* by clicking on the **Show Properties** button on the *Workspace Toolbar*.

Let's look at each of these elements in a little more detail.

The Workspace Toolbar

The *Workspace Toolbar* provides access to the primary functions in Instant Producer. The table below lists these buttons (from left to right) and explains their purpose.

Button		Purpose
	New Project	Create a new simulation project. How to do this is explained in *Recording a simulation project via Instant Producer* on page 198.
	Export Archive	Select one or more simulation projects and then click on this button to export the project(s) to an 'archive' file. You would normally only need to do this to create a backup, or to move your project(s) to another Workarea. Exporting projects is explained in *Exporting content objects* on page 543.

Button		Purpose
	Import Archive	Import simulation projects from a previously-created archive file. Importing projects is explained in *Importing content objects* on page 545.
	Check out Projects	Select one or more simulation projects, and then click on this button to check out the project(s). This will prevent other Authors from being able to change them.
	Save to Server	Select one or more simulation projects, and then click on this button to save the project(s) to the server and check them back in so other Authors can see your changes and change the project(s) if required.
	Delete	Select one or more simulation projects and click on this button to delete the project(s). Note that the projects must be checked in (saved to the server) to be able to do this.
	Settings	Click on this button to display (and optionally change some of) your default settings, and display some troubleshooting information about Enable Now.
	Show Properties	Toggle between showing and hiding the *Properties Pane*.

Server Access

The **Check out Projects** and **Save to Server** buttons are only available if you are connected to a Workarea—which you will be if you are using a cloud implementation and used a direct URL (ending in `/.ipro`) to access Instant Producer, as explained earlier in this chapter. If you are using an on-premises implementation you may need to log on to Manager and then click on the **Open Instant Producer** link from there.

The Project Manager

The Instant Producer *Project Manager* provides a list of:

- All of the simulation projects that have been assigned to you as workflow tasks

- All simulation projects that you created in Instant Producer, but that have not yet been adopted onto the server

- Any simulation projects that you created in Producer (not Instant Producer) and that are stored in your **Unsorted** folder

➕ As of the 1811 release, once a project has been edited in Producer it is no longer visible in Instant Producer.

The following information is provided for each project:

Column	Information provided
Project	The **Name** of the simulation project.
Date	The date on which the project was last changed.
Status	The current **Status** of the project.
Type	If development types have been defined by your Administrator, this field identifies the **Type** currently assigned to this content object. Types are typically used to differentiate between different types of development effort (for example, **Initial Creation**, **Update**, **Translation**, and so on).
Assignee	The person to whom the project (or workflow task for the project) has been assigned for completion. In Instant Producer, this should normally be you.

If the *Properties Pane* is not displayed, then three additional columns, containing action links of **Edit**, **Playback**, and **Open Documentation**, are provided on the right (in the space where the *Properties Pane*—which contains buttons for these functions—would otherwise be displayed). These perform exactly the same function as the buttons in the *Properties Pane*. Refer to that section (below) for details.

To edit a project that is listed in the *Project Manager*, you can either double-click on the project in the list, or single-click on the project and then click on the **Edit** button at the top of the *Properties Pane* (or on the **Edit** link in the *Project Manager*, if the *Properties Pane* is not currently displayed). In either case, you will be passed into the *Instant Producer Editor*, which is explained in *The Instant Producer Editor* on page 203.

The Properties Pane

The *Properties Pane* provides information about the project that is currently selected in the *Project Manager*. The table below lists the properties that are available and explains their purpose. Note that several of these properties are also shown in the columns in the Project Manager.

Column	Information provided
Status	The current **Status** of the project. This may be controlled by workflow.
Assignee	The person to whom the project (or workflow task for the project) has been assigned for completion. In Instant Producer, this should normally be you.

Column	Information provided
Type	If development types have been defined by your Administrator, this field identifies the **Type** currently assigned to this content object. Types are typically used to differentiate between different types of development effort (for example, **Initial Creation**, **Update**, **Translation**, and so on).
Keywords	Keywords can be used to associate a specific text with the simulation. This allows users to locate this content object by searching on the keyword text. Note that you would only enter words in here that do not already exist in the simulation texts, and that you want users to be able to search on.
Description	A description of the simulation. This typically takes up the largest portion of the rightmost side of the *Trainer* screen, and is therefore often used for providing context, concepts, or additional information about the simulation.
Attachments	A list of files that have been attached to this simulation. You can use the buttons below this field to add or remove files, open a file, or open the folder (within Enable Now) that contains the file. These files will be accessible by users in the Trainer, so you would not want to include 'working' documents in here.

Three buttons are available at the top of the **Properties Pane**. These are explained in the following table:

Link	Purpose
Edit	Open the selected project in the *Instant Producer Editor*. Refer to *The Instant Producer Editor* on page 203 for information on this.
Playback	Play the simulation in Demo mode (this is the only mode available from Instant Producer).
Open Documentation	Display any document output type that has been created for the project. Refer to *Chapter 12, Working with Documents* for more information on document output types. If a document does not currently exist, then the default document type will be created—although to do this you will need to check out the project (which you can obtain by opening the project for editing, or by selecting the project in the *Project Manager* and then clicking on the **Check Out Projects** button).

Preparing for recording

All of the preparation guidelines outlined for recording via Producer also apply to recording via Instant Producer. Refer to *Preparing for recording* on page 78 for details of these.

Recording a simulation project via Instant Producer

Instant Producer provides a 'simplified' method of recording a simulation (when compared to Producer). However, the actual recording process is largely identical to that used by the 'full' Producer. The only real difference is that there are less features available via the *Recording Toolbar*.

Step 1: Create a new project and select the application

Record a new project by following the steps shown below:

1. Either click on **Record New Project** from the *Welcome* dialog box displayed when you first start Instant Producer, or click on the **New Project** button from the *Workspace Toolbar*. The *Record New Project* dialog box is displayed.

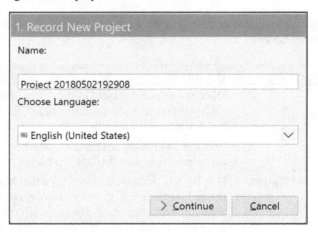

2. Enter a suitable name for your new simulation in the **Name** field.
3. Click **Continue**. The *Select Window and Profile* dialog box is displayed.

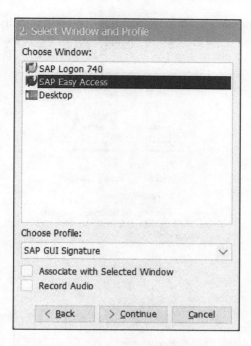

4. The *Choose Window* section of the dialog box lists all of the applications that are currently running on your PC. Click on the application that you want to record in this list.

5. The **Choose Profile** field automatically defaults to the most appropriate profile for the application that you have selected. The profile controls the context and object recognition, and you should not normally need to change this from the default selection. However, in some circumstances—such as for new, unknown applications—you may experience problems with the default selection, you can chose another profile (or the 'catch-all' **Standard** profile).

6. If you always want the selected profile to be used for the selected application, then select the **Associate with Selected Window** checkbox. This should only be necessary if you have changed the default profile selection.

7. If you want audio to be captured when you record the application, select the **Record Audio** checkbox. Note that refers to microphone-captured verbal explanations provided by you as you record. This is not the same as 'published audio', and is not normally left in the final simulation that is published. Effectively, audio captured during application recording is used purely as input to the editing process, and is therefore of most use when the person editing the simulation is not the same person as the person who recorded it. Audio is discussed in detail in *Chapter 14, Adding Audio to Your Content*.

8. Click **Continue**. The recording wizard displays the third step, *Define Recording Area*, and a red border is shown around the area of the screen

that will be captured during recording. This will initially correspond to the area occupied by the selected application, but you can change this in the next few steps.

9. In the upper part of the dialog box, you can choose exactly what you want to capture during recording. The options are:

   ♦ Click on **Region** to capture a specific area on the screen. This is the area bounded by the red recording marquee; you can change this area by dragging the marquee to a new location, or by dragging its borders to select a different area of the screen.

   ♦ Click on **Active Window** to capture the active window—regardless of where this window appears on the screen or whether it dynamically resizes itself (for example, in response to changes in screen content).

10. In the **Choose Size** field. Select the screen dimensions that you want to capture. You can either select one of the predefined sizes, or you can use the **Width** and **Height** fields to specify exact dimensions.

11. If you selected **Region** in Step 9, and selected a recording size and shape that is different from the current application size and shape, then you can click on the **Fit Application Window**, and the application will be resized to fit the recording marquee.

12. Click on the **Record** button. The *Recording Bar* is shown across the top of the screen.

You are now ready to record your application, as explained in *Step 2: Record the application* on page 201, below.

Step 2: Record the application

To record the application, simply perform the actions you want to have recorded, and Enable Now will automatically capture them.

Whenever Enable Now is busy capturing an action for you, the *Recording Bar* will turn red. Wait for it to turn green again, before performing the next action.

Other things you may find useful to do while you are recording are:

- Click the **Pause** button to temporarily pause recording. The *Recording Bar* turns gray. Click on the **Record** button to re-start recording.

- Click the **Undo** button to discard the last action you captured, so that it is not included in your project,

The following table shows the options that are on the *Recording Bar* and explains their purpose. Note that the availability of individual options will depend upon the status of the *Recording Bar*.

Button	Name	Purpose
❚❚	Pause	Temporarily pause recording. Any actions that you perform while recording is paused will not be captured. Everything that you have captured so far will be copied into the project.
⬤	Record	Re-start recording after you have previously paused it.
◼	Stop	Stop recording. Everything captured will be inserted into the project, and you will be returned to the *Project Editor*.
↺	Undo	Cancel the last action captured.

Once you have finished recording, click the **Stop** button to stop recording. The *Recording Bar* will close, and the *Finished Recording* dialog box is displayed. Continue with *Step 3: Save your recording*, below.

Step 3: Save your recording

The *Finished Recording* dialog box is displayed as soon as you stop recording.

Choose one of the following options:

- If you want to review your project, click on **Play Project**. The project is played back in Demo mode, which is described in *Demo mode* on page 9. When playback finishes, you are passed back to the *Finished Recording* dialog box (above) and can choose another option.

▲ Don't close the *Instant Producer Editor* window, as this will close Instant Producer completely (unless, of course, that's what you want to do...).

- If you want to edit your project, click on **Edit Project**. You are passed into the *Instant Producer Editor*. You can then edit your project as described in *The Instant Producer Editor* on page 203. Once you have finished editing your project, click **Save**, and then click **Explorer** to continue to the *Instant Producer Workarea*.

- If you want to keep your recording, click on **Save Project**.

- If you don't want to keep your recording, click on **Delete Project**.

Working from a placeholder

The above steps assume that you are recording a simulation from scratch. It is possible that empty 'placeholder' projects are created centrally, and then assigned (possibly via workflow) to Subject Matter Experts for recording. In such a scenario, the simulation should be recorded from the placeholder as follows:

1. Access the *Instant Producer Workarea* by selecting **Access Project Workarea** from the Instant Producer *Welcome* panel.

2. Locate the placeholder project that has been assigned to you, in the *Project Manager*, and *double*-click on it. The following message is displayed:

3. Click on the **Start Recording** button. The *Record New Project* dialog box is displayed. You can then record the simulation as explained in *Recording a simulation project via Instant Producer* on page 198.

The Instant Producer Editor

The *Instant Producer Editor* is effectively a slimmed-down version of the *Project Editor* in Producer. It is designed to allow the person recording via Instant Producer to check their recording and make some basic changes. Do not expect that you can make a recording 'training-ready' using just this editor; all recordings will typically need additional editing in the full Producer *Project Editor* before they are ready for use.

An example of the *Instant Producer Editor* screen is shown below:

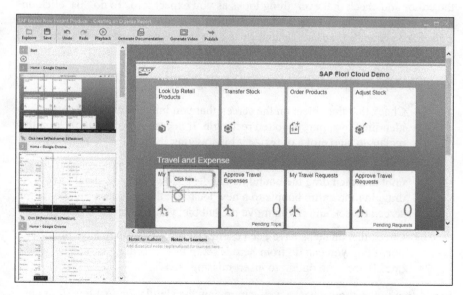

The *Project Editor* screen consists of four main components. These are identified in the graphic on the right, and explained below.

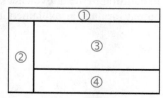

1. The *Project Editor Toolbar*.

2. The *Thumbnail View*, which shows a thumbnail image of the screen, and action captured, for each step in the simulation.

3. The *WYSIWYG Editor*, which shows a 'full-size' image of the screenshot selected in the **Thumbnail View**, with the 'bubble' for the captured action overlaid on it, just as it will be seen during playback of the simulation.

4. The *Notes Pane*, which provides two tabbed pages: *Notes for Authors*, and *Notes for Learners*. These are explained in *Adding notes to your recording* on page 205.

Unlike the *Project Editor* in Producer, you cannot change the layout of the *Instant Producer Editor* screen, in terms of which of the components are shown where, but you can change the relative size of these components by clicking and dragging the separator bars.

Reviewing your recording

As noted above, the primary purpose of the *Instant Producer Editor* is to allow you to check and review your recording before submitting it to an Author for full editing via the Producer.

The easiest way of reviewing your recording is to step through the screens in the editor and check that everything looks as you expect it to. To do this, click on a Step in the *Thumbnail View*, and check how this step looks in the *WYSIWYG Editor*. You can use the *PAGE UP* and *PAGE DOWN* keys or the cursor keys to navigate between Steps.

For each step, you should perform the following checks:

• Check that the object on the screen that you interacted with is correctly identified by a purple dotted rectangle. If necessary, you can click on this rectangle, and move or resize it by dragging its handles.

• Check that the 'bubble' is appropriately sized. If it is not, you can click on it and then drag the bounding handles. However, you should avoid dragging the entire bubble to a new location; the bubble is 'linked to' the screen object, and if you move the bubble, you will break this link.

• Check that all steps have been captured correctly. If they have not, the only thing you can do from here is scrap this recording, and create a new one. There is no option to insert missing steps

In addition to the above checks, you can review the simulation in a few different output formats, as explained in the following sections.

Adding notes to your recording

You can add text notes to your simulations in the *Notes Pane*. Notes can be specified per Step. Two types of notes are available:

Notes for Authors: These are effectively 'internal' notes that will be visible to Authors editing this simulation in Producer, but will not be visible in the final, published simulation. You would typically use these notes to advise Authors of things that need to be done to the simulation project, information that should be emphasized in the simulation, and so on. These notes will be added to the **Comments** field for the SCREEN macro in Producer.

Notes for Learners: These are notes that should be displayed to the users of the simulation. An EXPLANATION macro will be inserted into the simulation for these notes. The EXPLANATION macro is inserted as soon as you enter this category of notes, and will therefore be visible in any of the preview formats described above that you use.

To insert notes, simply click on the Step to which the notes should be added, select the appropriate notes category, and then enter your notes in the text area.

Playing your simulation

To play your simulation in Demo mode, click on the **Playback** button on the *Project Editor Toolbar*. The simulation will be played in a separate window, and the recording in the *Instant Producer Editor* will advance in sync with this, so you can make changes to the Steps as you identify them in the playback window.

Because the simulation is played in Demo mode (only; no other playback modes are possible from within Instant Producer), playback is hands-free and automatic. However, you can click on the **Pause** button to pause playback and make adjustments in the editor window (although these changes will not be reflected in the playback window unless you terminate playback and restart it).

Generating a printable document

If your simulations are typically also made available in a 'printable' document format, you may find it useful to generate a sample document, to see how this looks. To do this, click on the **Generate Document** button on the *Project Editor Toolbar*.

This will generate a **Standard Document** in Microsoft Word format. This may not necessarily be the document type or document format in which your simulation will ultimately be published, but it will at least give you an idea of how the simulation might look in print. This feature is also useful if you want your simulation to be reviewed by someone who does not have access to Instant Producer. This person can review the document, and optionally make comments in the Word document before passing it back to you (or to the Author) to have these comments incorporated into the final recording.

For more information on the Standard Document, including an example of this document type, refer to *The Standard Document* on page 483.

Generating a stand-alone video

If you want to share playback of the simulation with another user who does not have access to the Enable Now development environment, then you can export the simulation as a stand-alone video file that can be played back using Windows Media Player (or similar application). This will effectively be a video recording of Demo mode playback for the simulation.

To create a stand-alone video file for your simulation, carry out the steps shown below:

1. Click on the **Generate Video** button on the *Project Editor Toolbar*. The *Generate Video* dialog box is displayed.

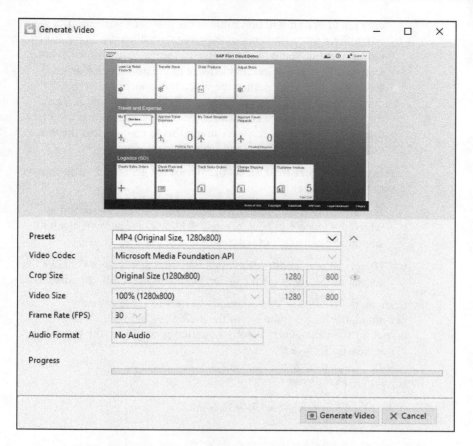

2. In the **Presets** field, select the size and format in which you want to generate the video. If you select a preset other than **User defined**, the video conversion settings (described below) will be defaulted for you. You can display these defaults by clicking on the **Settings** button (⚙) to the right of the **Presets** field, but you cannot change them.

If you select a preset of **User defined**, then the conversion settings fields are displayed below the **Presets** field, and you can change these as follows:

i. If you want to use a specific video codec, then select this in the **Video codec** field. Depending on the codec selected, further options may be available via the **Settings** button displayed to the right of the codec selection.

ii. In the **Crop Size** field, select the scale of the video image relative to the size of the captured screenshots. It is important to understand that the size selected here does not reflect the dimensions of the generated video—it defines how much of the screenshot will be shown in the video window. So if your original simulation was captured at 1280x800 and you select a size of 800x600 then the video will be generated at a scale of approximately 150%, so that only about ⅔ of it will be visible in the playback window. The video will always pan to the area of the screen in which the action is being performed, but you will not be able to see the entire screen at once. Conversely, if you select a video size of greater than the original screenshot dimensions, then the video will appear 'letterboxed' during playback, with a gray background shown around it. The image at the top of the *Generate Video* dialog box adjusts to reflect this, as you select a size. You can use this to confirm that the video will be generated at a size and scale that you want.

   iii. In the **Video size** field, select the size of the generated video relative to the **Crop size**.

   iv. In the **Frame Rate (FPS)** field, select the frames-per-second at which the video will be generated. A higher number will result in a smoother playback, but will result in a larger file.

   v. If you captured audio with your simulation then you can change the format of the audio for the generated file in the **Audio Format** field.

3.   Click on the **Generate Video** button. As the video file is being generated, the image at the top of the dialog box shows the current output for the video. Once video generation is complete, the following dialog box is displayed:

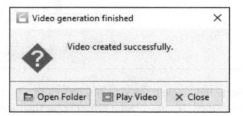

4.   Click **Open Folder** to open the folder intro which the video file has been saved (for example, so that you can send the file to another person for review), click **Play Video** to play the video now (to review it yourself), or click **Close** to just close the dialog box.

Publishing a playable simulation

As an alternative to creating a video file that you can send to other people for viewing, you can also publish a fully-functional playable version of your recorded simulation that other users can play (again, in Demo mode only). This is generated as a single executable file, which makes it suitable for e-mailing.

To publish a playable simulation, carry out the steps shown below:

1.   Click on the **Publish** button on the *Project Editor Toolbar*. The *Publish Object* dialog box is displayed.

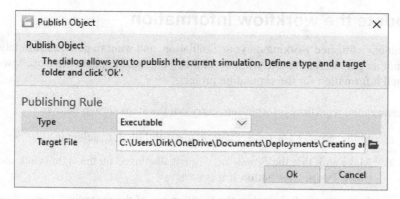

2. In the **Type** field, select the type of file that you want to generate. The options are **Executable**, which will generate a single `.exe` file, or **SLC**, which will generate a `.slc` file.

3. In the **Target File** field, navigate to and select the folder into which the file should be saved, and enter a suitable filename (the filename will default to the project name). Once the file has been generated, the following dialog box is displayed:

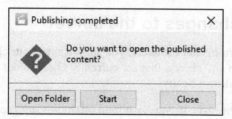

4. Click on **Open Folder** to open the folder to which the file has been saved, click on **Start** to launch the file, or click on **Close** to just close the dialog box.

Returning to the Project Explorer

Once you have finished reviewing your simulation, and have made any necessary changes, click on the **Explorer** button on the toolbar to return to the *Project Explorer*. Do not close the *Instant Producer Editor* window, as this will close the entire Instant Producer.

Finishing up

Once you have finished working on your simulation (at least for now), you can exit from Instant Producer. Depending on the current status there are a few things that you may need to do before exiting. These are described in the sections below.

Update the workflow information

If you have finished working on your simulation, and want to pass the simulation to another person for them to work on it, then you should update the workflow-related information for the simulation project.

To change the workflow information, carry out the steps shown below:

1. In the *Project Manager*, click on the simulation, to select it.

2. Make sure that the *Properties Pane* is displayed on the right (click the **Show Properties** button if it is not).

3. In the **Status** field, select the (new) status of the recording. Depending on whether a workflow process has been assigned to the project, you may be restricted in the values that are available for selection.

4. In the **Assignee** field, select the user to whom the simulation project should now be assigned. Again, depending on whether a workflow process has been assigned to the project, you may be limited in the people to whom you can assign the project.

Save your changes to the server

Before you exit from Instant Producer, you should save your changes to the server, and check in any objects that are currently checked out to you. To do this, carry out the steps shown below:

1. Click on the **Save to Server** button on the *Instant producer Toolbar*. The following message is displayed:

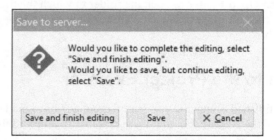

2. If you have finished working on the simulation, then click on the **Save and Finish Editing** button. Your changes will be saved to the server, and the simulation project will be checked in (which means that other people can edit the simulation).

    Caution:
    Once a simulation has been edited in Producer, it will no longer be accessible in Instant Producer. You should therefore be sure that you have completely finished with it before making it available to the Authors.

If you have not completely finished with the simulation, and will continue working on it later, then click on the **Save** button. Your changes will be saved to the server, but the object will remain checked out to you. This will prevent anyone else from editing the simulation in the meantime.

Exiting from Instant Producer

Once you have finished using Instant Producer, click on the **Close** button in the *Titlebar*. The Instant Producer window is closed.

Note that if you just close Instant Producer without first saving your changes to the server (as explained above) then your changes will be saved to your local repository (only).

Summary

Instant Producer is a simplified recording application that can be used to capture a recording of an application. It is easy-to-use and requires minimal training, which makes it suitable for use by Subject Matter Experts or other users who are not actual training developers.

Instant Producer includes a simplified editor that allows users of Instant Producer to make basic edits to captured recordings, and create documents and videos from this, for review.

Recordings captured (and optionally edited) via Instant Producer are typically not 'classroom ready' and will need editing by a trained Author, via the full Producer component of Enable Now.

7
Publishing Your Content

Developing your training content is undoubtedly the largest part of training, but the work does not stop once your content has been created (and approved). You still need to make this training content available to your users. Enable Now provides a number of different ways of doing this, depending upon your individual needs. This chapter describes the various formats in which you can provide your training content, and explains how to make these formats available.

In this chapter we will look at how to make your developed content available to your users. This includes:

- Publishing individual content objects
- Creating the *Trainer* for your entire Workarea
- Providing links to your content
- Providing context help in applications such as SAP ECC 6.0
- Generating full-motion video
- Publishing to a single executable

Delivery mechanisms

Enable Now provides a number of options for making your content available to your users. Broadly, this is split into 'training delivery', and 'performance support', although you can—and should—provide links between the two.

Training delivery involves providing content to users of a system (typically) before the system is available to the users. The purpose of this is to make sure that the users are able to perform their required business tasks when they get into the live system. Often, the majority of training delivery takes place before the new system has 'gone live', although there will always be the need to train new users (for example, new hires, or people moving into a new position) on an existing system.

Enable Now is perfectly suited to this type of (pre-go-live) training, as it provides simulations that allow the user to practice system activities before they actually get into the actual system. So here, you simply need to decide how to provide them with access to your simulations, so that they can review them (in the case of Demo mode) or carry them out (in the case of Practice mode) independently of the system. The simplest way of doing this is to *publish* your training content to a *Trainer*, and then provide the users with the URL of this *Trainer*. How to do this is explained in *Publishing to the Trainer in a cloud environment* on page 214.

Enable Now also allows you to publish training content in a format that can be loaded into a Learning Management System (LMS). This can be SAP Learning Solution (LS), SuccessFactors Learning, or any other LMS that supports the SCORM format or the AICC format.

For performance support, Enable Now provides a number of discrete options. It provides the Desktop Assistant for use with Windows applications (see *Chapter 10, The Desktop Assistant*), Web Assistant for browser-based applications (see *Chapter 11, The Web Assistant)*, and a Context File for use with other applications (see *Publishing Context Help* on page 239).

In addition, Enable Now allows you to generate video files which could be loaded into a video-sharing platform (such as YouTube), as explained in *Video output* on page 243, and allows you to generate single-file executables for easy distribution, as explained in *Publishing to an executable* on page 248.

Publishing to the Trainer in a cloud environment

In a cloud environment, there is not really a 'publishing process' that makes your content available to your users. You may recall from *Chapter 1, An Introduction to SAP Enable Now* that the *Trainer* provides access to all of your published content. The *Trainer* is effectively always available—as soon as you flag a content object as 'published', it will instantly be available in the *Trainer*; there is no need to publish your entire *Trainer* every time anything in it changes. This is extremely efficient; publishing is typically very fast (because you are only publishing one object at a time), and there is no period during which the *Trainer* is unavailable because it is being refreshed by the publishing process.

Preparing the Trainer

The *Trainer* presents all of the published content in the same hierarchical structure as your Workarea (see *Building your Workarea structure* on page 59). Your overall Workarea also contains a lot of other things in addition to your actual training content. For example, it will include Resources, probably a Toolbox, maybe some working Groups, and so on. Because you do not want this supporting content to be visible as-is in the *Trainer* hierarchy, you will typically have a high-level Group within your Workarea that contains all of your actual training content. This Group will then act as the **entry point** for your *Trainer*, and it is the URL of this Group that you will provide to your users, as explained in *Providing links to Enable Now content* on page 217.

It is therefore important that all of your content objects (that you want your users to be able to navigate to and select in the *Trainer*) are present within this entry point Group. As we saw in *Building your Workarea structure* on page 59, content objects can exist in multiple Groups, so you could define an entry point Group at any position within your Workarea and link selected user-facing content objects (potentially from 'higher up' in the Workarea hierarchy) into this as references, but there must be a copy of (reference to) all content objects that the user should see, somewhere below your *Trainer* entry point Group.

It is worth emphasizing here that this requirement of having content objects underneath your entry point Group applies only to *content objects* (typically, your simulations, Books, and Book Pages). You may have additional content that is included within (or referenced from) these content objects—for example, shared resources, common images, and so-on. These do not have to be located in your entry point Group as they will automatically be included in the published output—but they do have to be published. The best way to achieve this is to have all shared content included in a single Group within your Workarea (and outside of your entry point Group)—for example, a Toolbox Group), and then make sure that all objects in this Group are published.

Related to this, when you publish a content object, you need to make sure that the higher-level Groups containing this content object—all the way up to the entry point for your *Trainer*—are also published. If a Group is not published, then it—and any content objects it contains—will not be included in the *Trainer*, regardless of whether the selected content objects themselves are published.

Setting the Publish flag for a content object

To publish a content object in a cloud environment, all you need to do is tag it as 'Published'. There are effectively two points at which you can do this. The first point is when you finish editing the content object. This is done as follows:

■ If you want to publish all content objects in a Group, you will find it easier to first select the Group, and then use menu option **Server Workarea | Finish Editing All Objects**, or **Server Workarea | Change Workflow for All Objects** (as appropriate), instead of using the buttons. The remaining steps are the same, but will apply to all objects and not just the single object selected.

1. Click on the content object in the Workarea, to select it.

2. Click on the **Finish Editing** button. The *Finish editing* dialog box is displayed. Note that this will look slightly different depending on whether a workflow process is assigned to the content object or not. The example below shows a content object that does not have a workflow process assigned to it.

Finish Editing

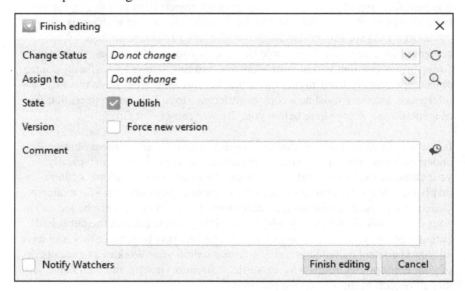

3. Next to the **State** label, select the **Publish** checkbox. This is the action that will make the content available—regardless of the **Change Status** setting.

4. Complete the other fields as necessary (see *Checking in a content object* on page 36).

5. Click **Finish Editing**.

If you do not currently have the content object checked out for editing, then you can use the second method of tagging an object as 'Published'. This is as follows:

■ Oddly, this method of setting the **Publish** flag via the **Change Workflow** button is not actually limited to only content objects to which a Workflow process has been assigned; you can also use it with any content object to change the **Publish** indicator without checking out the content object.

1. Click on the content object in the Workarea, to select it.

2. Click on the **Change workflow** button. The *Change workflow* dialog box is displayed. Again, note that this may vary slightly depending on whether a workflow process is assigned to the content object. For contrast with

Change Workflow

the example above, this screenshot (below) is for a content object that *does* have a Workflow Process assigned to it.

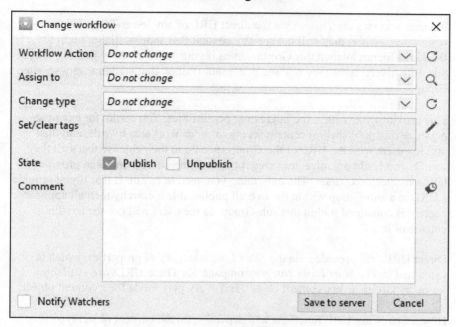

3. Next to the **State** label, select the **Publish** checkbox. This is the action that will make the content available—regardless of the **Workflow Action**.

4. Complete the other fields as necessary (see *Changing a workflow task without editing the object* on page 184).

    Typically, if you have a Workflow process assigned to the content object, you would select the 'final' **Workflow Action** (for example, "Approved", or "Published"), assign the content object to 'no-one' (select an **Assign to** value of **Unassign**), and change the **Change Type** (typically, to blank, now that the change is complete).

5. Click **Save to server**.

Regardless of which of the above two methods you use, once the **Publish** flag has been set for the content object, it will be visible to your users—assuming they know where to look, which is the subject of the next section.

▲ Although a content object can technically be published regardless of the object's **Status** (and independently of the Workflow Action if the object has a Workflow process assigned to it) the ability to publish a content object is controlled by permissions, and this permission should normally only be given to the role that can progress the object to having a **Status** of **Published** (or whatever your final Workflow step is).

Providing links to Enable Now content

Once you have published your content, you need to tell the users where they can find this content. Typically, you will want to direct users to the 'entry point' Group for your entire *Trainer*. However, one of the incredibly powerful features of SAP Enable Now is that you can effectively address any element in your

Workarea, from the highest-level Group to the lowest level content object—or even a specific delivery mode for a content object.

If a user accesses the *Trainer* via the direct URL of any lower-level Group within the *Trainer*, they will not see any content that appears higher up in the Workarea hierarchy than this Group—even if your 'official' entry point is above this. Effectively, what they will see is a 'mini-Trainer' that contains only selected Group.

This provides you with some interesting possibilities. You could, for example, organize the (publishable) content section of your Workarea by role, and then provide users with the URL of the Group specific to their role, so that's all they see. Or you could organize your content by training course, and then provide URLs to specific courses. The only thing you need to ensure is that if you provide a URL to a sub-Group within the overall publishable hierarchy then all applicable content is contained within this sub-Group, as the users will not see anything outside of it.

Direct URLs are provided via the *Start Links* category of properties, which is explained in *The Start Links category* on page 53. These URLs are available for every Group, every content object, and every play mode for a content object.

How a Start Link URL functions will depend upon the content object type to which the URL applies, as follows:

+ The *Start Links* category was introduced in the 1811 release. Prior to this, a single property of **Start Link** was available in the *Basic Properties* category, and this had to be manually edited to build a production URL by including `/~tag/published` after the Workarea identifier in the URL.

- For **Groups**, the URL will effectively open a full *Trainer* containing all of the content from the selected Group down.

- For **a simulation project**, the URL will open in a *Trainer* that contains only the selected simulation.

- For **a simulation play mode** (Demo mode, Practice mode, and so on), the simulation will be launched in the mode to which the URL applies, bypassing the *Trainer* completely.

- For **other files** (documents generated for a simulation project, or external content loaded into Enable Now) the file will be opened in the relevant helper application.

To provide a link to content in your published *Trainer*, carry out the steps shown below.

1. In the Workarea, navigate to the object to which you want to provide a link, and click on it to select it. This could be the entry point to your entire *Trainer*, a (sub-)Group within that *Trainer*, a simulation project, or even a specific play mode for a simulation project.

2. Go to the *Start Links* category of properties for the selected object, and use the **Copy Link** button to the right of the relevant property to copy this link to the clipboard.

Typically, you will want to copy either the **Published View** link if your *Trainer* is located in the Enable Now cloud, or the **Custom Location** if you publish your *Trainer* to another location (see *Publishing to outside of Enable Now* on page 219). Note that in order for the **Custom Location** property to contain a valid URL, the external location of your *Trainer* must be defined as explained in *Specifying the Custom Location prefix* on page 219.

3. You can now use this URL wherever necessary: distribute it to your users, use it as a link in a training presentation (typically for direct-launch links to specific play modes), and so on.

■ It is strongly recommended that you use a URL-shortening service to create a more manageable URL for distributing to users.

Specifying the Custom Location prefix

The **Custom Location** property in the *Start Links* category specifies the URL of the selected content object in an externally-published *Trainer*. To be able to generate this, Enable Now needs to know the location of this external *Trainer*. This is defined at the Workarea level.

To define the **Custom Location** prefix for your Workarea, carry out the steps shown below.

1. In your Workarea, click on the entry for the actual Workarea itself. This is the highest-level entry in the *Object Navigation Pane*.

Workarea Icon

2. In the *Object Editor*, navigate to the *Start Links* category of properties. An example of this is shown below.

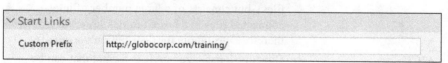

3. In the **Custom Prefix** field, enter the location of your external *Trainer*. This should be the exact same location as you specify as the **Target Folder** when publishing to the **Standard** format (see *The generic publishing process* on page 221).

Once specified, this prefix will be used in all **Custom Location** URLs for your content.

Publishing to outside of Enable Now

If you are not working in a cloud environment, whenever you publish your content, you will effectively be publishing your content to a location outside of Enable Now itself. This could be a local web server, another cloud service, an LMS, and so on. Even if you *are* working in a cloud environment you may have circumstances under which you want to publish to a location outside of Enable

Now—for example, to provide a review version of the *Trainer* before you make it available to your users.

Enable Now allows you to publish your content out in a number of formats (referred to as *types*, within Enable Now). Confusingly, it also provides several ways of doing this—sometimes identically, and sometimes with very minor differences. Some methods only allow you to publish certain formats, while others let you choose any of the formats available. And then there are publishing rules, which can be created in advance, or during publishing, and then used to provide yet another way of publishing. We'll try to add some clarity to this, in the following sections. We will first look at the most comprehensive publishing method, providing a full description of all of the available options. We'll then follow this with explanations of each of the other methods, referring back to the comprehensive description for the details where necessary.

Publishing types

Before you start the publishing process, you should know which publishing type you want to create (you can only create one at a time, but can re-execute the publishing process as many times as you like to create additional types). The available types are described in the table below

Type	Description
Standard	Generate a full *Trainer*. This is generated in a format that can be played back in any browser (it consists only of HTML, JavaScript, and image files), but consists of a large number of inter-connected files in a nested folder structure (and is therefore unsuitable for distribution via email).
AICC	Generate a package in AICC format that can be loaded into a compatible LMS. Note that only the AICC HACP format is supported. AICC PENS is not.
Documents	Take a copy of all currently-available documents and save these to a specified location. You can choose the document types to include at the time of publishing.
Executable	Generate a single executable file (`.exe`) that contains a complete *Trainer*. This is useful if you need to transfer or store the *Trainer* on a platform that does not easily support a folder structure containing thousands of individual files.
SAP Learning Solution	Publish your training content directly to an instance of SAP Learning Solution.

Type	Description
SCORM	Generate a package in SCORM format that can be loaded into a compatible LMS. SCORM versions 1.2, 2004 3rd Edition or 4th Edition, and SAVE 10 are supported.
SuccessFactors Learning	Publish the manifest file for your training package directly into an implementation of SAP SuccessFactors Learning. Note that you should have first published your actual content using the **Standard** output type; this output type only generates the manifest file.
SLC	Generate a single file that contains the entire *Trainer*, and that can be executed via a SAP Learning Content player. This player is typically available for SAP Learning Solution implementations, for off-line viewing of training content.

The generic publishing process

The instructions given in *Setting the Publish flag for a content object* on page 216 apply to a cloud-based installation, where users are accessing your Enable Now content objects directly from the cloud. In an on-premises implementation, you publish your content to a network location, and your users can access it from there.

You can also choose to publish your content to a network location even if you have a cloud-based implementation, and just want your users to access the content 'locally' instead of via the Internet. You may choose to do this, for example, if you have strict Internet access controls, or if you have locations with limited network availability.

This section provides a generic explanation of how to publish your training content to a location outside of SAP Enable Now itself. All options are covered, although you will likely pick one or two of these and use them exclusively.

To publish your training content, carry out the steps shown below:

1. Click on a Group (or a specific content object) in the Workarea, to select it. For a full *Trainer* (or equivalent), this should be your 'entry point' Group.

2. Click on the **Publish Selected Object** button on the *Producer Toolbar*. (Or click on the **Publish Selected Object** button on at the top of the *Object Editor* pane, or right-click on the Group and select **Publish Selected**

● Enable Now refers to this process as 'publishing a content object', as distinct from 'publishing your Workarea' (which is covered in the next section), but this process can also be used for publishing your full Workarea, so this book just refers to it as the "generic publishing process" that can be used for publishing just about any content.

Publish
Selected
Object

Object from the shortcut menu.) The *Publish Object* dialog box is displayed.

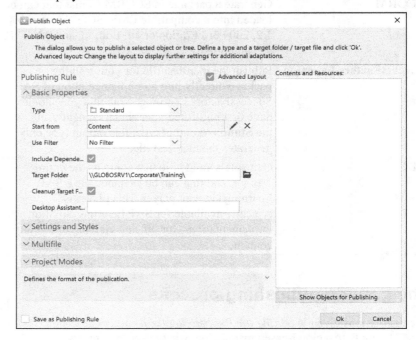

The *Publish Object* dialog box contains many parameters, organized into categories (these are the dark(er) gray bars that can be expanded or collapsed). The *Basic Properties* category is common to all publishing types, but the availability of the remaining categories depends upon the publishing type selected. The table below lists all of the available categories and identifies the publishing types to which they are applicable. Each category is described in its own sub-section below. You should refer to all of the relevant sections, according to the publishing type that you are generating—the page numbers of these sections are shown in the rightmost column of the table, for ease of reference.

Property Category	AICC	Documents	Executable	SAP learning Solution	SCORM	SuccessFactors Learning	SLC	Standard	See page
*Basic Properties**	✓	✓	✓	✓	✓	✓	✓	✓	223
Settings and Styles	✓		✓	✓	✓	✓	✓	✓	224
Multifile	✓		✓	✓	✓	✓	✓	✓	225
AICC	✓								226
Include Formats		✓							226
Project Modes			✓				✓	✓	228
SCORM				✓	✓	✓			228
SAP Learning Solution				✓					230
SuccessFactors Learning						✓			232

* Some properties in this category are only available for certain publishing types.

Note that the examples provided in the sections below show the *Advanced Layout* view. Category sections are described below in the order in which they appear in the *Publish Object* dialog box.

Basic Properties

Specify the publishing parameters in the *Basic Properties* category by following the steps shown below. Note that not all properties are available for all publishing types; if a property is listed in this book but isn't shown in your actual *Publish Object* dialog box for the selected type, then it isn't needed.

1. Make sure that the *Basic Properties* section is expanded. An example of this is shown below.

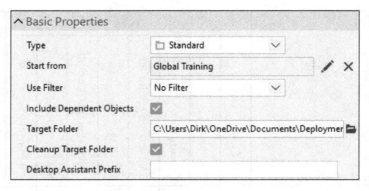

2. In the **Type** field, select the publishing type that you want to generate. Refer to *Publishing types* on page 220 for details of the available options.

3. The **Start from** field will default to the Group that you selected at the start of the publishing process. If you want to generate your output from a different entry point, then click on the **Edit** button to the right of this field, and navigate to and select the required entry point.

4. If you want to filter the selected content (for example, to publish only content with a specific keyword or tag) then select the appropriate filter in the **Use Filter** field. Note that this filter must have already been created in the Workarea, as explained in *Using Filters* on page 68.

5. Select the **Use Dependent Objects** checkbox. This will ensure that all files required by the content within your selection are automatically included, even if they are not located within your selected entry point. This typically includes such things as common resources or assets such as images and icons.

6. For the **Target Folder** field, click the **Open** button, and then navigate to and select the folder into which you want to publish your content.

7. Select the **Cleanup Target Folder** checkbox. This will cause any existing content of the target folder to be deleted before publishing starts, to ensure that no extraneous or unwanted files are included in your publishing output. Of course, if you have specifically included other content in this folder, then you should deselect this checkbox.

8. For on-premise installations (only), enter the URL of the web server on which the Desktop Assistant is located in the **Desktop Assistant Prefix** field.

Settings and Styles

The parameters in the *Settings and Styles* category control the overall appearance of the generated content.

For the applicable publishing types, specify the parameters in the *Settings and Styles* category by following the steps shown below.

1. Make sure the *Settings and Styles* category is expanded. An example of this is shown below.

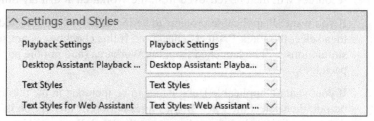

★ The configuration files selected in these parameters can be found in the **Resources | Adaptable Resources** Group, and can be maintained via menu option **Tools | Settings**.

2. In the **Playback Settings** field, select the resources file that defines the playback settings you want to use for playback of the published Trainer.

3. In the **Desktop Assistant: Playback Settings** field, select the resources file that defines the required appearance of the Desktop Assistant projects included in the published output.

4. In the **Text Styles** field, select the Text Styles resources file that you want to use (this will initially set to the default Text Styles; you will only need to change it if you have created your own custom set of Text Styles).

★ The Text Styles settings dictate the texts used in the interface (such as button names in the Trainer), and should not be confused with the Recording Dictionary, which governs simulation Bubble text.

5. In the **Text Styles for Web Assistant** field, select the resources file that defines the text styles to be used for Web Assistant content included in the published output.

Multifile

The settings in the *Multifile* category allow you to control which types of content are included your published output, versus being retrieved from the Workarea at display time. This allows the published content to be launched faster.

For the applicable publishing types, specify the parameters in the *Multifile* category by following the steps shown below.

1. Make sure that the *Multifile* category is expanded. An example of this is shown below.

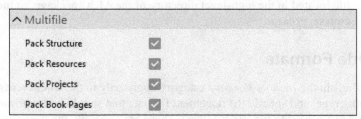

2. If you want details of the Workarea structure to be included in the publishing output then select the **Pack Structure** checkbox.

3. If you want all resources to be included in the published output then select the **Pack Resources** checkbox. If this checkbox is not selected, then some key resources will be included in the published output, and only information about the remaining resources will be included; these resources will then be retrieved from the Workarea at display time.

4. If you want all applicable projects to be included in the published output, then select the **Pack Projects** checkbox. If this checkbox is not selected, simulations will be launched from the Workarea (and not the published package).

5. If you want all applicable Book Pages to be included in the published output, then select the **Pack Book Pages** option. If this option is deselected then only information about the Book Pages will be published, and the Book Pages will be launched from the Workarea.

AICC

● AICC stands for **Aviation Industry CBT Committee**, and refers to a standards specification used for communications between training content and a Learning Management System.

★ The way in which AICC content is tracked and scored on the LMS is defined in **Tools | Settings | Playback Settings | trainer - Global | Tracking (AICC)**.

The settings in the *AICC* category are used only with the **AICC** publishing type. They allow you to specify a few parameters that are required for this format.

If you selected a publishing type of **AICC**, complete the parameters in the *AICC* category by following the steps shown below.

1. Make sure that the *AICC* category is expanded. An example of this is shown below.

2. In the **File Prefix** field, enter the full path prefix of the server location into which the AICC package will be loaded. This is prepended to the `index.html` files in the `lms.au` file located in the high-level directory of the AICC package, to identify the location of the training content.

3. In the **Creator** field, enter the name of the person or organization that owns this training content. This will be inserted into the in the `lms.cr` file located in the high-level directory of the AICC package, as the **course_creator**.

Include Formats

The settings in the *Include Formats* category apply only to the **Documents** publishing type, and specify the document formats that should be 'published' (actually, just copied to the target folder). These are generally the documents generated for simulations (see *Chapter 12, Working with Documents*), but you also have the option to include or exclude external documents (see *Importing content files* on page 551).

If you selected a publishing type of **Documents**, complete the parameters in the *Include Formats* category by following the steps shown below.

1. Make sure that the *Include Formats* category is expanded. An example of this is shown below.

2. If you want documents in native Microsoft Word and Microsoft Powerpoint format to be included in the publishing output, then select the **Word/PowerPoint Documents** checkbox. Otherwise, make sure this checkbox is not selected, and these documents will be omitted.

3. If you want documents in HTML format to be included in the publishing output, then select the **HTML Documents** checkbox. Otherwise, make sure this checkbox is not selected, and these documents will be omitted.

4. If you want documents in PDF format to be included in the publishing output, then select the **PDF Documents** checkbox. Otherwise, make sure this checkbox is not selected, and these documents will be omitted.

5. If you want 'external' documents (those documents created outside of Enable Now [versus documents generated for simulations] and imported into Enable Now) to also be included in the publishing output, then select the **External Documents** checkbox. Otherwise, make sure that this checkbox is not selected, and these documents will be omitted.

6. By default, the published documents will be saved in a folder structure that matches the Group structure in which they are stored in the Workarea. If you just want all documents to be stored in the **Target Folder** (and not using sub-folders) then select the **Flat Structure** checkbox.

7. If you selected the **Flat Structure** option, then you can select the **Sort By Type** checkbox to have the filename for each document prefixed with an indicator of the document type (*Standard Document*, *Work Document*, and so on), so that documents are effectively sorted by type.

Project Modes

The *Project Modes* category allows you to choose which play modes are included in the published output for each simulation project in your selection. This is useful if, for example, you have multiple play modes available in your standard *Trainer*, but want to create an **Executable** that only includes a single mode (for example, Demo mode), to reduce the size of the published file. You can also choose whether to include or exclude Desktop Assistant content and/or Web Assistant content.

Note that these modes must already exist for the selected project(s). Enable Now will not magically create these modes for you at publishing time. The selections here are therefore just a filter against existing content.

For the applicable publishing types, specify the parameters in the *Project Modes* category by following the steps shown below.

1. Make sure that the *Project Modes* category is expanded. An example of this is shown below.

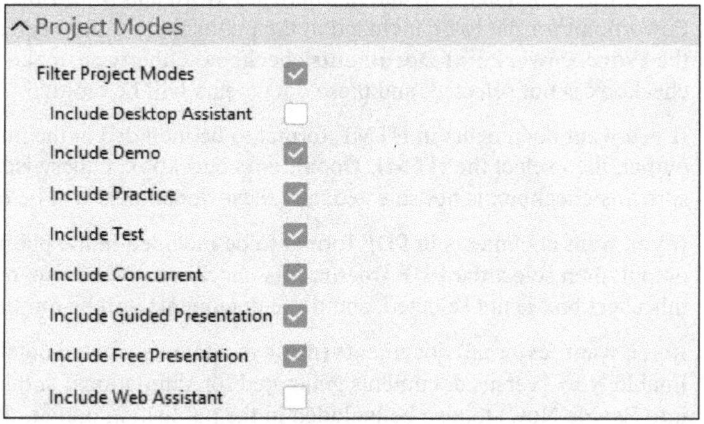

2. If you only want to include specific play modes in your trainer, then select the **Filter Project Modes** checkbox. This will result in additional fields being displayed—one for each possible play mode (although not all of these may necessarily be available for the selected content). Select or deselect the relevant checkboxes so that only the modes you want to include in your published output are selected. For an explanation of the various play modes, refer to *Simulations* on page 8.

SCORM

★ The way in which SCORM content is tracked and scored in the LMS is defined in **Tools | Settings | Playback Settings | trainer - Global | Tracking (SCORM)**.

The *SCORM* category allows you to control the generation of a SCORM-compatible package. Different LMS systems provide different levels of support for the SCORM 'standard', so make sure you know what is accepted (or required) by your specific LMS before setting these properties.

For the applicable publishing types, specify the parameters in the *SCORM* category by following the steps shown below.

1. Make sure that the *SCORM* category is expanded. An example of this is shown below.

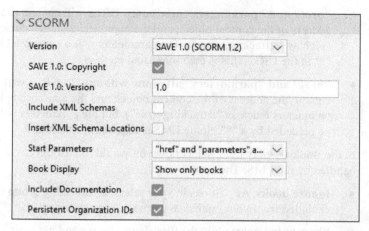

2. Select the SCORM version to use in the **Version** field. Currently, the following levels of SCORM compliance are supported:

    ♦   **SCORM 1.2**

    ♦   **SCORM 2004 3rd Edition**

    ♦   **SCORM 2004 4th Edition**

    ♦   **SAVE 1.0 (SCORM 1.2)**

    ● If you will subsequently publish to SuccessFactors Learning, you must select **SCORM 2004 4th Edition**.

3. If you selected a **Version** of **SAVE 1.0 (SCORM 1.2)** then specify the following parameters:

    i.   If the published content is copyrighted then select the **Save 1.0: Copyright** checkbox. This will cause a copyright statement to be included in the SCORM package.

    ● SAVE is a refinement of SCORM 1.2 which is used by the German insurance industry. It provides some SCORM 2004 features without requiring the full complexity of SCORM 2004.

    ii. Enter a version number for your content in the **SAVE 1.0:Version** field.

    These two parameters are not available for other SCORM versions.

4. If you want to include the XML schema definition files (which define the format of the SCORM manifest file) in the generated package then select **Include XML schemas** checkbox. Normally you would choose to include these.

5. If you want to include a reference to the location of the XML schema definition files (instead of the actual schema files) in the generated package then select the **Insert XML Schema Locations** checkbox.

6. In the **Start Parameters** field, select the appropriate option for building the URLs used to launch the actual training content. The options are:

   ♦ **Only "href" attribute**: URLs will only contain the address of the content object.

   ♦ **"href" and "parameters" attributes**: URLs will contain the address of the content object, and the appropriate launch parameters (such as "&tracking=true"). The parameters will be preceded by a "?" in the URL. This is the more usual method.

   ♦ **"href" and "parameters" attribute without '?'**: URLs will contain the address of the content object, and the appropriate launch parameters (such as "&tracking=true"), but the parameters will not be preceded by a "?". Some LMSes require this method.

7. In the **Book Display** field, select how you would like Books to be handled by the LMS. The options are:

   ♦ **Ignore books**: Any Books in your selected publishing group will be excluded from your published output.

   ♦ **Show only books**: Only the (first-level) Books and not their contents will be listed as objects in the SCORM contents.

   ♦ **Show books and direct sub objects**: The SCORM contents will show the first-level of books and the content immediately below these (either nested Books or, more usually, Book Pages).

   ♦ **Show books and all sub objects**: The SCORM contents will show all Books and their entire contents (including all nested Books and Book Pages).

8. If you want to include any generated document output formats (such as the **Standard Document**) in the SCORM package, then make sure the **Include Documentation** checkbox is selected. Note that included documents are for information only and their consumption will not be tracked in the LMS,

9. If you want the same IDs to be used each time you publish the same content, then make sure the **Persistent Organization IDs** checkbox (this is the default). Otherwise, deselect this checkbox and a unique ID will be generated each time you publish. Usually you would want to use Persistent IDs so that updates to the same course keep the same ID.

SAP Learning Solution

The settings in the *SAP Learning Solution* category apply only to the **SAP Learning Solution** publishing type, and allow you to specify the details of the LS system into which the content will be loaded. You will need to obtain the required values from your Learning Solution Administrator.

If you selected a publishing type of **SAP Learning Solution**, complete the parameters in the *SAP Learning Solution* category by following the steps shown below.

1.   Make sure that the *SAP Learning Solution* category is expanded. An example of this is shown below.

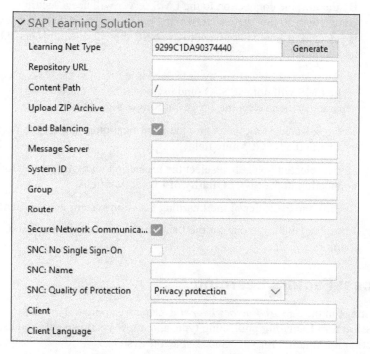

2.   The **Learning Type Net** defaults to a randomized, unique identifier for this publication. You should not need to change this, but if necessary you can click on the **Generate** button to generate a new one.

3.   Enter the URL of the Learning Solution repository in the **Repository URL** field.

4.   Specify the path of the location (relative to the **Repository URL**) used for uploading the published package in the **Content Path** field. This is the location in which the generated publication package will be stored.

5.   If a .zip file of the published package should also be uploaded to the LMS (in addition to the unpacked content, which is always loaded) then select the **Upload ZIP Archive** checkbox.

6.   Choose whether you want to hard-code a connection to a specific server, or allow load balancing to be used, as follows:

     ◆   If you want to use a direct connection to a specific LMS server, then deselect the **Load Balancing** checkbox, and specify the connection details in the **Application Server**, **System Number**, and **Router** fields.

♦ If you want to use load balancing (in which case the actual server accessed by the users may vary, depending upon network load and/ or user location) then make sure that the **Load Balancing** checkbox is selected, and specify the connection details in the **Message Server, System ID, Group,** and **Router** fields.

7. By default, the connection to the LMS server will use a secure connection, so the **Secure Network Communication (SNC)** checkbox is selected. If you do not want to use SNC then deselect this checkbox and continue with Step 11.

8. If you selected SNC, then by default Single Sign-On (SSO) is used. If the LMS will not use SSO (and users will be required to log on separately) then select the **SNC: No Single Sign-On** checkbox.

9. If you selected SNC, then enter the identification prefix for the back-end system in the **SNC: Name** field.

10. If you selected SNC, then select the protection level for the network connection in the **SNC: Quality of Protection** field.

11. Specify the identifier of the Learning Solution system in the **Client** field.

12. Enter the language code for the Learning Solution system in the **Client Language** field.

SuccessFactors Learning

The settings in the *SuccessFactors Learning* category apply only to the **SuccessFactors Learning** publishing type, and allow you to specify required connection information for your SuccessFactors system.

If you selected a publishing type of **SuccessFactors Learning**, complete the parameters in the *SuccessFactors Learning* category by following the steps shown below.

1. Make sure that the *SuccessFactors Learning* category is expanded. An example of this is shown below.

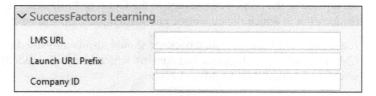

2. Enter the URL of your SuccessFactors LMS in the **LMS URL** field. Your published package will be loaded directly into this system.

3. Enter the launch URL prefix for the published content into the **Launch URL Prefix** field.

4. Enter your company's SuccessFactors company ID into the **Company ID** field.

Note that the **Content Package ID** will be included in the messages shown at the end of publishing. You should copy this ID and provide it to the SuccessFactors Learning Administrator, as they will need it when defining the course in SuccessFactors.

Continuing the generic publishing process

Once you have specified all of the required selection parameters for the selected publishing type, you can continue with the publishing process, as explained below.

1. If you want to save your settings as a re-usable Publishing Rule then select the **Save as Publishing Rule** checkbox, and then enter a meaningful name for this rule in the input field provided. See *Publishing Rules* on page 233 for more information on this functionality.

2. If you want to review the specific content objects that will be included in the *Trainer*, based on your selections, then click on the **Show Objects for Publishing** button. The objects will be listed in the *Contents and Resources* pane on the right of the *Publish Object* dialog box.

3. Click **Ok**. Your content will be published to the specified location. During publishing, a progress bar similar to the one shown below will be displayed:

Once publishing is complete, the following dialog box will be displayed:

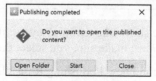

Here, you can choose to either open the destination folder (click **Open Folder**), launch the Trainer (click **Start**), or just close the dialog box (click **Close**).

Publishing Rules

As we have seen above, there are a lot of options that can be specified when publishing your content outside of Enable Now. If you always publish using the same set of options, you can save these as a **Publishing Rule** that you can re-use the next time that you publish. You can also use a Publishing Rule to publish via the command line—which means that you can then publish via a (possibly scheduled) batch job.

Creating a Publishing Rule

The easiest way to create a Publishing Rule is to select the **Save as Publishing Rule** checkbox when you publish using the generic method (how to do this is described above). Alternatively, if you have not yet published your content (or even if you have, and just want to create a new rule without immediately publishing using it) you can create a new rule at any time by following the steps shown below:

1. Select menu option **Workarea | Publish | Edit Publishing Rules**. The *Publishing Rules* dialog box is displayed.

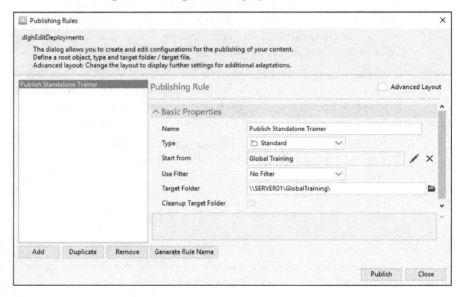

This example shows the 'simple' layout; if you want to see all of the available options, make sure you select the **Advanced Layout** checkbox.

2. To create a brand new Publishing Rule, click om the **Add** button at the bottom of the dialog box. Alternatively, if you want to base your new rule on an existing rule (for example, if you only want to make a few changes) then you can select an existing Publishing Rule in the list on the left, and then click on the **Duplicate** button.

3. Enter a suitable name for the rule in the **Name** field on the right. Alternatively, you can wait until you have specified all of the parameters, and then click on the **Generate Rule Name** button, to have Enable Now automatically create a name for you, based on these parameters.

4. Specify the required publishing parameters. Refer to *The generic publishing process* on page 221 for full details of all of these options (it

is exactly the same set of options as you see when publishing a content object).

5. If you want to publish immediately using this rule, then click on the **Publish** button. Otherwise, just click on the **Close** button to close the dialog box (your changes will be saved automatically).

Publishing using a Publishing Rule

When you create a Publishing Rule, this is saved as a menu entry on the **Workarea | Publish** menu. An example of this is shown below:

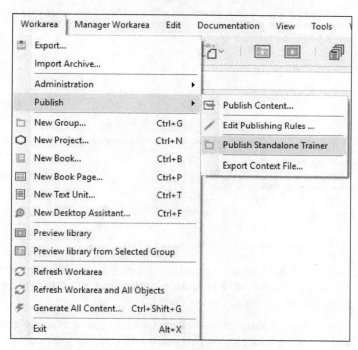

To publish using this Publishing Rule, simply select the menu option for that Publishing Rule. Publishing will start immediately, and the usual *Publishing completed* dialog box (see above) is displayed when this is complete.

Publishing your Workarea

The 'generic' publishing process outlined above allows you to publish any of the available publishing output types, from any level in your Workarea structure. Enable Now also provides a 'simplified' method of publishing the entire Workarea. Using this method you can only publish a **Standard** *Trainer*, an **Executable**, or an **SLC** file, but it does allow you to select the individual content objects for publishing.

⭐ Generating the **Executable** output format is explained in more detail in *Publishing to an executable* on page 248.

More significantly, this method of publishing a **Standard** *Trainer* allows you to perform **delta publishing**, where only new or updated content is actively published—but still incorporated within the previously-published *Trainer*—which could significantly reduce publishing time.

To publish your full Workarea, carry out the steps shown below.

1. Select menu option **Workarea | Publish | Publish Content**. The *Publish Content* dialog box is displayed.

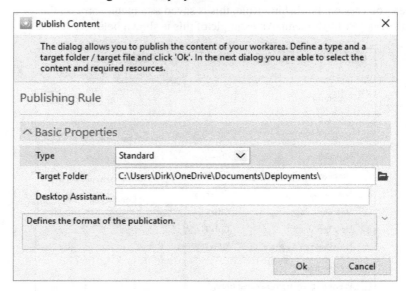

2. In the **Type** field, select the publishing type that you want to generate. This can be **Standard**, **Executable**, or **SLC** (refer to *Publishing types* on page 220 for an explanation of these).

3. In the **Target Folder** field, click the **Open** icon, and then navigate to and select the folder into which you want to publish your content. For delta publishing, this should obviously be the location of the existing published *Trainer* (or equivalent output format).

4. For on-premise installations (only), enter the DNS of the web server on which the Desktop Assistant is located in the **Desktop Assistant Prefix** field.

5. Click **Ok**. The *Publish Content* dialog box is displayed (yes, this has exactly the same name as the last one, but its content and purpose are entirely different).

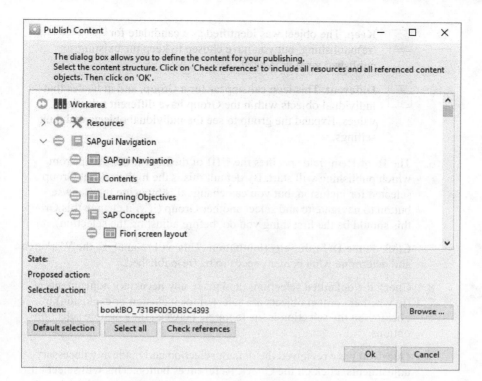

The main section of this *Publishing Content* dialog box contains a list of the full content of your Workarea, in its hierarchical structure. To the left of each object is an icon that indicates whether or not the object will be included in the incremental publish. Enable Now makes an initial determination of this, based on whether the object is newer than the last-published version, but you can override this, if necessary. The icons and their meaning are shown below.

● Incremental publishing is only possible for the **Standard** publishing type. For the **Executable** and **SLC** options, a checkbox is shown to the left of each object, and you simply select the objects to include in the published output.

Omit. The object will not be included in the published output. Typically, this is because it is does not have its **Published** flag The set. Resources and Local Trash Groups are also typically excluded by default.

Equal. The object in the Workarea is the same version as is currently published, so the object will not be re-published.

Update. The object has been updated since it was last published, and will be re-published.

Add. The object was not identified as a candidate for (re)publishing, but you have overridden this and selected it.

Remove. The object exist in the current publishing output but has since been deleted in the Workarea. It will be removed from the published output.

Keep. The object was identified as a candidate for (re)publishing, but you have chosen to keep the existing published version instead.

 Different. This icon can appear for a Group, and indicates that individual objects within the Group have different selection values. Expand the group to see the individual objects and their settings.

6. The **Root Item** field specifies the **UID** of the high-level Group from which publishing will start. By default this is the highest-level Group selected for inclusion, but you can change this by using the **Browse** button to navigate to and select another Group (if you change this Group, this should be the first thing you do, before adjusting the selection).

7. Click on the **Default Selection** button. This will re-analyze the Workarea and determine what content needs to be (re)published.

▲ When you click on an object, the **Proposed action** field shows the Enable Now determined action, and the **Selected action** field shows your override (if any). However, the **Selected action** field does not seem to be updated as soon as you select a new action. To refresh it, click on another object and then back on the object you just changed.

8. Check the defaulted selections, and make any necessary adjustments (to whether content objects are selected for inclusion or exclusion) by clicking on the selection icons to toggle between the possible selection options.

9. Once you have reviewed the default selection and made any necessary adjustments, click on the **Check References** button. This will select all objects referenced by the currently-selected objects. Typically, this will include resources, assets, and so on.

10. Click **Ok**. The selected content is published. Once publishing completes, a confirmation dialog box is displayed.

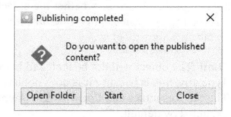

Here, you have the options to open the folder to which the content was published (click **Open**), launch the published *Trainer* (click **Start**), or just close the dialog box (click **Close**).

Publishing all Workarea documents

More recent versions of Enable Now have provided an additional method of publishing documentation (in effect, this just copies all of the currently-available generated documents to a specified local folder). This is effectively the same functionality as explained for publishing type **Documentation**, under *The generic publishing process* on page 221, but applies to your entire Workarea, and has less options. As such it is not particularly useful as standalone functionality, but for the sake of completeness, it is explained here.

To publish all generated (Enable Now format) documents in your Workarea, carry out the steps shown below.

1. Select menu option **Workarea | Publish | Publish Documents**. The standard Windows *Browse for Folder* dialog box is displayed.

2. Navigate to and select the folder into which the documentation should be published.

3. Click **OK**. All available documents are copied to the selected Windows folder. Once this finishes, a confirmation dialog box is displayed, giving you the option of opening this folder.

The documents are copied to a folder (within the selected folder) named `root`, and the full Workarea structure will be maintained below this. If you just want all documents in a single folder, it is better to use the generic publishing process (explained in *The generic publishing process* on page 221) to generate the **Documentation** publishing type).

Electronic Performance Support

An Electronic Performance Support System (EPSS) provides users with on-line, embedded help from within the application (for which they need help). This is typically context-sensitive, so that the help the user receives relates specifically to the task they are currently performing in the application, or the screen that is currently displayed.

Enable Now provides three possibilities for an EPSS:

- **The Desktop Assistant**. Publishing (generating) the Desktop Assistant is described in *Chapter 10, The Desktop Assistant.*

- **The Web Assistant**. Creating and publishing Web Assistant content is described in *Chapter 11, The Web Assistant*

- **Context Help**, which is described in this section.

Refer to *Web Assistant* on page 24 for an explanation of these components and the differences between them.

Publishing Context Help

A Context Help file effectively contains all of the context information from your simulations, along with links to the content objects in your *Trainer* that apply to these contexts. This file is then uploaded or linked into the application. When a user calls up the help function, the application checks the user's context (the context from within which help was invoked) against the contents of the Context Help file, and then launches the content object defined for that context.

A Context Help file can be used with SAPGui (HTML or Windows) and NetWeaver Enterprise Portal (Ajax Framework or Classic Framework).

To publish a Context Help file, carry out the steps shown below.

1. In the Workarea, select the Group that contains the content you want to be accessible via the embedded help system. This is normally the 'entry point' for your entire *Trainer*.

2. Select menu option **Workarea | Publish | Export Context File**. The *Export Context File - Settings* dialog box is displayed.

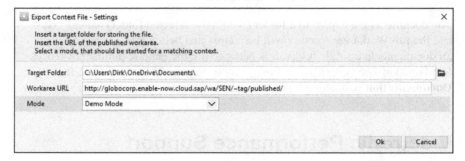

3. In the **Target Folder** field, navigate to and select the folder into which your Context Help file should be saved. Note that this needs to be outside of the Enable Now system—the intention is that it is stored within, or somewhere accessible to, the application itself, but see the comments under *Testing the Context Help file* on page 241.

4. In the **Workarea URL** field, enter the URL of your published *Trainer*. This is the location from which content will be launched.

5. If you want simulations (for the matched context) to be launched in a specific mode, then select this mode in the **Mode** field. Otherwise, make sure that **Project** is selected (this is the default), and the index page for the simulation will be displayed, allowing the user to launch any of the available modes.

6. Click **OK**. The *Export Context File - Parameter* dialog box is displayed.

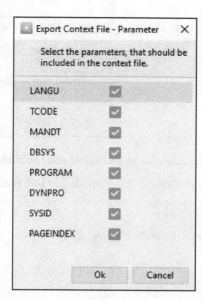

● The parameters shown here are for SAPGui. You may see different parameters for other applications.

7. This dialog identifies all of the context parameters that are contained in any of the selected content. Make sure that all of the parameters that you want to use are selected, and that all others are not selected. Typically, you would only select parameters that you know exist in the application from within which the context help will be provided.

8. Click **Ok**. The Context Help file is generated and stored in the specified location. Note that you will not receive a confirmation message that this has been done—just go and check the destination folder, and look for `context.html`.

Before implementing your Context File, you should test it, to make sure it is working as expected. How to do this is explained in the next section.

Testing the Context Help file

Enable Now provides a way for you to test your Context Help file, to confirm that it is working as expected, and that the context sensitivity is being correctly interpreted. You should do this before the Context Help file has been loaded to its final location and connected to the application.

To test your Context Help file, carry out the steps shown below.

1. Select menu option **Tools | Context Administration | Test Context File**. The Context file selection dialog box is displayed.

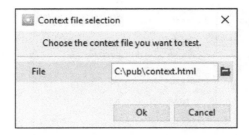

2. In the **File** field, navigate to and select your published Context Help file.

3. Click **Ok**. The *Parameter Selection* dialog box is displayed.

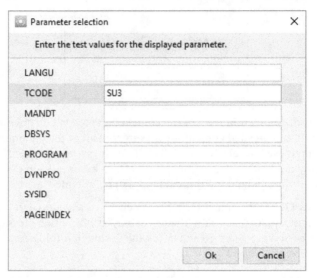

4. You will recognize that the fields available in the *Parameter Selection* dialog box are the same ones that you selected in the *Export Context File - Parameter* dialog box when you generated the Context File. Enter the context values that you want to test in these fields.

   In the example above, we are going to test that our sample simulation *Changing your User Options* is correctly identified as applicable content if we are in transaction **SU3**.

5. Click **Ok**. The Context Help file is searched for the specified parameter values, and the results displayed in a new browser window. An example of this is shown below.

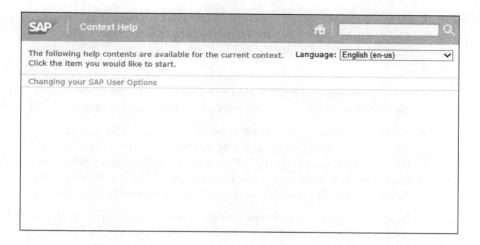

This window is exactly the same window that is displayed if our Context Help is called up from within the application itself. Clicking on the **Home** button in this window will launch your *Trainer* (from the location specified when you created the Context Help file).

Note that if there is only one matching simulation then this will be launched immediately. Otherwise, the window will list all of the matching simulations, and the user will need to click on the one they want, to launch it.

Implementing the Context Help file

Once you have tested your Context File, you need to store this file in a location from where your application can access it. This will normally be on a server accessible by your application, or within the application itself. Choose this location carefully, as you will need to re-generate and replace the Context Help file every time you create additional content that you want to be accessible via the application context help.

★ You can load the Context Help file back into your Enable Now Workarea, but will need to deselect the option **Tools | Settings | Producer | General | Forbid Active Content** first.

Once the Context Help file has been stored in its final location, you need to configure your application to use it. How you do that will be dependent upon the application itself, so is not described here.

Video output

The simulations created by SAP Enable Now can be played back for 'passive' consumption in Demo mode, but these are not pure 'video'. When a simulation is recorded, Enable Now effectively captures static screenshots, and the actions performed against them. Playback uses these same elements to create the impression of moving video, but it's not *really* a full-motion video. There may be occasions when you *want* a full-motion video of a simulation. Maybe you want a single file that you can transmit via email and that doesn't require any special software to display, or you want to load it to YouTube or some other video or file-sharing site. Enable Now provides the ability to create two types of full-motion video:

★ If any bubbles have a **Display Duration** property of -1 (infinite) then video recording will automatically progress after 8 seconds (by default, although this duration can be changed in **Tools | Settings | Playback Settings | General | Video**).

- A video recording of a simulation being played in Demo mode. This is captured using all of the Demo texts and bubbles, and all audio.

- **Screencast video**: A screencast video is effectively a full-motion video screen capture of the task that was performed when you created the simulation recording. It does not contain any bubbles or other information (that you would see in a simulation) but it will include any audio that was captured during recording (or entered during editing).

  In order to generate a screencast video, you must have captured all of the required information during the initial recording process, by selecting the **Record Screencast Video** checkbox in the *Select Window and Profile* dialog box during recording (see *Step 1: Create a new project* on page 80).

Both of these video formats are created in exactly the same way, as explained below.

Generating a video file

Generate a video file by carrying out the steps shown below.

1. In your Workarea, click on the simulation project for which you want to create a video.

2. Select menu option **Tools | Generate Video**. The *Generate Video* dialog box is displayed.

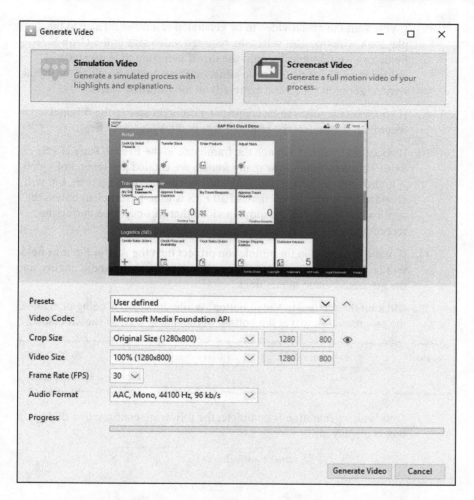

3. Click on the **Simulation Video** button or the **Screencast Video** button, depending on the type of video that you want to generate. The remaining steps are identical regardless of which option you choose.

4. In the **Presets** field, select the appropriate entry for the size (dimensions) and quality of the video that you want to create. Bear in mind that the larger the video dimensions, and the higher the quality, the larger the size of the generated file will be.

5. If you chose any preset other than **User Defined**, continue with Step 12. Otherwise (you *did* select **User Defined**), continue with Step 6. (You can also display the values associated with a preset profile via Step 6—even if you do not want to change these.)

6. Click on the drop-down button to the right of the **Presets** field, to display additional input fields (as shown in the example above).

7. If you want to use a specific video codec, then select this in the **Video Codec** field.

8. If you want the actual video to be generated at a different size to the playback window, then select the required video size in the **Crop Size** field. You would typically only use this if you want to leave space around the edge of the video to add a title or subtitles/captions, or if you want to zoom in (fixed and centered) on the recorded video.

9. If you want the video to be created at a different size to the original recording, then select the required size in the **Video Size** field.

10. If necessary, you can change the frame rate in the **Frame Rate (FPS)** field. This determines how many frames are created per second of video. A higher number will create smoother movement on the screen, but will create a larger file. The default of 30 FPS is usually sufficient unless the application itself contains moving video that was captured during the recording.

11. If audio is present in the simulation project then the **Audio Format** field will be available. If necessary, you can select a specific audio quality for the generated video in this field.

12. Click on the **Generate Video** button. While the video is being generated, the progress is shown at the bottom of the dialog box, as shown below:

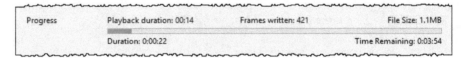

13. Once video generation is complete, the following confirmation dialog box is displayed:

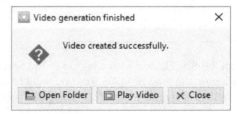

Select one of the following options:

♦ If you want to copy the file to somewhere outside of Enable Now, click on the **Open Folder** button to display the video file in Windows Explorer. You can then copy it to wherever necessary.

♦ If you want to play the video, then click on the **Play Video** button.

♦ Otherwise, click on the **Close** button to finish.

Your video will be stored as a 'deliverable' under the simulation project in the Workarea (just like for the simulation play modes). An example of this, for one of our sample exercises, is shown below:

Note that in this example, both the simulation video and the screencast video have been generated.

Although these files are not really intended as 'formal' Enable Now deliverables (why watch a video of Demo mode when you can just watch Demo mode itself?), they will be available in the *Trainer*, where they will be listed at the bottom of the index page for the simulation (where the documentation formats are also listed)—as shown in the example below:

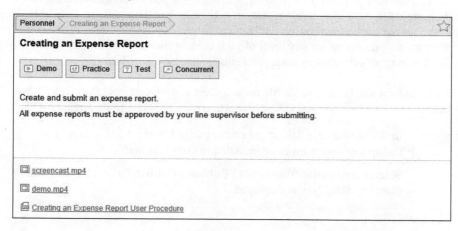

● If you do choose to make one or both of the video files available in the *Trainer*, you should rename them to be something more useful than the default (shown here). We have only left the defaults here so you can see which file is which.

Deleting the screencast files

The files captured during recording for screencast video can take up quite a bit of disk space (around 3MB per minute of video). Because these files are no longer required once the screencast video has been created, you can delete them, to save space. Note that this will not delete the generated screencast video itself (`screencast.mp4`) - which is actually significantly larger than the captured files (being around 12MB/minute).

★ Enable Now is remarkably efficient when it captures the information required to construct the video, capturing only the changed areas of screens and the data required to correctly position these.

To delete the (temporary) screencast files, carry out the steps shown below.

1. In the Workarea, click on the simulation project for which you want to delete the screencast files.

2. Select menu option **Tools | Delete Screencast Frames**. A warning message is displayed, asking you to confirm that you want to delete the files.

3. Click **Yes**. The files are deleted.

Publishing to an executable

By default, the Enable Now Trainer consists of a large number of small files. This is very efficient in terms of on-line delivery, but can present problems when distributing the content, as you need to zip up all of the files, and then make sure that the recipient successfully unzips them, retaining the exact same folder structure, and then locates and launches the correct file from within this.

If all you are trying to do is send a single simulation to a reviewer or other interested party, this can seem like a lot of effort, and prone to error. As an alternative, Enable Now allows you to publish your content to a single executable file (`.exe`) that can easily be emailed, and launched just by double-clicking on this single file. This executable is fully-functional, and all play modes available in the source content will be available in the single-executable version. You can generate an executable for any level of your content hierarchy (from any group), but it is most effective when done for a single simulation or Book.

To generate a single executable file for a content object, carry out the steps shown below:

1. In the Workarea, click on the content object (simulation or Book) or Group that you want to be included in your executable.

2. Select menu option **Workarea | Publish | Publish Content**. The *Publish Content* dialog box is displayed.

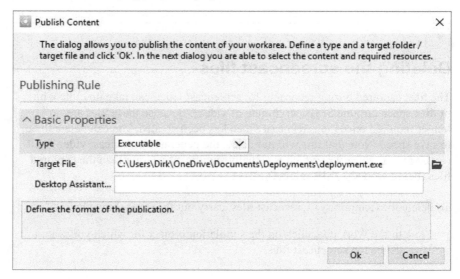

3. In the **Type** field, select **Executable**.

4. In the **Target File** field, navigate to and select the location to which the executable file should be saved, and enter a suitable file name (this defaults to `deployment.exe`).

5. In the **Desktop Assistant Prefix** field, enter the URL of your Desktop Assistant. This will be used for launching any Desktop Assistant content in the published output.

6. Click **Ok**. The *Publish Content* dialog box is displayed.

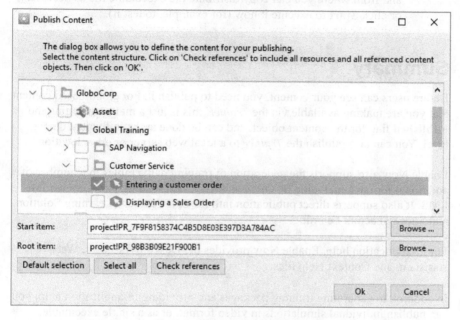

7. The *Publish Content* dialog box lists all of the content in your Workarea. Select (only) the checkboxes to the left of the items that you want to be included in your executable. (For some reason, this does not always default to the object selected in Step 1.)

8. Click on the **Check references** button. This will make sure that all content referenced by the selected content objects will also be selected for inclusion. This is typically styles and assets used by the content object(s).

9. Click **Ok**. The content is published. When publishing finishes, the *Publishing completed* dialog box is displayed.

10. Click on **Open Folder** to open the folder to which the output was saved and from where you can copy/distribute the executable file as necessary, or click **Start** to execute it now (for example, to test it).

Summary

Before users can see your content, you need to publish it. For cloud-based content that you are making available via the *Trainer*, this is just a matter of setting the **Published** flag for the content object, and can be done at the individual object level. You can also publish the *Trainer* to a local web server or other location.

Enable Now also supports the generation of training deliverables in a number of additional formats, including SCORM and AICC, for loading into a compatible LMS. It also supports direct publication into the SAP products Learning Solution and SuccessFactors Learning.

For in-application help, Enable Now provides the Desktop Assistant, Web Assistant, and Context Help files.

In addition to generating training packages and providing in-application help, you can publish individual simulations in video format, or as a single executable.

8

Books and Book Pages

So far in this book we have been looking almost exclusively at simulation projects. Yet Enable Now also includes robust functionality for building complete training presentations—whether these are used for classroom-based, Instructor-Led Training (ILT), or for self-paced Computer-Based Training (CBT). This functionality is provided by Books and Book Pages.

Conceptually, a Book is similar to a PowerPoint presentation, and a Book Page is similar to a slide within a PowerPoint presentation. However, there are some important differences. Most significantly, a single Book Page can be used in multiple Books, and related to this, a Book Page can exist entirely outside of a Book—and even be included in a simulation project.

In this chapter, we'll look at the many things you can do with Books and Book Pages. Specifically, we'll look at:

- Creating a Book
- Creating Book Pages
- Adding objects to a Book Page
- Basic animation
- Using a Book Page in a simulation project
- Using a Book Page as the 'concept' page

The Book Reader

Before digging into the details of how to create Books and Book Pages, it is worthwhile looking at a finished example of a Book, as it appears to users. This will allow you to better understand the options available for controlling the appearance of Books and Book Pages, as we come across them.

★ The Administrator can control the appearance of the Book Reader via **Tools | Settings | Playback Settings | book reader**.

Books are displayed in the *Book Reader*. This is effectively just a web page (not a specialized piece of software) and displays in the standard browser window. The following image shows an example of a Book, as it appears in the default *Book Reader*.

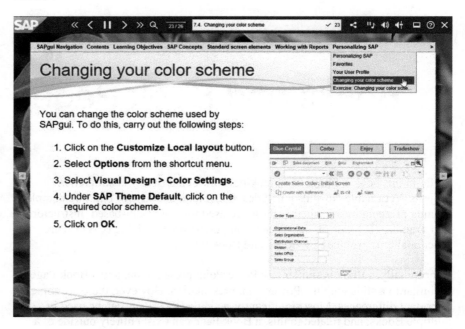

Things to note in this example:

- A **Background Image** has been used
- A **Shadow** has been applied to the Book Page
- The Book Page **Table of Contents** bar is displayed, with a **Position** of **Top of Book Page**, and a **Menu Structure** of **Indented contents**
- Book Page **Navigation Arrows** are shown

Don't worry if these things don't mean anything to you yet; we cover them all in this chapter. First, let's look at the overall contents of the *Book Reader*.

The bulk of the *Book Reader* window is taken up by the current Book Page. How you navigate between pages will depend upon the navigation methods enabled, but by default will be either via the navigation buttons on the *Book Reader Toolbar*, or via the Table of Contents drop-down list (also located on the toolbar). These controls, and all the other controls that may be enabled, are explained in the table below.

Control	Purpose
⌂	Variously referred to within Enable Now as the **Home** button, **Index Page** button, or **Content Page** button, clicking on this button will return the user to the page selected as the **Content Page** in the Book's properties. If no specific content page is selected, this control will not be displayed (regardless of the **Hide Index Page Control** property).
«	**Previous Chapter** button. If the Book contains nested Books, then clicking on this button will display the first page of the current (sub)Book. If the Book does not contain nested books, this control is not displayed.
<	**Previous Page** button. Goes back to the previous Book Page in the Book.
❚❚ ▶	**Pause / Play** toggle button. If playback is automated, this button will pause playback or resume playback, accordingly.
>	**Next Page** button. Advances to the next Book Page in the Book.
»	**Next Chapter** button. If the Book contains nested Books, then clicking on this button will advance to the first page of the next (sub)Book. If the Book does not contain nested books, this control is not displayed.
🔍	**Search** button. Clicking on this button will display the *Keyword Search* dialog box, which allows the user to search for a text string in the Book.
8 / 24	Progress indicator. The two numbers show the sequence number of the current page within the Book, and the total number of Book Pages in the Book, respectively. The progress bar above the numbers provides a visual indication of the position of the current page within the book (and not what proportion of the pages have been viewed).
4.5. Master Data ✓ 8	**Table of Contents** control. This is a drop-down list of all of the Book Pages in the Book. The user can select a page from this list to jump directly to that page.

Control	Purpose
	Share button. If the user clicks on this button, then they are presented with the *Share Content* dialog box, which contains the direct URL of the currently-displayed object, and a QR code of this URL. An example of this dialog box is shown below.

★ The availability of the **Feedback** button (and therefore the ability to submit feedback) is defined via **Tools | Settings | Playback Settings | Book Reader | Feedback | Show Feedback Functions**. The email address to which feedback is sent, is defined in the **Server Settings** in the Manager component, by the Administrator.

Control	Purpose
	Feedback button. If the user clicks on this button, they are presented with the *Your Feedback* dialog box, which allows them to submit feedback on the currently-displayed object. An example of the dialog box is shown below:

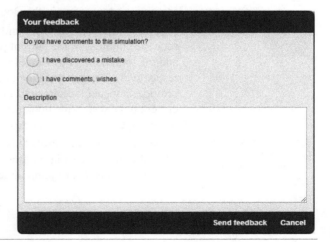

Control	Purpose
 	**Pause Audio / Play Audio** toggle button. Clicking on this button toggles between pausing and playing any audio included in the object. Note that this button (and the next two) are displayed (subject to the **Hide Audio Controls** property) regardless of whether the content object actually contains any audio.
 	**Audio Off / Audio On** toggle button. Clicking on this button toggles between suppressing and enabling audio for the object. Note that the button image actually shows the current state of audio playback, and not the state triggered by clicking the button.
	**Volume** button. Clicking on this button displays a dialog box that allows you to control the volume of any audio for the object. You can control the overall volume, or you can independently control sound effects and background music, and text-to-speech narration. An example of the *Volume* dialog box is shown below. 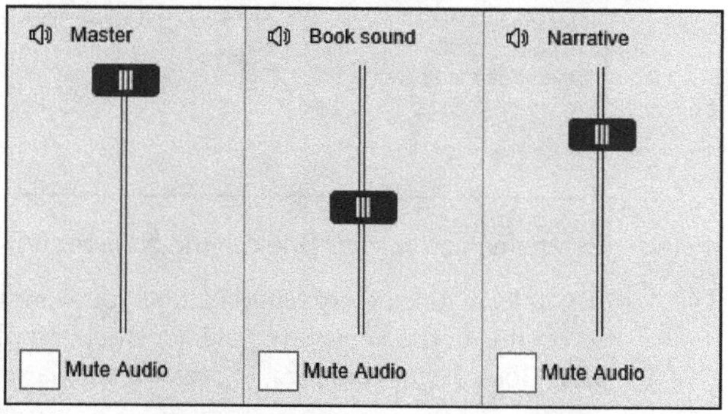

● For an explanation of the difference between Book sound versus Narrative sound, refer to *Chapter 14, Adding Audio to Your Content.*

Control	Purpose
 	**Bottom Bar / Top Bar** toggle button. Clicking on this button toggles between showing the *Book Reader Toolbar* at the top of the reader window and showing it at the bottom of the reader window.
	**Help** button. Displays the standard Enable Now help.
	**Close** button. Closes the current Book. Note that if this object was opened from another object (for example, another Book Page), then the current 'nesting level' is shown in the upper-right corner of this button—as shown in the example at the start of this section—and clicking on the button will close the current object and return to the previous object.

Now that we know what a Book looks like, and what features are available within it, let's create a Book for a sample course, and see how to control these features.

Creating a Book

To create a Book, carry out the following steps.

You can also click on the **New Object** button at the top of the *Object Editor* pane, and select Book from the drop-down menu.

1. In the *Object Navigation Pane*, click on the Group within which you want to create the Book.

2. Click on the **New Object** button on the *Producer Toolbar*. The *New Object* dialog box is displayed.

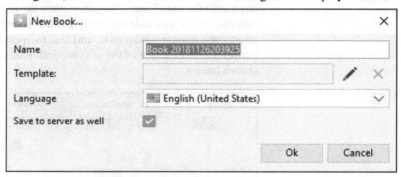

New Object

3. In the *Content Structuring* category of the *New Object* dialog box, click on **Book**. The *New Book* dialog box is displayed.

4. Enter a name for your Book in the **Name** field.

5. If you have an existing template that you want to use for this Book, then select this in the **Template** field. (A Book template can be pre-loaded with Book Page templates, to create a standard structure for Books.)

6. Select the default language for the Book in the **Language** field.

7. If you are creating the Book in a server-managed folder, then the **Save to server as well** checkbox will be selected and the simulation will also be created as server-managed. If you only want the Book to be saved locally (for example, to your Content Group) then deselect this checkbox. See *Server-managed vs. local objects* on page 34 for additional information on this subject.

8. Click **OK**.

Your new Book is created in the selected Group. Note that you are not immediately passed into an editor for this (as you are with for example, Book Pages or Projects). This is because a Book does not have any editable content—only Book Pages do. We'll look at editing the Book in *Working in the Book Page Editor* on page 261, after we have added some Book Pages to it, which we do in the next section.

Before we delve into Books in detail, let's see how our new Book (which we called "SAPgui Navigation") will appear in the *Trainer*, once it is published (we can test this, even though the Book doesn't contain any pages, we just can't open it). Let's assume we have inserted our new Book into our overall content structure. The following screenshot shows how this will look in the browser:

■ You can preview your content from any Group, by right-clicking on the Group in the *Object Navigation Pane*, and selecting **Group Options | Preview library from Selected Group** from the shortcut menu.

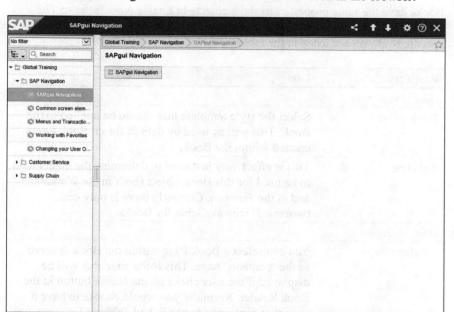

You will notice here that the way a Book is displayed in the Library is entirely consistent with the way any other content object is displayed. Once the Book is selected in the hierarchical outline on the left, its details are displayed on the right. These details include the Book **Name** at the top, with a 'play mode' button shown below this—although there is only one play mode for Books, which is opening the Book in the *Book Reader*. The Book's **Short Description** and full **Description** are also displayed (as they are for simulation projects) if these have been defined (which they have not been, in this example).

■ There is no **Library Autostart** option for Books.

You will see that there are no content objects shown hierarchically below the Book. This is not (just) because we haven't added any Book Pages to our Book—Books always appear as a single entity within the navigation outline, and their contents are only visible once you open the Book in the *Book Reader*.

To open a Book, simply make sure it is highlighted in the navigation outline, and click on the 'play mode' button for the Book—which has the same name as the Book itself. The Book is then opened in the same browser window—effectively 'on top of' the *Trainer* screen—as indicated by a numeric indicator of the number of open objects in the upper-right of the browser content area (see the example on page 252).

■ As an alternative to using the 'play mode' button you can set the Book to automatically open in the *Book Reader* when you click on it in the navigation outline (see the **Open Book Directly** Book property, in *Book Properties* on page 258).

Book Properties

Let's look at the Book's properties, which are displayed in the *Object Editor* pane when you select the Book in the Workarea.

Books have the same properties as most objects in Enable Now (refer to *The Object Editor* on page 49 for details of these); the object properties that are specific to Books are listed in the table below.

★ Book Styles are defined in **Resources | Book Styles**.

Property	Use
Basic Properties	
Book Style	Select the style template that should be applied to the Book. This will be used by default for all Book Pages created within the Book.
Subtype	This is effectively just used to determine the object icon to be used for this Book object (both in the Workarea and in the *Trainer*). Currently there is only one (unnamed) icon available for Books.
Book Reader	
Content Page	You can select a Book Page within the Book to serve as the 'contents' page. This is the page that will be displayed if the user clicks on the **Home** button in the Book Reader. Normally you would choose to have a page that contains a hyper-linked Table of Contents for the Book to be the Content Page.
Track Completion of Book	If the Book will be accessed via a Learning Management System (LMS), then select this option to pass information on how much of the Book has been viewed by the user back to the LMS.
Hide Book Panel	Select this checkbox to suppress the display of the entire *Book Reader Toolbar* in the *Book Reader*.
Open Book Directly	If this checkbox is selected then as soon as the user clicks on the Book in the content hierarchy in the Library, the Book is opened in the *Book Reader*.
Hide Audio Controls	Select this checkbox to suppress display of the three audio buttons on the *Book Reader Toolbar*. You would normally only (and always) want to do this if the Book does not contain audio.
Hide Navigation Controls	Select this checkbox to suppress display of the **Prior Chapter, Prior Page, Next Page,** and **Next Chapter** buttons on the *Book Reader Toolbar*.
Hide Play/Pause Control	Select this checkbox to suppress display of the **Pause / Play** toggle button on the *Book Reader Toolbar*.

Property	Use
Hide Index Page Control	Select this checkbox to suppress display of the **Home** button (which jumps to the Book Page selected as the **Content Page**—see above) in the *Book Reader*.
Hide Search Control	Select this checkbox to suppress display of the **Search** button on the *Book Reader Toolbar*.
Hide Table of Contents Control	Select this checkbox to suppress display of the drop-down list of Book Pages in the *Book Reader*.
Hide Progress Control	Select this checkbox to suppress display of the progress indicator (which shows the current page number and total number of pages below a progress bar) on the *Book Reader Toolbar*.

Creating a Book Page

There are a number of ways of creating a Book Page. This section explains the easiest; the others will be covered once we get into the *Book Page Editor*, on page 261.

To create a new Book Page, carry out the steps shown below.

1. In the *Object Navigation Pane*, click on the Group within which you want to create the Book Page.

    If you have an existing Book to which your Book Page will be added then you can select this Book, instead of a Group, to create the Book Page directly within the selected Book. This will save you having to link it in to the Book later.

2. Click on the **New Object** button and select **Book Page** in the drop-down panel (or click on the **New Object** button at the top of the *Object Editor* and select **New Book Page** from the drop-down menu). The *New Book Page* dialog box is displayed.

    ▪ You could also right-click on the Book and select **New Book Page** from the shortcut menu—or use keyboard shortcut *CTRL+P*.

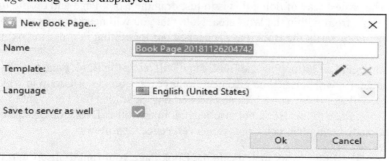

3. Enter a suitable name for the Book Page in the **Name** field. This will be used as the Book Page title (and appears in the Table of Contents and possibly also on the Book Page itself), so choose this name carefully.

4. If you have an existing Book Page template that you want to use, select this in the **Template** field. You would normally want to use a template for every Book Page, according to its purpose; several high-quality templates are shipped with Enable Now by default. The examples in this chapter use the 'Green' series of pre-built Book Page templates.

   Technically, you do not have to use an actual *template*—you can select any existing Book Page in this field. This will effectively take a copy of the selected Book Page to use as a start point for your new Book Page.

5. Select the default language for the Book Page in the **Language** field. This will determine the language used by the spell-checker.

6. If you are creating the Book Page in a server-managed folder, then the **Save to server as well** checkbox will be selected and the simulation will also be created as server-managed. If you only want the Book Page to be saved locally (for example, to your Content Group) then deselect this checkbox. See *Server-managed vs. local objects* on page 34 for additional information on this subject.

   If you are creating a Book Page from within a Book, this will default to the same synchronization behavior as the Book uses.

7. Click **Ok**.

The Book Page is opened in the *Book Page Editor*. You can start editing it immediately, or close the *Book Page Editor* to return to the Workarea.

Adding a Book Page to a Book

In *Creating a Book Page* on page 259, we looked at how to create a new Book Page from the Workarea. You can also create a new Book Page from within the *Book Page Editor*, as explained in *Creating a simple Book Page* on page 262

But what if you have an existing Book Page that you want to add to a Book (which will hopefully be the case reasonably often, as you re-use Book Pages)? The easiest way of doing this is to just drag the Book Page and drop it onto the Book, from within the Workarea. Note that you will need to have the Book (but not necessarily the Book Page) checked out for editing in order to do this.

Dragging and dropping the Book Page will *move* the Book Page to under the Book (in which case you also need to have the Book in or Group in which the Book Page is currently located checked out for editing). If you want to *add* the Book Page to this Book but also leave it in any other Books or Groups it may already be in, then you can create a **reference**, as follows:

1. In the Workarea, locate the Book Page you want to insert into your Book.

2. Right-click on the Book Page, and select **Copy** from the shortcut menu.

3. Right-click on your Book, and select **Paste** from the shortcut menu. The *Insert Object* dialog box is displayed.

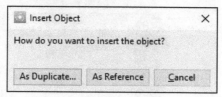

4. Click on **As Reference**. The Book Page is inserted into the Book as a reference (link). This means that there is still only one copy of the Book Page in the Workarea, but now it is visible in two places. Note that there is no function or visual difference between these copies—you can open either instance of the Book Page to edit it the single version that exists—and you can delete any instance without affecting any other instances.

   The other option in the *Insert Object* dialog box is **As Duplicate**. This will create a brand new Book Page that is an identical copy of the original one (that you copied in Step 2). Any changes made to this new object will not affect the original Book Page.

In addition to adding Book Pages to a Book, you can also add other Books to a Book, by using exactly the same method as described above. Typically, you would want to do this if you need to create a multi-level structure in your Book—for example, to group Book Pages into Lessons that are then grouped into a Course. The example Book that we are looking at in this chapter, *SAPgui Navigation*, has been built like this.

Working in the Book Page Editor

If you open a Book or a Book Page for editing, it is opened in the *Book Page Editor*. An example of a typical *Book Page Editor* screen is shown below. (Don't worry if this example is a little small—you don't need to be able to see the details; we're only concerned with the overall layout, and the components that comprise this screen.)

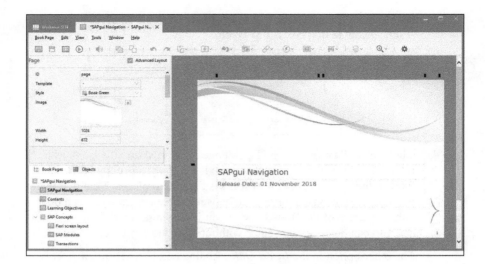

There are effectively four components of the *Book Page Editor*. These are identified in the graphic on the right, and explained below.

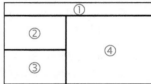

1. The *Book Editor Toolbar*. This provides access to the *Book Page Editor* functionality. Buttons on the Toolbar are grouped according to function, and you can show or hide specific groups via menu option **View | Toolbars**.

2. The *Object Editor* pane. This pane works the same way as the *Macro Editor* pane in the *Project Editor*, and provides access to all of the properties for a selected object.

3. The *Object Overview* pane. This pane contains two tabbed pages. The first of these is the *Book Explorer* page. This lists all of the Book Pages in the Book (or just the one Book Page, if you opened a Book Page that is not contained within a Book). Click on a Book Page to show that page in the *WYSIWYG Editor* (see below).The second tabbed page is the *Objects* page, which lists all of the objects on the selected page. Click on an object to show the properties for this object in the *Object Editor* pane.

4. The *WYSIWYG Editor* pane. This is similar to the *WYSIWYG Editor* pane in the Project Editor. It shows the selected Book Page, and all of the (visible) objects on it.

Let's look at some of the functionality offered by the *Book Page Editor* by way of a few simple examples.

Creating a simple Book Page

Most of the time, you will base your Book Pages on a template that includes placeholders for your content. In this example, we'll start from a completely blank page and add all of our content to that, working on the theory that if you can do this, you can do anything. We'll start by adding a new Book Page to our example Book.

To add a new Book Page to a Book that you currently have open in the *Book Page Editor*, carry out the steps shown below:

1. If your Book already contains Book Pages, make sure that the *Book Explorer* is displayed, and click on the page that is immediately before the position at which you want your new page to be inserted.

   If your Book does not contain any Book Pages, then the *WYSIWYG Editor* will be empty apart from a message that says "Click to create new book page...". Click on this, and continue with Step 3.

2. Select menu option **Book Page | New Book Page**. The *New Book Page* dialog box is displayed.

3. Complete the *New Book Page* dialog box, as explained in *Creating a Book Page* on page 259.

Setting the Book Page Properties

Make sure the Book Page is selected in the *Book Explorer*, so that its properties are shown in the *Object Editor*. A partial example of the *Object Editor* pane, showing the **General** properties, is shown below.

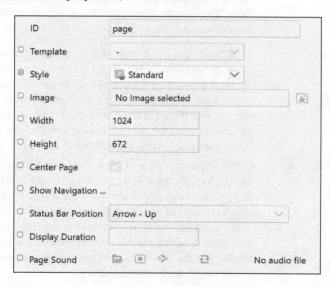

The table below provides a comprehensive list of all of the properties available for Book Pages, and explains their use.

Property	Use
General	
ID	This is the name of the page 'object' as it is listed in the *Object Overview* pane. This defaults to "page" and cannot be changed.
Template	If you specified a template in the *New Book Page* dialog box, then this template will be specified in this field. If not, or if you want to change the template assigned to the Book Page, you can select a new template from this field's drop-down list.
Style	This specifies the overall visual style to use for the Book Page. This differs from the Template, which specifies the default objects and placeholders to be included on the page, and instead specifies the overall color scheme and (most significantly) background image used for the page. **Standard** is an entirely blank style.
Image	This property can be used to select a background image for the page. You can use the **Edit Image** button to select or capture images as necessary. Refer to *Inserting images* on page 280 for additional information on working with images.
Width	These two fields specify the dimensions of the Book Page. You should make sure that you have set this to the correct size before adding content to your page.
Height	
Center Page	By default, the Book Page will be centered in the browser window (in which the Book is opened). If you deselect this option then the Book Page will be aligned to the upper-left corner of the browser window. This may be significant if the browser window is larger than the Book Page size, as the 'background' of the Book Reader will be visible around the Book Page.
Show Navigation Arrows	If this option is selected, then 'back' and 'forward' navigation arrows will be displayed in the *Book Reader* window, mid-way down the left and right sides (respectively) of the Book Page in the *Book Reader*. You would normally only choose to display these if you have disabled the navigation buttons (or the entire toolbar) in the *Book Reader* (see the **Hide Navigation Controls** property on page 264).
Status Bar Position	This property allows you to specify whether the *Book Reader Toolbar* should initially appear at the **Top** or **Bottom** of the *Book Reader* window. Note that this is only a default setting, and the user can override this themselves (and the user's choice is 'remembered').

★ Page Styles are defined in **Resources | Book Styles**. Enable Now ships with several standard styles, but the Administrator can define custom ones—for example to match corporate branding.

■ When choosing a Book Page size, you should consider the most common resolution of your user's screens, and allow for the screen space that will be taken up by the *Book Page Toolbar*.

Property	Use
Display Duration	If you want the Book Page to auto-advance to the next slide, then enter the number of seconds to wait (after displaying this page) before advancing to the next Book Page in the book. A value of **-1** indicates 'forever' (until the user manually advances).
Page Sound	Use the buttons for this property to manage audio for the Book Page. Refer to *Audio for Books and Book Pages* on page 575 for details of how to do this.
Page Sound Information	
Text to Speech Text **Text to speech Voice** **Editing Format** **Output Format**	If you have specified text-to-speech via the Page Sound property, then these read-only fields provide values related to this. Refer to Refer to *Audio for Books and Book Pages* on page 575 for details.
Design	
Page Color	Specifies the background color of the page.
Background Color	Specifies the color of the area behind the Book Page in the *Book Reader* (and the *WYSIWYG Editor* during editing).
Background Image	You can use this field to select an image to display behind the Book Page (as an alternative to using a **Background Color**). Note that this will be scaled to fit the full width or height of the area, so you should use a suitably-large image.
Border Width **Border Color** **Border Style**	Use these fields to add a border to the Book Page.
Shadow	
Show Shadow	Select this option to apply a 'drop shadow' to the Book Page. Once you select this checkbox, the remaining fields for this category are displayed.
Shadow Color	Select the color to use for the drop shadow.
Shadow Opacity	Select the opacity to apply to the drop shadow (this will let some degree of the **Background Color** or **Background Image** show through).
Shadow Blur	Indicates how many pixels it should take for the shadow to fade out from full color to no color (note that this may not be equal on all sides - see the **Shadow Horizontal** and **Shadow Vertical** properties).
Shadow Spread	Indicates how many pixels of full color there should be around the **Book Page** before it starts to fade out (see the **Shadow Blur** property).

▲ The **Display Duration** property isn't particularly smart, and will not take into account any animation, events, or timers. The Book Page will advance after the specified number of seconds regardless of whether any timers have completed or not. If your Book Page uses timers, make sure this value is sufficient to allow them all to complete before advancing.

■ For a 'traditional' drop-shadow (to the lower-right) use values of:
Shadow Color: Black
Shadow Opacity: 50
Shadow Blur: 10
Shadow Spread: 0
Shadow Horizontal: 10
Shadow Vertical: 10

■ Refer to the sample Book Page shown on page 252 for an example of these options.

Property	Use
Shadow Horizontal	Specifies the number of pixels by which the shadow should be 'offset' horizontally, relative to the Book Page itself. A negative number will shift the shadow to the left; a positive number will shift it to the right.
Shadow Horizontal	Specifies the number of pixels by which the shadow should be 'offset' vertically, relative to the Book Page itself. A negative number will shift the shadow up; a positive number will shift it down.
Table of Contents	
Show	If you want a hyperlinked 'Table of Contents' bar (containing the contents of the current Book) to be displayed for this Book Page, then select this option. Note that you would only normally select this if you have also selected the Book-level **Hide Table of Contents** property to suppress display of the Table of Contents drop-down in the *Book Reader Toolbar*.
Position	If you have selected Show, use this property to specify whether the Table of Contents bar should appear immediately above the Book Page, or at the top of the client area of the browser window.
Menu Structure	If you have selected Show, use this property to choose whether the Book Pages are listed on the Table of Contents bar as a flat list or an indented list (actually a flat list of the main contents, with drop-down lists for the sub-contents. The nested list is useful if you have nested Books.
Backward Compatibility	
Font Size in Pt	By default all font sizes you specify are in points. If you want to specify sizes in pixels, for backwards compatibility with some older browsers, deselect this option.
Version	No idea. It's read-only, anyway.
Actions	
On Click **On Page Loaded** **On Focus** **On Blur** **On Page Sound** **Finish**	Use these properties to assign events to specific actions for the Book Page. Actions are explained more fully in *Basic animation through Actions* on page 275.

Property	Use
Documentation	
Show in Documentation	By default, Book Pages are typically included in output formats—either in the Compound Document, or in any document that is created for a simulation that includes a Book Page. If you do not want this Book Page to be included in generated documents, then deselect this option.

Previewing a Book Page

Although the *WYSIWYG Editor* allows you to see all of your objects in place on the page, it does not necessarily reflect how the page will look to the user—especially if you have animations and overlapping elements. Enable Now provides two easy ways to preview a Book Page: **Preview**, and **Play with Book Reader**. These are available from the *Book Editor Toolbar*.

The **Preview** button displays the Book Page, as it will appear to the user, including all timing, animation, and other effects, in the *WYSIWYG Editor* pane. This allows you to review the appearance of the page without leaving the *Book Editor*. Nothing will be editable, and you need to click on the **Preview** button again, to exit from preview mode.

The **Display in Book Reader** button displays the page in the *Book Reader*, where you can test it using the full *Book Reader* functionality. This option is useful if you have set any properties for the Book Page that impact the layout of the Book.

Basic editing

Let's assume that we have now created a simple Book Page, using the **Book Green** style, and no template. This gives us a page that is empty apart from some green background graphics, as shown below.

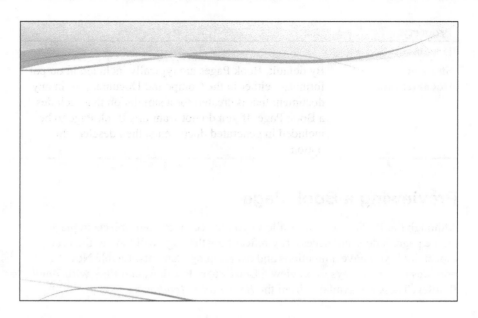

Clearly, we need to add some content to this. Enable Now provides a great many things that you can add to Book Pages to make them interesting and engaging. This includes:

- **Objects**, including bubbles, images, and text boxes - See *Inserting a Placeholder* on page 268, *Inserting a Text Box* on page 271, *Inserting images* on page 280, and *Additional Object Types* on page 300.

- **Shapes** - *Working with shapes* on page 283.

- **Media Objects**, including Flash animation and video - See *Inserting Media Objects* on page 294.

- **Links** - See *Inserting links* on page 290.

- **Actions** - See *Basic Interaction* on page 279, and *Advanced Actions* on page 306.

- **Quiz elements** - See *Chapter 9, Creating Tests*.

As noted, most of these are covered later in this chapter (or in the case of Quiz elements, in their own chapter), but we'll get started by looking at a few of the most frequently-used object types.

Inserting a Placeholder

The first thing we want to do for our sample file is insert a title at the top of the screen. We have already given our Book Page a suitable name ("Changing your color scheme" in our example) so let's just use this as the title. To keep things simple (and consistent) we can insert a placeholder for this.

To insert a placeholder, carry out the following steps:

1. With the Book Page displayed in the *WYSIWYG Editor*, click on the **Insert Object** button to display the drop-down panel of object types.

Insert
Object
button

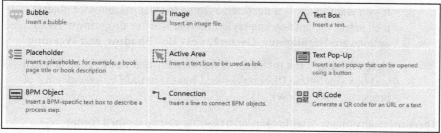

2. Click on **Placeholder**.

3. A new object is added to the upper-left corner of the Book Page. Use the handles on the object boundary to resize and reposition the object.

Now that we have added the object, let's maintain the basic properties for this object. Make sure the object is selected (click on it in the *Objects* pane, or the *WYSIWYG Editor*, if it is not), and then continue as follows:

4. In the **Name** property for the object, change the default name to something more meaningful. This is always a good idea, to make it easier to identify objects in the *Objects* pane.

5. In the **Placeholder** property, select the placeholder text that is to be displayed in the object. For our exercise, we will select **Book page title**. The full list of options is:

    ◆ **Book title**

    ◆ **Book description**

    ◆ **Book page title**

    ◆ **Book page description**

    ◆ **Chapter title**

    ◆ **Chapter title description**

    ◆ **Page number**

    ◆ **Page count**

    ◆ **Text to Speech text**

6. By default, scrollbars will be shown for a Placeholder text box (or any other text box) if the contents exceed the size of the box. To suppress the display of the scrollbars, select the **Hide Scroll Bars** property.

■ A 'Chapter' is the Book in which the Book Page is contained, where that book is itself contained within another Book. The 'Book' is the highest-level Book in which the Book Page is contained.

■ You would typically use the **Text to Speech text** placeholder to provide 'closed captions' where you have used text-to-speech for audio. See *Chapter 14, Adding Audio to Your Content* for additional information on providing audio in Book Pages.

7. To set the object to be hidden on the page, select the **Hide** checkbox. You may wonder why you would want to add an object to a page and then hide it so that it is not displayed. The simple answer is that you may want the object to be initially hidden, and then displayed as part of an animation sequence, or in response to a user action or other trigger (we will look at both of these cases later in this chapter).

8. If you want to apply a decorative frame to your placeholder object, then select the appropriate style from the **Border** drop-down. Available options are **Highlighter**, **Decor 1**, **Text Box Shadow**, and **Warning**.

   ★ Available frames are listed in **Resources | Adaptable Resources**. These can be edited, or new ones defined, via menu option **Tools | Customization | Edit Style Resources**.

   Note that this is not the same as the 'border' that can be assigned to a text box (including Placeholder text boxes) in the *Design* category of properties (see below).

There are many, many additional properties that can be defined for the Placeholder (or other text box objects) in the **Object Editor** pane. Most of these are self-explanatory, so we will not list them all individually here. Instead, let's just look at the overall categories of properties.

Category	Purpose
Design	This category includes properties for setting the overall appearance of any object that can contain text. This includes properties for font family, size, color, typographical emphasis, text alignment within the object, background, border, padding, and opacity.
	It is worth noting here that there are overall **Border Width** and **Padding** properties that apply to the entire object, but then separate properties for **Top**, **Right**, **Bottom**, and **Left**, in case you want to override the overall setting for individual borders.
Shadow	Use the fields in this category to apply a shadow effect to the placeholder object. (Note that initially only the **Show Shadow** option will be displayed; select this checkbox to show the additional options.) Refer to the description provided for Book Pages on page 265 for an explanation of these options.

Category	Purpose
Size and Position	Use the fields in this category to specify the exact (pixel-specific) location of the object on the page, and its size. Use the **Lock Position** property to prevent these from being changed (for example, by accidentally moving the text box in the *WYSIWYG Editor*). Of note here is the **Layer** property, which is assigned automatically, and determines which objects appear on top of which other objects (the higher the number, the nearer the 'top of the pile' the object appears). You cannot change this property directly, but can influence it by moving the relative position of the object in the *Objects* list, or by using the options on the **Change Layer** button.
Actions	Use the properties in this category to assign events to the various actions that can be performed against the object. These are discussed in *Setting actions for objects* on page 289.
Animation	Use the properties in this category to assign default animation effects to the object. Specifically, you can specify an animation effect to use when displaying ('animating in') the object, and an effect to use when hiding ('animating out') the object. Animation is discussed further in *Basic animation through Actions* on page 275.
Documentation	This category contains a single property, **Show in Documentation**, which you can deselect to prevent this object from appearing in any documentation output in which the Book Page is included.

Inserting a Text Box

Let's complete our example page by adding a text box, in which we can place our body text.

To insert a text box into a Book Page, carry out the following steps:

1. Click on the **Insert Object** button, and select **Text Box** in the drop-down panel.

2. Click in this text box in the *WYSIWYG Editor* (or click in the **Text** property for the object), and enter the required text in the *Text Editor* (see *Adjusting Bubble text* on page 111 for instructions on using the *Text Editor*).

3. Adjust the text box properties in the same way as explained above for the Placeholder text box (see *Inserting a Placeholder* on page 268).

So far so good. Our example Book Page appears in the *WYSIWYG Editor* as shown in the following screenshot:

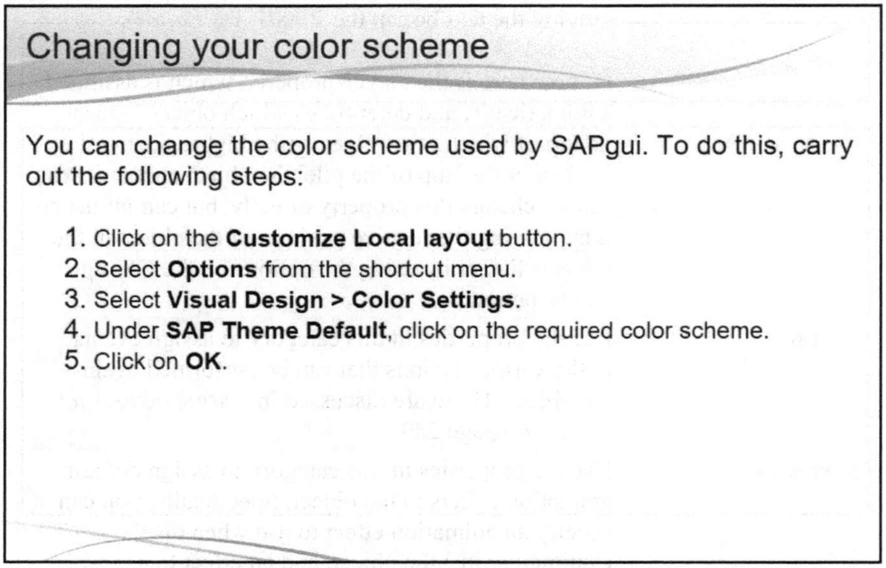

Changing your color scheme

You can change the color scheme used by SAPgui. To do this, carry out the following steps:

1. Click on the **Customize Local layout** button.
2. Select **Options** from the shortcut menu.
3. Select **Visual Design > Color Settings**.
4. Under **SAP Theme Default**, click on the required color scheme.
5. Click on **OK**.

Additional Object types

So far in this section, we have looked at the **Text Box** and **Placeholder Object** types. There are several more types of Objects available via the same **Insert Object** button. So as to not overwhelm you when we're just starting with the basics, we'll look at these Object types as we need them, throughout the rest of this chapter. If you,re impatient and want to learn about them *now*, refer to the following sections, as necessary:

- **Image**: See *Inserting images* on page 280.

- **BPM Object** and **Connection**: See *Inserting a Business Process Model chart* on page 297.

- **Bubble, Active Area, Text Pop-Up** and **QR Code**: See *Additional Object Types* on page 300

Our sample page is nice enough, but it's really just a bunch of words on the screen. Let's try and make it a bit more interesting by displaying the numbered list one item at a time. This is a simple enough task in PowerPoint, but is slightly more difficult in Enable Now—primarily because Enable Now animates things at the *object* level, and not (in the case of text boxes) one paragraph at a time.

If we want to introduce each line in our numbered list individually, each line needs to be a separate object—in this case, a separate text box. Let's assume that we have now done this, and we now have six text boxes on our page—one for the lead-in paragraph ("You can change...") and one for each list item.

Before we start animating them in, let's make sure they are all aligned consistently.

Object Alignment

When you start working with multiple objects on the page, you will likely discover that getting all of the objects consistently lined up and evenly spaced out can be tricky. Luckily, Enable Now has a few features to help with this.

Firstly, each Book Page has an invisible grid, which objects will be 'snapped to' when moving them on the page. Objects will also snap to other objects, and in alignment with other objects.

> ★ Grid and snap settings are defined in **Settings | Authoring Settings | Book Page Editor**.

Next, if the built-in grid isn't exactly where you want to align objects, you can add Guides to your Book Page. You can then align objects to these Guides. Note that Guides are not visible on the published Book Page.

To add a Guide to your Book Page, carry out the following steps:

1. Click on the **Change Alignment** button on the *Book Editor Toolbar*.

2. Select either **Insert Vertical Guide**, or **Insert Horizontal Guide** from the drop-down menu, as required.

Change Alignment

3. Position the Guide where you need it (either by dragging it in the *WYSIWYG Editor*, or via the **Top** or **Left** property (as appropriate) in the properties for the Guide object).

> ■ Guides are one of the few object types for which you can directly edit the **Layer** property. You might find it helpful to assign all Guides to layer **0**, so that they are always kept out of the way of other objects in the *Objects* list.

Note that Guides are specific to a page, so if you add a Guide to one Book Page, it won't automatically appear on all other Book Pages in the same Book. However, they are just objects, so you can copy and paste them between pages if necessary (Guides will be pasted in exactly the same location from which they were copied).

The following screenshot shows our example Book Page in the *WYSIWYG Editor*, after we have added a few Guides. These are shown in blue, with red 'handles' just off the visible page (to the top and left only). In this example, we have also selected every object on the page, just so you can see where the various object boundaries are.

Changing your color scheme

You can change the color scheme used by SAPgui. To do this, carry out the following steps:

1. Click on the **Customize Local layout** button.
2. Select **Options** from the shortcut menu.
3. Select **Visual Design > Color Settings**.
4. Under **SAP Theme Default**, click on the required color scheme.
5. Click on **OK**.

If you want to align objects in relation to other objects, and not in relation to the grid or Guides, you can do so via the options on the **Change Alignment** button. Just select the objects that you want to align and then select the relevant option from this menu, as described below:

Icon	Command	Use
	Left Align	Align the left side of all selected objects along the leftmost edge of the leftmost object.
	Top Align	Align the top edge of all objects along the upper edge of the object whose top edge is closest to the top of the page.
	Right Align	Align the right side of all selected objects along the rightmost edge of the rightmost object.
	Bottom Align	Align the bottom edge of all objects along the lower edge of the object whose bottom edge is closest to the bottom of the page.
	Same Width	Resize all selected objects so that they have the same width as the *first* object that you selected.
	Same Height	Resize all selected objects so that they have the same height as the *first* object that you selected.
	Same Size	Resize all selected objects so that they have the same height and width as the *first* object that you selected.

Icon	Command	Use
	Equal Horizontal Distribution	Set the horizontal space between each selected object and the next to be exactly the amount of space currently between the topmost object and the object immediately below it.
	Distribute Horizontally	Leave the topmost and bottom objects where they are, but adjust all objects between them so that there is the same amount of horizontal space between each object.
	Equal Vertical Distribution	Set the vertical space between each selected object and the next to be exactly the amount of space currently between the leftmost object and the object immediately to the right of it.
	Distribute Vertically	Leave the leftmost and rightmost objects where they are, but adjust all objects between them so that there is the same amount of vertical space between each object.
	Insert Vertical Guide	Insert a vertical Guide.
	Insert Horizontal Guide	Insert a horizontal Guide.

For our example Book Page, we will select our five list item text boxes, and then use **Left Align** and **Distribute Horizontally**. We'll also use **Same Size** to make them all consistently-sized (although that is more for this Author's OCD as on this example it makes no difference to the user how the text boxes are sized as long as all the text is the same size).

Basic animation through Actions

Now that we have our text in individual text boxes, and have made sure that these are aligned let's animate them in, so that the numbered list items are introduced one at a time. Every object has a set of properties that define how the object can be animated. These can be found in the *Animation* category for the object.

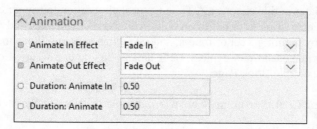

The table below explains the purpose of these properties.

Property	Use
Animate In Effect	Defines the animation effect that should be used to introduce the object to the visible page. This can be one of the following predefined effects: • **Fade In** • **Fly In - From Left/Right/Top/Bottom** • **Zoom In** (the object appears to grow from a point at the center of its final position) • **Bounce In** (the object moves onto the screen in an arc, and 'bounces' into position)
Animate Out Effect	Defines the animation effect that should be used to remove the object from the visible page. This can be one of the following predefined effects: • **Fade Out** • **Fly Out - To Left/Right/Top/Bottom** • **Zoom Out** (the object shrinks to a point at the center of its position) • **Bounce Out** (the object moves off the screen in an arc)
Duration: Animate In	Specifies how long, in seconds, it should take for the object to fully appear in its final position, from the start of the animation.
Duration: Animate Out	Specifies how long, in seconds, it should take for the object to disappear completely form the page, from the start of the animation.

It is important to understand that just setting an animation effect for an object will not result in the object being animated during playback. This is because it is necessary to *trigger* the animation. There are several ways that we can do this, but for now we'll use the easiest method—using a **Time Control** (we'll look at some other ways later in this chapter). A Time Control allows you to trigger events (such as the animation in or out of an object) after a predefined period of time. It does this by defining a set of timers, and assigning an action that should be performed when each timer expires. Let's look at how to use a Time Control, by way of our example Book Page.

To use a Time Control to animate objects, carry out the steps shown below.

1. Click on the **Insert Action** button, and select **Time Control** in the drop-down panel. A Time Control object is added to the page. This is represented by an icon

Insert Action

above the top-left corner of the page (outside the display area), as shown in the partial screenshot below.

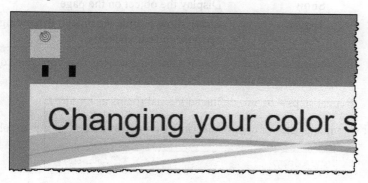

2. Make sure the Time Control is selected, so that its properties are displayed in the *Object Editor* pane. (An example of the object's properties pane is shown after Step 6, once we have specified the required properties.)

3. Enter a suitable name for the Time Control object in its **Name** property. This is only used internally, but you may find it useful to give it a name that reflects its purpose.

4. In the **Time 1** field, specify number of seconds after the Time Control starts at which the first timer should be triggered (and the action you specify in the next step is carried out). This is the number of seconds since the Time Control was started, and not the number of seconds since the last trigger (as is the case in, say, PowerPoint).

5. In the **On Timeout 1** field, click on the **Add** link, and then specify the following information:

   i. In the first column, use the drop-down list to select the object for which the action should be performed. In our example, this will be the first text box that we want to animate in (Step 1 of our numbered list).

   ii. In the second column, use the drop-down control to select the action that should be performed against this object (**Animate In**, in our example). The options available are:

Option	Use
Animate in	Use the effect defined in the **Animate In** property for the object
Animate Out	Use the effect defined in the **Animate Out** property for the object.
Animate Toggle	Either animate in, or animate out, depending on the current state of the object.
Hide	Remove the object from visibility.

Option	Use
Show	Display the object on the page.
Toggle	Either show or hide the object, depending upon its current visibility.

■ Being able to define multiple actions for a single timer is incredibly useful, as it allows you to trigger multiple effects at the same time, instead of having to define a timer per action (or object).

■ Defining multiple timers for a single Time Control allows you to trigger multiple events at different intervals. You can set up to eight timers within a Time Control. If you need more than eight timers, you can use the last timer in the Time Control to trigger another Time Control.

■ If you want to emulate PowerPoint's 'After Previous' animation control, then define multiple Time Controls, and have each one triggered by the previous Time Control.

    iii.   Repeat steps i and ii for all additional actions that you want to perform upon this timer being triggered.

6.   Repeat steps 4 to 5 to define additional timers as required.

For our example page, our completed Time Control properties appear as follows:

We're not done yet, though. There are a few additional things that we need to do, to animate in our texts. We need to prevent them from being visible when the page is first displayed, and we need to trigger our timer when the page loads. Continue with the following steps:

7.   For each of the objects that you want to animate in (the five 'list item' text boxes, in our example), select the **Hide** property checkbox. This will make sure that the object is not visible when the page is initially displayed, so that we can then animate it in.

Note that as soon as you do this, the object is 'faded out' in the *WYSIWYG Editor*.

8. In the *Objects* list, find the page object, and click on it to select it. (You can also click anywhere outside the viewable page in the *WYSIWYG Editor*.)

9. Locate the *Actions* category of the page's properties.

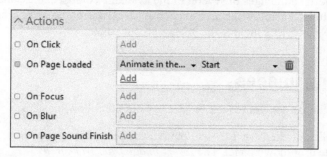

10. For the **On Page Loaded** property, click on the **Add** link, and then specify the following information:

   i. In the first column, use the drop-down control to select the object that should be acted upon when the page is initially displayed. In our example, this is our Time Control.

   ii. In the second column, use the drop-down control to select the action that should be performed against this object (**Start**, in our example).

   iii. Repeat steps i and ii for all additional actions that you want to perform when the page is displayed.

Now, in our example, when our page is first displayed, it will only contain the lead-in sentence. As soon as the page is loaded, our Time Control will be started. Two seconds into this, our first list item will be displayed, with the subsequent steps being displayed at one second intervals. (Obviously we can't show this on the printed page; just take my word for it—or better still, try it yourself!)

Additional Action types

In addition to the Timer Control used in this example, there are several other types of Action object that you can use with your Book Page. These could be considered part of 'advanced editing', and you probably won't need them until you have at least mastered the basics described in this section. Therefore, they are described in their own section, *Advanced Actions* on page 306.

Basic Interaction

Book Pages can do more than simply display information while the user passively consumes it. They can also include interactive elements, so that the user is required to interact with the Book Page (which always makes for more engaging and effective learning). In this section, we'll look at a simple example of interaction, by including a series of images on our example Book Page, and allowing the user to chose which one of these is displayed.

Our example page explains to the user how to change their color scheme in SAPgui. We'll add images of several of the available color schemes, and then provide buttons that allow the user to choose which one of the color schemes they want to see. First, let's include the images on our page.

Inserting images

To include images on your Book Page, carry out the following steps:

1. Click on the **Insert Object** button, and select **Image** in the drop-down panel. The *Insert Image from Workarea* dialog box is displayed.

Insert Object

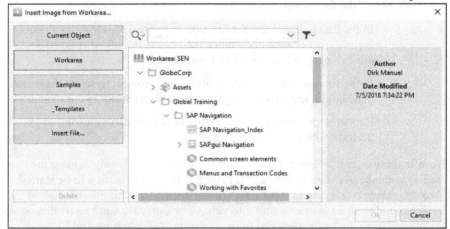

2. Use the buttons on the left to select the location from where you want to load the image. The options are:

   ♦ **Current Object**: Load an image that currently exists within this Book Page. Typically this will be image files that you have already imported via the **Insert File** option.

   ♦ **Workarea**: Load an image that exists within the Workarea.

   ♦ **Insert File**: Load an image from your PC.

   There may also be additional buttons for Groups within your Workarea for which shortcuts have been defined (see *Building your Workarea structure* on page 59).

3. Navigate to and select the image that you want to insert in your Book Page.

4. Click **OK**.

■ If you think there is any possibility you will use an image in more than one content object, you should import it into your Workarea as an asset (see *Importing images and other assets* on page 548), and then insert it in your Book Page from there. This will save unnecessary redundancy, and simplify maintenance.

5. Once the file has been imported, maintain its properties as explained below.

The following table lists the *general* properties available for images in Book Pages, and explains their use. You will likely need to change some of these, but probably not all properties in all cases.

Property	Use
Name	Enter a suitable name for the image object. This will make it easier to identify in the *Objects* list.
Image	This property provides a thumbnail of the image file. You can use the **Replace Image** button to the right of this thumbnail image to replace the image with a new one.
Image Roll-Over	If required, select another image that will be displayed in place of this image when the user moves the cursor over this image.
Image Click	If required, select another image that will be displayed in place of this image, when the user clicks on this image.
Keep Aspect Ratio	If this option is selected (which it is, by default) then if you resize the image, the original height-width ratio is maintained.
Zoom	If this option is selected, then an icon is shown in the upper-right corner of the image that the user can click on to display a full-size copy of the image, centered on the book page. Another button is provided on this full-size copy to close it. You would normally only do this if you have significantly reduced the size of the image (for example, to provide it as a thumbnail on the book page) but still want users to be able to see the full version if they want to.
Hide	Select this option if you want the image to initially not be displayed on the Book Page. You would normally only select this if you will animate in the image, or display it in response to some other interaction.

As with most object types, there are many additional properties that can be defined for Images in the *Object Editor* pane. We will look at some of these as we continue to enhance our example Book Page, but in the meantime, the table below lists the overall categories of properties that are available, and describes a few of the most useful properties within these categories.

Category	Purpose
Design	This category includes properties for setting the overall appearance of the image. This includes background, border, padding, and opacity.
Shadow	This category contains a single property—**Show Shadow**—that can be used to apply a drop shadow to the object. This always appears on the bottom and right edges of the image; you cannot change this.
Size and Position	Use the fields in this category to specify the exact (pixel-specific) location of the image on the page, and its size. Use the **Lock Position** property to prevent these from being changed (for example, by accidentally clicking on the text box in the *WYSIWYG Editor*).
	The **Layer** property is assigned automatically, and determines which objects appear on top of which other objects (the higher the number, the nearer the top the object appears). You cannot change this property directly, but can influence it by moving the relative position of the object in the *Objects* list.
Link	These properties allow you to define the image as a hyperlink, so that another file is opened when you click on the image.
New Window Properties	These properties allow you to define the format of the window in which any linked file is opened. You would only use this category if you also use the *Link* category.
Actions	Use the properties in this category to assign events to the various actions that can be performed against the object. These are discussed in detail in *Basic Interaction* on page 279.
Animation	Use the properties in this category to assign default animation effects to the object. Specifically, you can specify an effect to use when displaying ('animating in') the object, and an effect to use when hiding ('animating out') the object. Animation is discussed further in *Basic animation through Actions* on page 275.
Documentation	This category contains a single property—**Show in Documentation**—that you can deselect to prevent this object from appearing in any documentation output in which the Book Page is included.

For our ongoing example, let's assume that we have inserted four images of different SAPgui Themes (Blue Crystal, Corbu, Enjoy, and Tradeshow) into our Book Page. We have positioned them all at exactly the same location on the page, and set three of them to initially be hidden. Now we want to add some buttons so that the user can display the hidden images. How to do add buttons and assign actions to them is covered in the next few sections.

Working with shapes

Enable Now supports a number of standard shapes that you can add to your Book Page. These are added via the **Insert Shape** button. The following diagram shows the shapes that are available.

Insert
Shape

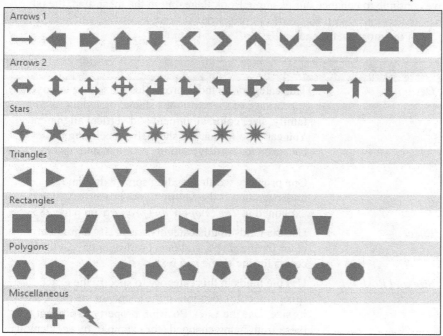

The following table lists the *general* properties available for shapes in Book Pages, and explains their use.

Property	Use
Name	Enter a suitable name for the image object. This will make it easier to identify in the *Objects* list.
Type and Orientation	You can use this property to change the object from one shape to another, if necessary.
Text	Enter any text that should be displayed in the object. You can apply default text formatting (that applies to all text in the object) via the *Design* category of properties, or apply direct formatting to text, via the standard *Text Editor*.

Property	Use
Hide	Select this option if you do not want the shape to initially be displayed on the Book Page when the page is loaded. You would normally only select this if you will animate in the shape, or display it in response to some other interaction.

As with most object types, there are many additional properties that can be defined for shapes, via the *Object Editor* pane. We will look at some of these as we continue to enhance our example Book Page, but in the meantime, the table below lists the overall categories of properties that are available, and describes a few of the most useful ones.

Category	Purpose
Design	This category includes properties for setting the overall appearance of the text in the shape, including its font family, size, color, alignment and vertical alignment. You can also format the shape, by specifying the background, border, padding, rotation, and opacity. One property worth spending some extra time understanding is the **Shape Value** property, which is explained in *The Shape Value property* on page 285.
Effect	Use the fields in this category to specify a gradient color for the shape, and/or set roll-over or on-click colors for the shape and text.
Size and Position	Use the fields in this category to specify the exact (pixel-specific) location of the shape on the page, and its size. Use the **Lock Position** property to prevent these from being changed (for example, by accidentally clicking on the text box in the *WYSIWYG Editor*). The **Layer** property is assigned automatically, and determines which objects appear on top of which other objects (the higher the number, the nearer the top the object appears). You cannot change this property directly, but can influence it by moving the relative position of the object in the *Objects* list.
Link	These properties allow you to define the object as a hyperlink, so that another file is opened when you click on the shape.
New Window Properties	These properties allow you to define the format of the window in which any linked file is opened. You would only use this category if you also use the *Link* category.

Actions	Use the properties in this category to assign events to the various actions that can be performed against the image (including on click, on mouse roll-over/roll-out, on show/hide, and on visible/hidden).
Animation	Use the properties in this category to assign default animation effects to the object. Specifically, you can specify an effect to use when displaying ('animating in') the object, and an effect to use when hiding ('animating out') the object. Animation is discussed further in *Basic animation through Actions* on page 275.
Documentation	This category contains a single property—**Show in Documentation**—that you can deselect to prevent this object from appearing in any documentation output in which the Book Page is included.

The Shape Value property

The **Shape Value** property is interesting in that what it does depends upon the type of shape to which it applies. In general terms, it defines one attribute (x) of a shape as a percentage of another attribute (y)—typically the distance from the center line to the outer edge of the shape. This is better understood visually, so the following images show where these two attributes (x) and (y) are measured. The **Shape Value** property is then determined to be **(x) as a percentage of (y)**.

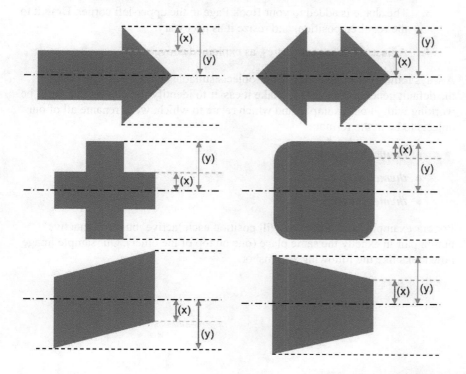

▲ Note that although all shapes have a **Shape Value** property, for some shapes (such as squares, circles, polygons, and triangles) this property has no effect. The examples shown here are a sample of the shape types that *do* have working **Shape Value** properties. (And yes, the single-arrow and double-arrow versions *are* implemented inconsistently.)

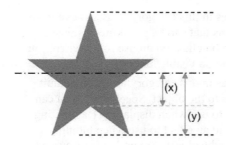

Inserting shapes

For our example page, we want to provide four buttons: one for each of the graphic images we have. To make things simple for our users, we want these buttons to have an 'active' (darker) appearance when the image associated with that button is displayed, and an 'inactive' (lighter) appearance when another image is displayed. This means that we effectively need *eight* buttons: four for the 'active' state, and four for the 'inactive' state.

To insert a shape into your Book Page, carry out the following steps:

1. Click on the **Insert Shape** button on the *Book Editor Toolbar*, to display the list of available shapes.

2. Click on the shape that you want to insert.

3. The shape is added to your Book Page in the upper-left corner. Drag it to the required position, and resize it as necessary.

4. Adjust the shape properties, as explained above.

Always remember to give all of your objects suitable names (don't just rely on the default generated name). To make it easier to identify the objects that we'll be working with in our example, and which relate to which, we'll rename all of our objects to be in the format:

*   *theme*_**Screenshot**

*   *theme*_**Active**

*   *theme*_**Inactive**

For our example Book Page, we will position each 'active' button / 'inactive' button pair in exactly the same place (one on top of the other). Our sample image now looks like the following screenshot.

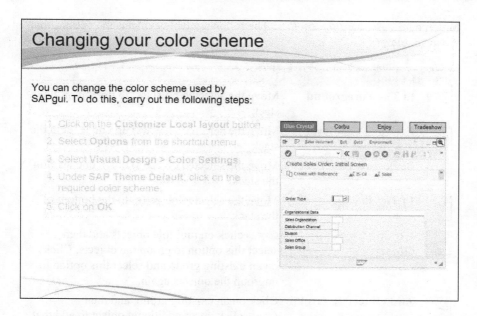

Now for the hard part: displaying the relevant image, depending on the button on which the user has clicked. We'll look at how to do that in *Using Groups* on page 288, but first, we'll look at some functionality that will make that easier, in the next section, *Organizing your Objects*.

Organizing your Objects

There are two key things that you can use to organize the objects on your page: **Groups** and **Layers**. You can use Layers to define which objects are 'in front of' or 'behind' other objects on the Book Page. You can use Groups to perform actions (such as Show and Hide) for multiple objects at the same time.

Using Layers

As you have probably noticed as we have been adding new objects to our Book Page, each object is placed in its own layer (the **Layer** property is unique). A layer can be thought of as a transparent sheet the size of the Book Page, which contains a single object on it—positioned where you place it. If you stack all of these sheets on top of each other and look at them, you'll see the complete page.

● Older readers can visualize a stack of viewfoil sheets!

Objects are assigned to layers in the order that they are created, and each new layer is placed 'on top of' the existing layers. This corresponds to the order in which the objects are listed in the *Objects* list. You can change the order of objects by dragging them into the required order in the *Objects* list. You can also reorder objects via the **Change Layer**

■ A **Layer** property value of **1** indicates the lowest level in the stack—effectively, the background.

Change Layer

button on the *Book Editor Toolbar*. The following table explains the options that are available.

Icon	Command	Use
	In The Foreground	Move the selected object(s) to the top of the stack.
	Forward one Level	Move the selected object(s) up one level in the stack.
	Backward One Level	Move the selected object(s) down one level in the stack.
	In The Background	Move the selected object(s) to the bottom of the stack.
	Group / Ungroup Objects	*CTRL*+click on multiple objects and then select this option to group the objects. Click on an existing group and select this option to ungroup the objects again.
	Add Object To Group	Click on an existing group, and then *CTRL*+click on an additional object to add that object to the group.
	Remove Object From Group	Click on an existing group, and then *SHIFT*+click on an object within that group to remove that object from the group.

For our example, we'll keep things simple by placing all our **Active Buttons** in the foreground, and all our **Inactive Buttons** below (behind) them. That way we only need to worry about showing or hiding the relevant 'active' buttons; whenever an 'active' button is hidden, the 'inactive' button underneath it will automatically be displayed—we don't need to worry about showing or hiding the 'inactive' buttons. We'll also select the **Hide** property for the 'active' buttons for all images except for the image that is initially displayed.

Using Groups

■ Unlike in Microsoft PowerPoint, you can still uniquely address objects within a group, as well as being able to address the group as a unit.

You can use Groups to be able to address and affect (show, hide, animate, and so on) multiple objects at the same time.

In our example, because we don't know which image is currently displayed (and therefore which 'active' button should be displayed and which ones should be hidden), we'll set up three groups: one for the active buttons, one for the inactive buttons, and one for the images. We can then show or hide these a Group as necessary, to show or hide all of the objects within the group with a single command.

To group objects on a Book Page, carry out the following steps:

1. Select all of the objects that you want to include in the group. You can either drag a marquee on the *WYSIWYG Editor* that touches them all, or *CTRL*+click on them in the *WYSIWYG Editor* or the *Objects* list.

2. Click on the **Change Layer** button on the *Book Editor Toolbar*, and select **Group / Ungroup Objects** from the drop-down menu.

3. Give the group a suitable name in its **Name** property.

To ungroup objects (that you have previously grouped), simply select the group (it will be shown with a green dotted boundary) and then select **Change Layer | Group / Ungroup Objects** again.

Setting actions for objects

In this section, we will look at how to allow users to perform actions on the Book Page by clicking on objects on the page.

For our example, our basic approach is to define our buttons so that if a user clicks on an inactive color scheme button, the following things will happen:

a. Hide all of the 'active' buttons (it's easier to just hide the group that contains them all, rather than try to figure out which one is currently displayed and hide that).

b. Display the associated 'active' button for the 'inactive' button that the user clicked on.

c. Hide all images (again, it's easier to just hide all of the images and then display the one we want).

d. Display the relevant image for the button that was clicked on.

To set an action for an object, carry out the steps shown below:

1. Select the object for which you want to define an action.

2. Go to the *Actions* property category, and activate the **On Click** property (or one of the other available Actions, as required).

3. Click the **Add** link, and then specify the following information:

    i.   In the first column, use the drop-down control to select the object for which the action should be performed.

    ii. In the second column, use the drop-down control to select the action that should be performed against this object (see the instructions on page 277 for a list of the available actions).

    iii. Repeat steps i and ii for all additional actions that you want to perform when this object is clicked.

For our example page, we set up the following set of actions. (This screenshot is for the **Enjoy_Inactive** button.)

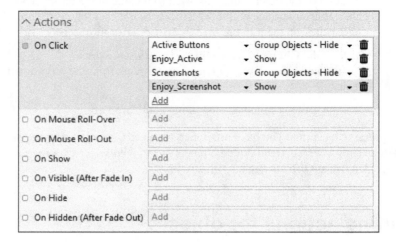

Once we have defined similar actions for all four of our 'inactive' buttons, we will have a completed, working, interactive Book Page! Each time the user clicks on an 'inactive' button, the corresponding 'active' button and image are displayed. Obviously we can't show you this on a printed page (it looks the same as the example provided on page 287), but you can try it yourself; it's really not as daunting as it seems, to set up.

Inserting links

Let's look at some of the other things that you can add to Book Pages. In this section we'll look at how to launch our simulations (or other deliverables) from a Book Page.

Firstly, why would you want to do this? The simplest scenario is that you want to embed simulations into a training course that you have built using Books and Book Pages. Alternatively, as we shall see in *Using a Book Page as an object index* on page 317, you may want to use Book Pages as the launch page for your simulations in the *Trainer*, to provide a more aesthetically-pleasing interface.

Let's look at this by way of another example. Throughout this book, we have been developing a *SAPgui Navigation* course, and earlier in this chapter we created a Book Page that explains how the user can change their color scheme. Suppose we have also recorded a simulation project for this functionality, and now want to include this in our course, as a hands-on exercise.

First, we need a Book Page from which we will launch this simulation. How to build a basic Book Page is covered earlier in this section, so we won't repeat it here. Let's assume that we have built this Book Page, and it currently looks like the example shown below:

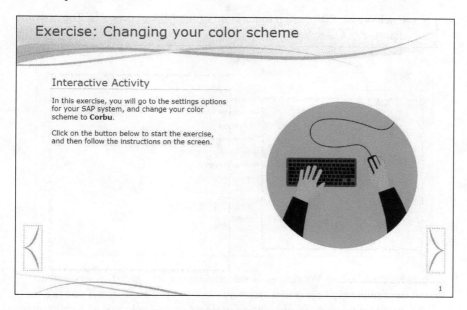

Now we can place a link to the simulation onto this Book Page. To insert a link to a content object in your Workarea, carry out the steps shown below:

1. Click on the **Insert Link** button on the *Book Editor Toolbar*. A panel of available options is displayed.

Insert Link

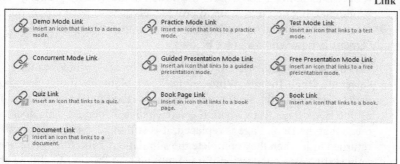

2. Click on the relevant option in this panel for the type of link that you want to add to the page.

    For our example, we want to provide a link to the simulation in Practice mode, so we click on the **Practice Mode Link** option.

3. A button is added to the Book Page. Note that the color and format of this may differ depending on the template (if any) used for the Book Page. Drag this button to the appropriate place on the page.

4.   In the *Object Editor* panel, go to the *Link* category of properties for the new button.

5.   Click on the **Edit** button to the right of the Link to property. The *Link to* dialog box is displayed.

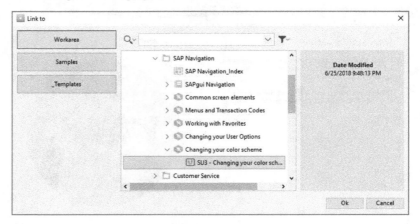

6.   Make sure that **Workarea** is selected on the left, and then navigate to and select the object to which you want to link. Note that if you are providing a link to a simulation project (as we are in this example), you will need to expand the simulation project to see the play modes below it. The only play mode that will be listed will correspond to the mode selected in Step 2.

7.   Click **Ok** to confirm your selection.

8.   If necessary, enter a ToolTip for the button in the **Tooltip** property. This is optional, but you may want to provide a hint as to what will happen when the user clicks on the button—for example, "Practice mode" or "Opens in new window" (see below).

9.   If you want the simulation to open in a new browser window, then select the **Open In New Window** checkbox. Note that if this checkbox is deselected then the simulation will play in the same browser window as the Book Page from which it is launched is displayed. This does not mean that the Book Page is replaced; it is still there, and the user will be returned to it when they complete the simulation. Therefore, you should only really select this option if it is important for the user to still be able to refer to the Book Page (or its containing Book) at the same time as they are carrying out the simulation.

     If you choose to open the simulation in a new window then you should also review the properties in the *New Window Properties* category, and make any necessary adjustments. These properties are explained in *Setting New Window Properties* on page 293.

Your button is now fully-functional, and when the user clicks on it in the *Book Reader*, the object will be launched directly. Note that there is no text associated with the button, so you might want to add a text box alongside this.

Our example Book Page now appears as follows:

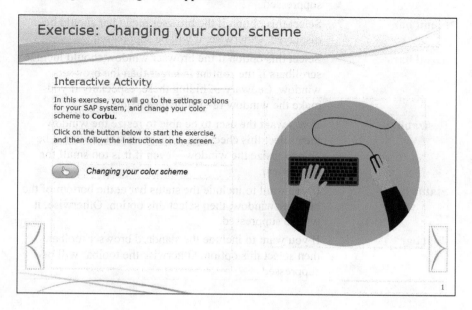

Setting New Window Properties

If you select the **Open In New Window** property for an object link (or any other type of link—whether you are linking to a Workarea object, or an external document or URL), the target of the link will be opened in a new browser window. You can control the format of and features provided for this new window via the *New Window Properties* category of properties for the object link.

The table below lists the properties that are available in this category, and explains their use.

Property	Use
Top / Left	Specify the position (in pixels) of the upper-left corner of the window on the user's screen.
Width / Height	Specify the size (in pixels) of the new window. If you are launching a simulation in Practice Mode or Demo Mode then this should be large enough to hold the simulation and the toolbar.
Fullscreen	Select this checkbox if the window should be launched in full-screen mode (no toolbars, no menus, and so on).

Property	Use
Location bar	Select this option if the browser location bar (which contains the Address field, forward/back buttons, and so on) should be displayed. Otherwise, it will be suppressed.
Menu bar	Select this option if the browser menu bar should be displayed. Otherwise, it will be suppressed.
Scroll bars	Select this option if the browser window should include scrollbars if the content is larger than the browser window. Be \wary of hiding these, especially if you make the window re-sizable (see below).
Resizable	If you want the user to be able to resize the window then select this checkbox. Otherwise, they will not be able to resize the window—even if it is too small for the content.
Status bar	If you want to include the status bar at the bottom of the browser window, then select this option. Otherwise, it will be suppressed.
Tool bar	If you want to include the standard browser toolbar, then select this option. Otherwise the toolbar will be suppressed.

Inserting Media Objects

In addition to building your own animation, you can also add interest by inserting multimedia objects into your Book Pages. You can add:

- Flash animation objects
- Video
- Audio
- 'HTML files' (actually any other type of file, but oddly not an `.html` file)

Audio files are handled a little differently to the other three types of object (which are visible and placed directly onto the Book Page), and so are explained separately in *Chapter 14, Adding Audio to Your Content*.

Note that the "HTML File" object does not actually allow you to insert the content of an HTML file into your Book Page (which would undoubtedly be useful). Instead, it allows you to almost any supported file into your Book Page—although most of these seem to be opened automatically as soon as the Book Page is loaded, so this feature should be used with care.

To insert a Flash object, video, or other file into a Book Page, carry out the steps shown below.

1. Make sure the page onto which you want to insert the object is displayed in the *WYSIWYG Editor* in the *Book Editor*.

2. Click on the **Insert Media Object** button on the *Book Editor Toolbar*, to display the drop-down panel of available media object types.

Insert Media Object

Flash Animation	Video
Insert a flash file in an embedded flash player.	Insert a video file in an embedded video player.
Audio	HTML Document
Insert an audio file.	Insert an HTML document in an iFrame.

3. Click on the required object type from the drop-down panel.

4. A large, rectangular placeholder is placed on the Book Page. Resize and reposition this as necessary.

The object placeholder is initially empty. Its contents and appearance are controlled via the object's properties—just like for any other type of Book Page object. Make sure this placeholder object is selected, so that its properties are displayed in the *Object Editor*, and the continue as follows:

■ Some key properties are shown in the placeholder itself, but you cannot edit them from there; you can only edit them in the *Object Editor*.

5. Enter a suitable name for this object in the **Name** property. This is only used internally to the *Book Editor*, but you will find it helpful to change the default name to something more meaningful.

6. Click on the **Edit** button to the right of the **Source** property, and navigate to and select the file that you want to be displayed on the Book Page (in the frame currently occupied by the placeholder object).

   As with other objects (such as images) you can select a file in your Workarea, or a file on your PC or at another network location (including the Internet). If this is a file that you will use more than once, you should import it into the **Assets** Group of your Workarea and then link to it from there.

7. The remaining properties are object-type-specific. Refer to the relevant section, below:

   Flash objects:

   i. If necessary, select the quality level at which the Flash animation should be played, from the **Quality** property's drop-down list. Note that a higher quality will result in an exponentially larger file.

ii.   Select the way in which information behind the object should (or should not) appear, in the **Window Mode** property.

iii. If the Flash file should start playing as soon as the Book Page is displayed, then select the **Start Automatically** property.

iv.   If the Flash file should be played in a continuous loop, then select the **Repeat** property.

v.   If you want the object to initially be hidden (in which case you will need to control its display via animation or events) then select the **Hide** property.

Video:

i.   You can select up to two alternative sources for the video file, in the **Alternative Source 1** and **Alternative Source 2** properties. If Enable Now cannot find the file at the primary source (specified in Step 6) at display time, it will try the alternative sources. This is useful if the video is on a website out of your control, but you know it is replicated at other locations.

ii.   If you want playback controls (pause, play, and so on) to be included in the video window, then select the **Show Control** checkbox.

iii. If the video should start playing as soon as the Book Page is displayed, then select the **Start Automatically** property.

iv.   If the video should be played in a continuous loop, then select the **Repeat** property.

v.   If you want to prevent users from downloading a copy of the video file, then select the **Hide Download Button** checkbox.

vi.   If you want the object to initially be hidden (in which case you will need to control its display via animation or events) then select the **Hide** property.

HTML file:

i.   If the file should always be downloaded (instead of being displayed in the browser window, where applicable) then select the **Enforce a download of the linked content (Manager)** property. This is useful if you are attaching files that should be saved and not opened (such as executable files or ZIP files).

ii.   If you want the object to initially be hidden (in which case you will need to control its display via animation or events) then select the **Hide** property.

In addition to these basic properties, different media types support different properties in the *Design, Size and Position, Link, New Window Properties, Actions,* and *Documentation* categories. These all work exactly the same way as for other Book Page objects, and are therefore already described elsewhere in this chapter.

Although it's hard to appreciate in a printed book, below is an example of a video media object embedded into a Book Page, as it appears in the Book Reader.

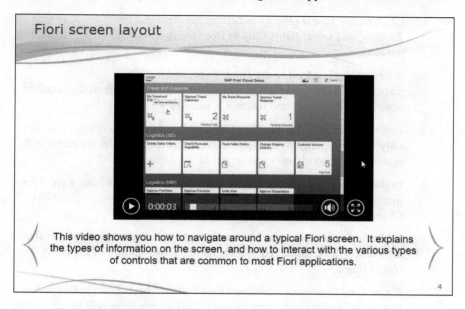

In this example, the **Show Control** property has been selected, and the cursor is currently hovering over the video, so that the video control bar is displayed at the bottom of the video area (it is hidden as soon as the cursor moves off the video).

Inserting a Business Process Model chart

Enable Now provides some very rudimentary business process modeling (BPM) capabilities. Specifically, it allows you to create a (slightly feature-rich) BPM flowchart on a Book Page.

To illustrate this, we'll take a very simple process that should be familiar to most readers of this book: creation of training content using Enable Now. We'll consider this process to be simplified as follows:

1. A Subject Matter Expert records a simulation
2. An Author edits this simulation and makes it classroom-ready
3. The Content Owner reviews and approves it
4. The Training Team Lead publishes the content

Now let's look at how to chart this on a Book Page.

A Business Process Model chart in Enable Now is basically made up of a series of **BPM Object** elements (each of which represents a step in the process), connected via **Connection** elements (which represent the path from one step to the next).

To add one of these elements to your Book Page, carry out the steps shown below.

1. Click on the **Insert Object** button on the *Book Editor Toolbar*, and select **BPM Object** from the drop-down panel.

   Insert Object

2. A new shape is added to the Book Page, and initially positioned in the upper-left corner of the page. Drag this to the required position on the page, and resize it if necessary.

3. Enter a suitable name for this BPM step in the **Name** property. This is only used internally within Enable Now, but using a relevant name will make it easier to identify this object in the *Objects* list.

■ See the example at the end of this section to see where these various elements appear.

4. In the **Process Step** property, enter a short description of this step. Bear in mind this text has to fit within the larger, upper section of the BPM Object shape, so be concise.

5. In the **Role** property, enter the name of the role that carries out this step. This text will be displayed in the smaller, lower section of the BPM object shape.

6. If you need to provide additional information about the step, then enter this in the **Annotation** property field. This information will be accessible to the user via a clickable 'bubble' icon in the upper-right corner of the shape.

7. You can provide a link to another Book Page from the BPM Object. This is useful if the flowchart provides only a simple summary and you expand on each step with further Book Pages. To do this, use the **Link to** property to navigate to and select the Book Page to which you want to link. If a link is provided, then an arrow is shown in the upper-left corner of the shape; the user can click on this icon to jump to the linked page.

8. If necessary, you can attach up to ten additional objects to a BPM object (for example, to provide request forms, sample documents, and so on). These attachments will be accessible via a (single) clickable 'paper clip' icon in the upper-left corner of the shape (clicking on this icon will display a list of the attachments). To attach an object, go to the *Attachments* category of properties, and complete the following fields:

   i. Enter a short text description of the attached file in the **Caption x** field.

   ii. In the **Attachment x** field, navigate to and select the object to attach. You can select any content object in the Workarea, or you can upload a new file from your PC.

   iii. If you want the attachment to be downloaded to the user's PC (instead of the attached file opening in the browser) then select the

Enforce a download of the linked content (Manager) checkbox. This is useful for files that cannot be displayed in the browser, or files that you want the user to have a local copy of.

iv. Repeat steps i to iii for all additional attachments you want to include.

v. If you want files that are opened in the browser (versus those you set to download) to be opened in a new browser window, then select the **Open in New Window** checkbox. Note that this is a single setting that applies to all attachments for the step.

Repeat the above steps to add BPM Objects for all of the steps in your process. You can then connect these by adding Connection elements, as follows:

1. Click on the **Insert Object** button on the *Book Editor Toolbar*, and select **Connection** from the drop-down panel.

2. A line is drawn on the Book Page, and initially positioned in the upper-left corner of the page. Drag this so that it is linking two of the BPM Object boxes.

   Note that these connectors do not 'glue' to the BPM Object boxes (although they will snap to the edges), so if you move the boxes you will have to manually move the connectors.

   Note also that connectors cannot 'turn corners', and you cannot draw a diagonal connector (only pure horizontal or vertical connectors). This means that if your flowchart is more than a simple one-row linear progression, you will need to connect multiple connectors together, at right-angles, to connect some boxes.

3. The connector line will initially not have arrowheads. You will normally want arrowheads, so use the **Arrow Head 1** (left end) and **Arrow Head 2** (right end) fields to select the type of arrow head to use. You can change the size of the arrowheads in the *Advanced* category of properties.

4. Repeat these steps for all additional connections that you need to make between your BPM Objects.

Let's assume that we have now completed our rudimentary Business Process Model flowchart, and that our Book Page now appears as follows:

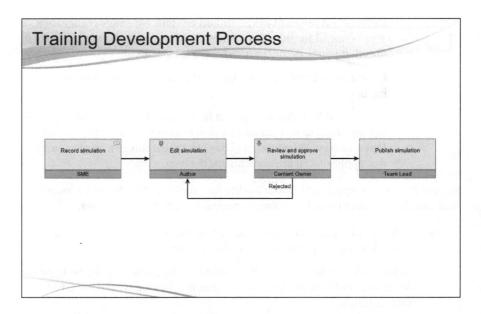

A few things to note about this example:

- We have re-colored the shapes to better match our green Book Page style. The color and formatting options for the process description (in the upper portion of the shape) can be found in the *Design Process* category of properties, and the color and formatting options for the role (in the lower portion of the shape) can be found in the *Design Role* category of properties.

- The first step (the leftmost box) in our process has an annotation.

- The second step has an attachment.

- The third step has a link.

- We have added a 'reject' loop to the third step. We had to use three Connection objects to loop back to the preceding step (but only added an arrow to the last of these). We also added a Text Box object containing the text "Rejected" to clarify the purpose of the loop back.

Additional Object Types

There are a few object types available on the **Insert Object** panel that we have not looked at in our examples above. For the sake of completeness, let's quickly look at these.

Bubble

Bubble objects are extremely similar to Bubbles in simulation projects; they look exactly the same, but there are a few unique properties that we'll look at below. Bubbles are useful if you want to provide 'overlay' information (particularly on screenshots) and want this to match the format used in the associated simulations.

The properties that are available for Bubble objects, and an explanation of how to use them, are described in the table below.

Property	Use
Name	Unique object name, used in the *Objects* list.
Text	The contents of the Bubble.
Title	An optional tittle for the Bubble. For most Bubble Styles, this will be placed in a 'header bar'. For the **Sidebar** style, it will just appear as a bold heading above the Bubble Text.
Style	The Bubble style to use. All styles available in simulation projects are also available here.
Alignment	The position of the Bubble relative to the bubble 'pointer'. This is comparable to the **Orientation** property for simulation Bubbles, but here all 16 standard compass points can be selected, or you can use **Center** to hide the Bubble pointer.
Movable	If this checkbox is selected, the user can move the Bubble, during playback in the *Book Reader*.
Closable	If this checkbox is selected, the user can close the Bubble, during playback in the *Book Reader*. The **Close** button is shown in the upper-right corner of the Bubble (within the 'header bar', if the Bubble style provides this).
Hide	If this checkbox is selected, the Bubble is hidden when the Book Page is initially displayed, and you will need to trigger its display through an action or timer (for example, when the user hovers over the object (or area) to which the Bubble relates).
Opacity	This property can be used to make the bubble background see-through to varying degrees.

An example of a Book Page that includes a Bubble object is shown below.

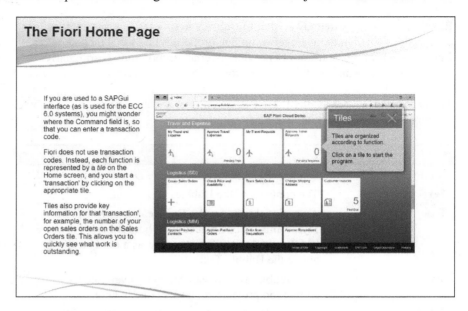

Things to note in this example:

- **Style** is set to **Green Meadow**, to be consistent with our example Book Style.
- A **Title** ("Tiles") has been specified.
- **Closable** is selected.
- **Opacity** is set to **80**.

Active Area

The Active Area object allows you to identify a specific area on your Book Page that can be used to link to something else (such as an external website), or trigger some other action (for example, displaying a Bubble when the user hovers over the Active Area). The Active Area can contain text, and by default is transparent, although all of the usual formatting options can be applied to it.

The table below lists the key properties that are applicable to Active Areas (although most of these are also available with other types of objects).

Property	Use
Name	Unique object name, used in the *Objects* list.
Text	An optional text to show inside the Active Area. This text can be formatted by using the properties in the *Design* category.

Property	Use
Hide Scroll Bars	If the Text content cannot fit within the visible area of the Action Area, then scrollbars will automatically be added to the area. Select this option to suppress the use of scrollbars (and if the text is too large for the area, some text will simply not be visible).
Hide	If this checkbox is selected, the Action Area is hidden when the Book Page is initially displayed, and you will need to trigger its display through an action or timer.
Border Style	If necessary, you can select one of the predefined border styles to use with the Action Area.

⋆ Border Styles are defined in **Resources | Adaptable Resources**, and have an Object Type of **frame_style**.

To have the Action Area link to another file, website, or object, use the properties in the *Link* category and the *New Window Properties* category, if necessary (see *Inserting links* on page 290). To trigger some other action, use the properties in the *Actions* category (see *Setting actions for objects* on page 289).

Text Pop-Up

A Text Pop-Up allows you to provide additional information in a text box that is displayed in response to an 'info' icon being clicked (or hovered over). You could achieve the same thing with an image, a Bubble, and some basic action triggers, but this built-in functionality does all of the hard work for you.

The table below lists the key properties for the Text Pop-Up object, and explains how to use them. Note that there are a lot of other 'common' properties that can also be used with Text Pop-Up objects, as explained elsewhere in this chapter.

Property	Use
Name	Unique object name, used in the *Objects* list.
Text	The text that is to be shown in the pop-up. Note that you can use all of the simulation Bubble formatting options in this field, including adding tables, images, and placeholders. See *Adjusting Bubble text* on page 111 for details.
Pop-Up Style	By default, the pop-up will use a style that is visually compatible with the Book Page Style, but if necessary you can select one of the other available styles via this property.

⋆ The **Pop-up Styles** and **Type** icons are defined in **Resources | Adaptable Resources | Book ***, and have an Object Type of **popup_style**.

Property	Use
Type	This property controls the visual appearance of the icon that is clicked on (or hovered over) to display the Text Pop-Up. This can be one of the following: **Tip**　　**Standard**　　**More Info** The color is taken from the Book Page Style, and cannot be changed.
Title	An optional title for the pop-up. This will be placed in a 'header bar'.
Hide Scroll Bars	If the Text content cannot fit within the visible area of the pop-up box, then scrollbars will automatically be added. Select this option to suppress the use of scrollbars (and if the text is too large for the area, some text will simply not be displayed).
Show on Roll-Over	By default, the pop-up box will be displayed when the user clicks on the pop-up icon. If you want the pop-up to be displayed as soon as the user hovers the cursor over the icon, select this option.
Fade In/Out	By default, the pop-up box will be displayed instantly, as soon as the user clicks on (or hovers over) the icon, and be hidden as soon as the user re-clicks on the icon (or moves the cursor off it). If you select this option, then the bubble will fade in and fade out.
Hide Pop-up in Editor	Because the Text Pop-Up is typically overlaid on top of other objects on the Book Page, this can make it difficult to edit the objects underneath it. You can select this option to hide the pop-up box (but not the icon) in the editor (only) to make it easier to work with the underlying objects. This does not affect the display in the *Book Reader*.
Hide	If this option is selected, the Text Pop-Up is hidden when the Book Page is initially displayed, and you will need to trigger its display through an action or event.
Shadow	
Show Shadow	Select this option to apply a drop shadow to the pop-up icon. Additional properties for precisely defining the shadow are made available once you select this option. Refer to the description for Book Pages on page 265 for more information on these properties.

Property	Use
Text Pop-Up Shadow	
Show Shadow	Select this option to apply a drop-shadow to the pop-up box itself. Additional properties for precisely defining the shadow are made available once you select this option.

By default, the pop-up box is displayed overlaying the icon. You may prefer to have the pop-up box shown clear of the icon, to make re-clicking on the icon (to hide the pop-up box again) easier. To do this, you need to change the position of the pop-up box in the *Text Pop-Up Position* category of properties. This is independent of the icon position, which is controlled by the properties in the *Size and Position* category.

A partial example of a Book Page that includes a Text Pop-Up object is shown below.

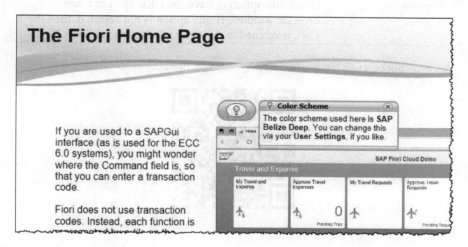

Things to note in this example:

- The **Pop-up Style** was left as the default, to use the Book Page style.
- **Type** is set to **Tip**.
- A **Title** ("Color Scheme") is specified.

QR Code

QR Codes allow you to provide a link (typically a URL) that a user can scan using their mobile device (or other QR reader) to open the link on that device. This is useful for allowing users to open your content (such as a simulation in Concurrent mode) on a second device, while they perform the actions on their primary device.

- QR Codes are also generated by the **Share** button in the *Book Reader* or the *Trainer*.

The table below lists the key properties that are applicable to QR Code objects.

Property	Use
Name	Unique object name, used in the *Objects* list.
QR Code Data	The URL that is encoded into the QR Code.
Hide	If this checkbox is selected, the QR Code is hidden when the Book Page is initially displayed, and you will need to trigger its display through an action or timer.
Open Link on Click	QR Codes are designed to be scanned with a camera or other optical reader. However, your users may not have such a device available. If you select this option then the QR Code effectively works as a link object as well, and the user can click on it to open the destination of the URL.
Open in New Window	If you select the **Open Link on Click** property, then select this option to have the URL open in a new browser window. If this option is not selected, then the URL is opened in the same window as the Book Page.

An example of a QR Code generated by this functionality is shown below:

Advanced Actions

Earlier in this chapter, we looked at the Timer Action object as a way of triggering some basic animation on our Book Page. Enable Now provides a number of other Action types that you can use to provide further animations and interactions on your Book Pages. In this section, we'll look at what these are, and how to use them.

Using a Counter

● Technically, you can use multiple trigger objects, but that scenario is better suited to a Collector object, covered later in this chapter.

The Counter object allows you to trigger different actions based on the number of successive clicks made on a specific object. Each click on the 'trigger object' increases the counter, and then a different action can be assigned to each 'count' (value of the counter).

Let's look at this through an example of a simple scenario. We'll re-work our *Changing your color scheme* Book Page to allow the user to 'page through' the sample images on the page using a single button, instead of having to click on individual buttons for each image. First, we'll remove the existing buttons above the screenshots, and replace them with a single Next button. We'll also add a text to identify the currently-displayed theme. Our page then looks like this:

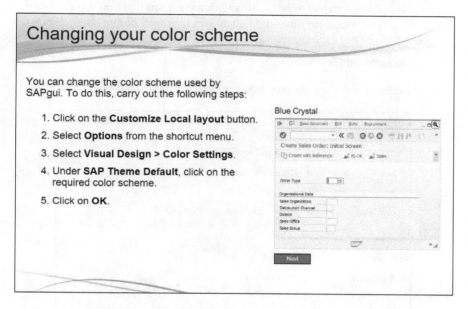

To use a Counter object on your Book Page, carry out the steps shown below.

1. Click on the **Insert Action** button, and select **Counter** in the drop-down panel. A Counter object is added to the page, and appears on the upper-left, outside of the page display area.

Counter object

First, you need to set the actions for the Counter. (Actually, whether you set the counter or the trigger objects first doesn't really matter, but it's more logical to define the Counter first as you should give the Counter a logical name that you will then select when defining the triggers.) Continue as follows:

2. Make sure the Counter object is selected, to display its properties.

3. Enter a suitable name for the Counter in the **Name** property.

4. In the first (or next free) **Count** field, select the value that the counter should have, to trigger the action you will specify in the next step.

5. In the first (or next free) **On Count** field, select the action that is to be performed when the Counter reaches this value, as follows:

    i. Click on the **Add** button to add a new action entry.

> ii. In the first column, select the object against which you which you want the action to be performed (for example, the image that will be displayed).
>
> iii. In the second column, select the action that should be performed against this object.
>
> iv. Repeat steps i to iii for all additional actions that you want to be performed for this action count (for example, hiding other objects).

6. Repeat Steps 4 and 5 for all additional count values (you can specify up to eight values).

For our example, our Counter properties are now defined as follows:

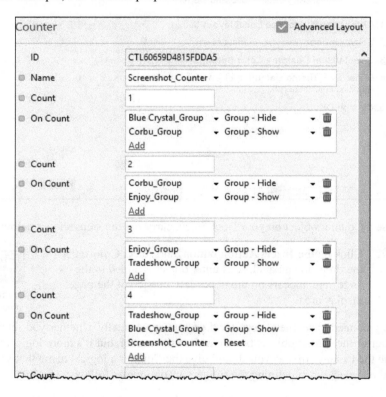

Note that for each click on the button we hide the currently-displayed theme, and then show the next one. When the last image is displayed, we show the first one again, and then reset the counter (to **0**)—this will allow the user to cycle through again. We have also used Groups (see *Using Groups* on page 288) for each screenshot/label combination, to simplify the process.

■ If you initially set a Group to **Hide**, you should make sure that the objects within the Group are *not* set to **Hide**, otherwise even though you show the Group, the objects within it will remain hidden because of their own **Hide** properties.

Once you have set up your Counter object, you can set up the triggers. Thankfully this is a little easier, as we only have one triggering object. Continue as follows:

7. Click on the object that you want to increase the counter, and go to its *Actions* property category.

8. In the **On Click** field, specify the action that should be performed when this object is clicked, as follows:

i. Click on the **Add** button to add a new action entry.

ii. In the first column, select your Counter object.

iii. In the second column, select **Count Up**.

- Unfortunately, there is no **Count Down** action.

For our sample exercise, we have set up our Next button to be the trigger object. Its properties are now set as follows:

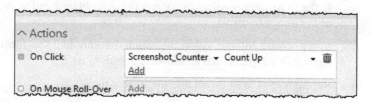

And that's it! We have now effectively created a slideshow within our Book Page! (Obviously, we can't show it here, but you should be able to recreate it yourself easily enough.)

Using a Collector

The Collector object allows you to use multiple objects to trigger one or more actions against other objects. It is similar to a Counter, in that actions are triggered based on the number of collective clicks (or 'flags') on the various trigger objects, but the Collector object is different in that each trigger 'flag' can only be used once. This presents some interesting possibilities—although it is limited in that there are only ten possible 'flags'.

Let's look at this by way of a slightly-more complex example. Let's say we want to provide a quick interactive example of how to match incoming payments against an invoice. Users are required to select a combination of payments that will match the value of the invoice. We'll do this by creating a Collector object that will represent the 'value of the invoice consumed', and then trigger one or more 'flags' for this, depending on the payment the user clicks on—so the higher the value of the payment, the more 'flags' are triggered. Each successive flag will trigger the display of an additional graphic that represents a portion of the invoice being 'matched' by the selected payment.

To set up a Collector Action object on your Book Page, carry out the following steps.

1. Click on the **Insert Action** button, and select **Collector** in the drop-down panel. A Collector object is added to the page, and appears on the upper-left, outside of the page display area.

Collector object

2. Make sure the Collector object is selected, to display its properties.

3. Enter a suitable name for the Collector object in the **Name** property.

■ Most commonly., a 'flag' is triggered by an object being clicked, but as we shall see in this example, clicking on a single object can trigger more than one flag.

4. In the first (or next free) **Count** field, select the number of 'flags' that will trigger this specific action.

5. In the **On Count** property, specify the action (or actions) that should be carried out when this number of flags have been triggered, as follows:

   i. Click on **Add** button to add a new action entry.

   ii. In the first column, select the object that should be acted upon (such as the image to display).

   iii. In the second column, select the action that should be performed against this object (such as showing or hiding it).

   iv. Repeat steps i to iii for all additional actions.

6. Repeat Steps 4 and 5 for all additional flag value that you want to use as triggers.

In our example, we have seven objects, representing $10 increments of the invoice amount, and the display of each of these is triggered by a separate count. Our Collector's properties therefore appear (in part) as follows:

■ "1/6" and "2/6" are simply our object names, reflecting the portions of the 'invoice' object filled.

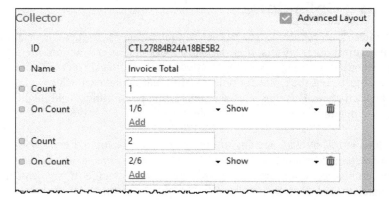

Now you need to specify which flags will be triggered by which objects. Continue as follows:

7. Click on the trigger object, and go to its *Actions* property category.

8. In the **On Click** property, select the flag(s) that should be triggered when this object is clicked on, as follows:

   i. Click on **Add** button to add a new action entry.

   ii. In the first column, select your Collector object.

   iii. In the second column, select the flag that should be triggered when this object (selected in Step 7) is clicked on.

iv. Repeat steps i to iii for all additional flags.

It is important to understand that a 'flag' does not correspond to a specific 'count' in the Collector object. Although there are ten flags, each flag will increase the counter by 1. You can use the same flag for multiple objects, but each flag can only be triggered once—which means that if a flag has been triggered by one object to which it is assigned, it then becomes 'inactive' for any other objects to which it has been assigned and cannot be triggered again by those objects.

9. Repeat steps 7 and 8 for all additional objects that you want to trigger flags for this Collector object.

In our example, we set up each 'payment' object to trigger the number of flags corresponding to the payment amount. This will then show the invoice amount being 'consumed' by the selected payment(s). Our properties for our $40 payment with therefore appear as follows:

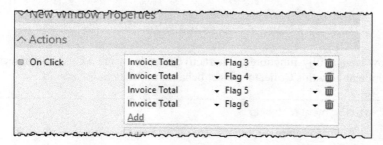

Note that because there are only ten available triggers, we had to do some creative assignment of these to the trigger options (which is why we do not just trigger Flags 1, 2, 3, and 4 for a $40 payment), so that a combination of small payments can be selected.

If necessary, you can also create a mechanism for 'resetting' the Collector object. This will clear all of the flags, so that the user can try again. Note that you will likely also need to 'undo' any actions performed by the Collector count triggers (such as hiding all of the objects that were displayed in response to the various Count actions).

To reset a Collector object, carry out the following steps:

1. Click on the object that will reset the Collector (such as a "Try Again" button in our example), and go to the *Actions* property category.

2. In the **On Click** property, define the reset for the Collector, as follows:

i. Click on **Add** button to add a new action entry.

ii. In the first column, select your Collector object.

iii. In the second column, select **Reset**.

3. Add any further actions, to undo the actions triggered by the Collector object, as necessary.

For our example Book Page, we will add a button below the Invoice object that resets the Collector, and hides all of the 'invoice increment' objects. Our properties for this button are defined as follows:

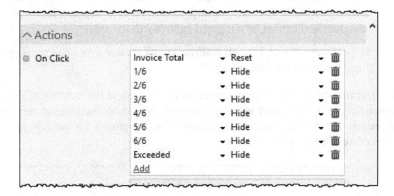

We now have a fully-functioning interactive exercise using a Collector object. Let's look at how this Collector object behaves in the *Book Reader*.

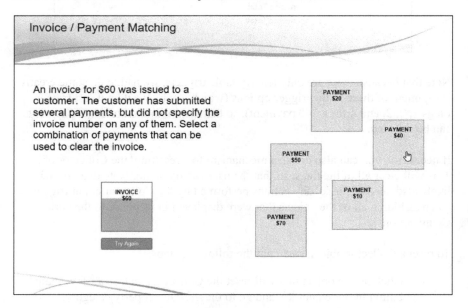

In this example, the user has clicked on the $40 payment. This triggered four flags (as noted above), which gave us a count of 4, which means that the first four of our 'invoice increment' objects (the green bars in the Invoice box) are displayed. Note that each Count value is triggered in turn—so triggering four flags will trigger the Count 1, Count 2, Count 3, and Count 4 events in the Collector.

The user can click on any combination of the payments and are told if they exceed the invoice quantity (by a red 'invoice increment' object displayed on Collector Count 7). At any point, they can click on the Try Again button to restart.

Using Object Visibility

The Object Visibility object allows you to control the visibility (or not) of a number of (usually related) objects in a fairly simplified manner. You can achieve the same thing in a variety of other ways, but what makes this object useful is that only one of the objects assigned to this control is displayed at a time, and the control takes care of ensuring that all of the other objects associated with this control are hidden (so you do not need to define **Hide** actions yourself).

Again, let's look at this by way of a simple example. We'll amend our *Changing your color scheme* Book Page again, so that instead of clicking on the Next button (which we set up in *Using a Counter* on page 306), we'll allow users to click on the actual screenshots themselves to page through the images.

To use an Object Visibility Action object on your Book Page, carry out the following steps.

1. Click on the **Insert Action** button, and select **Object Visibility** in the drop-down panel. An Object Visibility object is added to the page, and appears on the upper-left, outside of the page display area.

Object Visibility object

2. Make sure the Object Visibility object is selected, to display its properties.

3. Enter a suitable name for the Object Visibility object in the **Name** property.

4. If you want the images to fade in and out when they are triggered for display, then select the **Fade In/Out** property.

5. In the **Object x** fields, select up to ten objects (or object groups) for which you want to trigger the display.

For our sample exercise, we will assign our four screenshot/label groups to this Object Visibility Action object. The properties for this are therefore defined as follows:

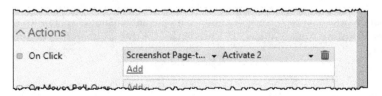

Next, you need to define the trigger actions for each of these objects (in our case, to trigger the display of the next screenshot in the sequence). Continue as follows:

6. Select the **Hide** property for all but the first of the objects assigned to this Object Visibility object.

● You can't set an **On Click** action for a Group—you need to select an object within the Group.

7. For each object, set the 'on click' action to display the *next* object, as follows:

   i. Select the object, to display its properties, and go to the *Actions* category.

   ii. In the **On Click** property, click on **Add** to add a new action row.

   iii. In the first column, select your Object Visibility object.

   iv. In the second column, select the **Activate x** value corresponding to the **Object x** assigned to this Object Visibility object. Make sure that you are selecting the *next* image to be displayed—so for the object defined as **Object 1** in your Object Visibility object, you would select **Activate 2** here.

   Repeat this step for all objects assigned to the Object Visibility object.

In our example, the properties for our first object now appear as follows:

Now, in our example, when the user clicks on a theme screenshot the screenshot (and name) for the next theme is displayed. And because we set the action for the last screenshot to display the first one again, the user can loop through as many times as they like.

Our example page now looks as shown below. Note that we also added a text to tell the users that they need to click on the screenshots to scroll through—otherwise they may never realize that's what they have to do.

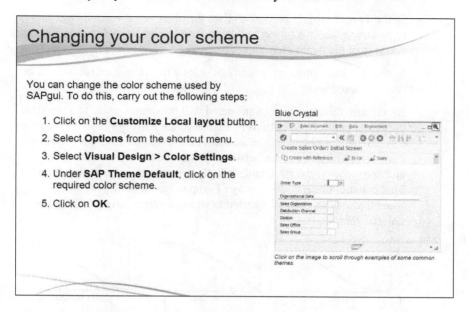

Again, you can't really appreciate this on the printed page, but it is easy enough to recreate it, if you want to create it for yourself.

Using an Animation object

The Animation Action object allows you to move and/or resize an object on the Book Page. This object can be an image, shape, media object, or even a text box.

To use an Animation object on your Book Page, carry out the steps shown below.

1. Click on the **Insert Action** button, and select **Animation** in the drop-down panel. A light-blue rectangle is added to the Book Page, and positioned on the upper-left of the page.

2. This rectangle represents the 'end position' of the object that you will animate. Drag it to the required location, and resize it if necessary, by dragging the handles on its boundary.

Tip:
If you only want to move the object, and do not want to resize it, then you should make sure that the Animation object rectangle is exactly the same size as the object to which it will be applied. The easiest way to do this is to position it on top of the object, and resize it so that the edges of the Animation object snap to those of the object itself.

3. Enter a suitable name for the object in its **Name** property. As always, this should be meaningful, as you will need to select this name when defining the animation trigger.

4. In the **Target Object** property, select the object on the Book Page that is to be animated. This object will be moved and/or resized to the location and size of the Animation object rectangle.

5. In the **Duration** property, specify how long the animation (move and/or resize) should take.

■ Watch a demonstration of the various Easing options.

6. By default, the object being animated will move and resize at a constant pace. You can use the options available on the **Easing** property to change this, so that the object accelerates and decelerates at different speeds over time. You can choose between Quadratic, Sine, or Cubic easing, and apply this to the start, end, or both start and end of the animation. This is better understood by way of graphs, so the following images show the various options, charted to show distance traveled (d) by the object over time (t).

Sine In	Sine Out	Sine In/Out
Quadratic In	Quadratic Out	Quadratic In/Out
Cubic In	Cubic Out	Cubic In/Out
None		

7. Select the **Show Debug Information** checkbox to display a time counter during preview playback. This can be useful to check where the object appears after a specific period of time. This will not be displayed in the *Book Reader*.

You have now added animation to your object. Note that you will still need to trigger this animation—on page load, on a timer, or in response to some other action or event.

An example of a Book Page to which an Animation object has been added—as it appears in the Book Editor—is shown below. In this example, the avatar image will grow to occupy the area identified by the larger, light-blue box.

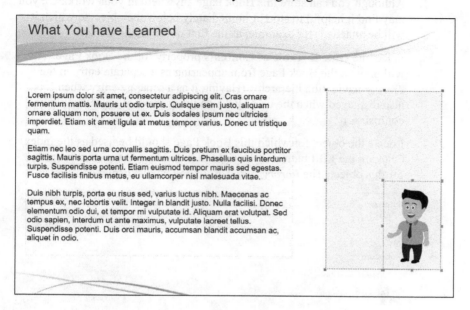

Using a Book Page as an object index

Within the *Trainer*, when a content object is selected in the navigation hierarchy, its details, including its **Short Description**, **Description**, and play mode buttons are displayed on the rightmost side of the *Trainer* screen. Although you can include a reasonable amount of feature-rich information (including tables, images, and text formatting) in either or both of these fields, they are still largely text-based. If you want to make a bit more of a splash, then you can display a Book Page in this area, instead.

This is a great way of adding a touch of interest and (perceived) 'professionalism' to your *Trainer*—especially for Groups, which don't really have content of their own. However, bear in mind that the default index page for content objects contains the 'play mode buttons' that let you launch the content objects. If you replace the default index page for a simulation with a Book Page, you need to implement these buttons yourself (thankfully Enable Now makes this very easy, as explained in *Inserting links* on page 290).

To use a Book Page as the index page for a Group or content object, carry out the steps shown below.

1. Create the Book Page that you want to use as the index, as explained in this chapter. You can name this Book Page anything you like (the name will not be visible in the *Trainer*), but you may find it useful to give it

the same name as the object to which it will be attached, suffixed with "**_index**".

2. Although you can store this Book Page anywhere in your Workarea, you may find it helpful to store it immediately below the object to which it will be attached (for example, as the first object in the Group).

3. Select the **Hide in Table of Contents** property for the Book Page. This will prevent the Book Page from appearing as a separate entry in the *Trainer* navigation hierarchy. (Having it as a separate entry when it is also displayed when the user clicks on the associated object would be confusing.)

4. Locate the object for which this Book Page should be used as the index. Click on the **Edit** button to the right of the **library Autostart** property for this object. The *library Autostart* dialog box is displayed.

A thumbnail image of the selected Book Page is shown on the right-hand slide of this dialog box. You can use this to confirm that you have selected the correct Book Page. You can also click (and hold) on this thumbnail image to show the Book Page full size.

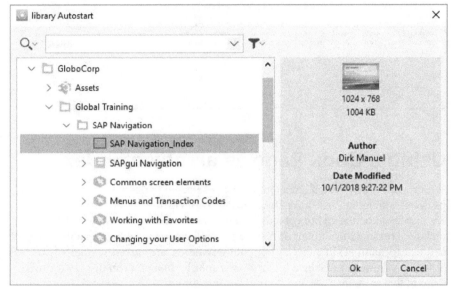

5. Navigate to and select the Book Page that you created in Step 1. If you followed the advice in Step 2, this will be the first thing you see under the current object (as is the case in the example above).

6. Click **Ok** to save your selection.

Now when the user navigates to the object (to which the Book Page has been attached), the Book Page will be displayed instead of the object's **Short Description** and **Description**. An example of this is shown below.

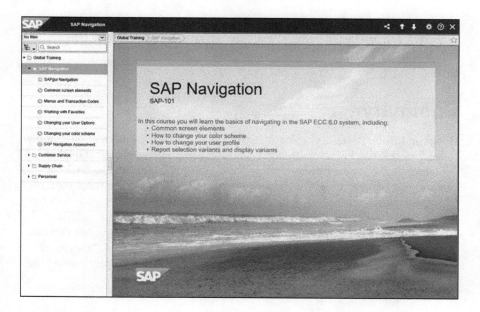

Note that the Book Page is not listed in the Table of Contents—the first thing listed under the **SAP Navigation** Group (to which the Book Page has been attached) is the course Book. This is because we selected the **Hide in Table of Contents** property for the Book Page.

Using a Book Page in a simulation project

You can insert a Book Page into a simulation project, where it acts as a separate step. This is useful if you want to provide some conceptual information (or links to other content) during the playback of a simulation. However, it can disrupt the playback of the simulation, so this feature should be used sparingly.

To insert a Book Page into a simulation project, carry out the following steps:

1. Open the simulation project in the *Project Editor*.

2. Select the existing Step after which the Book Page should appear.

3. Select menu path **Insert | Insert Page Macro | Book Page**. A new Step is inserted into the simulation project. This contains only a single BOOK PAGE macro.

4. Click on the **Edit** button on the left of the **Book Page** property for the BOOK PAGE macro, and navigate to and select the Book Page that is to be inserted.

5. Maintain the other BOOK PAGE macro properties as necessary.

During playback of the simulation, the Book Page will be displayed in the *Book Reader*, within the simulation playback window. The Book Page will appear in the *Progress Bar* (using the name specified in the BOOK PAGE macro's **Name** property), and can be navigated to and selected just like any other Step in a simulation.

Summary

Books and Book Pages are typically used to create 'training presentations' similar to Microsoft PowerPoint presentations and slides. You can add a great deal of content to Book Pages, including text, shapes, images, video, and so on. You can also use triggers, timers, and actions to control how and when these objects appear on the screen.

Books and Book Pages are typically displayed via the *Book Reader*, but you can also use Book Pages as the 'index page' for simulations or Groups. You can also use Book Pages within simulation projects, or as 'stand-alone' objects within the *Trainer* outline.

9
Creating Tests

A necessary component of any training program is ensuring that knowledge transfer has been successful. The surest way of doing this is by testing the trainee to confirm that they do indeed possess the knowledge or skills imparted through the training course. Traditionally, this is achieved through administering a test.

Enable Now provides two possibilities for testing users:

a. Simulations carried out in Test mode

b. 'Written' questions, provided either as a stand-alone test, or embedded within other content as 'knowledge checks'.

In this chapter, you will learn:

- How to prepare a simulation for use in Test mode
- How to create a Quiz
- What types of Quiz Question are available and how to build them

Deciding what to test

Before developing a test it is worth taking a moment to consider what you want to achieve through the use of the test. Do you just want to confirm that the user has consumed the training material, or do you want to confirm that they have obtained the skills and knowledge taught by the training material? This is an important distinction.

Most of the time you are probably building training for users in the corporate workplace. These are adults who, in theory, are capable of taking responsibility for their own work and their own education. So you *should* be able to just have a one-question 'attestation' at the end of training of "I confirm that I have received and understood this training". Alternatively, if you are using a Learning Management System, you may be able to simply track that the material has been viewed, and take this as confirmation.

In some cases, such simple confirmations may be sufficient. However, it may be that you are 'certifying' users as having a certain level of knowledge, or being able to perform certain tasks, and in these cases you absolutely need to confirm that they do indeed have this knowledge or ability. Here, you will want a robust test that covers all aspects of the training material.

You should also consider what the 'pass mark' should be set to. Quite often, the default pass mark for computer-based tests is 80%. This is reasonable with a simulation of a software application, where an errant mouse-click (or, more likely, the tester trying to perform an action in a way that is valid, but not the exact one that was captured in the simulation recording) is unfortunate but not the end of the world. However, with a plant control system, this could be disastrous, and in these cases, you might consider anything less than 100% accuracy to be a failure. Even with question-based tests, if you set the pass mark to 80% a user (or more likely an auditor or controls specialist) could reasonably ask which 20% of the material is irrelevant and doesn't even need to be remembered.

That said, you don't really want a user to fail—effective training is the transfer of knowledge, and if the user does not have the requisite knowledge after completing the training, then this could be a failure of the training, and not necessarily a failure on the part of the user. Furthermore, if a user fails (or repeatedly fails) this will disenfranchise them from trying again, and possibly from taking any of the training material again. For go-live training, it is sometimes just as important for the user to leave training feeling confident and empowered—especially if they will have additional support in the system (for example, through in-application help, such as Desktop Assistant or Web Assistant).

You should also consider the use of tests for 'pre-testing' (or 'testing out') for courses, whereby if a user takes a test before taking the associated course and passes the test, then they do not need to take the course at all—because they have verified that they already have the knowledge being taught by the course. In these cases, the test must absolutely cover all of the training material.

Regardless of the purpose of your testing, SAP Enable Now includes the functionality to meet these needs. In the following sections, we will look at this functionality.

Editing a simulation for Test mode

All simulation projects can be carried out in Test mode—they just need to be saved in Test mode format. This is typically the case by default, but if not, you can 'activate' Test mode for any simulation by selecting menu option **Tools** |

Settings, navigating to **Producer** | **Save** | **Project Overrides**, and then selecting the **Test** checkbox under *Simulation*. This will then ensure that the Test mode output is generated whenever you save this simulation project.

It is important to understand that there are no Bubbles displayed in Test mode. Instead, all instructions must be provided via the **Task Description**, which is defined in the properties for the SIMULATION START macro. This is displayed in an 'always on top' *Task* dialog box when the simulation is launched (in Test mode), and remains displayed until either the user closes it or the test ends.

All of the properties available for the SIMULATION START macro are listed in the table below, along with descriptions of how each of them should be used for Test mode.

Property	Use
General Properties	
Comment	You can enter a text comment for the START macro in this property. This is used internally in Enable Now and is not visible to users in any delivery mode.
	For Test simulations, by default the text shown for the macro in the *Step View* is taken from the **Task Description** property (see below). If text is entered in the **Comment** property then this is used instead (unless preceded by a backslash ("/")—see *Information on the macro bar* on page 106).
UID	The Unique identifier of this macro. This is generated automatically and cannot be changed.
Maximum Score	This is calculated automatically, as the number of *interaction* macros in the simulation, multiplied by 3. There are three possible points available for each interaction. If the user performs the action correctly, they are awarded all three points. Each time they get it wrong, one point is deducted. If they get it wrong three times, they score zero points for the step.
Required Score	This is the number of points the user must score in order to pass the Test. It is calculated automatically as 80% of the **Maximum Score**, but you can change this percentage by clicking on the **Update** button at the top of the *Macro Editor* and then entering the required percentage in the **Minimum Scores** field in the pop-up dialog box.
Application Response Time	This property is not relevant for Test mode.

Property	Use
Task Description	
Task Description	The **Task Description** is displayed during Test mode, as a replacement for the bubbles that are displayed in other modes. It is therefore extremely important that **all** information the user needs to successfully complete the simulation is provided here.
	To help with this, you can auto-populate this field with a list all of the input fields (**Object Name**) and values (**Input Text**) for every STRING INPUT macro in the simulation, by clicking on the **Generate Values for Task Description** button at the top of the *Macro Editor*. However, this information alone will probably not be sufficient, and you will likely need to provide additional instructions on how to navigate through the system—especially if there are multiple valid paths through the application.
Translate Manually	If you do not change the **Task Description** from the default value, then this text (at least the "Use the following data" lead-in sentence can be translated 'automatically' if you port this simulation to another language. However, if you make any changes to the description, you should select this checkbox, to indicate that the description should not be translated automatically. You will then need to arrange for manual translation. See *Chapter 15, Localizing Your Content* for additional information on translating content.
Window Width **Window Height**	Specify the initial width and height of the *Task* dialog during test mode playback. You can also drag the boundaries for the dialog box in the *WYSIWYG Editor*. The user cannot resize the dialog box during playback; if it is too small to accommodate the text then scrollbars will be available.
Orientation	Select the initial position of the *Task* dialog box during test mode playback. This can be set to the eight primary compass points, which correspond to the four corners of the screen and the (center of) the four edges. The user can move the dialog box during playback if necessary—for example, if it is obscuring a part of the screen that they need to see.
Background	Set the background color for the *Task* dialog box.

Property	Use
In Practice Mode	By default, the *Task* dialog box is only visible in Test mode. If you want it to also be visible in Practice mode (in addition to the Practice mode bubbles—unless you explicitly hide these) then select this checkbox. If you are not using Test mode, then this is a good way of providing additional instructions, or perhaps a descriptive 'scenario' to the user for the duration of the simulation.
In Test Mode	By default, the *Task* dialog box (containing the **Task Description**) is visible in Test mode. If you don't want the *Task* description to be displayed, then deselect this checkbox (but be aware that you will almost certainly need to provide instructions some other way (for example, through data sheets or exercise guides).

A partial screenshot of the playback of a simulation in Test mode, showing the *Task* dialog box, is provided below. In this example, only the default (generated) **Task Description** has been used, and the *Task* dialog box has been dragged from its default position along the edge of the screen.

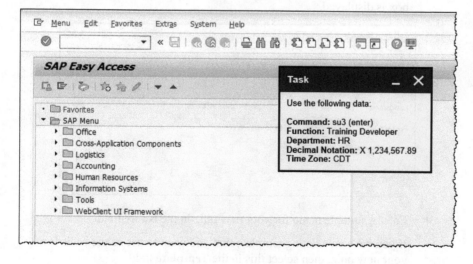

● You cannot change the Bubble style of the Task dialog box (either in the simulation or via style customization).

Creating a Quiz

A Quiz can be created as its own learning object within your Workarea structure, or it can be included within a Book.

To create a Quiz, carry out the following steps:

1. In the *Object Navigation Pane*, click on the Group within which you want to create the Quiz.

2. Click on the **New Object** button on the *Producer Toolbar*, to display the *New Object* dialog box.

3. Click on **Quiz** in the *Rapid Learning* category. The *New Project* dialog box is displayed.

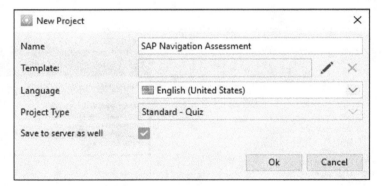

4. Enter a suitable name for your new quiz in the **Name** field.

5. If you have an existing template that you want to use as the basis for your new quiz, then select this in the **Template** field.

6. The **Language** field defaults to your default authoring language. If you want to create your new quiz in another language, then change this field accordingly.

7. The **Project Type** field defaults to **Standard - Quiz** (because you selected **Quiz** in Step 3). Do not change this.

8. If you are creating the Quiz within a server-managed Group, then the **Save to server as well** checkbox is available. Assuming you want your quiz to be saved to the server, then leave this option selected. Otherwise, deselect it and the Quiz will only be created in your local storage. See *Server-managed vs. local objects* on page 34 for additional information on this.

9. Click **Ok**.

A new Quiz project is created and opened in the *Project Editor*. This is exactly the same editor as used for simulation projects, so how to use it will not be repeated here—refer instead to *The Project Editor* on page 104. Instead, we'll look at only those aspects that are specific to Quiz projects.

The project will include a START macro and an END macro, just like any other project. Although there are a few properties of the START macro that look as though they may be applicable to a Quiz (**Maximum Score**, **Required Score**, **Task Description**) these are not actually used for a Quiz—they are used only for simulations—and can be ignored.

Adding questions to your Quiz

It is recommended that you insert a new Step between the two default steps (use menu option **Insert | Add Step**), and place all of your Questions within that single step. This is not strictly necessary (you could have each Question in its own Step), but it will keep your project organized and easy to maintain.

Furthermore, you may want to use a Quiz Section to randomize the order of the Questions and/or randomize the questions presented to the user, and you can only create a Section within a single Step. How to use Quiz Sections is explained in *Defining a Quiz Section* on page 346.

To add a Question to your Quiz, carry out the following steps:

1. Click on the Step within which you want to add the Question.

2. Click on the **Insert Quiz Item** button on the *Project Editor Toolbar*, to display the *Question Type* panel.

Insert Quiz
Item

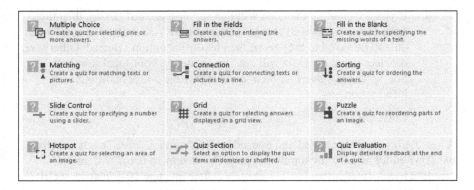

3. Click on the type of Question that you want to add to the Quiz. A brief explanation of each type is shown in the panel, but you may find it helpful to refer to the sections in this chapter for information about, and examples of, each type of Question.

When you add a Question to a Quiz, a macro of this Question type is added to the Step. The *WYSIWYG Editor* appears blank. This is normal—the appearance of the Question is controlled by the Template, and the content is controlled by the Question properties, which are editable via the *Macro Editor*, as usual.

The following properties are common to all Question types, and should be completed as noted. Properties specific to individual question types are explained in the relevant section following this table.

Property	Use
Basic Properties	
Comment	This is purely internal to the Quiz, and does not appear anywhere (not even in the Step View, as is the case for simulation projects).
Template	By default, a Question will use the template (if any) specified for the containing Quiz. If you want to use a different template for this individual Question, then select the template here.
UID	This is the internal identifier of this macro.
Points	Specify the number of points that should be awarded for answering this question correctly. This defaults to **1**, but you can enter any other number, to provide a 'weighting' for Questions. By default, the number of points available for a question is not visible to the user when the Question is displayed, but the user's cumulative points awarded and possible points are typically (depending upon the template used) shown in the lower-left corner of the Question page.

Property	Use
Title	This is a one-line text title for the Question, and is distinct from the question itself. This appears in the Page header during playback, and can be any text you like, but you may find it useful to specify the subject being tested by the Question—especially the Quiz is testing across a range of subjects or topics.
Task	This is the actual question that the user has to answer. The wording of this will depend upon the type of Question, but should clearly and unambiguously explain what the user needs to do, to answer the question correctly.
Options	
Time Limit	If the user should only be given a limited amount of time to answer the question, then enter the number of seconds they have. A countdown will be displayed to the user (unless this has been suppressed by the template). Make sure you provide enough time to read the question and answers, as the countdown will start as soon as the Question is displayed.
Media	
Media File	You can include a media file—a sound clip, image, or a video—in the Question (or in place of the Task text). This is useful if the user is expected to identify a specific sound or object. Use this field to select the media file. This can be a file in your Workarea, or a file from your PC.
Width **Height**	If necessary, specify the overall width and height of the media. Note that the media will initially be displayed as a fixed-size thumbnail, and will only be displayed at the size specified here (over the top of the Question page) if the user chooses to display it larger.
Show Instead of Task	If the selected media file is to be displayed instead of (as opposed to as well as) the Task text, then select this checkbox.
Feedback	
Show Feedback	If the user should be provided with feedback as soon as they answer the question to indicate whether they got the question correct or wrong, then select this checkbox. If you do not provide feedback at the question level, then you should use a QUIZ EVALUATION macro at the end of the Quiz, to provide feedback then. See *Inserting a Quiz Evaluation* on page 348 for details.

Property	Use
Quiz Passed	You can use this property to provide specific feedback to the user if they answered the Question correctly. If you do not specify any text, then only an image (by default, a green check-mark) will be displayed.
Quiz Failed	You can use this property to provide specific feedback to the user if they answered the Question correctly. If you do not specify any text, then only an image (by default, a red cross) will be displayed.
Quiz Timeout	If you set a Time Limit for the Question, then specify the text that is to be displayed if the user does not answer the Question in time. If you do not specify any text, then only an image (by default, a red cross) will be displayed.
Documentation	
Show Title in Documentation	Questions will automatically appear in some output document types. If the Title should also be included in the generated document, then select this checkbox. See *Chapter 12, Working with Documents* for more information on output documents.

Defining a Multiple Choice Question

A MULTIPLE CHOICE Question presents the users with a list of possible answers, and the user has to select the correct answer(s) from this list.

The table below lists the additional properties (over and above those listed at the start of this section) that are applicable to MULTIPLE CHOICE questions, and explains how to use them.

Property	Use
Answers / More Answers	
Answer x	Specify up to eight possible answers for the user to select from.
Answer Correct	Select the checkbox for each answer that is correct. Note that if you only select one correct answer, the user has to select their choice via radio buttons; if you select multiple correct answers, the user selects their choices via checkboxes (but see the Force Multiple Choice property, below).

Property	Use
Options	
Shuffle Solutions	Select this option to shuffle the order on which the possible answers are displayed. This is a useful thing to do if the user will be allowed to take the Quiz multiple times, as it prevents them from just remembering the position of the correct answer.
Force Multiple Choice	Select this option if there is only one correct answer, but you want the list of possible answers to use checkboxes and not the default radio buttons. This is a useful option if you do not want to give the users a clue that there is only one correct choice.

An example of a MULTIPLE CHOICE Question, as it appears during playback, is shown below. In this example, the Question was defined with five possible answers and only one of these is correct. **Force Multiple Choice** was selected, and the **Time Limit (Seconds)** was set to **10**. This screenshot was captured with the answer selected but not committed.

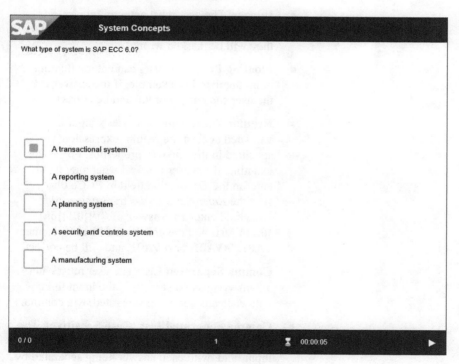

Defining a Fill in the Fields Question

With a FILL IN THE FIELDS question, the user is asked a question, and has to type in their answer. If there are multiple expected answers, multiple input fields will be available—unless you set the **Input Type** to **Comma Separated List**, in which case only one input field will be provided, and the user must enter all answers, separated by commas, in this one field.

The table below lists the additional properties (over and above those listed at the start of this section) that are applicable to FILL IN THE FIELDS questions, and explains how to use them.

Property	Use
Basic Properties	
Input Type	Select the type of input that the user must enter into the input field(s). This can be one of the following: • **Text**: The user must enter the exact text specified in the **Answer** properties. • **Text (case sensitive)**: The user must enter the exact text specified in the **Answer** properties, and the case must match the case of the specified answer(s). • **Integer**: The user must enter an integer. For example, if the answer is **9** and they enter **9.0** they will be marked wrong. • **Floating Point**: The user can enter a floating point number. For example, if the answer is **9** the user can enter **9** or **9.0** and be correct. • **Regular Expression**: The user's input is validated against the regular expression(s) specified in the **Answer** properties. For example, if the user is asked what they would enter in the Transaction field in ECC6.0 to start the *Enter Sales Order* transaction, then you could enter an **Answer** of /[\V]{0,1}[on]{0,1}VA01/ and the user would be able to enter **VA01**, **/nVA01**, or **/oVA01**, and still be correct. • **Comma Separated List**: The user must enter all answers as text strings, in the input field, with each answer being separated by a comma. • **Comma Separated List (Case-Sensitive)**: The user must enter all answers as text strings, in the input field, with each answer being separated by a comma, and the case must match the case of the specified answer(s).
Answers / More Answers	
Answer x	Specify up to eight answers. The user will be required to enter all answers.

An example of a FILL IN THE FIELDS Question, as it appears during playback, is shown below. In this example, the Question was defined with one possible answer, the **Input Type** is set to **Integer**, **Show Feedback** is selected, and a **Quiz Failed** text has been provided. This screenshot was captured after the question was attempted, and the answer was incorrect.

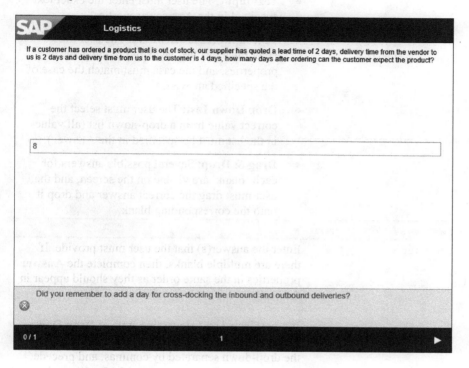

Defining a Fill in the Blanks Question

With a FILL IN THE BLANKS question, the user is presented with a sentence (or set of sentences) and the user has to specify the missing words.

The table below lists the additional properties (over and above those listed at the start of this section) that are applicable to FILL IN THE BLANKS questions, and explains how to use them.

Property	Use
Basic Properties	
Text	Enter the sentence that the user has to complete. For the 'blanks' that the user has to fill in, type three underscores (___).

Property	Use
Interaction	Select the way in which the user should specify their answer(s). The options are:
	• **Text input**: The user must enter the exact text specified in the **Answer** properties.
	• **Text input (case sensitive)**: The user must enter the exact text specified in the **Answer** properties, and the case must match the case of the specified answer(s).
	• **Drop Down List**: The user must select the correct value from a drop-down list (all values in the list must be specified in the **Answer**).
	• **Drag & Drop**: Several possible answers for each 'blank' are visible on the screen, and the user must drag the correct answer and drop it onto the corresponding blank.
Answers / More Answers	
Answer x	Enter the answer(s) that the user must provide. If there are multiple blanks, then complete the **Answer** properties in the same order as they should appear in the **Text**.
	If you selected an **Interaction** type of **Drop Down List**, then enter all of the texts that should appear in the drop-down separated by commas, and precede the correct answer with an asterisk. For example, **A,B,*C,D**
Options	
Shuffle Solutions	Select this option to shuffle the order on which the possible answers are displayed. This is a useful thing to do if the user will be allowed to take the Quiz multiple times, as it prevents them from just remembering the position of the correct answer.
Use Answer 1 Only	If you selected an **Interaction** type of **Drag & Drop** but there is only one blank, make sure that you enter the answers in **Answer 1**, select **Shuffle Solutions**, and then select this property, so that **Answer 1** is recognized as the correct answer.

■ **Drop Down List** and **Drag & Drop** are only effective if you have multiple blanks. (I'd suggest at least three.)

An example of a FILL IN THE BLANKS Question, as it appears during playback, is shown below. In this example, the Question was defined with three blanks and three **Answers**, and with the **Interaction** set to **Text Input**.

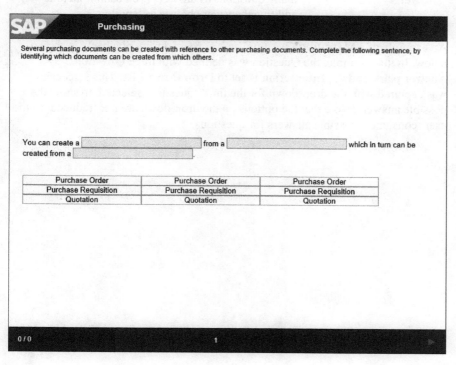

Below is another example of the same question, but with the **Interaction** set to **Drag & Drop**.

Defining a Matching Question

With a MATCHING question, the user is presented with two lists of up to eight words or phrases, and has to pair up the phrases from each list. This can be set up to use drag and drop, or selecting from a pick-list.

The table below lists the additional properties (over and above those listed at the start of this section) that are applicable to MATCHING questions, and explains how to use them.

Property	Use
Basic Properties	
Interaction	Select the way in which the user should specify their answer(s). The options are: • **Drop Down List**: The user must select the correct value from a drop-down list. • **Drag & Drop**: Several possible answers for each 'blank' are visible on the screen, and the user must drag the correct answer and drop it onto the corresponding blank.
Answers / More Answers	
Question x Answer x	Enter the correct pairs of terms. You must have as many questions as answers (you cannot include additional answer choices as 'spoilers').

An example of a MATCHING Question, as it appears during playback, is shown below. In this example, the Question was defined with three **Question / Answer** pairs, and the **Interaction** is set to **Drop Down List**. This screenshot was captured with the drop-down for the third 'question' selected, to show the possible answers. Note that the options on the drop-down are not 'reduced' as the user 'consumes' possible answers for questions.

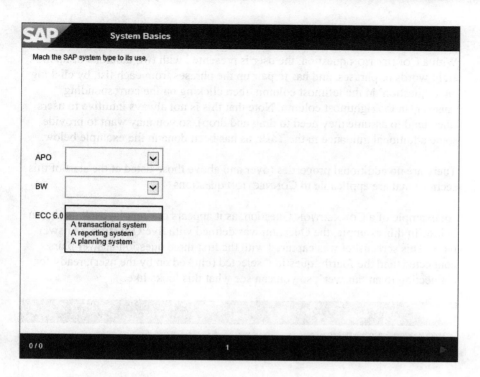

Below is another example of the same question, but with the **Interaction** set to **Drag & Drop**.

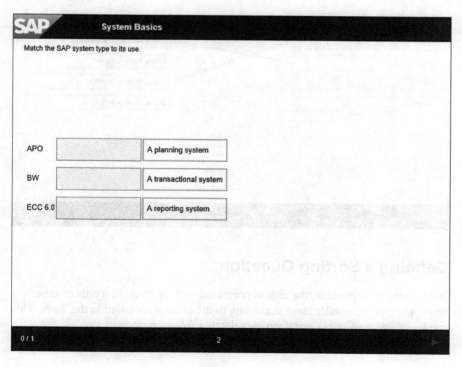

Defining a Connection Question

With a CONNECTION question, the user is presented with two columns of up to eight words or phrases, and has to pair up the phrases from each list, by clicking on a 'question' in the leftmost column, then clicking on the corresponding 'answer' in the rightmost column. Note that this is not always intuitive to users (they tend to assume they need to drag and drop), so you may want to provide some additional guidance in the Task, as has been done in the example below.

There are no additional properties (over and above those listed at the start of this section) that are applicable to CONNECTION questions

An example of a CONNECTION Question, as it appears during playback, is shown below. In this example, the Question was defined with five Question / Answer pairs. This screenshot was captured with the first three question/answer pairs connected, and the fourth 'question' selected (clicked on by the user), ready for connecting to an 'answer', so you can see what this looks like.

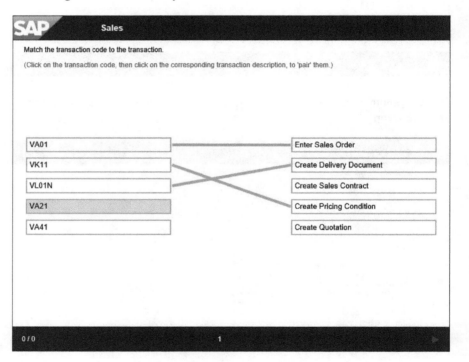

Defining a Sorting Question

With a SORTING question, the user is presented with up to eight words or other texts, and has to re-order these according to the criteria specified in the Task. This can be set up to use drag and drop, or selecting from a pick-list.

The table below lists the additional properties (over and above those listed at the start of this section) that are applicable to CONNECTION questions, and explains how to use them.

Property	Use
Basic Properties	
Interaction	Select the way in which the user should specify their answer(s). The options are: • **Drop Down List**: The user is provided with as many drop-down lists as there are options, and has to select a different option for each of these, in the correct order (top to bottom, or left to right, depending upon the **Alignment** property. • **Drag & Drop**: The user drags the options into the correct order.
Alignment	Select whether the options should be displayed **Horizontally** or **Vertically**.
Answers / More Answers	
Question x **Answer x**	Enter up to eight texts that are to be reordered.

An example of a SORTING Question, as it appears during playback, is shown below. In this example, the Question was defined with five **Answer** options, using an **Interaction** of **Drag and Drop**, and the **Alignment** set to **Vertical**.

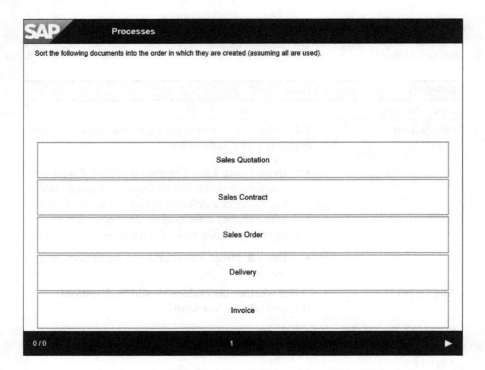

Here is another example of the same Question, but with an **Interaction** of **Drop Down List**, and **Alignment** set to **Horizontal**. This screenshot was captured with the drop-down list for the first option selected, so you can see how that works.

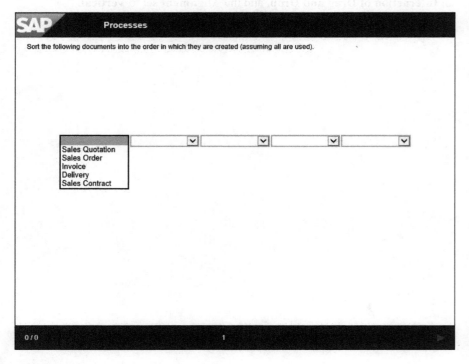

Defining a Slide Control Question

With a SLIDE CONTROL Question, the user answers the question by selecting a numerical value on a slider. The value range can be any range of whole numbers, and can apparently be as large as you like (I've tested 1-1,000,000) but be careful because the slider is not sensitive enough to identify very small percentage changes. Probably 1-100 is as far as you'd want to go. The currently-selected number is shown below the slide control. This type of question is arguably no more effective than a FILL IN THE FIELDS question in that it only accepts a single integer as an answer, but there are perhaps some creative options when combined with media files.

The table below lists the additional properties (over and above those listed at the start of this section) that are applicable to SLIDE CONTROL Questions, and explains how to use them.

Property	Use
Basic Properties	
Range	Specify the range of integers that should be reflected on the slide, separated by a hyphen.
Answer	Specify the correct answer.

An example of a SLIDE CONTROL Question, as it appears during playback, is shown below. In this example, the **Range** was defined as **0-7**, and the **Answer** set to **2**. We also included a **Media File** (an image) in the Question. Note that this is displayed as a 'thumbnail' in the question area. There is an **Expand** button in the upper-right corner of this thumbnail (pointed to by the cursor in this example), which the user can click on this to display the image full size (it will be overlaid on the middle of the page).

This example was taken after the question was attempted. The **Show Feedback** option was selected, and you can see the **Quiz Passed** text at the bottom of the screen. If you do provide feedback at the Question level, it is always worth including more than just "Correct" or "Incorrect"—especially for the **Quiz Failed** text, where you might want to refer the user back to the relevant section of the training material.

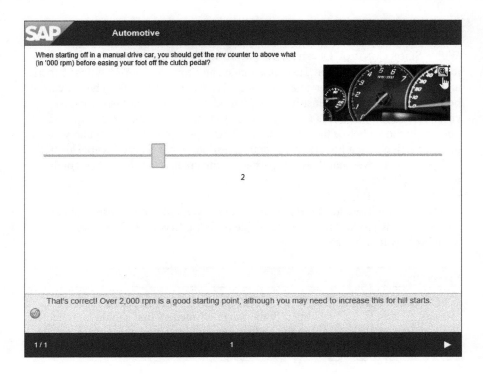

Defining a Grid Question

With a GRID question, the user is presented with a table populated with only row and column headers. The rows can be thought of as questions, and the columns as possible answers, and the user has to select the correct answer for each question, by clicking on the radio button in the relevant column. (Because the cells contain radio buttons, only one answer can be selected in each row or column.) This type of question is useful for categorization tasks.

The table below lists the additional properties (over and above those listed at the start of this section) that are applicable to GRID Questions, and explains how to use them.

Property	Use
Basic Properties	
Possible Answers	Enter all of the possible answers (the column headers in the grid), separated by commas.
Answers / More Answers	
Question x	Enter the 'question' (a row in the grid).
Position of Correct Answer	Enter the number of the column that contains the correct answer for this question.

Property	Use
Options	
Shuffle Solutions	If you want the order of the columns to be randomized each time the Question is displayed, then select this checkbox. Otherwise, leave this option deselected, and the columns will appear in the order defined in the Possible Answers property.

An example of a GRID Question, as it appears during playback, is shown below. In this example, four Questions and three Answers were defined, giving a 4x3 grid. This screenshot was taken after the Question was attempted, to emphasize that only one selection is possible in each row or column.

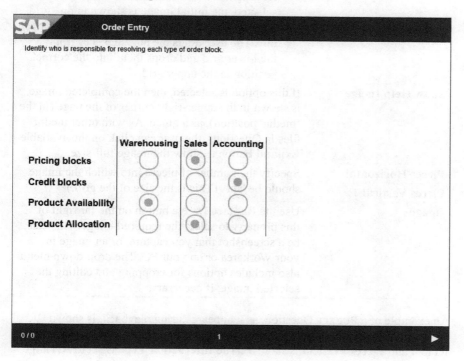

Defining a Puzzle Question

With a PUZZLE Question, the user is presented with a 'jumbled up' image, and has to rearrange the pieces (via drag-and-drop) to form the correct image. This type of Question is useful for testing object recognition—and also for providing a bit more 'fun' than some of the other question types.

The table below lists the additional properties (over and above those listed at the start of this section) that are applicable to PUZZLE Questions, and explains how to use them.

Property	Use
Basic Properties	
Interaction	This property has two options:
	• **Arrange in One Field**: If this option is selected, the initial image is shown in a single grid, and the user must drag and drop the pieces within this grid. (As they drop a piece into a position, the puzzle piece currently in that position is moved into the position from which the piece being dropped was originally dragged.)
	• **Arrange in Second Field**: If this option is selected, the initial image is shown in one grid, and an empty grid is shown immediately above this. The user drags the puzzle pieces from the lower grid and drops them into the correct position in the upper grid.
Show Help Image	If this option is selected, then the completed image is shown in the upper-right corner of the page (in the 'media' position), as a guide. As with other media files in Questions, the user can click on the available **Expand** button to show the image full-size.
Pieces Horizontal **Pieces Vertical**	Specify the number of pieces into which the image should be 'cut'. (This is the size of the grid.)
Image	Use the **Replace Image** button on the far right of this property to select the required image. This can be a screenshot that you capture, or an image in your Workarea or on your PC. The drop-down menu also includes options for cropping and editing the selected image, if necessary.

An example of a PUZZLE Question, as it appears during playback, is shown below. In this example, the image was split into a 4x3 grid (**Pieces Horizontal** is set to **4** and **Pieces Vertical** is set to **3**). The **Interaction Type** is set to **Arrange in One Field**, and the **Show Help Image** checkbox is not selected.

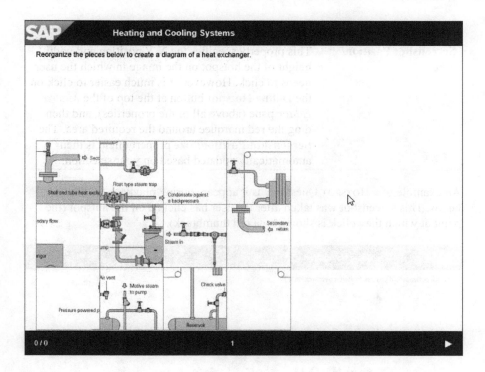

Reorganize the pieces below to create a diagram of a heat exchanger.

0 / 0   1   ▶

Defining a Hotspot Question

With a HOTSPOT Question, the user is required to identify a specific point on an image.

The table below lists the additional properties (over and above those listed at the start of this section) that are applicable to HOTSPOT Questions, and explains how to use them.

Property	Use
Basic Properties	
Image	Use the **Replace Image** button on the far right of this property to select the required image. This can be a screenshot that you capture, or an image in your Workarea or on your PC. The drop-down menu also includes options for cropping and editing the selected image, if necessary.

Property	Use
Screenshot Position/ Size	This property specifies the X,Y position and width/ height of the hotspot on the image in which the user needs to click. However, it is much easier to click on the **Define Hotspot** button at the top of the *Macro Editor* pane (above all of the properties), and then drag the red marquee around the required area. The **Screenshot Position/Size** property field is then automatically updated based on your selection.

An example of a HOTSPOT Question, as it appears during playback, is shown below. This screenshot was taken after the user has clicked on the hotspot (the point at which they click is shown by a red thumbtack).

Defining a Quiz Section

So far, we have looked at how to create the various sorts of Questions that you can include in a Quiz. By default, the user will be required to answer each Question in the Quiz, in the order they are defined. However, there is also a way to randomize the Questions, or to present only a set number of Questions chosen at random from a 'bank' of questions. Both of these things are achieved through the use of a Quiz Section.

To add a Quiz Section, carry out the steps shown below.

1. Make sure all Questions you want to include in the Section are located within the same Step. You can drag Questions into the same Step if necessary.

2. Click on the QUIZ START macro, or on the Question after which the section should start.

3. Click on the **Insert Quiz Item** button on the *Project Editor Toolbar*, and then select **Quiz Section** from the *Question Type* panel.

4. A QUIZ SECTION BEGIN macro is added immediately after the selected element, and a QUIZ SECTION END macro is added as the last macro in the Quiz. An example of this, showing all of the questions defined in this chapter in a single Quiz Section, is shown below.

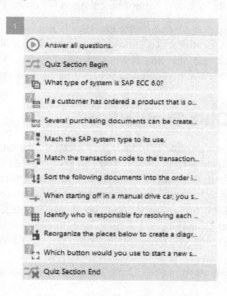

5. Click on the QUIZ SECTION BEGIN macro, to select it and show its properties in the *Macro Editor*.

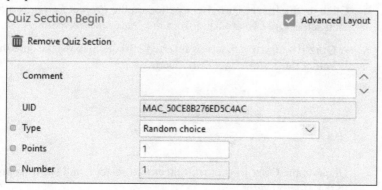

6. In the **Type** property, select one of the following options:

   ♦ **Random Choice**: Select this option to have (only) one Question selected at random from all of the Questions in the Quiz presented to the user.

   ♦ **Shuffle Quizzes**: Select this option to have all of the Questions in the Quiz Section presented to the user, but in a random order.

   ♦ **Shuffle Quizzes (number)**: Select this option to have a defined number of Questions selected at random from the Quiz, and then presented to the user in random order. The number of Questions to select is specified in the **Number** property.

7. If you chose a **Type** of **Random Choice**, you can change the number of points awarded for a correct answer to the Question in the **Points** field. This defaults to 1, and cannot be changed for other **Type** options.

8. If you chose a **Type** of **Shuffle Quizzes (number)**, then specify the number of Questions that should be selected in the **Number** field. During playback, this number of Questions will be selected from the Quiz Section, and presented to the user in random order.

Inserting a Quiz Evaluation

You have the option to provide feedback per Question, depending on whether the user gets the answer correct or not. You can also provide feedback at the end of the Quiz, in the form of a Quiz Evaluation. You would normally want to do this if you want to inform the user of whether they have passed the entire Quiz or not (and especially if this information is being passed back to an LMS). If you provide feedback per Question, and don't need to record the overall result (or pass this to an LMS) then you can probably omit the Quiz Evaluation.

To insert a Quiz Evaluation in your Quiz, carry out the steps shown below.

1. Click on the last Step in your Quiz (this will have only the SIMULATION END macro in it).

2. Click on the **Insert Quiz Item** button on the *Project Editor Toolbar*, and then select **Quiz Evaluation** from the *Question Type* panel.

3. A QUIZ EVALUATION macro is inserted into the Step. Make sure that this is before the SIMULATION END macro.

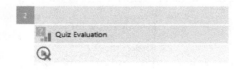

4. Click on the QUIZ EVALUATION macro, to select it and show its properties in the *Macro Editor*.

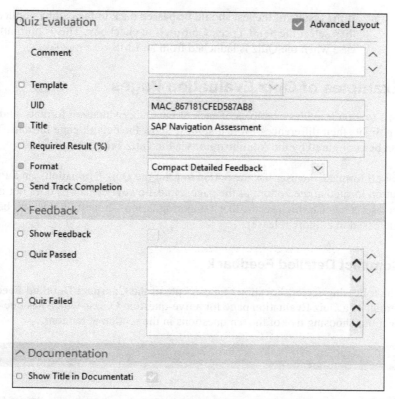

5. The **Title** property defaults to the **Name** of the Quiz. This will be displayed on the Quiz Evaluation page, and can be changed to some other title, if necessary.

6. Specify the percentage (of the total points available) that the user must score to pass the Quiz in the **Required Result (%)** field.

7. In the **Format** field, select the format in which the results should be displayed, as follows:

   ♦ **Compact Detailed Feedback**: Show the Questions and whether the user answered each one correctly. The user can expand the Questions to see both their answer and the correct answer.

   ♦ **Extended Detailed Feedback**: Show the Questions and whether the user answered each one correctly, as well as all of the user's answers and the correct answers.

   ♦ **Extended Short Feedback**: Show the Questions (but not the answers) and the points awarded/available for each question.

   ♦ **Total Score Only**: Show only the user's final score, the available points and the required pass level.

   It is much easier to appreciate the difference between these four options when you see them, so an example of each, along with an extended description, is provided in the next section.

8. If the results of the test should be passed back to the calling application, then select the **Send Track Completion** checkbox. This is normally the case when the Quiz is launched from an LMS.

Examples of Quiz Evaluation Pages

This section provides examples of each of the Quiz Evaluation formats, and highlights their differences. Note that these show the default page formats. These can be configured by the Administrator via the Quiz Template.

For all formats, the user has the option to print the Quiz Evaluation, via a **Print** button located at the bottom of the page. Note, however, that this does not include the user's name (which seems like a major omission—hopefully this will be addressed in a future release).

Compact Detailed Feedback

The following screenshot shows an example of the **Compact Detailed Feedback** format of a Quiz Evaluation page for a five-question Quiz—which has one Quiz Section, choosing five of the ten questions in the section at random.

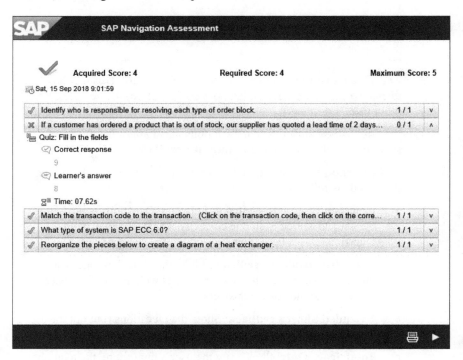

At the top of the page you can see a pass/fail indicator (either a green check-mark or a red 'x'), the user's score, the required passing score, and the maximum score. Immediately below this is the date and time at which the Quiz was started.

This is followed by a list of the Questions. For each question, you can see the pass/fail indicator, the question (the Question's **Task** property), the acquired and available points for the question, and (on the far right) an 'expand button' (actually, a lowercase 'v'). The user can click on the expand button to see the following information for the question:

    a.   The question type.

    b.   The correct answer.

    c.   The user's answer.

    d.   How long the user took to answer the question.

In the example above, the second question has been expanded.

Extended Detailed Feedback

The following screenshot shows an example of the **Extended Detailed Feedback** format of a Quiz Evaluation page for the same five-question Quiz.

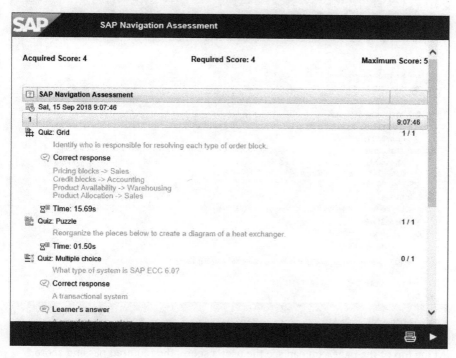

At the top of the page you can see the user's score, the required passing score, and the maximum score (there is no pass/fail indicator). Below this is a row showing the Quiz Title ("SAP Navigation Assessment" in this example), followed by the date and time at which the Quiz was started.

This is followed by numbered sections for each Quiz Section—even if there is only one Quiz Section. The time taken to complete the section is shown on the right of the section line. Within each section, the following information is provided for each Question:

    a.   The question type.

    b.   (On the right) The user's score and the maximum score for the question.

    c.   The question (the Question's **Task** property).

    d.   The correct answer, preceded by the text "Correct response".

    e.   The user's answer, if they answered incorrectly, preceded by the text "Learner's answer". If they answered correctly, this section is omitted.

    f.   How long the user took to answer the question.

Extended Short Feedback

The following screenshot shows an example of the **Extended Short Feedback** format of a Quiz Evaluation page for our five-question Quiz.

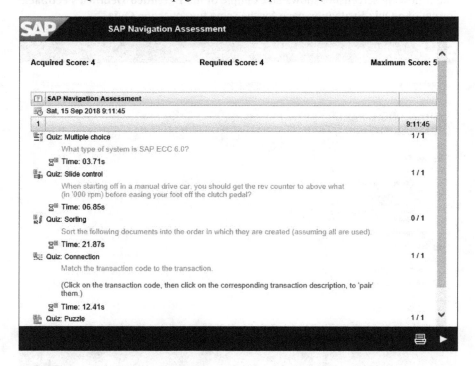

At the top of the page you can see the user's score, the required passing score, and the maximum score (there is no pass/fail indicator). Below this is a row showing the Quiz Title ("SAP Navigation Assessment" in this example), followed by the date and time at which the Quiz was started.

This is followed by numbered sections for each Quiz Section—even if there is only one Quiz Section. The time taken to complete the section is shown on the right of the section line. Within each section, the following information is provided for each Question:

   a.   The question type.

   b.   (On the right) The user's score and the maximum score for the question. Note that this is the only indicator as to whether the user answered the question correctly or not.

   c.   The question (the Question's **Task** property).

   d.   How long the user took to answer the question.

Total Score Only

The following screenshot shows an example of the **Total Score Feedback** format of a Quiz Evaluation page for our five-question Quiz.

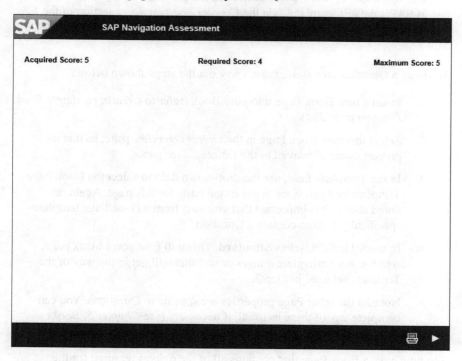

True to the type name, this feedback format only gives you the user's score, the required passing score, and the maximum score.

Using Questions outside of a Quiz

Although the primary use case for Questions is for them to be used within the context of a Quiz, you can also use Questions within a Book, and even within a simulation project.

Using Questions in Books

You can place a Question onto a Book Page. The user can then answer it before progressing to the next Book Page in the Book. This is useful for providing 'knowledge check' activities during the overall flow of the training course—for example, at the end of each section.

It is important to understand that Questions on Book Pages work differently on Book Pages than they do within a Quiz. Specifically, the Question itself (only the question—no correct/incorrect indicators, not even a 'submit' button) is inserted onto the page. All of the other objects provided by the template selected for the Question macro in the Quiz must similarly be provided by a Book Page template.

● If you will use Questions in Book Pages extensively, you may want to ask your Administrator to define a Book Page Template for each Question type, pre-populated with the Question, and with the various actions pre-configured. Then you can skip most of this section, and should only need to specify the actual Question properties.

Book Page templates for questions are extremely complicated, and outside the scope of this book. If your Administrator has not provided one, you can download one of SAP's default templates, via the *Content and Templates* section of the *Info Center* (which you can access via menu option **Help | Info Center** in Enable Now).

To create a Question on a Book Page, carry out the steps shown below:

1. Insert a new Book Page into your Book (refer to *Creating a simple Book Page* on page 262).

2. Select this new Book Page in the *Object Overview* pane, so that its properties are displayed in the *Object Editor* pane.

3. In the **Template** field, use the drop-down field to select the Book Page Template that you want to use as the basis for this page. Again, as noted above, it is important that you start from a Book Page template specifically built to contain a Question.

4. In the **Style** field, select **Standard**. This will give you a blank page, without any boilerplate images or text that will get in the way of the Template selected in Step 3.

5. None of the other Page properties are specific to Questions. You can complete any of these as usual, if necessary (see *Chapter 8, Books and Book Pages*).

You now have a Book Page that contains all of the objects required for the question (such as a 'submit' button, 'correct'/'incorrect' texts and images, and so on)—all of these will be provided by the selected Template. You are now ready to insert the Question into this. Continue as follows:

● Unlike Questions in a Quiz, you *can* see the Question in a Book Page, along with all of the question objects that may or may not be displayed,, taken from the Template.

6. With the Page selected in the *Object Overview* pane, click on the **Insert Quiz Item** on the *Book Editor Toolbar*, and select the required Question type from the drop-down panel.

7. Make sure that the Question is selected, so that its properties are displayed in the *Object Editor* pane. (You may find it easies to do this from the *Object Overview* pane.)

8. Enter a suitable name for the Question in the **Name** property. This will default to the Question type followed by a sequential number (to differentiate between multiple instances of the same Question type), but you will find it easier to locate the Question in the Object Overview pane if you give it a more meaningful name.

9. The Question placeholder does not include the question **Title** or **Task**. These should be provided by objects in the Template (if they are not, you can insert a **Text Box** object for each of them). Locate these objects, and specify the **Title** and **Task** as appropriate.

10. Specify the Question answers, and other properties, as explained earlier in this chapter (refer to the relevant sub-section under *Adding questions to your Quiz* on page 327).

11. Locate the *Actions* category of properties, and expand it so you can see the individual properties.

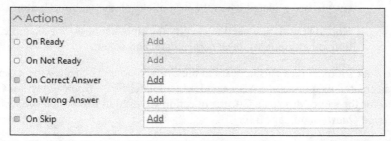

12. In the **On Correct Answer** property, specify what should happen when the user specifies the correct answer. This will typically be to display a confirmation text or image, but could also be to move to the next Book Page, or perform some other action.

13. In the **On Wrong Answer** property, specify what should happen when the user specifies an incorrect answer. This will typically be to display a text or image, but could also be to return the user to a previous Book Page to review the material, or perform some other action.

14. If the user will be able to skip the Question without answering it (this is typically dictated by the template) then specify what should happen when the user skips this Question.

15. Locate the 'submit' button in the objects brought in from the Template. The name of this may vary, but it should be relatively easy to locate it based on its name (which may be **Submit**, **Next**, or something similar). Click on this object, to display its properties.

16. Locate the *Actions* category of properties, and expand it so that you can see the individual properties.

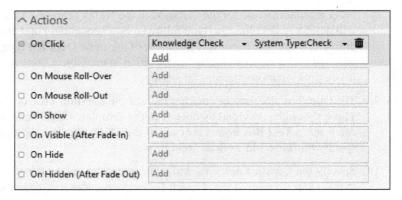

17. In the **On Click** property, **Add** a new row, select the Question object (created in Step 6) in the first field, and select an action of **System Type:Check** in the second field. This will cause the user's answer (if any) to be validated when the user clicks on the 'submit' button.

Note that you may need to specify multiple actions—for example, to hide other graphics, reset screen data, and so on.

Now let's look at how this appears in the *Book Reader*. The following example was created using one of SAP's standard templates (**TP - Book Question Comic**), and for the same MULTIPLE CHOICE question we used in *Defining a Multiple Choice Question* on page 330.

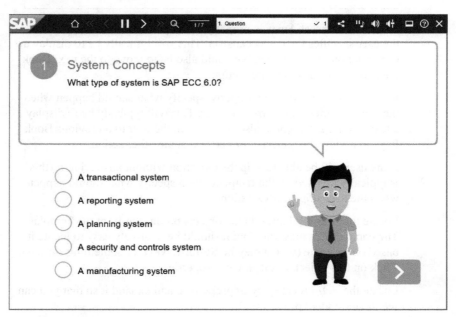

There are many other things that you can do with questions on Book Pages; the information provided above is simply to get you started with the basics, in case you do not have a suitable Template that does all of these things for you.

Using Questions in simulation projects

You can insert a Question into a simulation project. Although this could disrupt the overall flow of the simulation (which should generally reflect exactly what the user sees in the actual application), it can be useful for performing a quick 'knowledge check' or reinforcing key learning points, before continuing with the rest of the simulation.

If a Question is inserted in a simulation, then it is available in all modes, including Demo (where you would normally not want 'interaction'), and Practice Mode, as well as Test mode. If used in Test mode, you may want to set the Points awarded for the Question appropriately, as this defaults to **1**, which gives the Question as much weighting as getting an interaction wrong once (out of a default of three possible attempts).

To insert a Question into a simulation project, carry out the steps shown below.

1. In the *Project Editor*, click on the macro after which the Question should appear, to select it.

2. On the *Project Editor Toolbar*, click on the **Insert Quiz Item** button, and then select the required Question type from the drop-down panel (see the section *Adding questions to your Quiz* on page 327 for more information on this, if necessary).

Insert Quiz Item

3. The relevant Question macro is added to the simulation.

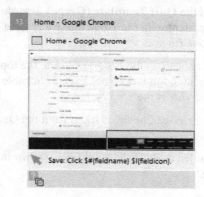

Click on this macro to select it and show its properties in the *Macro Editor*.

4. Edit the Question macro's properties as necessary. These are exactly the same as for Question macros within a Quiz, so you should refer to the relevant sub-section under *Adding questions to your Quiz* on page 327 for full details of the available properties and how to use them.

■ There is no 'show in mode' property for a Question, but if you don't want the Question to appear in certain modes, you can use a JUMP TO STEP macro that is enabled only for specific modes to jump around it. See the example in the section *Using a Branch* on page 164 for details.

■ You can also insert QUIZ SECTION macros and a QUIZ EVALUATION macros into a simulation; they work in exactly the same way as for within a Quiz.

Now let's look at how a Question within a simulation appears during playback. This example is taken from Demo mode, after the user has selected their answer, but before submitting this.

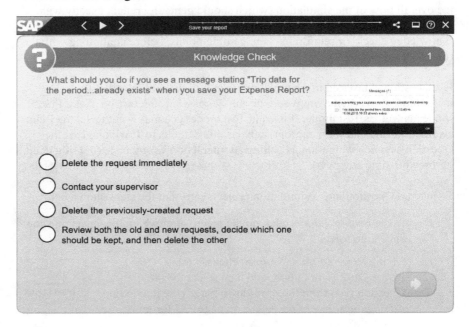

A few things to note about this example:

- We have used the **Quiz Template (Green) Template** for the Question—just to be consistent with our Book that we created in *Chapter 8, Books and Book Pages.*

- The question appears in the *Progress Bar* at the top of the screen (in Demo mode), although it does not have a clickable 'dot'. The text shown in the *Progress Bar* is the Step **Name**.

- The text "Knowledge Check" is taken from the Question macro's **Title** property.

- We have included a **Media File**, which is shown in the upper right of the question area.

■ If you want the Question to have a clickable 'dot' in the *Progress Bar*, then place it in its own Step, and make sure the **Show in Progress Display** property is selected for that Step.

Summary

Enable Now provides two primary methods of testing users. The first of these is through the use of a simulation project played in Test mode. This is very easy to produce (assuming you have already created the simulation in Demo mode or Practice mode), but you will need to check the **Task Description** and make sure that this contains all of the information that the user needs to be able to successfully complete the simulation.

The second method of testing users is through the use of Questions. Questions can be assembled into a standalone Quiz, or can be included in Book Pages, or even in simulations. Enable Now provides ten different types of Questions, and a variety of customizable templates to fully meet your individual requirements.

10

The Desktop Assistant

The Desktop Assistant is the component of Enable Now that provides in-application, context-sensitive help for Windows applications. The Desktop Assistant can be used to provide Guided Tours, which walk the user through a task in the application, and Context Help, which provides a help bubble for a specific object on the screen (or for the screen as a whole). The Desktop Assistant can also provide access to other (context-applicable) training content, such as simulation projects and Books and Book Pages.

In this chapter you will learn how to:

- Convert a simulation project into a Desktop Assistant project
- Record a Desktop Assistant Guided Tour
- Create Desktop Assistant Context Help
- 'Genericize' context
- Record context for Books and Book Pages
- Generate the Desktop Assistant

Components of the Desktop Assistant

The Desktop Assistant is effectively a separate application that runs 'on top of' a 'target' application, and provides help for that application. Before digging into *how* to create Desktop Assistant content, it is worth looking at an example of Desktop Assistant content, so you understand *what* you are creating.

The Desktop Assistant effectively monitors what the user is doing on their PC, and when the user is working in a context (typically, a specific screen in a specific application) for which Desktop Assistant has some help content, the Desktop Assistant will inform the user that help is available, and provide access to this content. In order for Desktop Assistant to be able to do this, it needs to be running on the user's PC. This is best achieved by having Desktop Assistant automatically started when the user starts up their PC. How you do this will depend on whether you are running an on-premise version of Enable Now or are running a cloud instance. Either way, this is something that your Administrator should take care of.

The Desktop Assistant Sidebar

Assuming the Desktop Assistant is running, the *Desktop Assistant Sidebar* will be displayed. This will initially be docked to an edge of the screen, but the user can drag it to any other edge (and to any position along that edge). The user can also minimize the sidebar to show only the 'drag bar' (the leftmost example, below).

★ Which buttons are available on the *Desktop Assistant Sidebar* and what they do is defined via **Tools | Settings | Desktop Assistant: Playback Settings | Desktop Assistant | Desktop Assistant - Sidebar**.

The icons present on the *Desktop Assistant Sidebar* will depend upon your configuration, but can include the following:

Button	Name	Use
	Content	This is the primary indicator in the Desktop Assistant, and indicates whether or not help is available for the current context. The user clicks on this button to display the *Desktop Assistant Content Panel*.
	Search	Allows the user to search the content of the Desktop Assistant.
	External Search	Allows the user to search an external training library for applicable content. Typically this points to your *Trainer*, and the current context (executable and page key) are passed as parameters on the search call.
	Context Help	Allows the user to disable the display of Context Help bubbles.
	Add Sticky Note	The user can click on this icon to add a sticky note to the current application. Note that this sticky note is tied to the *application*, and not the screen within the application.

Button	Name	Use
✉	**Request Content**	If no content is found for the current context then the user can click on this button to send an email to the Enable Now administrator to request content. This is done by opening the default mail client and pre-populating this with some default text, including the current context.
⏺	**Recording**	Allows the user to create a recording of the application. This can be saved as either (or both of) a Microsoft Word document or a video. These recordings cannot be used as the basis for a simulation (or Desktop Assistant) project, but will appear on the *User* tab of the *Desktop Assistant Content Panel*, and can be shared with other users via email.
⏻	**Exit**	Closes the Desktop Assistant.

⭐ The e-mail address to which this request will be sent is defined in **Tools | Settings | Desktop Assistant: Playback Settings | Desktop Assistant | Desktop Assistant - Sidebar | E-mail**. These settings can also be defined to direct the user to a separate URL to provide feedback.

The Desktop Assistant Content Panel

When the Desktop Assistant has applicable help content for the current context, it alerts the user to this by 'lighting up' the **Content** indicator (the light-bulb) on the *Desktop Assistant Toolbar*. The user can then click on this icon to display the applicable content in the *Desktop Assistant Content Panel*. An example of this panel is shown below.

★ The default size and position of the Desktop Assistant Content Pane are defined via **Tools | Settings | Desktop Assistant: Playback Settings | Desktop Assistant | Desktop Assistant - Style and Windows**.

The *Desktop Assistant Content Panel* is initially docked to an edge of the screen, and at a default size. However, the user can drag it to another location (even to another screen, if they are using multiple monitors), and resize it by dragging its boundaries, if necessary.

Let's look a little closer at the contents of the *Desktop Assistant Content Panel*, and the things we (as Authors) can do to influence this.

The Content List

If you look at the example of the *Desktop Assistant Content Panel* above, you will see that there are a few different types of content listed. In the example above, you can see two Desktop Assistant Guided Tours, and a simulation project. The types of content object that can appear is dictated by the content types selected when generating the Desktop Assistant. See *Generating the Desktop Assistant* on page 412 for more information on this.

★ Whether the **Description** or the **Short Description** is used is defined in **Tools | Settings | Desktop Assistant: Playback Settings | Desktop Assistant | Desktop Assistant - Content and Behavior | Use Text From**.

For each content object listed, the object **Name** is shown, along with a short text description. This text may be taken from either the object's **Short Description** property, or its **Description** property.

The user can click on an object in the *Content List* to display a list of the modes in which the simulation can be launched (even if this is only one, as will the case for Guided Tours). The user can also click on a pop-up icon on the rightmost side of the object entry in the *Content List* to launch that object in the default playback mode.

Using Content Categories

★ In order to group your content by the **Content Categories**, this option must be enabled, via **Tools | Settings | Desktop Assistant: Playback Settings | Desktop Assistant | Desktop Assistant - Content and Behavior | Consider Content Categories**.

In the example of the *Desktop Assistant Content Panel* shown above, the content is shown under two headings: **GloboCorp Logistics** and **GloboCorp Services**. These are the values in the **Content Categories** property for the content objects.

Categories are expandable/collapsible, and a user's selection is typically remembered across executions of the Desktop Assistant. A content object can have multiple categories assigned to it (separated by semicolons in the **Content Categories** property), and will appear under each category in the Desktop Assistant Content Panel.

Often, this property is used to identify different *types* of content, but it is simply a text field, and can really be used for anything. In the example above, the **Content Categories** property is used to differentiate between content for different parts of the company, each of which may use the same system functionality in different ways. However you (or your Training Lead) choose to use it, just make sure that you are consistent—both in terms of the categories you use, and in terms of applying categories to all content objects that will appear in the Desktop Assistant (objects without a category will be listed under a catch-all category of **Other Content** at the bottom of the *Content List*).

Filtering by Roles

If you have assigned roles to your content, then users will also be able to filter the contents of the *Desktop Assistant Content Panel* to show only content that has been tagged for their specific role (or roles). Roles are assigned to content objects via the helpfully-named **Roles** property.

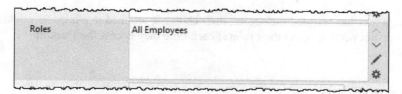

Note that the **Roles** property is a simple text field, and there is no validation against what you enter into it. This means that you (and all of the other Authors) need to be very careful to use exactly the same name for the same role.

■ Consider defining a master list of roles in a **Text Unit** in your **Assets** Group, and ensure that all Authors only ever use the role names present in this master list.

A Few Words on Roles

Because roles are really just text labels, you (or your Team Lead) can decide exactly what constitutes a 'role'. You could use job titles or access profiles, but you could just as easily use organizational names, or department names. It is important to strike a balance between using enough roles to usefully reduce the number of role-filtered content objects to only those that are applicable to a user, and still keeping the number of roles to a manageable list, so that the user isn't having to scan through hundreds of roles just to find the one role (or, even worse, the specific combination of roles) that applies to them. You should also strive to use role names that are meaningful to the users themselves, and not use 'technical' or system role names.

★ The *Filter Help Content by Role* section is only available on the **Settings** tab if this has been enabled via **Tools | Settings | Desktop Assistant: Playback Settings | Desktop Assistant | Desktop Assistant - Content and Behavior | Consider Roles.**

● The **Show All Suppressed Help Again** option is for use with Context Help. See the **Hide Option** on page 401 for details.

Users can select their role(s) on the *Settings* tab of the *Desktop Assistant Content Panel*. An example of this tab is shown below.

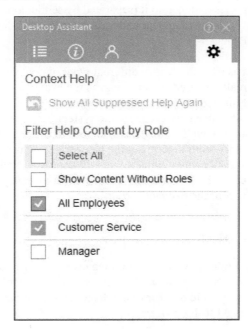

Once a user has selected their roles, their choice is retained in a browser cookie; they do not need to select their role(s) each time they access the Desktop Assistant.

The Info tab

★ The **Info** tab is only displayed if this has been enabled via **Tools | Settings | Desktop Assistant: Playback Settings | Desktop Assistant | Desktop Assistant - Content and Behavior | Show 'Info' tab,** *and* the Desktop Assistant object's **Info Description** property has some content.

The *Desktop Assistant Content Pane* may also contain an *Info* tab, if this has been enabled by the Administrator. The content of the *Info* tab is taken from the **Info Description** property of the **Desktop Assistant** object in the Workarea. You can use this to provide any information that you think may be useful to your users. An example of this tab is shown below:

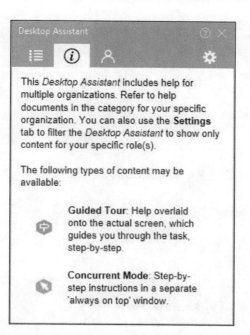

The User Area

The last section of the *Desktop Assistant Content Panel* is the *User Area* tab. This tab is only present if users have the ability to record their own content, in which case it contains a list of all of the content they have created, along with a **Record Document** button. This same button will also be present in the *Desktop Assistant Sidebar*, if the user content creation feature is enabled.

An example of the *Desktop Assistant Content Panel*, showing the *User Area* tab, is shown below.

★ The ability for users to generate their own content, and therefore the visibility of the *User Area* tab and the **Recording** button is controlled via **Tools | Settings | Desktop Assistant: Playback Settings | Desktop Assistant | Desktop Assistant - Sidebar | Position: Recording Control.**

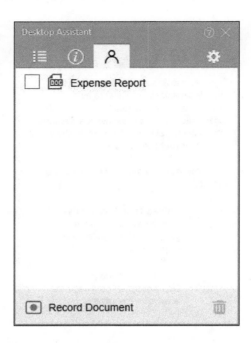

User-generated content is not strictly a part of Enable Now development (as the content generated by users cannot be incorporated into Enable Now projects (as it can be in some applications), but for the sake of completeness, it is covered in *User-generated content* on page 418.

Desktop Assistant project types

The Desktop Assistant supports two distinct types of project: **Guided Tours** and **Context Help**. A Guided Tour provides step-by-step instructions on how to complete a specific business task in the application. A Guided Tour is therefore extremely similar to a simulation project, but provides the instructions overlaid on the application screen, as opposed to providing playback in its own window with its own screenshots (as is the case with a simulation).

Context Help, on the other hand, provides 'targeted help' for a specific screen object. This may well be exactly the same instructions as would be provided by a Guided Tour, but the difference is that with Context Help the instructions are provided 'all at once' (for all objects on a screen) instead of one step at a time, and—depending on the Author's choices—the user must explicitly choose to display the instructions.

You would typically not choose to use both Context Help and a Guided Tour on the same screen, as this could lead to information overload—especially if they both provide the same basic instructions. You should therefore decide upon which you want to use, and how, before recording either of them (as you cannot change content from being one type to another).

One approach, used by this Author, is to provide Guided Tours for each business task, and then provide Context Help only for specific fields on a strictly temporary basis. For example, you could use Context Help to draw the user's attention to a new field, or new field value, for (say) the first month of its availability after implementation (this is the scenario we will use in one of our examples later in this chapter).

There is a lot of commonality between developing Guided Tours and developing Context Help. However, there are also significant differences - both in terms of the recording process and the properties available for controlling the way the content is displayed within the Desktop Assistant. In this book, we will cover these two project types separately, and include all—and only—the applicable functionality in each section. This may result in some slight repetition, but this is deemed preferable to co-mingling the content and/or providing copious cross-references. All that said, you may find it easier to go through the section on Guided Tours first, and then go through the Context Help section—which is most likely the order in which you will develop them, and is therefore also the order in which they are presented in this book.

Before we delve into the project type specifics, let's look at one part that is at least consistent: converting a simulation project into a Desktop Assistant project—regardless of whether it is being converted into a Guided Tour or Context Help.

Converting a simulation project into a Desktop Assistant project

Typically, the first thing you will do with Enable Now, is create simulations for use as exercises and/or demonstrations in pre-go-live training—whether this is instructor-led training in the classroom or self-paced training using CBTs. Your application help, whilst no less important, will typically be created second—maybe to allow any clarifications or updates identified during training to be incorporated, or simply out of expediency as Authors concentrate on what is needed soonest. This works out well with Enable Now, as you can create a Desktop Assistant project directly from a simulation project.

When you use a simulation project as the basis for a Desktop Assistant project, all of the simulation's bubbles and texts are copied over, along with all of the context-sensitivity and object linking that is present in the original simulation. This significantly reduces development time, and also ensures that your in-application help is consistent with what was taught during training, Of course, you can still edit the converted project as required, post-conversion.

To convert a simulation project to a Desktop Assistant project, carry out the steps shown below.

1. Open the simulation project in the *Project Editor*.

2. On the *Project Editor Toolbar*, click on the **Generate Desktop Assistant Project** button. The *Generate Desktop Assistant Project* dialog box is displayed.

3. The *Project Name* field defaults to the name of the simulation project. If necessary, you can change this. Note that this is the name that the user will see in the Desktop Assistant itself.

4. The Desktop Assistant typically ties instructions to specific objects on the screen. If your simulation project contains HOTSPOT macros (where the recording simply captured a click on a location on the screen, and not on a specific object) then Desktop Assistant does not have an object to which it can attach this action. If you want these instructions to be retained in your Desktop Assistant project, then make sure that the **Convert Hotspot to Explanation** checkbox is selected, and the simulation's HOTSPOT macros will be converted to EXPLANATION macros (which are not tied to objects anyway) in the Desktop Assistant project. If you deselect this checkbox, then any HOTSPOT macros in the simulation project will simply be ignored, and will not be included in the Desktop Assistant project.

● For an explanation of the difference between Guided Tours and Context Help, refer to *Desktop Assistant project types* on page 368.

5. A Desktop Assistant project can be either a Guided Tour or Context Help (but not both). If you want your simulation project to be converted to a Guided Tour, then select the Guided Tour checkbox. Otherwise, make sure that this checkbox is deselected, and the simulation project will be converted into Context Help.

6. As noted above, Desktop Assistant content (either Guided Tour steps or Context Help panels) are 'tied' to screen objects—and therefore point to the relevant object during playback. If you do not want the content to point to the specific objects (for example, because the screen configuration does not readily allow for this) then select the **Interactive Mode** checkbox, and the Desktop Assistant content will be displayed on the screen independently of any specific object. Note that if you choose this option, you need to make sure that all of your interaction bubbles explicitly and unequivocally identify the relevant screen object to which they apply (typically by including the **Object Name** and possibly the **Object Image** within the bubble).

7. Click **Ok**. The Desktop Assistant project is created, and then opened in the *Project Editor*.

You can now edit the Desktop Assistant project as explained in *Editing a Guided Tour* on page 376, or *Editing a Context Help project* on page 397, as appropriate. Note that the original simulation project remains open; you will need to close this.

Guided Tour projects

Guided Tours provide step-by-step instructions on how to perform a task in the application. They are created and edited largely in the same way as simulation projects are.

Recording a Guided Tour

If you do not have a simulation project that you can convert into a Desktop Assistant Guided Tout, then you can record a new Guided Tour from scratch, as described in this section.

> If you are recording a simulation of a browser application, then you must record this using Microsoft Internet Explorer (or Edge). The recording can be *played back* against the application in Google Chrome (as long as the SAP Enable Now plug-in is installed and active) but it must still be *recorded* against Internet Explorer for correct object recognition.

To record a new Guided Tour, carry out the steps shown below.

1. Click on the Group within which you want to create the recording. Ideally, you should check this Group out for editing first; if you do not, it will be checked out to you when you create the recording, anyway. No matter where you create your Guided Tour, it must ultimately be located within your **Desktop Assistant** Group, in order to be included in the Desktop Assistant. To avoid conflicts with other Authors, you may want to create the recording in the **Unassigned** Group, and then move it to your **Desktop Assistant** Group when it is ready to be published.

2. On the *Producer Toolbar*, click on the **New Object** button, and then select **[Desktop Assistant] Guided Tour**, under *In-App Help*. The *New Project* dialog box is displayed.

New Object

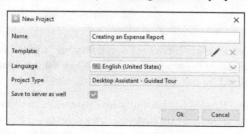

3. In the **Name** field, enter a suitable name for this Guided Tour.

4. If you have an existing Desktop Assistant project that you want to use as a template for this new project, then click on the **Edit** button to the right of the **Template** field, and navigate to and select the required project.

5. If you want the simulation to be created in a language other than the default one then change the **Language** field, as appropriate. This will determine the language in which the default bubble texts are generated.

6. The **Project Type** field will default to **Desktop Assistant - Guided Tour**—because that's what you selected in Step 2. You cannot change this.

+ The **Save to Server as well** checkbox was introduced in the 1811 release. Prior to that, the **Synchronization behavior** option was used instead.

7. If you are creating this Guided Tour within your Root structure, and want it to be managed on the server, then make sure the **Save to server as well** checkbox is selected. Otherwise, deselect this checkbox, and the project will only be saved to your local storage. For more information on this, refer to *Client-Server functionality* on page 35.

8. Click **Ok**. The project is created, and opened in the *Project Editor*, as a separate tab within *Producer*.

9. On the *Project Editor Toolbar*, click on the **Record Guided Tour Step** button. The *Select Window and Profile* dialog box is displayed.

Record Guided Tour Step

Select Window and Profile

Choose Window:

- Home - Microsoft Edge
- Desktop

Choose Profile:

SAP UI5

☐ Associate with Selected Window

Record Screencast Video

[⦿ Record] [Cancel]

10. The *Choose Window* section of the dialog box lists all of the applications that are currently running on your PC. Click on the application that you want to record, in this list.

11. The **Choose Profile** field automatically defaults to the most appropriate profile for the application that you have selected. The profile controls context and object recognition, and you should not normally need to change this from the default selection. However, in some circumstances—such as for new, unknown applications—you may

experience problems with the default selection and can chose another profile (or the 'catch-all' **Standard** profile) instead.

12. If you always want the selected profile to be used for the selected application, then select the **Associate with Selected Window** checkbox. This should only be necessary if you have changed the default profile selection.

13. Click on the **Record** button. The selected application window is brought to the front (of your open windows), and the *Recorder Toolbar* is displayed across the top of the screen.

You are now ready to record the application. How you do this for a Guided Tour is slightly different from how you record a simulation project, so pay careful attention to the instructions provided below. But before jumping into recording, lets' take a quick look at the *Recorder Toolbar*.

The *Recorder Toolbar* for Desktop Assistant content contains the following buttons that you may need to use during recording.

The following table describes the purpose of these buttons.

Button	Name	Purpose
❚❚	Pause	Temporarily pause recording. Any actions that you perform while recording is paused will not be captured. Everything that you have captured so far will be copied into the project.
▣	Record	Re-start recording after you have previously paused it.
▪	Stop	Stop recording. You will be returned to the *Project Editor*, which will now contain all of the recorded content.
↺	Undo	Cancel the last action captured.
💬	Insert Explanation	Insert an EXPLANATION macro.

Button	Name	Purpose
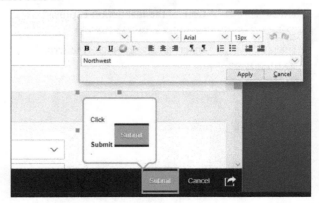	**Execute Mouse Actions**	You record your application by performing the actions in the actual application. If you want an action to be captured, but do not want to actually perform the action in the application, then (de)select this option. The action will still be captured, along with its full context, but the action will not be executed in the application. This is very useful if you do not want to 'consume' the data used in the recording. Select this option again to return to performing the actions in the application.
	Minimize	Hide the *Recording Bar*. A single icon will be visible in the System Tray, instead. This will be one of: ● Pause ● Record ● Stop These have the same function as the same buttons on the full *Recording Bar*.
	Close	Close the *Recording Bar* and return to the *Project Editor*. You should only do this once you have finished your recording.

To record your Guided Tour, carry out the steps shown below.

1. After making sure that the *Recorder Toolbar* is green (which signifies that it is ready to capture your action), click on the screen object (typically a button or input field) for which you want to record a Guided Tour step.

   As soon as you click on a screen object, three distinct elements are overlaid onto the application screen. These are shown in the partial screenshot below.

● If you click on an area of the screen that is not a screen object, a dialog box containing the message `No object available at clicked position` is displayed. Click on the **Add Explanation** button in this dialog to add an Explanation.

These elements are (from top to bottom, in the example above):

◆ The *Bubble Formatting* dialog box. This is similar to the *Text Editor* in the *Project Editor*, and allows you to format the (selected) bubble text. However, it does not allow you to edit the actual text itself— you can only do that directly in the bubble itself

◆ The **bubble**. This is shown in the approximate position it will appear in the Desktop Assistant (relative to the screen object to which it relates), and contains the defaulted text for the action that you performed.

◆ The **Action Area**. This is shown as a blue rectangle, and identifies the border of the screen object on which you clicked. You should not need to adjust this.

Note that at this stage your action has not yet been captured (that only happens in Step 4, below). This gives you the opportunity to adjust the bubble for this step, before committing it. Also note that the action is not actually performed in the application until you commit this action in the recorder, so don't be surprised if clicking on a button doesn't actually seem to do anything. Just hold tight until we get to Step 4.

> Before continuing, it is worth taking a closer look at how the Desktop Assistant recorder handles input text fields. Because you typically do not want the actual entered data to be included in your in-application help (because users seeing this bubble are using the actual system, and will therefore have their own 'live' data), as soon as you click in an input field, the three capture elements identified above are displayed, and a default bubble text of "Fill out the XXX field" is generated, as shown in the following partial screenshot.

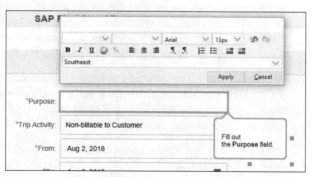

At this point, you should enter your text in the input field (you could also do this after Step 2 or after Step 3, but in any case before Step 4). It may seem logical to commit the 'click in' action before doing this, but don't! If you commit this action now, when you type your text Enable Now will interpret this as a new action, capture the first character you type as a keyboard action, and ignore all subsequent characters that you type (even though they appear on the application screen).

Even though it is not included in the bubble by default, your input text *is* captured, and is stored in the **Input Text** property for the INPUT TEXT macro. If you really want it to be included in the instructions (for example, because users should always enter this exact value) then you can include it via a **Placeholder** during editing, as explained in *Inserting a Placeholder* on page 115.

2. If you want to change the bubble text, click in the bubble, and then change the text as required. You can use the formatting options provided in the *Bubble Formatting* dialog box to apply styles or direct formatting, just as you can with the *Text Editor* (refer to *Adjusting Bubble text* on page 111 for more information on this).

3. To adjust the size of the bubble, click on it to show its bounding box, and then drag the available handles to the required position. Do not move the bubble to a new position on the screen by dragging it, as this will break the link between the bubble and the object, which you do not want to do. If you want to change the *position* of the bubble relative to the object, then you can select the orientation of the bubble from the drop-down list at the bottom of the *Bubble Formatting* dialog box (which shows **Southeast** in the example above).

■ As per the instructions on the leftmost side of the *Recorder Bar*, you can also press *CTRL+ENTER* on the keyboard to commit the action. However, in my experience, this sometimes doesn't work—whereas clicking **Apply** *always* works.

4. Once you have finished making any adjustments to the captured action, click on the **Apply** button in the *Button Formatting* dialog box. This will capture the action in your recording, and also perform the action in the application.

Alternatively, if you decide that you do not want this action to be captured in your Guided Tour then click on the **Cancel** button in the *Button Formatting* dialog box (or press the *Esc* key), and the action will be discarded. This means that the action will also not be performed in the application (because you did not 'commit' it). If you want to perform the action but not capture it, click on the **Pause** button on the *Recorder Toolbar*, perform the action, and then click on the **Record** button again.

5. When you commit or cancel your action in Step 4, the screen is cleared (of the Desktop Assistant elements) again, and you are ready to record the next step in the Guided Tour. Repeat steps 1 to 4 for all additional steps that you want to capture.

6. Once you have captured all required steps, click on the **Stop** button on the *Recorder Toolbar*. You are returned to the *Project Editor*.

You can now edit the project as explained in *Editing a Guided Tour*, below.

Editing a Guided Tour

Once you finish recording a Guided Tour (or once conversion from a simulation project completes) you are passed into the *Project Editor*. If you want to edit an existing Guided Tour, simply locate it in the Workarea, and double-click on it to open it in the *Project Editor*.

The *Project Editor* used for Desktop Assistant projects is very similar to the *Project Editor* used for simulation projects, so we will not repeat the basics here. If you are not familiar with the *Project Editor*, you should refer to *The Project Editor* on page 104 before continuing. However, there are enough differences and inconsistencies to make it worth looking at a few things in detail. We'll do this by editing a sample Guided Tour for entering an expense report. This Guided Tour was recorded as a Desktop Assistant project, and not converted from a simulation project, although the content and how to edit it is almost identical in both cases.

Let's first look at the types of macros that are generated for a Desktop Assistant Guided Tour. Here's the first few Steps for our Guided Tour project:

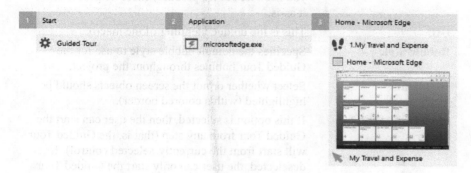

The first Step in any Desktop Assistant project is the **Start** Step, which contains a single macro of GUIDED TOUR STYLE.

The second Step is the **Application** step, which contains a single APPLICATION macro. This identifies the application that was recorded to create this Desktop Assistant project (even if this was by way of a simulation project). In the example above, the Guided Tour project was captured in the Microsoft Edge browser, so the application shown is **microsoftedge.exe**. The properties for this macro provide technical information about the capture profile used. You should normally not need to change any of these properties.

These two standard Steps will be followed by a Step for each action you performed. Each Step will contain:

1. A sequentially-numbered GUIDED TOUR STEP macro.

2. A SCREEN macro, containing a screenshot of the screen against which the action was performed. This is largely for internal reference only, as it is not displayed during playback in the Desktop Assistant.

3. An interaction macro—typically a MOUSE ACTION macro or an INPUT TEXT macro.

4. Any EXPLANATION macros captured during recording.

Controlling the appearance of a Guided Tour

★ The overall appearance of the Desktop Assistant is defined via **Tools | Customization | Edit Style Resources | Desktop Assistant Style** (although your Administrator may have created a custom version of this). Desktop Assistant style definitions are stored in the **Resources | Adaptable Resources** Workarea Group.

In addition to the overall color scheme and global settings defined for the Desktop Assistant itself, you can also control the visual appearance of a specific project. This is done via the properties of the GUIDED TOUR STYLE macro. The following table lists the properties that are available, and explains their use.

Property	Use
Basic Properties	
Comment	This defaults to "Guided Tour". This text is used in the macro in the *Step View*. You can change this if you need to, but it's probably more helpful to leave it as-is.
UID	This is the unique identifier of the macro.
Bubble Style *	Specifies the default bubble style to use for the Guided Tour bubbles throughout the project.
Highlights *	Select whether or not the screen objects should be highlighted (with a colored border).
Start from Arbitrary Step	If this option is selected, then the user can start the Guided Tour from any step (that is, the Guided Tour will start from the currently-selected control). If deselected, the user can only start the Guided Tour from the first step.
Focus Layer *	If selected, the 'focus layer'—where all screen content except the current control is grayed out—is used.
Restricted Mode *	If this option is selected, the user can only perform the action dictated by the current step of the Guided Tour.
Interactive Mode	If selected, Guided Tour bubbles are not 'attached' to screen objects (no context sensitivity is performed, and the bubbles do not have pointers). This is a useful option if context was not captured accurately or consistently during the recording, or if the project was created from a simulation that was itself created outside of Enable Now and imported.

▲ Be very careful about using **Restricted Mode**—especially at the project level—as if the user is unable to perform the required step for some reason, they cannot proceed without closing down the Desktop Assistant.

Property	Use
Window	
Style	If necessary, you can use this property to specify a Desktop Assistant Style that should be used for this specific Guided Tour, overriding the style resource specified for the Desktop Assistant as a whole. Note that this will only apply to Desktop Assistant dialog boxes that are Guided Tour specific—namely, the *Step List*, the *Guided Tour Step not found* dialog box, and the 'current step cannot be displayed' message box.
Alignment	Specify the relative location on the screen at which Desktop Assistant dialog boxes specific to this Guided Tour should appear.
Position	If the **Alignment** (above) is set to **Free**, then specify the initial position and size of the Guided Tour specific Desktop Assistant dialog boxes.
Size	
Tour End	
End Window	By default, as soon as a user completes the last step of a Guided Tour, the Guided Tour simply closes. If necessary, you can have a final Bubble displayed—for example, to mention next steps. To have this end Bubble displayed, select this option.
Text	If you selected the **End Window** option, then enter the text to be displayed in the end Bubble. The full *Text Editor* is used for this, so all the usual formatting options are available to you.
Next Project	If another Guided Tour should be started as soon as the current Guided Tour ends, then select this next Guided Tour in this field. Note that if you select a next Guided Tour no end Bubble will be displayed, even if you selected the **End Window** option.
Advanced	
Source	If this Guided Tour was created from a simulation project, then this field contains the **UID** of this source simulation project. This is for information only, and cannot be changed.

★ Desktop Assistant Styles are defined via **Tools | Customization | Edit Style Resources**.

* Setting can be overridden at the macro level.

Controlling macro display behavior

In addition to the properties that can be specified at the Guided Tour level to control the display of the Guided Tour as a whole (identified in the previous section), there are a few properties that can be defined at the macro level, to control the display of individual macros (STRING INPUT, MOUSE ACTION, KEYBOARD, and EXPLANATION macros). These are summarized in the table below.

Property	Use
Display Behavior	
Set Value Automatically	For INPUT TEXT macros only. If selected, the **Input Text** will automatically be entered into the field. See additional information on page 389.
Optional	Select this checkbox to indicate that an action is optional. The only impact of this is that the step is flagged with a specific icon in the *Step List*, as shown (for Step 6) below: 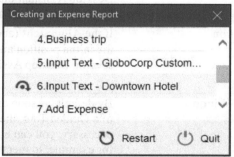 Note that this property is not available for EXPLANATION macros.
Focus Layer	Select this checkbox to use the 'focus layer'—where all screen content except the current control is grayed out—for this control.
Restricted Mode	Select this option to prevent the user from skipping this step and clicking elsewhere on the screen. This is best used in conjunction with the **Focus Layer** property.

▲ Be very careful about using **Restricted Mode** because if the user is unable to perform the required step for some reason, they will not be able to proceed without closing down the Desktop Assistant.

Controlling the Highlight

The Highlight is (by default) the border that is shown around the screen object to which the instruction currently being displayed applies. For Desktop Assistant projects this works in exactly the same way as the Highlight in a simulation project. However, whereas for simulation projects most Highlight properties can only be set globally (typically centrally for all projects by the Administrator, although some settings can be overridden at the project level by the Author), for Desktop Assistant projects the Highlight properties can be defined at the individual object/action level (as well as at the global/project level). The table below explains the options that are available.

★ The global Highlight settings are defined in **Tools | Settings | Desktop Assistant: Playback Settings | General | Highlights**.

Property	Use
Highlight	
Show Highlight	Select this checkbox if the Highlight should be visible during playback of the Guided Tour.
Offset	You can use this property to provide some padding between the screen object and the Highlight. Click on the **Edit** button for this property to display the following dialog box:

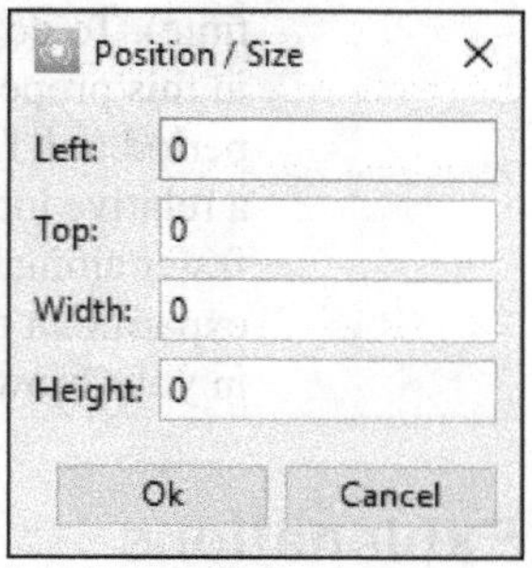

> **Position / Size**   ✕
>
> Left: 0
>
> Top: 0
>
> Width: 0
>
> Height: 0
>
> [Ok]   [Cancel]

Ignore the field labels, which are misleading; these fields should be interpreted as follows:

- **Left**: Number of pixels to leave to the left of the object

- **Top**: Number of pixels to leave above the object

- **Width**: Number of pixels to leave to the right of the object

- **Height**: Number of pixels to leave to the bottom of the object

Note that positive values will result in the Highlight being larger than the object area, whereas negative values will result in the Highlight being smaller than the object area.

Property	Use
Effect	Choose the type of Highlight that should be used. This can be one of:

- **Frame**: A rectangle (this is the default)

- **Underline**: A solid line under the object

- **Circle**: An ellipse

Property	Use
Border	Specify the width of the line for the Highlight. This defaults to **4** (pixels). Be very careful about changing this, as the position of most bubbles is predicated on a Highlight width of 4.

Property	Use
Color	Change the color of the Highlight, if necessary. If you change this, change it consistently, and change it to a color that is easy to see against the application color scheme.
Animation Steps	By default, Highlights appear as soon as the associated instruction bubble is displayed. If necessary, you can have the Highlight 'animate in' (so that it appears as if it is being drawn, in real time). To do this, enter the 'speed' of the animation in this property. Note that this isn't an actual period unit (such as second, or millisecond), but a relative indicator; a smaller number results in a faster animation. (Tip: Start with a value of **20** and experiment until you find something that works well in your browser.)

Inserting Explanations

As with simulation projects, EXPLANATION macros are also available in Guided Tour projects. However, they are handled significantly differently, so it is worth looking at them in detail, here.

Firstly, note that there is no **Insert Explanation** button on the *Editor Toolbar*. Instead, there is a button available at the top of the *Macro Editor* for some macro types. These determine the *level* at which the Explanation is defined, which in turn determines the period during which it is displayed on the user's screen in the Desktop Assistant. This is summarized in the following table:

Macro level	Explanation duration
Guided Tour Style	The Explanation bubble is displayed before the first processing Step is displayed, and includes a **Start** button. The user must click this **Start** button to start the Guided Tour. This effectively functions as a 'start page' and is a useful option for proving some introductory text, process information, prerequisites, and so on.
	Do not use more than one Explanation at this level, as they will both contain **Start** buttons, either of which will start the Guided Tour but still leave the other bubble displayed, which could confuse users.

Macro level	Explanation duration
Application	The Explanation bubble is displayed for the entire duration of the Guided Tour (and not just for steps within the selected application, if the tour spans multiple applications—the Explanation is not actually tied to the application). This is useful for providing information that you always want to be displayed—perhaps a summary of the process, common reference codes, and so on.
Screen	The Explanation bubble is displayed as long as the application screen (for which the Explanation was defined) is displayed. It is displayed as soon as the user navigates to this screen, and is hidden as soon as the user navigates away from this screen.

To insert an EXPLANATION macro into a Guided Tour during editing, carry out the steps shown below.

1. Click on the appropriate existing macro, depending on the level at which you want the Explanation to be defined (see above).

2. Click on the **Insert Explanation** or **Add Explanation** button, depending on which is available. The *Explanation* dialog box is displayed.

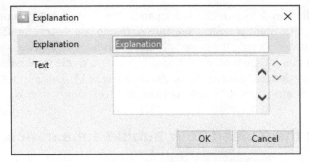

Insert Explanation

3. For **Guided Tour** and **Application** level Explanations, the **Explanation** field is included in the dialog box, and defaults to "Explanation". This is used for the **Comment** property of the EXPLANATION macro, and therefore appears in the *Step View*. You can change this here, if necessary (but you can also change it in the **Comment** property after you have added the Explanation). This is not visible to the user in the Desktop Assistant.

4. Click in the **Text** field. The *Text Editor* is displayed. Use this to enter the required text, and format it as required. Refer to *Adjusting Bubble text* on page 111 for full details of the functionality available in the *Text Editor*.

   Once you have finished editing the text, click on the **OK** button in the *Text Editor* to return to the *Explanation* dialog box.

▲ In this author's experience, the sequence of Screen-level Explanation macros within a single screen/Step is extremely buggy. Sometimes an Explanation inserted after an interaction macro will only appear once that interaction has been performed, but at other times all Explanations on a screen are displayed at the same time, for as long as the screen is displayed.

● Inconsistently, the button to add an Explanation is named **Insert Explanation** on the GUIDED TOUR and APPLICATION macros, and **Add Explanation** on the SCREEN macro.

● Confusingly, the **Explanation** field is not provided in the dialog box for Screen-level Explanations, but you can still change it in the **Comment** property (which still defaults to "Explanation").

5. Back in the *Explanation* dialog box, click on the **OK** button to confirm your changes and insert the EXPLANATION macro into your project.

6. If necessary, move and/or resize the Explanation bubble, either in the *WYSIWYG Editor*, or via the EXPLANATION macro's properties.

Because Explanation bubbles can be displayed at the same time as instructional bubbles, you need to be very careful with the positioning of them, to make sure that they are not obscuring other Bubbles (by default every Explanation bubble will initially be positioned in the center of the screen). This is particularly true if you use Explanations on all three of the above levels, and/or have multiple Explanations for a single screen. A simple fix to this is to just use a different **Bubble Alignment** parameter value for concurrently-displayed bubbles.

There is a further problem with this, in that Explanation bubbles cannot be tied to an object, and are therefore always positioned relative to the screen. Because you cannot guarantee that the user's screen will be the same dimensions as the screen you recorded on you should avoid using bubble pointers altogether in Explanation bubbles (leave the default setting of **Center**, or select the **No Spike** property—see *Adjusting the Guided Tour bubble appearance* on page 384).

Adjusting Bubble Text

Unlike simulation projects (which have separate **Demo Text** and **Practice Text** fields), Desktop Assistant projects have only have one bubble text field: **Text**. This can be edited in exactly the same way as for simulation projects, so we won't duplicate all of that information here. Instead, you should refer to the extensive instructions provided in *Adjusting Bubble text* on page 111. This applies to EXPLANATION, STRING INPUT, MOUSE ACTION, and KEYBOARD macros.

Adjusting the Guided Tour bubble appearance

Bubbles in Desktop Assistant projects are comparable to bubbles in simulation projects (and can be resized and repositioned in the same way). However, the properties available for controlling their appearance are vastly different, owing to the different way in which they are presented to the user. It is therefore necessary to explain these separately (and to explain the options for Guided Tours and Context Help separately, for the same reason).

The full range of options for formatting Guided Tour bubbles is shown in the table below. These are available for all Explanation bubbles, regardless of the level for which they are defined (or were captured during recording), and for all bubbles for interaction macros, regardless of whether these are STRING INPUT macros, MOUSE ACTION macros, or KEYBOARD macros.

Property	Use
Basic Properties	
Icon	For Explanation bubbles (only), you can select an icon to be shown in the upper-left corner of the Bubble. The following icons are available:

    Note   **Tip**   **Info**   **Warning**

You can also select None to have no icon.

Property	Use
Object Bubble	
Style	If necessary, you can override the project-level (or Workarea-level) bubble style by selecting the bubble style you want to use for this bubble.
Width	The bubble will resize automatically to accommodate the text, but you can specify an absolute size (in pixels) if necessary (although just dragging the boundary handles in the *WYSIWYG Editor* would likely be quicker).
Height	
Bubble Alignment	Explanation Bubbles only. Select the position of the bubble relative to the screen, or select **Free** to be able to position it via the **Bubble Position** parameter.
Bubble Position	Explanation Bubbles only. If you selected a **Bubble Alignment** value of **Free**, then use this field to specify the absolute position of the bubble on the screen. Because playback may be on a screen with a different resolution to the captured screen, positions can only be specified as a percentage of the overall screen width and height at which the bubble anchor point [the blue block, during editing] appears—so **50,50** would be the absolute center of the screen (50% along the X axis and 50% down the Y axis).
Orientation	This property specifies the position of the bubble relative to the screen object. It is only relevant if your bubble has a pointer; otherwise, it should be set to **Center**.
Offset	You can use this field to specify an (X,Y) offset to shift the icon or bubble anchor point relative to the specified **Orientation** point. Note that this property is ineffective for Explanations as there is no screen object from which to offset the bubble.

● With simulation project Bubbles, you have both a **Position** property that identifies the position of the bubble anchor point relative to the screen object, and an **Orientation** property that defines the position of the Bubble relative to this anchor point. For Desktop Assistant Bubbles, the single **Orientation** property effectively fulfills both of these purposes.

Property	Use
No Spike	Select this option to suppress the bubble 'spike' (the pointer that extends from the bubble). This would seem like a pointless option as setting the **Orientation** to **Center** would achieve the same thing, but given that the **Offset** option is ineffective for EXPLANATION macros, this option can be used in conjunction with an **Orientation** of anything except **Center** to move an Explanation bubble off the bubble anchor point and still avoid pointing to a particular place on the screen (which will likely shift during playback). Note that the spike still appears during editing, and is only suppressed during playback.
Minimizable	If selected, the bubble includes a **Minimize** icon (in the header) during playback. The user can click on this to 'minimize' the bubble. This replaces the bubble with the **Help Mini Icon**, which appears at the (current) reference point for the bubble. The user can click on this icon to re-display the bubble.
Closable	If selected, the bubble includes a **Close** icon (in the header), during playback. The user can click on this to close the bubble (it can not be reinstated). Note that closing the Explanation at the Guided Tour level will close the entire Guided Tour.
Next Button	If selected, the bubble includes a **Next** button (in the lower-right corner of the bubble) during playback. The user can click on this to progress to the next Step in the Guided Tour. This is not available for Guided Tour level Explanations, as they have a **Start** button instead.

▲ Don't think that you can change the icon used for the minimized bubble via the **Mini Icon Type** parameter. That parameter only works with Context Help, and if you select it for a Guided Tour Explanation, inexplicably no icon at all (not even the default **Help** one) is displayed when the user clicks on the **Minimize** button.

The following graphic shows an example of a bubble for a Desktop Assistant Guided Tour, and highlights a few of the optional elements.

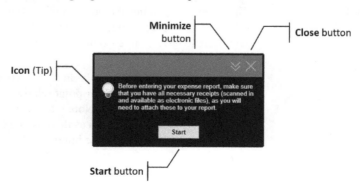

Note that this example is of an Explanation bubble (which is why there's an Icon) at the Guided Tour level (which is why the **Start** button is present), and using the **Big Title Bar** bubble style.

Validating Input Text

Because the Desktop Assistant provides context-sensitive field-level help, it is able to interact directly with screen objects (typically, buttons and input fields). This means that it can see exactly what a user enters into an input field, and validate this. In this section, we'll look at the functionality that Enable Now provides to perform this validation.

By way of example, let's assume that HR has reported that employees always forget to specify the purpose of their expenses when creating an expense report. The Purpose field isn't a mandatory field in the system, but we want to make sure that the user always enters some text anyway. To do this, we need to use a **condition**.

To define a condition for an input field, carry out the steps shown below.

1. In the *Step View*, click on the INPUT TEXT macro for the input field, to show its properties in the *Macro Editor*, and go to the *Condition* category (an example of this is shown at the end of these steps).

2. In the **Condition Pattern** field, select the condition that you want to apply to the input field. There are several standard options to choose from (such as **Is equal to**, **Is greater than**, and so on), or if you need something more complex, you can select **Regular Expression** and use the full functionality of regular expressions. (For slightly more information on regular expressions, see page 130.)

    For our example, we will select a **Condition Pattern** of **Minimum number of characters**.

3. Enter the value for this condition in the **Condition Value** field. What you enter here will depend upon the **Condition Pattern** chosen. For example, if you chose a **Condition Pattern** of **Is Equal To**, then you would enter the expected value (that the field should be equal to) in this field. If you selected **Regular Expression**, you would enter the regular expression itself into this field.

    For our example, we will enter a value of **1** which, in conjunction with our **Condition Pattern** of **Minimum number of characters** will make sure that the user enters *something*.

4. If processing should continue with a specific Step (other than the default next sequential Step) if the user enters a value that *matches* this condition, then select this step in the **Jump Target** field. This could be a useful option if you want to perform (or avoid) specific steps depending upon the value entered (for example, if additional fields need to be completed if the user enters a negative price on an invoice).

▲ That's the theory, but in this author's experience if you select *anything* in the **Jump Target** field, the Guided Tour just stops as soon as the user enters a valid value.

5. In the **Condition Text** field, enter a message that should be displayed to the user if they *do not* enter a correct value. This will be displayed in a pop-up bubble on the screen. You should always specify a text—otherwise the user will not know why their input is not valid.

6. If the user's input should also match the text *case* of the **Condition Value**, then select the **Case Sensitive** checkbox.

■ Consider using a different bubble type (than the type used for instructions) and/or a different highlight color to emphasize to the user that this is a break-in validation message and not just a regular part of the Guided Tour.

7. In the **Bubble Style** field, select the type of bubble that you want to use for the **Condition Text** message.

8. If a highlight is displayed for this input field (the **Show Highlight** property for the macro is selected) then select the color that should be used for this highlight when the condition is not met in the **Highlight Color** field.

For our example scenario, the *Condition* category of properties for our Purpose field's INPUT TEXT macro now appears as follows:

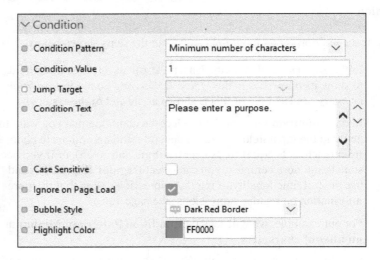

Now let's see what this would look like during playback. The following partial screenshot shows our example Guided Tour if the user does not enter a text in the Purpose field.

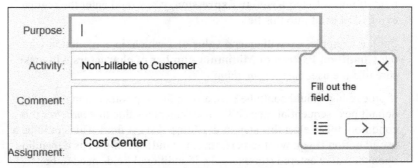

Example 1: When the Guided Tour Step is first displayed.

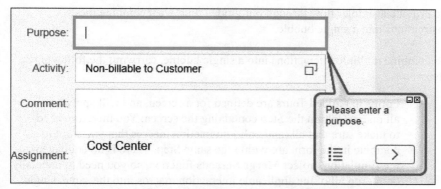

Example 2: If the user attempts to skip to the next step without input.

Note that in this example we have used a different **Bubble Style** and **Highlight Color**, to draw the user's attention to the fact that they have done something wrong.

Before we finish with the subject of input field validation, there is one more setting that you may find useful. This is the **Set Value Automatically** property, which can be found in the *Display Behavior* category. If you select this checkbox, then the value entered in the **Input Text** property (which is [by default] the value that you entered during recording) is automatically entered into the input field as soon as the user reaches this Step in the Guided Tour. This is useful if the user should always enter a specific value in a field, as you can pre-populate the field for them, and then apply a condition to make sure they don't change it.

▲ Use this option (of pre-populating fields) with caution. Some companies are (rightly) wary of training systems updating production data.

Using a Form

By default, each interaction in a Guided Tour will be placed in a separate Step, along with the associated screenshot. This means that each interaction will be displayed in its own bubble. As an alternative to this, you can have multiple interactions included in the same, single bubble by using a **Form**.

● Forms in Guided Tours are not the same as Forms in simulation projects; they are constructed differently and display differently.

Let's look at how to do this by way of an example, using our recording of *Creating an Expense Report*. Within this recording, we have a couple of steps where we select an expense category and then click OK to add this to our report. Here are the initial instructions, in separate bubbles, as they appear during playback.

To provide a simpler flow through our guided tour, we'll combine these instructions into a single bubble.

To combine multiple interactions into a single bubble, carry out the following steps:

1. Forms in Guided Tours are defined for a screen, and will apply to all macros within the Step containing the screen. You therefore need to make sure that all (and only) interaction macros that you want to combine in the form are within the same Step. There is no equivalent to the simulation project **Merge Screens** function, so you need to manually drag/drop all of the applicable interaction macros into the same, single Step, below the SCREEN macro.

   In our example, we will drag the macro for the second bubble above into the same Step as the first bubble. Here, sequencing is important, as the bubble texts will appear in the combined (Form) bubble in the same order as they appear in the *Step View*.

2. Delete any Steps that now no longer have an interaction macro (that is, the Steps from which you dragged the macros into your consolidated step). Technically it won't cause any problems to leave them in the project, but they aren't needed, so to keep things tidy you may as well delete them.

3. Go to the *last* action in the (combined) Step and set its **Next Step** property (in the *Next Guided Tour Step* category) to the next Step of the Guided Tour. (This property is always set automatically during recording, but for some reason it is blanked out when you combine action macros in a single Step.)

4. Select the SCREEN macro in the combined Step, and then select the **Form Mode** property in the *Macro Editor*.

5. Update the **Comment** and **Name** properties for all subsequent Steps (that is, Steps after the Step that now contains the Form Mode) to reflect the correct Guided Tour step numbers. (Enable Now automatically inserts a sequentially-numbered step identifier during recording, but if you delete [or add] Steps, this is not updated automatically.)

Now, when the user reaches this screen during playback, an additional dialog box is displayed showing all of the actions for this screen. However, the standard bubble is still displayed, showing the text for only one action—and to see the bubble for the other action, the user has to display the *Step List* and select another action. The following two screenshots show the 'form structure' for our example exercise. In these examples, the *Step List* is also displayed, so you can see the different actions being selected.

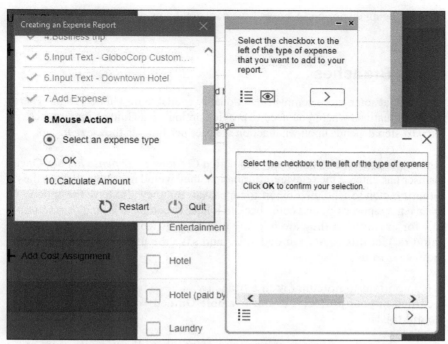

Example 1: The first action in the Step is selected

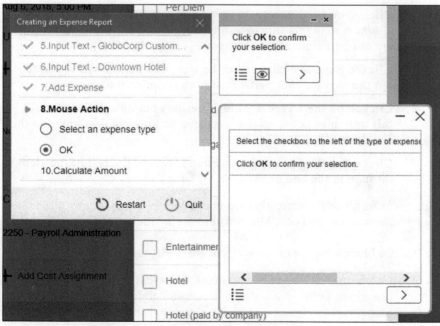

Example 2: The second action in the Step is selected

This is far from an ideal solution, and doesn't really achieve the stated objective
of having the text for all actions in a single bubble (actually resulting in more

'bubbles' being displayed...), but at least now you know what this functionality does.

Using Branches

Let's look at some more complex functionality available for Guided Tours. There may be situations where you need to provide options in a Guided Tour—where the *next* step depends upon what action the user performs in the *current* step.

We have an example of this in our simulation *Creating an Expense Report*. Once the user has entered the relevant information, they would normally click on the **Submit** button to send their report for approval. But they also have the option to *save* the report as-is, and come back to it later to complete it (and *then* submit it)—for example, if they are missing a receipt. It would be better if we could reflect this in our Guided Tour, and give the user the option of what they want to do.

It is important to note that with a branch you need to have *both* branches recorded in your project. For our example Guided Tour project, here's how we did this:

1. Recorded all steps up until the point where the user can save or submit, as usual.

2. Clicked on the **Execute Mouse Actions** button on the *Recorder Toolbar*, to toggle this option to off, so that the captured actions are not performed in the system.

3. Clicked **Save** and committed the step. The action was captured, but the step was not performed in the application.

4. Clicked on the **Execute Mouse Actions** button again, to toggle this option back on, so that captured actions *are* performed in the application.

5. Clicked on the **Submit** button, and recorded the rest of the steps through to the end of the task.

This gives us all of the steps that we need, but obviously this would make no sense as a linear activity. That's where the **branch** comes in.

To insert a branch into your simulation, carry out the following steps:

1. Combine the two (or more) interactions that will constitute the branching point into a single Step and delete any now-empty Steps.

    For our example, we will drag the MOUSE ACTION macro for clicking **Submit** into the same Step as the MOUSE ACTION macro for clicking **Save**, and then delete the Step that originally contained the Submit interaction (which is now empty except for the screenshot).

2. Click on the interaction for the first branch (in our case, clicking on **Save**), to display its properties in the *Macro Editor*, and set its **Next Step** property (in the *Next Guided Tour Step* category) to the first step of the branch for this action.

   Repeat this step for all additional branches.

3. Update the **Comment** and **Name** properties for all subsequent Steps (after the Step that now contains the Form Mode) to reflect the correct Guided Tour step numbers.

Now, during playback—and assuming that the user has the *Step List* displayed—the user can choose which branch to follow by selecting it from the task list. Once they select a branch, the instructions for that action are displayed. The following two screenshots show how this manifests itself in our example Guided Tour.

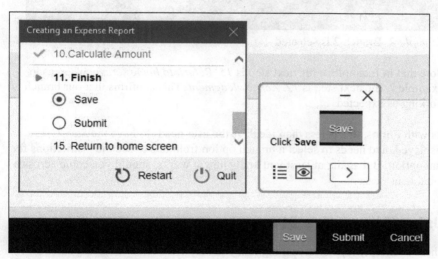

Example 1: Branch 1 is selected

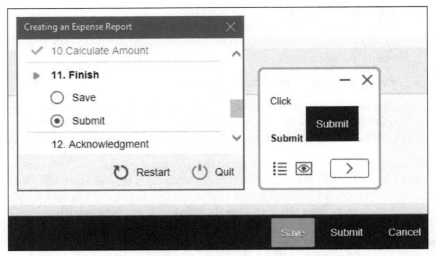

Example 2: Branch 2 is selected

Note that in Example 1, the next step is *15. Return to home screen*, whereas in Example 2, the next step is *12. Acknowledgment*. This confirms that our branch is working as expected.

As with Forms, this is less than ideal, as the user needs to have the *Step List* displayed, and needs to select a branch option from this to see the instructions for that option. But again, at least you know how it works, should you come across a suitable use case.

Using Alternative Steps

There is another type of branching that you may want to cater for in your Guided Tour. This is where the user performs an action and may see one of two (or more) possible screens next. Consider our current example, where we are entering an expense report. If we have previously started an expense report, then when we try to create a new report, we are asked if we want to continue working with this previously-started report. It would be good if we can cater for this scenario. To do this, we can use an **Alternative Step**.

Alternative Steps allow us to say how the Guided Tour should proceed if the *expected* next step cannot be performed because the context for that step is not found. You can define up to three Alternative Steps for a macro, in the *Next Guided Tour Step* category of the macro's properties. The Guided Tour will attempt to continue with each step in turn until it finds a context in these alternative steps that matches the context on the actual application screen.

In our example, assume that we have recorded the following steps:

1. (Prior steps.)

2. Click on the **New** button.

3. If prompted to continue an existing report click **Yes**.

4. Enter the expense details.

5. (Subsequent steps.)

Step 3 may or not be displayed. To cater for this, we would add an Alternative Step to Step 2, stating that if the context for Step 3 is not found when we perform the action for Step 2, then the Guided Tour should go directly to Step 4, effectively skipping Step 3.

The definitions to support this are shown in the sample screenshot below. Here, the Step Names have been changed to match the descriptions above, to make it easier to correlate the Steps to our scenario.

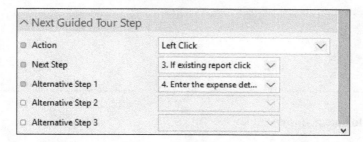

The **Action** and **Next Step** properties are automatically filled in with the recorded Action for this step and the logical next Step upon completion of this macro. To define an Alternative Step, simply select the required Alternative Step from the drop-down list for the **Alternative Step 1** field (and **Alternative Step 2** and **3** if necessary).

Context Help projects

Context Help is in-application help that is presented as a stand-alone bubble tied to a specific screen object (that is, not as a Guided Tour). This is most useful for providing targeted help for a specific field or button.

For Context Help bubbles to be displayed, Desktop Assistant must be running, but the user does not have to click on the **Content** button in the *Desktop Assistant Toolbar* to display the help—it is automatically displayed as soon as the user navigates to screen for which the Context Help was recorded (and the specific screen object is visible on the screen).

An example of a typical Context Help bubble is shown below:

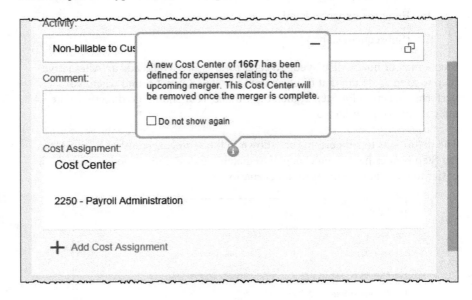

Things to note in this example:

- The bubble **Orientation** is set to **North**.
- The **Mini Icon Type** is set to **Info**.
- The **Minimizable** option is selected.
- The **Hide Option** option is selected.

These options are described later in this section, so don't worry if they don't mean anything to you yet.

Recording Context Help

To create a Context Help project, carry out the steps shown below. Note that the first few steps are almost identical to recording a Guided Tour, so information is only summarized below (refer to *Recording a Guided Tour* on page 371 for full instructions, if necessary).

1. Click on the Group within which you want to create the project.

2. On the *Producer Toolbar*, click on the **New Object** button, and then select **[Desktop Assistant] Context Help**, under *In-App Help*. The *New Project* dialog box is displayed. This is exactly the same as the example shown under *Guided Tour projects* on page 371, but the **Project Type** is **Desktop Assistant - Context Help**. Complete this dialog box as explained in that section, and then click **OK**. The project is created, and opened in the *Project Editor*, as a separate tab within *Producer*.

3. On the *Project Editor Toolbar*, click on the **Record Object** button. The *Choose Application* dialog box is displayed. Again, this is the same as for Guided Tours. Complete this dialog box, and then click on the **Record** button. You are passed into the application.

Record
Object

4. Click on the screen control for which you want to provide Context Help. The same three capture elements (*Bubble Formatting* dialog box, Action Area, and bubble) are displayed. Adjust these as necessary, and then click on **Apply**. Repeat this step for all additional screen objects for which you want to provide help.

5. Once you have captured all required elements, click on the **Stop** button on the *Recording Toolbar*. You are passed back into the *Project Editor*.

You can now edit this project as explained in the next section.

Editing a Context Help project

Once you finish recording a Context Help project (or once conversion from a simulation project completes) you are passed into the *Project Editor*. If you want to edit an existing Context Help project, simply locate it in the Workarea, and double-click on it to open it in the *Project Editor*.

As with Guided Tours, the Project Editor for Context Help projects is similar to the Project Editor for simulation projects. If you are not familiar with the *Project Editor*, you should refer to *The Project Editor* on page 104 before continuing.

The screen layout and basic navigation is the same as for other projects (both simulations and Guided Tours), and so won't be repeated here. However, although the macros available for Context Help projects are largely the same as for Guided Tour projects, the properties that are available are generally different, so we will examine them more closely in this section.

The example we will use for this project is for the scenario where a new Cost Center has been defined, and we want to alert our users to this fact and advise them when to use it. This is information that we will only need to provide temporarily (until they get used to its availability), so Context Help is the perfect vehicle for providing this information—and right at the point that users will need it.

The image below shows the entire content of our Context Help project:

You can see that this project consists of three Steps. The first two are always provided for a Context Help project. The third is repeated for every screen object for which help is being provided. Let's look at these three types of Steps in a little more detail.

The first Step in any Context Help project is the **Start** Step, which contains a single macro of CONTEXT HELP STYLE. This macro provides options that apply to the project as a whole. These are explained in *Controlling the overall appearance of Context Help* on page 399.

The second Step is the **Application** step, This identifies the application that was recorded to create this Desktop Assistant project (even if this was by way of a simulation project—see *Converting a simulation project into a Desktop Assistant project* on page 369). In the example above, the Context Help project was captured in the Microsoft Edge browser, so the application shown is **microsoftedge.exe**. The macro properties for this step provide technical information about the capture profile used. You should not normally need to change any of these properties.

These two standard Steps will be followed by a Step for each Context Help bubble captured. Each Step will contain:

1. A SCREEN macro, containing a screenshot of the screen against which the action was performed. The screenshot itself (and the associated application key) are largely for reference only and should not need to be changed. There are no properties for this macro that have a direct influence on the *appearance* of the Context Help, so we will not describe them here.

2. An interaction macro—typically a MOUSE ACTION macro or an INPUT TEXT macro. The ways in which you can control this macro are explained in *Controlling the appearance of a Context Help bubble* on page 400.

Controlling the overall appearance of Context Help

The overall appearance of the Context Help help content is controlled by the
CONTEXT HELP STYLE macro. The table below lists the properties available for
this macro and explains their purpose.

Property	Use
Comment	This defaults to **Context Help**. This text is used in the macro in the *Step View*. You can change this if you need to, but it's probably more helpful to leave it as-is.
UID	This is the unique identifier of the macro.
Display Variant *	This property defines how the Context Help will initially be displayed. This can be one of: • **Icon**: An icon will be displayed alongside the screen object to which the help applies. The user clicks on this to display the Context Help bubble. • **Tooltip**: The content of the Context Help bubble will be displayed when the user hovers the cursor over the screen object to which the help applies. Unless you select the **Highlights** option, there is no indication that help is available until the user hovers over the object. • **Bubble**: The Context Help bubble will be displayed as soon as the screen object is visible. If the user chooses to 'minimize' the bubble it is replaced by the **Icon**.
Mini Icons Style	If you a **Display Variant** of **Icon** then you can select the specific icon set to be used. Note that the individual icon is specified at the bubble level via the **Mini Icon Type** property.
Highlights *	If this option is selected then the Highlight will be shown for the screen object as soon as the object is visible on the screen (and regardless of the **Display Variant** used).

* Setting can be overridden at the macro level.

Controlling the Bubble Text

Similar to Guided Tours, there is only one bubble text type for Context Help. This
is specified in the **Text** property for the interaction macro. This can be edited in
exactly the same way as for simulation projects, so we won't duplicate all of that

information here. Instead, you should refer to the extensive instructions provided in *Adjusting Bubble text* on page 111. This applies to all interaction macros.

Controlling the appearance of a Context Help bubble

Typically, a Context Help project will consist of one Step per screen, and one or more interaction macros within this: one for each screen object for which help is being provided. In many cases—especially if you are providing temporary help on a new feature—you will have one screen and one macro in each Step.

Because the possibilities with Context Help are relatively few (versus a Guided Tour), *all* of the properties that apply to interaction macros in a Context Help project are explained in a single table, below.

Property	Use
Object Bubble	
Display Variant	This property can be used to override the project-level **Display Variant** property (see page 399). If it is left with the default value of **Global**, then the project-level setting will be used.
Style	Select the bubble style you want to use for this Context Help bubble. Note that there is no project-level **Style** setting for Context Help, as there is for Guided Tours.
Mini Icon Type	If you are using a **Display Variant** of **Icon** (or **Bubble**, in case the user minimizes this), select the icon that is to be displayed alongside the screen object. The following icons are available: ? **Help** (Default) ↻ **Update** ◯ **Link** ⓘ **Info** ✉ **Training** 💡 **Tip** ⚠ **Warning** ★ **New** ☰ **Note** ⚒ **Maintenance** 📎 **Attachment** § **Compliance**
Width	The bubble will resize automatically to accommodate the text, but you can specify an absolute size (in pixels) if necessary (although just dragging the boundary handles in the *WYSIWYG Editor* would likely be quicker).
Height	
Orientation	This specifies the position of the Context Help icon and/or the bubble pointer relative to the screen object. It is only relevant if your bubble has a pointer; otherwise, it should be set to **Center**.

★ The icons shown here are from the default **Desktop Assistant: Mini Icons** set. Administrators can define other sets via menu option **Tools | Customization | Edit Style Resources**.

Property	Use
Offset	You can use this field to specify an (X,Y) offset to shift the icon or bubble pointer relative to the specified **Orientation** point.
Minimized	Select this option if you want the bubble to initially be minimized. This is presumably only relevant for a **Display Variant** of **Bubble**.
No Spike	Select this option to suppress the bubble 'spike' (the pointer that extends from the bubble).
Minimizable	If this option is selected then the bubble includes a **Minimize** icon (in the header) during playback. The user can click on this to 'minimize' the bubble. This replaces the bubble with the **Help Mini Icon**, which appears at the (current) anchor point for the bubble. The user can click on this icon to re-display the bubble.
Hide Option	If this option is selected then the bubble includes a checkbox labeled **Do not show again**. The user can select this to prevent this Context Help bubble from being displayed again when they access the same screen.

● If a user has hidden one or more Context Help bubbles, they can reinstate them all (there is no 'individual bubble' option) by clicking on the **Show All Suppressed Help Again** option on the *Settings* tab of the Desktop Assistant *Content Panel*.

A new Cost Center of **1667** has been defined for expenses relating to the upcoming merger. This Cost Center will be removed once the merger is complete.

☐ Do not show again

This is useful if you have used a **Display Variant** of **Bubble** to ensure that users see this information at least once, but want the user to be able to dismiss it once they have seen it.

Highlight	
Show Highlight **Offset** **Effect** **Border** **Color** **Animation Steps**	These properties work in exactly the same way as for Guided Tour bubbles. To avoid unnecessary duplication in an already-large book, please refer to *Controlling the Highlight* on page 380 for details.

Display Behavior	
Enabled	If you want to suppress this help bubble from being displayed, you can select this checkbox. This is useful if you want to temporarily remove this help.

Property	Use
Force Display	Users can suppress the display of all Context Help by toggling off the **Context Help** button on the *Desktop Assistant Sidebar*. If you want this Context Help bubble to be displayed anyway (and override the user's settings) then select this checkbox.

Extending a Context Help Project

If you have created a Context Help project and subsequently decide that you need to provide Context Help for additional screen objects, you can extend your Context Help project as explained in the subsections below.

Note that these sections are listed in the order you are most likely to use them, but in practice, the logical (hierarchical) progression is **application → screen → object**. Technically, you can just use the first section below (adding an object), as the application and screen will also be captured if they do not already exist in the project.

Adding help for another screen object

If you want to provide Context Help for an additional object on a screen that already exists in your Context Help project (for example, because you have already provided Context Help for other objects on the same screen) then you can do this by following the steps shown below.

■ Selecting the screen in Step 1 is pretty much optional; if you don't, Enable Now will identify the correct SCREEN macro for the control selected in Step 3 anyway, and add the new control to this same screen.

1. In the *Project Editor*, click on the Screen macro for the application screen that contains the object for which you want to capture new Context Help.

2. On the *Project Editor Toolbar*, click on the **Record Object** button. The standard *Choose Application* dialog box is displayed. Complete this dialog box, and then click on the **Record** button. You are passed into the application. Record Object

3. Click on the screen control for which you want to provide Context Help. Adjust the capture elements as necessary, and then click on **Apply**. Repeat this step for all additional screen objects for which you want to provide help.

4. Once you have captured all required elements, click on the **Stop** button on the *Recording Toolbar* to return to the *Project Editor*.

(Note that Steps 2 to 4 are identical to the steps for the initial Context Help recording.)

Adding help for another screen

If you want to provide Context Help for an object on a screen that does not yet exist in your project (for example, because you haven't provided Context Help for any objects on that screen yet) then you can do this by following the steps shown below.

1. In the *Project Editor*, click on pretty much any Step or macro. The new Screen will be added in a new Step immediately following the currently-selected Step, but screen order is not significant in Context Help projects anyway.

2. On the *Project Editor Toolbar*, click on the **Record Screen** button. The *Choose Application* dialog box is displayed.

Record Screen

3. Complete the *Choose Application* dialog box , and then click **Record**. The *Record Screen* dialog box is displayed.

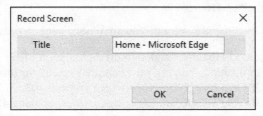

● If you select a screen that already exists in your project then Enable Now will simply add it again, resulting in two identical screens being added to your project. This may be valid (for example the same screen used with two different display variants), but in general you would normally only want each screen to appear once, so watch out for this.

4. The **Title** field defaults to the title of the screen in the application. You can change this, if necessary. This name is only used internally within the *Project Editor*, and will not be seen by users, so this is largely for the Author's reference.

5. Click on the **OK** button. You are passed back into the *Project Editor*.

A new Step is added to your project, which contains only a SCREEN macro for the application screen that you selected. You can now capture Context Help for objects on this screen as explained in *Adding help for another screen object* on page 402.

Adding help for another application

You can include Context Help for multiple applications within the same project. You would probably not normally want to do this, but there may be circumstances under which you want to provide temporary help relating to the same new functionality or change that impacts multiple applications, and providing all of this help in a single project will make it easier to discontinue this help—by deleting this single project—when it is no longer required.

To include another application in your project, carry out the steps shown below.

1. In the *Project Editor*, click on any Step or macro.

2. On the *Project Editor Toolbar*, click on the **Record Application** button. The *Choose Application* dialog box is displayed.

Record Application

3. Complete the *Choose Application* dialog box as usual, and then click **Choose**. The *Record Application* dialog box is displayed.

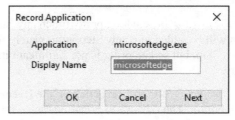

4. The **Application** field defaults to the name of the application. You can change this, if necessary. This name is only used internally within the *Project Editor*, and will not be seen by users, so this is largely for the Author's reference.

5. Click on the **OK** button. You are passed back into the *Project Editor*.

A new APPLICATION macro is added to the Application Step (Step 2), specifying the selected application. You can now capture Screens for this application, as explained in *Adding help for another screen* on page 403, and/or objects, as explained in *Adding help for another screen object* on page 402.

Note that any screens you subsequently add for this application will simply be added into the body of the project, and not immediately below the APPLICATION macro (because all APPLICATION macros are grouped together into a single Step at the start of the project). If you're wondering how Enable Now knows which screens go with which application, the link is provided by the **Application** property of the SCREEN macro, which ties to the same property in the APPLICATION macro.

Capturing context for non-Desktop Assistant content objects

Whenever you record a Desktop Assistant Guided Tour or Context Help, Enable Now captures the context of this, so that it can display this content whenever the user is working within the same context (for example, within the same application/screen). However, there may be times when you want additional content (other than a Guided Tour, Context Help, or a simulation project) to be listed in the Desktop Assistant Content Panel as 'applicable information'. To do this, you have to assign the same context to this additional content.

Let's look at this by way of an example. We have a Guided Tour for *Creating an Expense Report*. Suppose we also have a training course called *Travel and*

Expense Guidelines that we would like to make available to users when they are entering their expense reports. To do this, we will assign the same context as is assigned to the Guided Tour to the Book for this training course.

To capture context for a non-Desktop Assistant content object carry out the steps shown below.

1. In the application, navigate to the context (application and screen) for which the content object should be proffered as applicable help.

2. In Producer, navigate to and select the content object for which you are capturing the context (a Book, in our example). Make sure that you have this checked out for editing.

3. Click on the **Record Context** button at the top of the *Object Editor* pane, and select **Record Desktop Assistant Context** from the drop-down menu. The standard *Select Window and Profile* dialog box is displayed.

Record Context

4. Click on the application window from which you are capturing the context. This window is displayed on the screen (with the *Select Window and Profile* dialog box still overlaid on top of it).

5. Check the profile in the **Choose Profile** field, and then click on the **Record** button.

6. The context is captured from the current screen of the selected window and saved into the **Context: Desktop Assistant** property of the content object. Note that this may take a few moments, and there is no confirmation message to indicate when it is complete.

7. Don't forget to save the updated content object to the server, and check it in if you have finished editing it.

Now that the context has been correctly assigned to the content object, it will appear in the Desktop Assistant when the user navigates to this context, as shown in the example below.

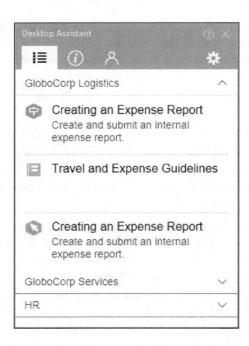

Note that the content object must be included in a Group that is located below your **Desktop Assistant** Group, and you need to make sure that the content object type (in this example **Books**) is selected for inclusion when you generate the Desktop Assistant (see *Generating the Desktop Assistant* on page 415).

Updating assigned context

If you subsequently need to attach an additional context to the same content object (for example, if it spans multiple screens), or if you want to replace the context, or delete the context so that the content object no longer appears in the Desktop Assistant (for this context), then repeat the steps provided above, but after Step 3, you will be prompted with the following dialog box:

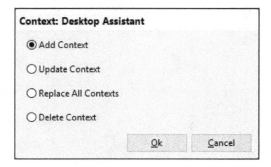

Select the appropriate option, and continue as before.

Editing context

When you record content for the Desktop Assistant, Enable Now captures the exact context of the screen. This context is comprised of a combination of elements (depending on the application), for example:

- The application (executable)
- The transaction code (for SAP systems)
- The screen name

Whenever a user accesses the same context, this content is proffered as applicable content in the Desktop Assistant. Normally, this is what you want, but there are a few situations where you *don't* want to do this. Let's look at a couple of examples.

Excluding context from the Desktop Assistant

In our example recording of *Changing your User Parameters* (SAP ECC 6.0 transaction code SU3) we included steps demonstrating how parameters worked, showing an example of a screen from transaction VA01. This resulted in the context for transaction VA01 being captured in our recording, which means that every time a user accesses (this specific screen within) transaction VA01, our *Changing your User Parameters* Guided Tour will appear in the Desktop Assistant as applicable content. This clearly isn't what we want, so we need to get Enable Now to ignore this (VA01) context for the Desktop Assistant.

To prevent a captured context in a project from being considered for context matching in the Desktop Assistant, follow the steps shown below.

1. Open the project (simulation project or Desktop Assistant Guided Tour project) in the *Project Editor*.

2. Navigate to the Step for the context that you want to remove from the project, and click on the SCREEN macro to show its properties in the *Macro Editor*.

3. Expand the *Rerecord* category, and select the **Exclude from Desktop Assistant** checkbox.

Rerecord	
Object Type	screenshot
Executable	saplogon.exe
Screendump Configuration File	SAPGUISignatureDesign
Page Key	`<PageAtt type="title" value="Create Sales Order: Initial Screen" langdep="1"/>` `<PageAtt type="transaction" value="VA01" langdep="0"/>` `<PageAtt type="type"`
Exclude from Desktop Assistant	☑
Recorded Window ID	0

4. Save your changes.

The context for this screen will now be excluded from context matching in the Desktop Assistant

Genericizing page key attributes

Enable Now is very pedantic about the context that it captures, and this can cause problems with some screens or other elements. For example, say we have recorded a project of *Displaying a Sales Order* (transaction VA03 in SAP ECC 6.0). Now suppose when we recorded this simulation we used an order with an SAP document number of 12345678. The screen (context) captured for the recording will be "Display Order: 12345678". Now, if the user is displaying a sales order with a document number of 98765432 our content will *not* be proffered as context-sensitive help, because the screen context does not match. Clearly this is a problem. Fortunately, Enable Now (as always) has a solution: 'genericizing' the screen name context so that the document number is ignored (technically, so *any* number is considered a 'match'). You do this by changing the attributes of the context page keys.

To change the page key attributes for a project, so that variable data is not considered to be a part of the context, carry out the following steps.

▲ When replacing page key attributes you must have the object checked out for editing—otherwise it won't do anything, but will look like it has because there is no error message generated.

1. In the Workarea, click on the content object for which you want to edit the context. You can also select a Group (at any level—even the entire **Desktop Assistant** Group) and edit the context for all of the content within it at the same time.

2. Select menu option **Tools | Context Administration | Replace Page Key Attributes**. The *Replace Page Key Attribute* dialog box is displayed.

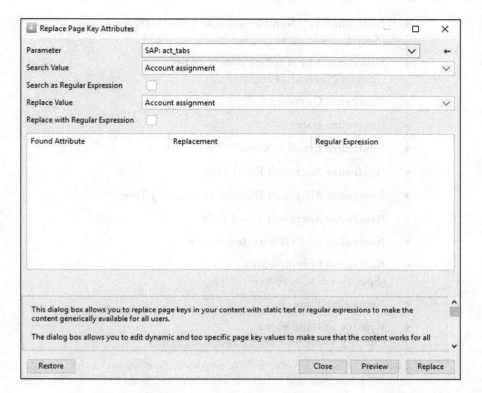

| Replace Page Key Attributes | — □ × |

Parameter	SAP: act_tabs ∨	←
Search Value	Account assignment ∨
Search as Regular Expression	☐
Replace Value	Account assignment ∨
Replace with Regular Expression	☐

Found Attribute	Replacement	Regular Expression

This dialog box allows you to replace page keys in your content with static text or regular expressions to make the content generically available for all users.

The dialog box allows you to edit dynamic and too specific page key values to make sure that the content works for all

| Restore | | Close | Preview | Replace |

When you first display the *Replace Page Key Attributes* dialog box, it is shown in Standard Mode, which includes a **Preset** drop-down (in place of the Search and Replace fields) that provides access to a number of preset replacement rules for common scenarios. The example above shows the Advanced Mode of this dialog box, which you can access by clicking on the *Advanced Mode* button (🔆) on the simplified form of the dialog box. (My reasoning here is that if you learn how to manually genericize context, using the presets will be a cinch.)

3. In the **Parameter** field, select the context parameter for which you want to change the attribute values. The available parameters will depend upon the application, and you may need to cycle through each of them in turn, looking for variable data.

   For our example, we will use the **SAP: title** parameter, as that is the one that contains our sales order document number in the screen title.

4. If you are using Standard Mode, select the appropriate predefined replacement rule from the **Preset** drop-down (and additional parameters as noted below) and then continue with Step 8. If you are using Advanced Mode, continue with Step 5.

   The following presets are available:

   ♦ **Neutralize All Numbers**

➕ The *Replace Page Key Attribute* dialog box was reworked to include **Presets** in the 1811 release.

- ◆ **Neutralize Any Number With At Least X Digits**
  (Specify **Number of Digits**)

- ◆ **Neutralize Any Number with X Digits**
  (Specify **Number of Digits**)

- ◆ **Neutralize Currency**

- ◆ **Neutralize Date**

- ◆ **Neutralize Email Address**

- ◆ **Neutralize Microsoft Excel Title**

- ◆ **Neutralize Microsoft Outlook (Calendar) Title**

- ◆ **Neutralize Microsoft Word Title**

- ◆ **Neutralize SAP GUI System Name**

- ◆ **Neutralize Specific Value**
  (Specify **Value to Find**)

- ◆ **Neutralize Time**

- ◆ **Replace Specific Value**
  (Specify **Value To Find** and **Replace With**)

5. Click on the **Search Value** field to display a list of current values for the selected parameter, and select the value that you want to change from the drop-down list.

6. When you select a value in the **Search Value** field, the same value is automatically copied into the **Replace Value** field, so that you can change only the parts that you need to. Update the **Replace Value** field as necessary.

   For our example, we want to replace the actual document number with effectively "anything". To do this, we can use a Regular Expression. Regular Expressions are beyond the scope of this book, but in this scenario the expression we want to use is **\d+**. This matches any number.

■ You can also use Regular Expressions in the **Search Value** field (as long as you select the **Search as Regular Expression** checkbox). This is useful if (for example, there are several numbers and you want to replace all of them with the same replacement value..

7. If you are using a regular expression in the **Replace Value** field (as we are in our example) then make sure you select the **Replace with Regular Expression** checkbox. Otherwise, the literal text specified in the **Replace Value** field will be used in the replacement.

8. Click on the **Preview** button. (It is recommended that you always preview your changes.) The area in the center of the dialog box is populated with all of the changes that will be made. Check this information carefully.

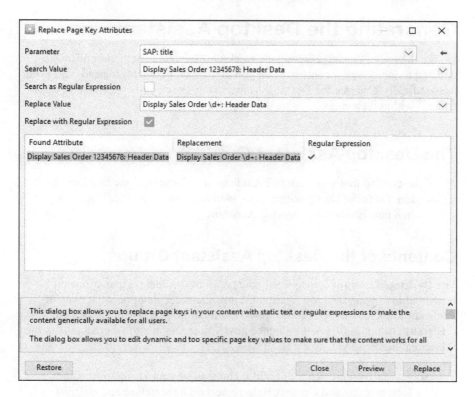

9. Once you have confirmed that these are the changes you want to make, click on the **Replace** button. The key values are changed. A progress bar is displayed while this is being done, but this may be very quick if there are only a few changes to make, and no final confirmation message is displayed.

10. Click on the **Close** button to close the *Replace Page Key Attribute* dialog box.

Now, regardless of the specific sales document that the user is displaying, our project of *Displaying a Sales Order* will be suggested as context-applicable help.

Restoring page key attributes

If things go horribly wrong, and your changes to the page key attributes do not work the way you intended, then you can effectively back out your changes and revert to the original values, via the same functionality. To do this, either select the specific parameter and value that you want to revert and click on the **Restore** button in the *Replace Page Key Attribute Value* dialog box, or click on the **Restore All** button to restore all of the page keys for the entire project.

Generating the Desktop Assistant

Unlike the (cloud-based) *Trainer*, the Desktop Assistant is not automatically updated to include new content when you publish that content. Instead, you need to specifically generate the Desktop Assistant any time content is added to it, or content within it changes.

The Desktop Assistant Group

All of the content that you want to include in your Desktop Assistant must be included in a specific Group within your Workarea, and it is this Group that you select when publishing your Desktop Assistant.

Contents of the Desktop Assistant Group

The **Desktop Assistant** Group must contain all of the content that you want to be available in your Desktop Assistant. You should decide upon what content you want to include in your Desktop Assistant before you create the **Desktop Assistant** Group, as this will influence how you create it, and whereabouts in the Workarea hierarchy you create it.

Typically, your Desktop Assistant will include all of your Desktop Assistant Guided Tour projects and Context Help projects. The structure and order of content objects within the Desktop Assistant Group is effectively irrelevant, because content is never displayed in this structure (content is displayed in a flat list in the *Desktop Assistant Content Panel*, depending on the application context). This means that you *could* have all of the content objects in the single **Desktop Assistant** Group, with no subgroups—although, as always, you will find maintenance much easier if you do structure your content objects.

In addition to including your Guided Tours and Context Helps in your Desktop Assistant Group, you may want to include other content objects. For example, you may want to include simulation projects in your Desktop Assistant, so that your users have access to them within the application's EPSS. Although you probably wouldn't want the *entire* contents of your *Trainer*—including all play modes—to be available in the Desktop Assistant, you may decide that you want to provide access to one or more specific play modes, to provide another level of help if the user needs it. For example, you may choose to provide access to the Demo mode so that users see a complete demonstration of a task. Or you may choose to provide access to the Concurrent Mode, as an alternative to the Guided Tour.

Alternatively, depending on your development mode, you may well create simulation projects first, and then create Desktop Assistant projects from these (see *Converting a simulation project into a Desktop Assistant project* on page 369). In this case, you may want to have a simulation mode available in the

Desktop Assistant as a backup in case a Guided Tour has not yet been created for the task or transaction.

If you choose to include specific play modes for a simulation in your Desktop Assistant, then you need to include the *entire* simulation project in your Desktop Assistant Group—you will select the required play modes at the time of publishing (as explained in the next section). You can include specific simulations, or you can just include the Group that contains the simulations. In fact, because the Desktop Assistant will include everything under the Desktop Assistant Group, you could quite easily create the Desktop Assistant Group as a level *above* the 'entry point' Group for your entire *Trainer*, and all of your *Trainer* content will then automatically be included in the Desktop Assistant.

In the example below, you can see that we have created our Desktop Assistant Group inside our primary **GloboCorp** Group, at the *same level* as the entry point Group for our **Global Training** *Trainer*.

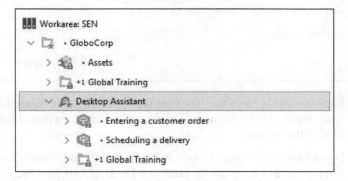

This Desktop Assistant Group contains our (two) Guided Tours, and also contains the entire **Global Training** Group. This will allow us to include (selected output modes for) our simulation projects in our Desktop Assistant. You can see that this is a reference to the 'primary' folder under **GloboCorp**, because the reference counter shows as **+1**.

Note that it is not just projects that you can include in your Desktop Assistant. You can also make Books and Book Pages in available to users in the Desktop Assistant by including them in your Desktop Assistant Group. The only caveat with this is that because the Desktop Assistant relies on the application context to determine what content to display, you must set the required context for the Book and/or Book Pages (as explained in *Capturing context for non-Desktop Assistant content objects* on page 404)—otherwise they will never appear in your Desktop Assistant, even though they are included in your **Desktop Assistant** Group.

Creating a Desktop Assistant Group

Once you have decided upon the content of your Desktop Assistant, you can create the **Desktop Assistant** Group that will contain this content.

To create a **Desktop Assistant** Group, carry out the steps shown below.

1. In your Workarea, click on the Group within which you want to create the Group (or select **Workarea** itself to create the Group at the highest level).

2. Click on the **Create Object** button on the **Workarea Toolbar**, and select **Desktop Assistant** from the drop-down panel. The *New Desktop Assistant* dialog box is displayed.

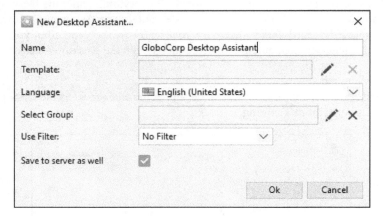

3. Enter a suitable name for your Desktop Assistant in the **Name** field. This name is not seen by the users, so you can use anything that makes sense to you (the Author).

4. If you have an existing Desktop Assistant within your Workarea that you want to use as a template for your new Desktop Assistant, then use the **Edit** button for the **Template** field to navigate to and select this.

5. Select the language for your Desktop Assistant in the **Language** field. This determines the interface language for the Desktop Assistant.

6. If you want to include all of the content objects from a specific existing group in your Desktop Assistant, then navigate to and select this Group in the **Select Group** field. Note that this is effectively just a convenience during initial set-up; you can add Groups to or remove Groups from the Desktop Assistant Group at any time—without affecting the source Group (selected here).

   If you do not choose a specific Group here, then you will need to manually copy all of the specific content that you want included in the Desktop Assistant into this Group, later.

7. If you want to filter the selected content (for example, to publish only content with a specific keyword, or tag) then select the appropriate filter in the **Use Filter** field. Note that this filter must have already been created in the Workarea, as explained in *Using Filters* on page 68.

8. Assuming that you want your **Desktop Assistant** Group to be managed on the server (and it would be very odd not to), make sure that the **Save to server as well** checkbox is selected.

9. Click **Ok**.

If you specified a Group in Step 6, then once you click on the **OK** button in the *New Desktop Assistant* dialog box, you are passed directly into publishing the Desktop Assistant, and should continue with Step 3 of *Generating the Desktop Assistant* on page 415.

If you did not select a Group then you are effectively done with the creation of your Desktop Assistant Group. You can now add the required content to this Group. Once this is done, you can generate the Desktop Assistant as described in *Generating the Desktop Assistant*, below.

Generating the Desktop Assistant

To generate your Desktop Assistant, carry out the following steps.

1. In the Workarea, click on your **Desktop Assistant** Group, to select it.

2. Click on the **Generate Desktop Assistant** button on the *Object Toolbar*. The *Desktop Assistant Configuration* dialog box is displayed. This dialog box includes checkboxes for all of the content types that are contained within your **Desktop Assistant** Group (recursively, through all of its sub-Groups).

Generate Desktop Assistant

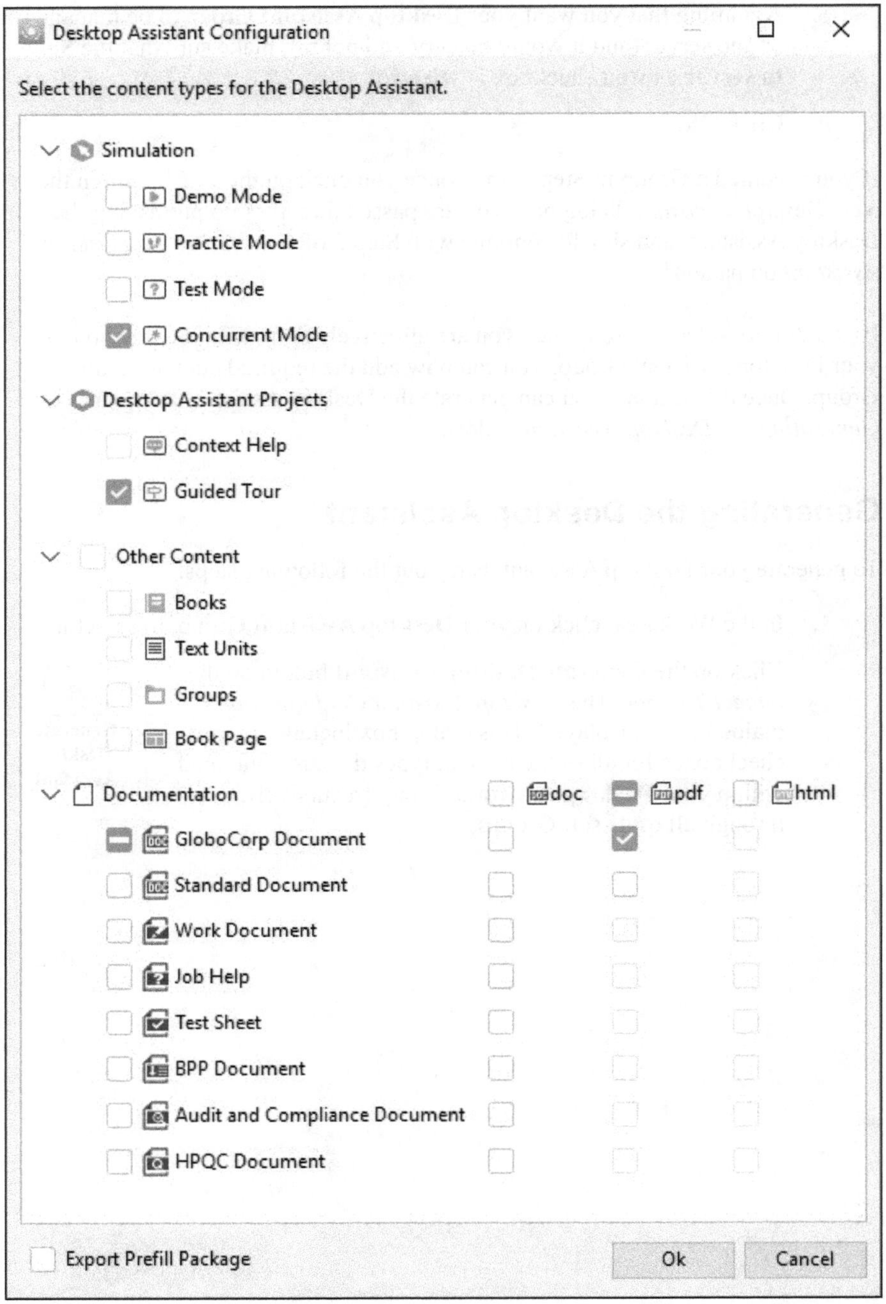

Desktop Assistant Configuration — □ ×

Select the content types for the Desktop Assistant.

∨ 🔵 Simulation
    ☐ ▶ Demo Mode
    ☐ 🔟 Practice Mode
    ☐ ❓ Test Mode
    ☑ 🔁 Concurrent Mode

∨ ⬡ Desktop Assistant Projects
    ☐ 🖥 Context Help
    ☑ 🖥 Guided Tour

∨ ☐ Other Content
    ☐ 📒 Books
    ☐ 📄 Text Units
    ☐ 📁 Groups
    ☐ 📖 Book Page

∨ ☐ Documentation	☐ 📄doc	☑ 📄pdf	☐ 📄html
➖ 📄 GloboCorp Document	☐	☑	☐
☐ 📄 Standard Document	☐	☐	☐
☐ 📄 Work Document	☐	☐	☐
☐ 📄 Job Help	☐	☐	☐
☐ 📄 Test Sheet	☐	☐	☐
☐ 📄 BPP Document	☐	☐	☐
☐ 📄 Audit and Compliance Document	☐	☐	☐
☐ 📄 HPQC Document	☐	☐	☐

☐ Export Prefill Package   Ok   Cancel

● If you select **Books**, then all Book Pages within the Books will also be included; you only need to select **Book Page** if you have stand-alone Book Pages that are not included in a Book (or if you do not want to include the Book but do want to include the Book Pages contained within it).

● Once you have generated the Desktop Assistant your selection will be listed in the **Desktop Assistant Configuration** property for the Desktop Assistant Group object.

3. Select the checkboxes to the left of all content types that you want to include in your Desktop Assistant, and make sure that all other checkboxes are not selected. Again, note that checkboxes are only selectable for those object types for which content exists in the **Desktop Assistant** Group.

4. If you want to generate a Desktop Assistant pre-fill package, then select the **Export Prefill Package** checkbox. A pre-fill package is a `.zip` file that contains all of the content (including resources, styles, and so on) for the Desktop Assistant. This can then be loaded onto the users' workstations, so that the Desktop Assistant uses this content (effectively as a pre-loaded cache) instead of requesting the content from the server. This is useful for sites that have low-bandwidth issues, as it reduces (or effectively eliminates) network traffic, but the downside is that if the content changes, you need to re-create and re-deploy the pre-fill package.

5. Click **OK**. The Desktop Assistant is (re)generated. There is no completion message displayed for this (although a progress dialog box is displayed during the generation).

Creating a Prefill Package

If you chose to create a Prefill Package, then once creation of the Desktop Assistant itself finishes, the *Publish Object* dialog box is displayed, as shown below:

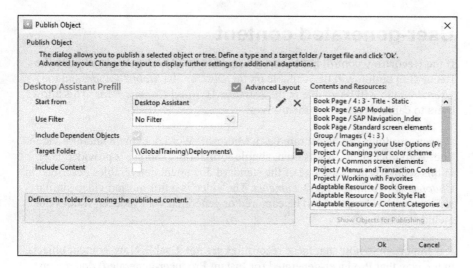

Create the Prefill Package by carrying out the steps shown below:

1. By default, the Prefill Package will be generated for the same Group as the one for which you generated the Desktop Assistant. This is what you would normally want, but if you want to use another Group, then use the **Edit** button for the **Start From** field to select the required Group.

2. If you want to filter the selected content objects prior to generating the Prefill Package, then select this filter in the **Use Filter** field.

3. In the **Target Folder** field, navigate to and select the folder into which the Prefill Package should be saved.

4. By default the Prefill Package will be generated containing only the *resources* required by the content objects (for example, the style files, common images, and so on) but not the actual content objects themselves. If you also want to include the content objects, then select the **Include Content** checkbox.

Caution:
Although including all of the content objects will cause the Desktop Assistant to load significantly faster, the Prefill Package could be massive, taking up a lot of space on the user's PC, and taking significant time to update. Including only the resources is usually a better option, as the package will be relatively small, and the resources shouldn't change very often.

5. Click **Ok**.

Once the Prefill Package has been created, you can find it in the folder you specified in Step 3, and distribute this to the user's PCs. By default, it should be placed in the `%appdata%/Roaming/NavigatorCache` folder, but could be different depending upon your specific environment.

User-generated content

If the **Recording** control has been activated for the Desktop Assistant, then the **Recording** button will be available on the *Desktop Assistant Toolbar*, and the *User Area* tab will be visible in the *Desktop Assistant Content Pane*. This allows users to capture recordings themselves.

These recordings can be captured as a Microsoft Word document and/or a video. The Word document uses its own, simple format (an example is provided later in this section) and is not one of the standard document deliverables described in *Chapter 12, Working with Documents*. The video is a full-motion video similar to screencast videos that can be captured or generated via Producer. It does not include audio.

★ The location to which videos are saved is defined in **Tools | Settings | Desktop Assistant: Playback Settings | Desktop Assistant | Desktop Assistant - Sidebar | Video Recordings Folder**. Confusingly, documents are not saved to the same (or even a comparable) place, but instead are stored in the Producer cache under `AppData\Roaming\ NavigatorCache`.

It is important to note that these recordings are not 'Enable Now' content objects, in the way that Producer-generated (or Instant Producer-generated) documents and simulations are. They are not stored in the Workarea (they are stored on the user's PC), and they cannot be imported into the Workarea and converted into Enable Now content. Instead, this feature is provided to allow users to capture recordings of activities that they perform in the system for their own reference.

As noted earlier in this chapter, this is not really 'Enable Now development', but for the sake of completeness, and in case you need to educate your users on this functionality, it is explained here.

To create user-generated content from within Desktop Assistant, carry out the following steps:

1. Click on the **Recording** button either on the *Desktop Assistant Sidebar* or on the bottom of the **User Area** tab of the Desktop Assistant *Content Pane*.

Recording

2. The *Select Recording Output* dialog box is displayed.

Click on the relevant option, depending on what you want to create: A Word **Document**, a **Video** file (in .mp4 format) or both **Document and Video**.

3. The *Recording Area* dialog box is displayed, and a bounding box identifying the area that will be captured, is displayed on the screen.

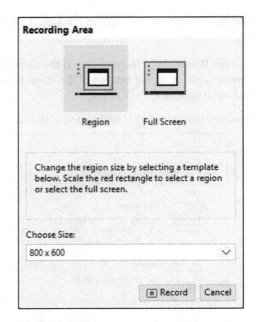

In the upper part of the dialog box, you can choose exactly what you want to capture during recording. The options are:

♦ **Region** to capture a specific area on the screen. This is the area bounded by the red recording marquee; you can change this area by dragging the marquee to a new location, or by dragging its borders to select a different area of the screen.

♦ **Full Screen** to capture the entire contents of the screen.

4. If you chose **Region** in Step 3, then you can select one of the predefined screen sizes in the **Choose Size** field, or leave the default value of **800x600**.

   All portions of the screen outside of the selected or specified region will be grayed out during recording (in Step 7), so that you can easily see what is being captured. Make sure that any pop-up dialog boxes or drop-down lists that you interact with are within this area, or they will not be visible in the final recording.

5. Click on the **Record** button at the bottom of the *Recoding Area* dialog box.

6. The recording marquee is hidden and the *Recording Hin(ts)* dialog box is displayed.

● Note that unlike recording in Producer or Instant Producer, there is no option to capture a specific window. This means that if you are not using the **Full Screen** option you should be very careful to ensure that the full application window is contained within the red bounding area.

Click on the **Thanks** button.

7. Perform the required actions in the application. When you have finished, press the *END* key on the keyboard.

8. Recording stops, and the *Generate Content* dialog box is displayed, prompting you to enter a name for the recording.

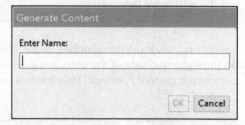

Enter a suitable name for the recording. You can change this later, if necessary.

9. Click **OK** to confirm the name and close the *Generate Content* dialog box. Progress bars will be shown with messages of:

♦ *Analyzing actions*

♦ *Generate Documentation* or *Generate Video* (as appropriate).

Once generation of the output finished, you are returned to the Desktop Assistant.

You can find the output from the recording(s) on the *User Area* tab of the *Desktop Assistant Content Panel*. An example of this, showing a Document and a Video, is shown below:

When the user hovers the cursor over a recording in the *User Area*, a set of action buttons appear on the rightmost side of the entry for that recording, as shown for the Document entry in the example above. These buttons are explained in the table below:

Icon	Object Type	About
	Rename	Rename the recording.
	Display	Display the generated document, in either Microsoft Word or your default video player, as appropriate.
	Share	Share your recording with another user, via your default email client, with a default subject line of "Recommended content". The .doc or .mp4 file will be included as an attachment to the email.

To delete a recording, click on the selection box to the left of the recording, and then click on the **Delete** button in the lower-right corner of the *User Area* tabbed page, and then confirm the deletion when prompted.

Sample Document output

An example of the Document captured during user-generated content recording is shown below.

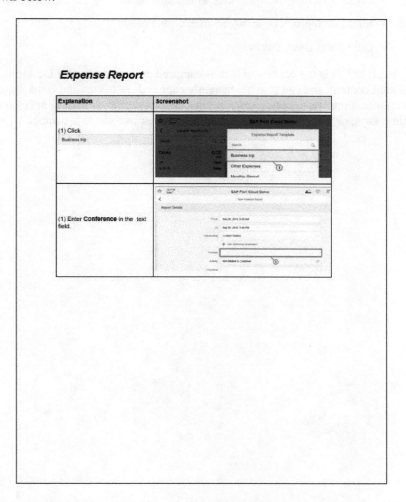

The document consists of a single table, containing columns for the action performed and the associated screenshot, including the highlight and step reference (although the step number is always **1**). This document can be edited and saved to the same location.

Summary

Desktop Assistant is the Enable Now component that provides EPSS (Extended Performance Support System) capabilities for Windows-based applications. It does this by providing in-application, context-sensitive help content, overlaid onto the application screen.

The *Desktop Assistant Content Panel* can provide access to:

- Guided Tours, which walk users through a task, step-by-step
- Context Help, which provides a help bubble for a specific screen element
- Simulation projects, in any available play mode
- Books and Book Pages

Key to all of this is the context, which is captured during creation of Desktop Assistant content, and can also be manually captured for Books and Book Pages. Sometimes it may be necessary to edit this context—either by adding or removing context keys, or by 'genericizing' context keys to remove variable content.

What does Web Assistant provide?

11

The Web Assistant

This chapter is dedicated entirely to the Web Assistant. Web Assistant is the
Enable Now component that provides in-application help for web-based
applications. Web Assistant has been developed for use with SAP's web-based
systems such as S/4HANA and its Fiori interface, and SuccessFactors, but is
being actively extended to cover other (SAP and non-SAP) applications. If
you will not be using these applications, or have decided to just use Desktop
Assistant for providing in-application help for web-based applications as well as
for desktop applications, then you can probably skip this chapter—but you'll be
missing out on some great functionality!

Web Assistant looks and feels like an entirely separate application, and does not
share much more than a few concepts with Desktop Assistant or even Producer,
so if the only thing you will be using is Web Assistant, this could be the only
chapter of this book that you need to refer to.

● In fact, Web Assistant
effectively *is* a separate
application, evolving out
of an SAP-internal product
called X-Ray, whereas the
rest of Enable Now evolved
out of an acquired product
called Datango.

In this chapter, you will learn:

- What Web Assistant provides

- How to create a Web Assistant Guided Tour

- How to create a Help Tile

- How to create a Link Tile

- How to provide content via the Learning Center

- How to enhance SAP-provided content in the Learning Center

- How to add enhanced functionality to your Web Assistant content
  through the use of the *Web Editor*

What does Web Assistant provide?

Web Assistant provides in-application help directly on top of the application screen. It does this via the *Carousel*, which users can display by clicking on the **Open Help** button (the question mark) on the application screen. (This button is present in SAP Fiori-based applications as soon as the application is connected to your Enable Now system. You will need your Enable Now Administrator—and probably also your Fiori Administrator—to set this up.)

An example of a Fiori screen, showing the *Carousel*, is shown below. The *Carousel* is the blue panel along the rightmost side of the screen, although (for Fiori; not SuccessFactors) it can be configured to use a different color scheme, or to be located along the bottom of the screen instead of down the side.

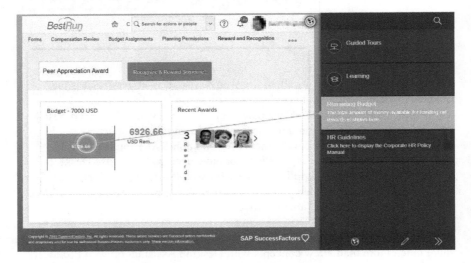

The *Carousel* can effectively provide three types of content:

- **Guided Tours**, which provide step-by-step instructions on how to perform an activity in the application
- **Help Tiles**, which provide a single panel of information and optionally a bubble containing more information
- **Link Tiles**, which link to additional content objects

Help Tiles and Link Tiles may be 'tethered' to a specific object on the screen (identified by a Hotspot) as shown for the 'Remaining Budget' tile in the example above, or can provide stand-alone help.

In addition to these three types of help content, the *Carousel* may contain a **Learning** tile (see *The Learning Tile* on page 450), and/or a **What's New** tile (see *The What's New Tile* on page 448).

If your application has been configured to use Web Assistant in **extensibility mode** then some or all of the SAP-delivered, pre-built help may already be visible in the Web Assistant. In this case, you can either edit this existing content, or you can add your own help on top of this. How to do this is explained later in this chapter, in the section *Editing SAP-provided content* on page 456.

Guided Tours

A Guided Tour provides the user with step-by-step instructions on how to complete a task in the application. It is possible to have multiple Guided Tours for a single screen or function—for example, to cover multiple scenarios.

Creating a Guided Tour

To create a new Guided Tour, carry out the steps shown below.

1. In your web application, navigate to the screen from which you want to start the Guided Tour.

2. Click on the **Open Help** button. The *Carousel* is displayed. This may appear on the rightmost side of the screen, or across the bottom of the screen, depending on configuration settings.

3. Click on the **Edit** button. (This button allows you to toggle between Display mode and Edit mode—when you are in Edit mode the button appears 'selected' [lowlighted].)

Edit

4. You may see a message stating **Help Content Not available**, similar to the example shown below.

▲ When editing an existing Guided Tour, make sure the Guided Tour is not currently being displayed (as help). If it is, you will not be able to edit it.

■ If the **Edit** button is not visible, it is because editing is currently not enabled. To enable it (assuming you have the required permissions), add a parameter of **&edithelp=true** to the URL and then reload the web page.

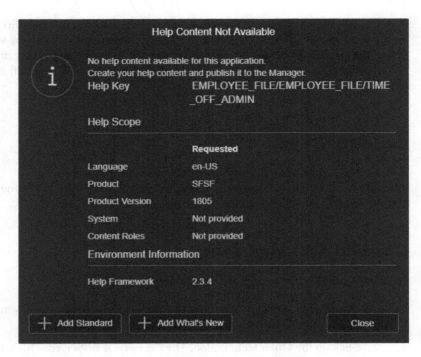

This simply indicates that no help project exists for the current context (shown in the **Help Key**). Click on the **Add Standard** button to create a new help project for this context, and continue with Step 5.

5. Click on the **Add** button. A pop-up bubble is shown, providing you with a number of options for what you can add to the *Carousel*.

Add

Add What's New

Add Tour

Add Help Tile

Add Link Tile

6. Select **Add Tour**. The *New Tour Name* dialog box is displayed.

7. Enter the name you want to give to your new Guided Tour in the **Enter Tour Name** field, and then click **Apply**. A new Tile is added to the *Carousel*. This is your Guided Tour. It will initially be empty; you now need to record the steps for this.

8. Click the **Add Tour Step** button (this looks exactly the same as the **Add** button you clicked in Step 5, but now it has been contextualized for use within a Guided Tour, and will have an appropriate ToolTip). The *Edit Content* dialog box is displayed.

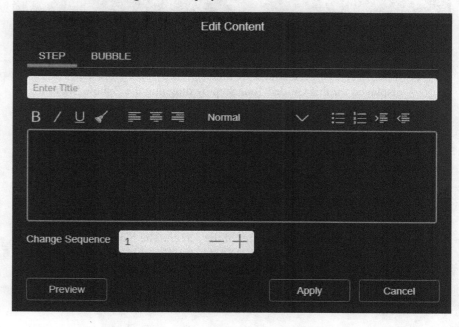

➕ Prior to the 1811 release, the **Title** and **Text** fields were on separate tabbed pages (*Tile* and *Text*, respectively).

9. On the *Step* tabbed page, enter a short text title for the step in the **Enter Title** field. This will appear as a header (in bold) in the Guided Tour Step bubble (see the example under *Reviewing a Guided Tour* on page 434).

10. In the text area on the *Step* tabbed page, enter the text that you want to appear in the help bubble for this Step. The toolbar above the text area provides some standard functions for formatting your text. More functionality is available—for example, to include objects, tables, links and so on—just not from here. See *Editing Web Assistant content in the Web Editor* on page 463 for details.

11. By default, this new step will be added to the end of the list of currently-defined steps (if any). If you want the step to be inserted at another position within the Guided Tour, then select the step at which it is to appear in the **Change Sequence** field. (Don't worry if you don't know the exact step number - you can always change this later.)

12. Click on the **Bubble** tab.

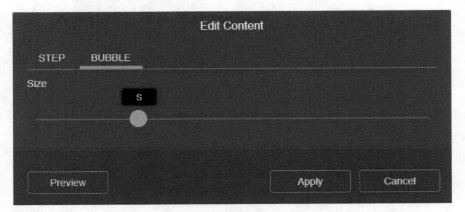

13. If necessary, you can adjust the dimensions of the bubble that will be displayed for this Guided Tour Step by dragging the Bubble Slider to **XS**, **S**, **M**, **L**, or **XL** as necessary. Bubbles are always automatically sized to accommodate the **Tile Title** and **Tile Text** entered on the *Step* tabbed page. This setting defines the relative *width* of the Bubble, so a value of **XL** will result a very wide but relatively short (height) Bubble, and a value of **XS** will result in a relatively narrow, but taller Bubble. These are 'relative' values (not absolute pixels) so you may need to play around to find the size that works best for this particular bubble.

14. Click **Apply**. Your step is added to the Guided Tour in the *Carousel*. A 'hotspot' is added to the center of the screen. The number of this step is shown within this hotspot. Do not worry that this has not been added to the correct object—that's just because you haven't selected a screen object yet.

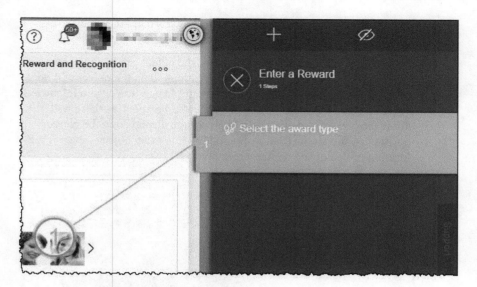

You will notice that an icon is now shown on the upper left of the *Carousel*. This is the **Status** icon, and indicates that your changes have not yet been published. If you are not in Edit mode, you can click on the **Toggle Editor/ Published Stage** button to toggle between showing your latest (unpublished) edits and the currently-published version of help for the current screen.

Toggle Editor/ Published Stage

At this stage, the Guided Tour Step has not been assigned to an object on the screen, and the Bubble will be displayed in the center of the screen during playback. If you do not want to associate this bubble with a specific object (maybe it applies to several objects, or is just a general explanation) then you can skip the next several steps and jump directly to Step 24. Otherwise, continue as follows.

15. Click on the Tile for this new Step in the *Carousel*. The *Step Actions* pop-up is displayed.

16. Select **Assign Hotspot**.

17. The cursor changes to a cross-hairs. Move the cursor over the object on the application screen to which the Tile for this Step should be connected. As you move the cursor over an object on the screen, the

● If you are changing a content object extended from the SAP-provided Workarea, then the **Remove Tile** button will be replaced by a **Revert to Original** button.

■ If you subsequently decide that you do not want the Guided Tour Step to be associated with a specific object, you can return to the *Step Actions* pop-up and select **Center on Screen**, to center the Bubble for the Guided Tour Step on the screen.

object will be highlighted and a border drawn around the object's boundary. You need to pay careful attention to this.

If the object is a 'stable' object—that is, the object can be uniquely and consistently identified within this application—then the object will be highlighted in green, as shown in the example below. You should always strive to select stable objects as the target for hotspots, as these will allow the context-sensitive help to always be displayed in the correct position on the screen (that is, pointing to this exact object—even if the location of this object on the screen changes).

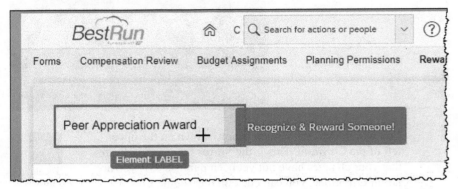

If the object *cannot* be consistently identified (for example, it is an optional object that may not always appear when the screen is displayed) then the object is highlighted in yellow. You should avoid selecting such objects as the target for hotspots if another, more suitable control can be selected. In some cases a better object may not be available; you can select the unstable element, but should bear in mind that during playback the Guided Tour Bubble may not be positioned as accurately as it would otherwise be (it will still be displayed, but may not point to the exact object—or, indeed, to any object).

Even if a content object is highlighted in green, you should move the cursor around slightly, to make sure that you are selecting exactly the right object. This is because some objects may be nested within other objects (even if they are the only thing in the containing object) and you want to make sure that you are selecting the correct object to which the help tile should apply. To help you with this, the 'context' of the object is displayed immediately below the identified object area (as shown in the examples above).

18. Once you have identified the correct object, click on it to select it. The *Edit Content* dialog box is displayed. This is ostensibly the same dialog box that you saw in Step 12, but now additional fields related to the Hotspot have been added to the *Bubble* tabbed page.

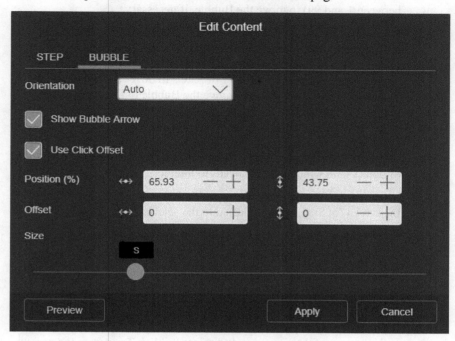

Prior to the 1811 release, the hotspot-related fields were located on their own tabbed page (of *Hotspot*). In 1811 they were merged onto the *Bubble* tabbed page.

19. The **Orientation** field defines the position of the Bubble relative to the object (that you clicked on in Step 17). This defaults to **Auto**, which means that Enable Now will determine the optimal position for the Bubble. If you want the Bubble to use a specific orientation, then select this from the drop-down list. The options available are **North**, **East**, **South**, and **West**.

20. If you want the Bubble to have a pointer that points to the screen object on which you clicked, then make sure that the **Show Bubble Arrow** checkbox is selected. Otherwise, deselect this checkbox.

    Note: If you choose not to show the pointer, then the Bubble will still be positioned near (and possibly overlapping) the object; if this is not what you want, then you can use the **Position (%)** and **Offset** fields to move the Bubble to another location (see Steps 21 and 22, below), or just select **Center on Screen** from the *Step Actions* pop-up to position the Bubble in the middle of the screen.

21. By default, the Bubble pointer (or Bubble edge, if no pointer is displayed) will be located exactly where you clicked on the screen. The **Use Click Offset** checkbox is automatically selected to reflect this (the Bubble pointer is *offset* from the center of the object, to be where you *clicked*), and the exact position within the object at which you clicked is shown in the **Position (%)** fields. The first of these specifies the

percentage of the way along the X axis of this object that you clicked, and the second specifies the percentage of the way down the Y axis that you clicked (so values of 50 and 50 would be exactly in the middle of the screen object). You can change these position percentages (to a value between 1 and 99) to move the Bubble, if necessary.

22. If you want to 'shift' the Bubble pointer (either relative to the center of the screen object, or relative to the clicked position if the **Use Click Offset** option is selected, then you can do so via the **Offset** fields. The first of these specifies the number of pixels to offset the Bubble on the X axis (a negative number will move the Bubble to the left; a positive number will move it to the right). The second field specifies the number of pixels to offset the Bubble on the Y axis (a negative number will move the Bubble up; a positive number will move it down). Adjust these as necessary. This is useful if the Bubble would otherwise obscure the area of object with which the user needs to interact.

23. Click **Apply**. The hotspot that was initially positioned in the center of the screen (in Step 14) is relocated to the selected object.

24. Repeat Steps 8 to 23 to add all additional steps to your Guided Tour.

25. Once you have recorded all of the steps for the Guided Tour, click on the **Save Changes** button to save these changes. Note that your changes have not yet been published, and are only visible to Authors.

Save Changes

▲ It is strongly recommended that you test your Guided Tour thoroughly, before you publish it.

26. If you are ready to publish your tour now, click on the **Options** button at the bottom of the *Carousel*, and select **Publish Tour** from the pop-up bubble. Alternatively, skip this step and you can come back to it later (as explained in *Publishing Help Content* on page 466).

27. Click on the **Enter/Leave Editing** button to exit from Edit mode.

Reviewing a Guided Tour

✚ Enable Now Release 1811 added a **Preview** button to the *Edit Content* dialog box that you can use to preview a single tile during editing, but to review the complete Guided Tour, you need to follow the steps described here.

Now that we've created this Guided Tour, let's see how it appears to the user. First, assuming that the user has clicked on the **Help** button to display the *Carousel*, clicking on the *Guided Tours* Tile will display a list of available Tours.

If the user clicks on a Guided Tour, then the tour is launched, and they are positioned on Step 1. The tour appears as shown in the following example:

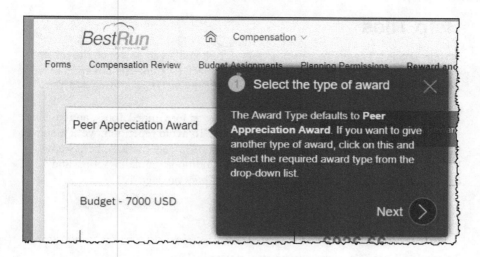

There are a few things to note here. Firstly, in the upper-left corner of the bubble is a small, round progress indicator. This contains the current step number, and the darker blue segment around the outside of the circle provides a visual indication of how far through the Guided Tour you are.

Next, you can see that the bubble contains a title at the top ("Select the type of award" in this example) which is the text entered in the **Title** field (see Step 9 above). This is followed by the bubble **Text** (which was entered in Step 10, above).

Finally, note that in this example the bubble has a pointer on the leftmost edge. This is because the **Show Bubble Arrow** property is selected for the bubble (see Step 20). The pointer points to the object that we clicked on in Step 17.

The bubble contains a **Next** button at the bottom to allow the user to progress to the next Step in the Guided Tour. Subsequent bubbles will have a **Previous** button as well, allowing the user to go back to the previous step, but that isn't shown in this example because we are on Step 1, so there is no previous step.

Progress through each of the Guided Tour steps in turn, and make sure they work as expected—that the text is correct, that the Bubble is correctly sized and in the correct sequence, and that the Bubble points to the correct object (where Hotspots are assigned).

Once you have tested your help content and confirmed that it is working correctly, you can publish it as described in *Publishing Help Content* on page 466.

Help Tiles

A Help Tile is a Tile on the *Carousel* that is 'tethered' to an object on the screen. It provides information about or help on that object. (A Link Tile is a specialized form of Help Tile, and is covered separately under *Link Tiles* on page 444.)

Many of the settings for Help Tiles are the same as for Guided Tours, and involve similar (and sometimes identical) dialog boxes. To avoid repetition, we'll assume that you have already read through the section on Guided Tours, so here we will just describe the basic steps, and you can find additional guidelines, tips, and caveats for carrying out these steps in *Guided Tours* on page 427.

Creating a Help Tile

To create a Help Tile, carry out the steps shown below.

1. In your web application, navigate to the screen for which you want to provide a Help Tile.

2. Click on the **Open Help** button. The *Carousel* is displayed.

3. Click on the **Edit** button. (This button allows you to toggle between Display mode and Edit mode—when you are in Edit mode the button appears 'selected' [lowlighted].)

   Edit

4. Click on the **Add** button. A pop-up bubble is shown, providing you with a number of options for things you can add to the *Carousel*.

   Add

5. Select **Add Help Tile**. The *Edit Content* dialog box is displayed.

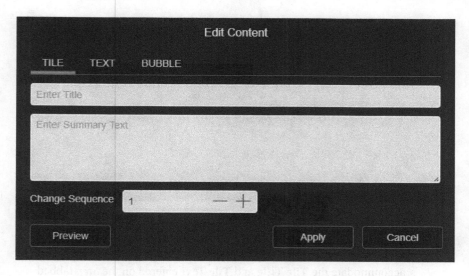

6. On the **Tile** tab, enter the text that you want to appear as the title in the Help Tile into the **Enter Title** field. You should limit this to one (very short) line. (Tip: Consider using the name of the screen object to which the Help Tile relates.)

7. In the **Enter Summary Text** field, enter the additional text that should appear in the Tile, below the title. You should limit this to a single, short sentence, if possible.

8. By default, this new Help Tile will be inserted after any existing Help Tiles on the *Carousel*. If you want the Tile to appear in a specific sequence, then select the sequential position at which it is to appear in the **Change Sequence** field.

9. Click on the **Text** tab.

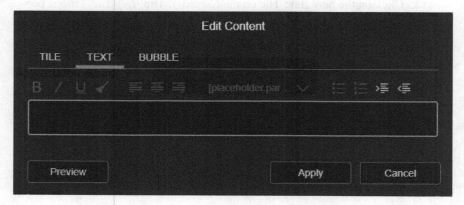

10. In the text area on the *Text* tabbed page, enter the text that you want to appear in the bubble for this Help Tile.

11. Click on the **Bubble** tab.

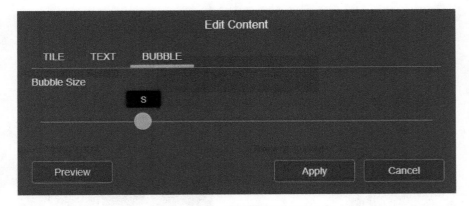

12. If necessary, you can adjust the dimensions of the bubble that will be displayed for this Help Tile by dragging the **Bubble Size** slider to **XS**, **S**, **M**, **L**, or **XL** as necessary. Bubbles are always automatically sized to accommodate the **Tile Title** and **Tile Text** entered on the *Step* tabbed page. This setting defines the relative *width* of the Bubble, so a value of **XL** will result a very wide but relatively short (height) Bubble, and a value of **XS** will result in a relatively narrow, but taller Bubble. These are 'relative' values (not absolute pixels) so you may need to play around to find the size that works best for this particular bubble.

13. Click **Apply**. Your Help Tile is added to the *Carousel*.

At this stage, the Help Tile has not been assigned to an object on the screen. Assuming that you do want to tether your Help Tile to a specific object on the screen, continue with the following steps. If you do *not* want to tether the Help File to an object, then you can jump ahead to Step 26. Otherwise, continue with the following steps.

14. Click on the new Help Tile on the *Carousel*. The *Help Tile Actions* pop-up is displayed.

15. Select **Assign Hotspot**.

16. The cursor changes to a cross-hairs. Move the cursor over the object on the application screen to which this Help Tile should be connected, and once the appropriate object is identified, click on it to select it. As with Guided Tour Hotspots, you should make sure you select a uniquely-

identifiable object (which will be highlighted in green). When you click on the object, the *Edit Content* dialog box is re-displayed, now showing the *Hotspot* tabbed page.

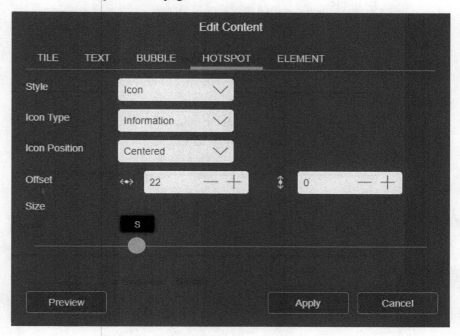

■ The combination of fields and options available on the *Hotspot* tabbed page will depend upon the value selected in the **Style** field. Examples of the *Edit Content* dialog box for each Style type can be found on enablenowexpert.com, or via the following QR code:

➕ The *Element* tabbed page was introduced in the 1811 release. It contains technical information relating to the hotspot, and does not need to be changed.

➕ Prior to the 1811 release, **Circle** was the only style available. The **Style**, **Icon Type**, **Icon Position**, **Offset**, and **Modify Size** settings were therefore not available.

17. In the **Style** drop-down, select the way in which the Hotspot should appear in the application. The following options are available:

♦ **Circle**: A circle is overlaid on the object. This is the default.

Example:

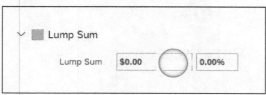

♦ **Rectangle**: A rectangle is drawn around the entire object, with the lower-right corner shaded.

Example:

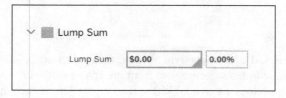

♦ **Underline**: A line is drawn along the bottom edge of the object, and the lower-right corner of the object is shaded.

Example:

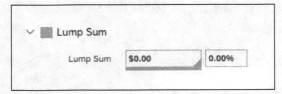

♦ **Icon**: An icon is displayed at the outer edge of the object. The exact position is determined by the **Icon Position** property (see Step 19).

Example:

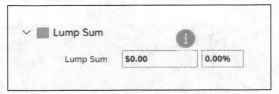

18. If you selected a Hotspot **Style** of **Icon**, then select the icon to use from the **Icon Type** drop-down. The following options are available:

19. If you selected a Hotspot **Style** of **Icon**, then select the position of this icon relative to the screen object from the **Icon Position** drop-down. The following options are available (the icon on the left of each option shows the approximate position of the icon relative to the screen object):

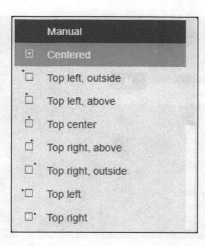

| Manual |
| Centered |
| Top left, outside |
| Top left, above |
| Top center |
| Top right, above |
| Top right, outside |
| Top left |
| Top right |

If you choose **Manual** then the icon will be centered on the object, and you will probably need to use the **Offset** fields (below) to adjust the position of the icon relative to the object.

20. If you selected a Hotspot **Style** of **Circle** then by default the Hotspot will be positioned directly in the middle of the object. You can use the **Offset** fields to adjust the position of the Highlight relative to the center of the object. You can also use these fields in conjunction with a Hotspot **Style** of **Icon**, to fine-tune the position of the icon.

21. If you selected a Hotspot style of **Rectangle** or **Underline**, then you can use the **Change Size** fields to increase or decrease the width and/or height of the Highlight (for example, to increase the space between the Highlight and the object).

■ Use even numbers to 'balance' the space around the object.

22. If you selected a Hotspot **Style** of **Circle** or **Icon** then you can adjust the size of the Hotspot by dragging the **Hotspot Size** slider to **XS**, **S**, **M**, **L**, or **XL** as necessary.

23. Click on the **Bubble** tab. Now, the **Orientation** field is available. This field was not available earlier (in Step 12) because you hadn't assigned a Hotspot to the Tile at that stage.

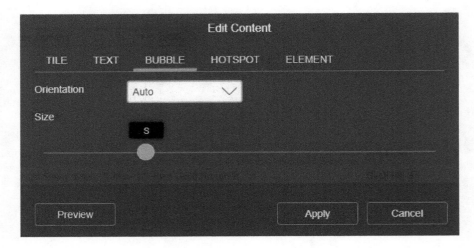

24. If you want the Bubble to be located in a specific position relative to the Hotspot (or Icon), then select this position in the **Orientation** field. You can choose **Auto** (to have Enable Now automatically determine the best position), **North**, **South**, **East**, or **West**.

25. If you select an **Orientation** of anything other than **Auto**, then an additional field of **Offset** is available. You can use this to shift the location of the Bubble reference point (the tip of the pointer) relative to the Hotspot (or Icon).

26. Click **Apply**. A 'Hotspot' icon is shown in the upper-left corner of the Help Tile to indicate that it has been assigned to a screen object.

27. Click on the **Save Changes** button to save your changes. Your changes have not yet been published.

28. Click on the **Edit Mode** button to exit from the editor.

Save Changes

Note that you still need to publish your Help Tile (as explained in *Publishing Help Content* on page 466), but for now let's just check how will look to the users.

Reviewing a Help Tile

➕ Enable Now Release 1811 added a **Preview** button to the *Edit Content* dialog box that you can use to preview a single tile during editing, but that will not show you the tether or the Tile—only the Bubble itself.

Once you have created a Help Tile, you should review it the way users will see it, before you publish it. We'll do that now, to better see exactly what is provided by Web Assistant and how this ties back to the settings we made when creating the Tile.

Assuming the user has clicked on the **Help** button to display the *Carousel*, they will see the new Help Tile listed below (or to the right of) any **What's New**. **Guided Tour**, and **Learning** tiles (and in the sequence specified, if there are multiple Help Tiles).

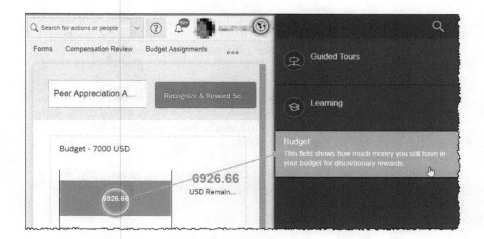

The Tile contains the **Title** and **Summary Text** entered during editing, and the Hotspot is shown over the associated screen object. If the user hovers over the Tile, then a *tether* line is drawn from the Tile to the Hotspot, as shown in the image above (this line disappears as soon as the user moves the cursor out of the Tile).

● The SAP documentation sometimes refers to this line as a "laser" or "laser pointer", but "tether" seems more appropriate, as the tile is tethered to the *object*.

If the user clicks on the Help Tile (instead of just hovering the cursor over it) then the Bubble for this Help Tile is displayed (and the tether is still displayed as long as the cursor is still over the Tile). The user can also click on the Hotspot itself to display the Bubble. In either case, the Bubble is displayed as shown below.

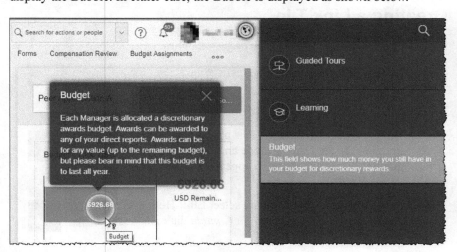

● If you chose not to tether your Tile to an object on the screen (you skipped Steps 14-25), then there is obviously no Hotspot, and no tether line. In this case, the user can only display the Bubble by clicking on the Tile itself. The Bubble is then displayed immediately to the left of (or above, for a horizontal *Carousel*) the Tile, and the Bubble pointer points directly to the Tile.

There are a few things to note, here. Firstly, if the user hovers the cursor over the Hotspot, the cursor appears with a question mark (to indicate that help is available) and a ToolTip is displayed below the cursor. The text of this ToolTip is the Tile **Title**.

Next, in this example, the Hotspot is positioned directly in the middle of the object, because we deselected the **Use Click Offset** option. Also, the Bubble is positioned above the Hotspot area, because the **Bubble Orientation** is set to **North**.

Finally, the Bubble itself contains the Tile **Title** (again), followed by the Bubble **Text** (specified in Step 10). The Bubble also contains a **Close** button in the upper-right corner; the user can click on this to hide the Bubble again (or they can click on the Tile or the Hotspot to hide the Bubble).

Once you have confirmed that the Help Tile is being displayed correctly, you can proceed with publishing it, as explained in *Publishing Help Content* on page 466.

Link Tiles

A Link Tile is very similar to a Help Tile, but instead of the Tile providing a Bubble that contains (typically) text, clicking on the Tile (or the Hotspot) displays a linked object instead. This object can be a Book or Book Page, a non-Enable Now file that you imported into your Workarea (such as a PDF or PowerPoint presentation), or even a website. This is a good way of providing additional—possibly external to Enable Now—information to your users.

Creating a Link Tile

To create a Link Tile carry out the steps shown below:

1. In your web application, navigate to the screen for which you want to provide a Link Tile.

2. Click on the **Open Help** button. The *Carousel* is displayed.

3. Click on the **Edit** button. (This button allows you to toggle between Display mode and Edit mode—when you are in Edit mode the button appears 'selected' [lowlighted].)

Edit

4. Click on the **Add** button, and select **Link Help Tile** from the drop-down menu. The *Edit Content* dialog box is displayed.

Add

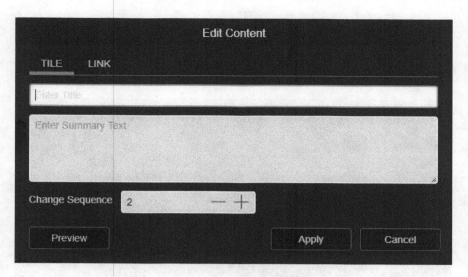

5. In the **Title** box, enter a short title for the Tile. This should be short enough to fit on one line in a Tile on the Carousel.

6. In the **Summary Text** box, enter a slightly longer text that explains the purpose of the tile. This should be no longer than can fit in a single Tile (because Tiles do not expand). For Link Tiles you may find it useful to explain what document or other object will be displayed if the user clicks on the Tile.

7. By default, this new Link Tile will be inserted after any existing Help Tiles on the *Carousel*. If you want the Tile to appear in a specific position within the existing tiles, then select the sequential position at which it is to appear in the **Change Sequence** field.

8. Click on the **Link** tab. The *Link* tabbed page is displayed, as shown below.

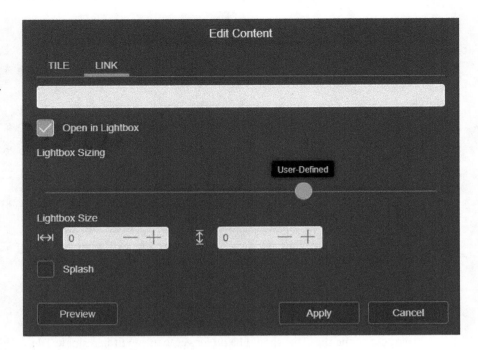

9. In the **URL** field, enter (or paste) the URL of the object, document, or web page that should be displayed when the user clicks on the Tile. If you are linking to a content object in Enable Now, then you should use the URL provided by the object's **Published View** link (in the *Start Links* category)—see *Providing links to Enable Now content* on page 217).

10. By default, the linked object will be opened in a new browser window. If you want it to be opened in a 'lightbox' (an overlay on top of the application screen), then complete the following fields:

    i. Select the **Open in Lightbox** option.

    ii. Use the **Lightbox Sizing** slider to select the *option* that controls the way in which the lightbox will be sized. The following options are available:

    ◆ **Full**: The lightbox will be displayed as large as possible, within the entire browser window.

    ◆ **Client**: The lightbox will be displayed as large as possible within the client (application) area of the screen (that is, excluding the *Carousel*, so that the *Carousel* remains visible). Note that if the object is larger than can fit within just the client area, it will extend over the Carousel anyway.

    ◆ **User-Defined**: The lightbox will be displayed centered within the client (application) area of the screen (that is, excluding the *Carousel*, and at the size specified in the **Lightbox Sizing** fields (see below).

- ◆ **User-Defined (Overlay)**: The lightbox will be displayed centered on the entire browser window, and at the size specified in the **Lightbox Sizing** fields (see below).

iii. If you selected a **Lightbox Sizing** of **User-Defined** or **User-Defined (Overlay)** then use the **Lightbox size** fields to specify the height and width of the lightbox, in pixels. If you are linking to a Book Page, then it would be sensible to specify the size of the Book Page, so that the full Book Page can be displayed within the lightbox area, without the need for scrollbars.

11. If you want the linked object to be opened automatically when the user first accesses the application screen (with which the Link Tile is associated) then select the **Splash** option. Otherwise, make sure that this option is not selected, and the user will need to click on the Link Tile itself to display the object.

    Note that if you have multiple Link Tiles on the same application screen that have this option selected, then only the first one of these (in **Sequence** order) will be displayed as a 'splash screen'.

12. Click **Apply**.

13. Click on the **Save Changes** button to save your Tile. Note that your changes have not yet been published.

14. Click on the **Edit Mode** button to exit from the editor.

Save Changes

Your Link Tile has now been created. To see how it looks to the users, continue with *Reviewing a Link Tile* on page 447.

Reviewing a Link Tile

Let's look at how a Link Tile appears to the user. Assuming that the user clicks on the Link Tile in the *Carousel*, they will see something similar to the following example.

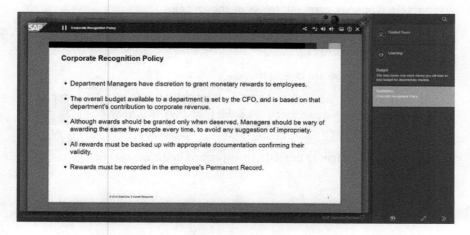

In this example, the Link Tile has been set to link to a Book Page in our Workarea. The **Show in Lightbox** setting was used, and the **Lightbox Size** was specified as **Client**. Although this example is a little small, you can see that the linked object is shown full-size (there are no scrollbars) over the 'application' portion of the screen (the *Carousel* is still fully visible).

Once you have confirmed that the Link Tile is being displayed correctly, you can proceed with publishing it, as explained in *Publishing Help Content* on page 466.

The What's New Tile

The What's New Tile is a specialized Tile that the user can click on to display content that has been created specifically to showcase new features or functionality in the application.

When the user clicks on this Tile, the *Carousel* is populated with (only) content that has been created within the scope of this feature (as explained in this section). This can be best thought of as a way to *temporarily* highlight key changes, or to provide delta training that you will subsequently discard. This last point is important: you should plan on eventually deleting any content created under the What's New Tile (for example, when it is no longer considered 'new').

Adding the What's New Tile

The What's New tile is not automatically available. To add it to the *Carousel* for a given screen (context), carry out the steps shown below:

1. In your application, navigate to the screen for which you want to provide the What's New Tile.

2. Make sure you are in Edit mode.

3. Click on the **Add** button, and select **Add What's New** from the drop-down menu. The What's New tile is added to the *Carousel*.

Add

You can now add content to this Tile, as explained in the next section.

Adding content to the What's New Tile

All of the help types discussed so far in this chapter (**Guided Tour**, **Help Tile**, and **Link Tile**) can be added to the What's New Tile. You create them in exactly the same way as described above, and they all work the same way for the users. The only difference is that the content is only visible if the user explicitly clicks on the What's New Tile (at which point all they see is the contents of the What's New Tile; any Help Tiles on the 'regular' *Carousel* will be hidden).

To add content to your What's New Tile carry out the steps shown below.

1. Make sure the *Carousel* is displayed, and that you are in Edit mode.

2. Click on the What's New Tile in the Carousel. The icon to on the left of the tile changes to a **Cancel** button; this is a useful indicator that you are editing What's New content (as opposed to standard help content).

3. Click on the **Add** button, and select the appropriate option, depending on the type of help that you want to add.

4. How you proceed depends upon the type of help that you are adding to the What's New Tile. Refer to one of the sections listed below, as appropriate:

   ◆ *Creating a Guided Tour* on page 427.

   ◆ *Creating a Help Tile* on page 436.

   ◆ *Creating a Link Tile* on page 444.

5. Once you have created the help content, click on the **Cancel** button in the What's New Tile to return to the 'regular' *Carousel*.

6. Exit from Edit mode, test the Tile(s), and then publish your changes as explained in *Publishing Help Content* on page 466.

Removing the What's New Tile

If (when!) you subsequently decide that you no longer need the What's New Tile, then you can remove it by selecting it in the *Carousel* (in Edit mode) and then selecting **Options | Remove Help**. To do this you will first have to remove all of the help content that currently exists within the What's New Tile. If you want to keep this content, you will need to manually copy the Help Tiles and Guided Tour Steps, and paste them into a non-What's New project with exactly the same context. You will need to do this in Producer (you can't do it from within the Web Assistant Editor).

The Learning Tile

If a Workarea has been linked to the Web Assistant as the **Learning App**, then the Learning Tile will be displayed in the *Carousel*. This functionality is only available for selected systems—initially only SAP SuccessFactors, but additional ones are being added by SAP.

● Simulations will always launch in Practice mode.

The Learning Tile provides users access to additional training content (simulations, Books, and Book Pages) located in the connected Workarea. This is context-sensitive, so the help that the user will (initially) see is applicable to the specific screen that they are on (we'll look at how to make this connection later). When a user clicks on the Learning Tile, they are presented with a *Recommended Learning* dialog box similar to the one shown below:

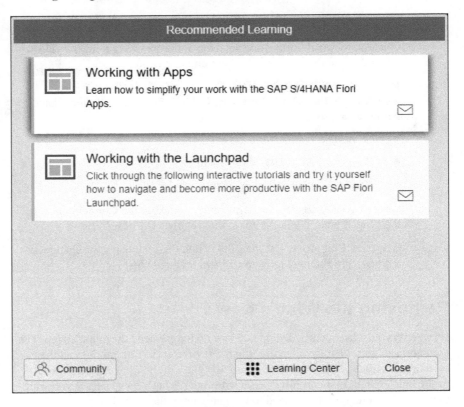

If the user clicks on a content object in this list, the object is opened in the appropriate display application (in this example, the *Book Reader*), in a new browser tab.

Let's quickly look at the other options available via the *Recommended Learning* dialog box. Firstly, if the user clicks on the **Learning Center** button, they are passed into the full *Learning Center*.

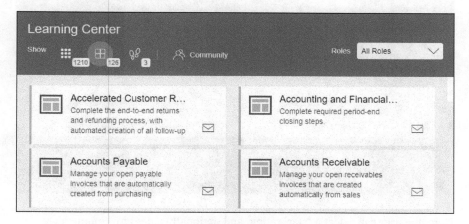

The *Learning Center* provides access to *all* additional learning content that is available in the Workarea (that is, not just the context-filtered content shown in the *Recommended Learning* dialog box). If the content objects in the Workarea have been correctly categorized (see *Assigning Categories to your content* on page 455) then users can filter this content by category, via the **Show** option buttons. (The number of content objects in each category is shown in the lower-right corner of the button.)

Users can also use the **Roles** drop-down to filter the screen to show only content applicable to their role (assuming that content has been tagged for roles—see the **Roles** property on page 52).

The other option available via the *Recommended Learning* panel is the **Community** button, which may appear in the lower-left corner of the panel (if this has been activated). This can be configured to open a specific social/support community, such as a SAP JAM site, a Yammer group, or other shared resource (basically, anything with a URL). This is extremely useful if you have a culture of users helping each other out, or a strong Power User network. If activated, the **Community** button is also available from the bar at the top of the *Learning Center* screen, as shown in the example above.

There's another feature here that is worth taking a quick look at. This is the *feedback* feature. You may have noticed that there is a small 'envelope' icon in the lower-right corner of the object tile. This is the **Send feedback to author** button, and users can click on this to provide feedback on this particular content object. This is similar to the feedback feature provided via the *Trainer*.

Send feedback to author

● In Edit mode, the **Send feedback to author** button is replaced by the **Edit in Manager** button (which in this case *does* actually pass you to the Manager component).

If the user clicks on the **Send feedback to author** button, the following dialog box is displayed:

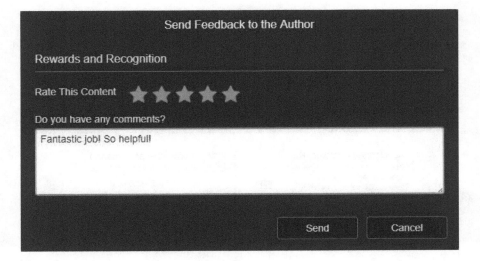

Here, the user can select a 'star' rating, and optionally enter any comments they have, before clicking the **Send** button to submit their feedback. Note that although the dialog box title implies the feedback will be sent to the Author, it will not actually be sent to anyone. Instead, an entry is created in the *Event Log*, and this entry will only be visible on the *Tasks* tab for the object in the Manager, and not in Producer, which is less than helpful (I've put in a feature request for a consolidated report).

Contextualizing a content object

In order for content objects to appear in the list of available content (either in *Recommended Learning* or in the *Learning Center*) it must be tagged with the exact context for the application (and screen, for *Recommended Learning*) with which you want it to be associated. You need to do this in the Producer (in the Workarea that your Web Assistant is using for additional content). Let's look at how to do this by way of an example.

Suppose we have a Book that we want to make available to users when they are using the **Recognize and Reward Someone** screen within our SuccessFactors system (this is the screen for which we built our help earlier in this chapter). Let's add the context for this screen to our Book.

To add context to a content object, carry out the following steps.

1. In the application (SuccessFactors, in this example), navigate to the screen for which this content object should be suggested as applicable learning content.

2. Make sure you are in Edit mode, and then click on the **Options** button at the bottom of the *Carousel* and select

Options

Show Context information from the pop-up menu. The *Help Context Information* bubble is displayed.

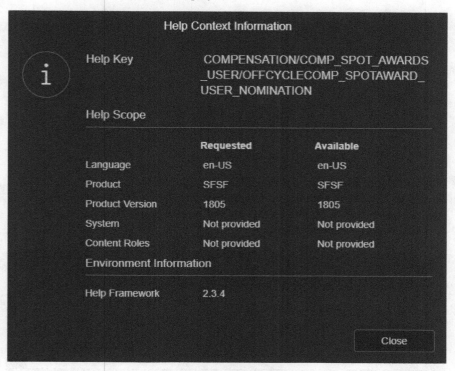

3. Locate the **Help Key** shown at the top of the screen ("COMPENSATION... through ...NOMINATION" in this example), and copy the entire text for this to your clipboard. You should also make a note of the (**Available**) **Product, Product Version,** and **System** settings, as you will also need this information. Once you have done this, you can click **Close** to close the *Help Context Information* bubble.

4. Open the Producer for the Workarea that is linked to the Web Assistant as additional content.

5. In the *Object Navigation Pane*, select the content object that is to be linked into your Web Assistant content. Make sure that you have this checked out for editing.

6. Paste the copied **Help Key** value into the **Context** property for the content object, and enter the **Product, Product Version,** and **System** values into the properties of the same names in the *Web Assistant Context* category. The object's properties will now look similar to the following partial example:

★ The Workarea containing this content does not necessarily have to be the same Workarea as the one in which your Web Assistant help content exists. The Workarea to use is configured in the application itself (for example, in SuccessFactors, this is defined in the **Additional Content | Display Learning Center | Enable Now Workarea ID** setting).

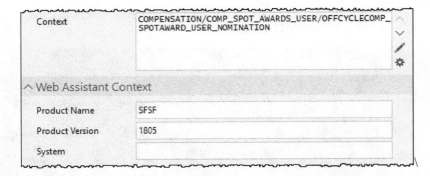

7. Check in the object, and publish it.

Now let's look at how this appears in Web Assistant. If the user clicks the **Learning** button from within the screen for which we copied over the context (the SuccessFactors **Recognize and Reward Someone** tile, in our example), the user will see the following panel:

● The bold title here is the object's **Name**. The text below this is taken from the object's **Short Description** property.

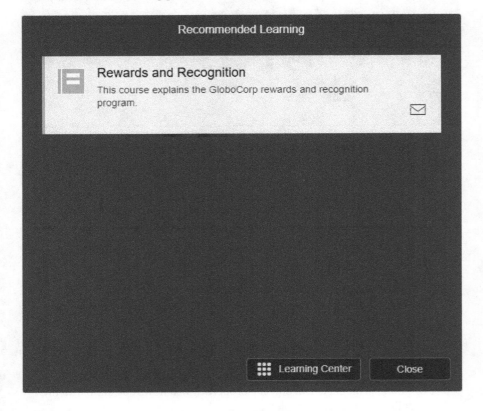

Note that this capability is not just for Books or Book Pages—you can link to simulations (in any mode), Guided Tours, and so on.

Alternative method of capturing context

In the 1811 Release, SAP introduced the ability to capture Web Assistant content directly from within Producer, instead of having to manually copy and paste it. To do this, carry out the following steps:

1. Open the Producer for the Workarea that is linked to the Web Assistant as additional content.

2. In the *Object Navigation Pane*, select the content object that is to be linked into your Web Assistant content. Make sure that you have this checked out for editing.

3. Click on the **Record** button at the top of the *Object Editor* pane, and select **Record Web Assistant Context** from the drop-down menu. The standard *Select Window and Profile* dialog box is displayed.

Record Context

4. Click on the application window from which you are capturing the context. This window is displayed on the screen (with the *Select Window and Profile* dialog box still overlaid on top of it).

5. Check the profile in the **Choose Profile** field, and then click on the **Choose** button. The context is captured from the current screen of the selected window and saved into the **Context** property of the content object, and the application details are saved into the properties in the *Web Assistant Context* category. Note that this may take a few moments, and there is no confirmation message to indicate when it is complete.

6. Don't forget to save the updated object to the server, and check it in if you have finished editing it.

Assigning Categories to your content

If you have a Workarea attached to the Web Assistant as the Learning App, then you can assign Categories to the content in this Workarea, so that the user can filter the *Learning Center* to show only content for a specific Category. The image below shows a snippet of a *Learning Center*, showing two Category buttons: **Learning Package** and **Get Started** (the leftmost button is "All"). The Category is shown as a ToolTip when you hover over the button, and the number of objects in the category is shown in the lower-right corner of the button.

To assign a Category to a content object (Project, Book, or Book Page), carry out steps shown below.

1. In Producer, open the Workarea that is attached to Web Assistant as the Learning App.

2. Navigate to and select the content object to which you want to assign a Category. Make sure that you have this checked out for editing.

3. In the *Object Editor*, navigate to the *Learning App Context* category of properties.

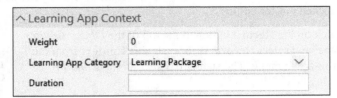

4. In the **Weight** field, enter the 'weighting' that should be given to this context object. The weighting is a value between 1 and 100, and determines how near the top of the *Recommended Learning* list this specific object will appear. This is a good way of making sure that users see the 'most important' content first.

5. In the **Learning App Category**, enter the Category that should be assigned to the content object. This can be one of:

   ◆ **Learning Package**

   ◆ **Get Started**

   ◆ **Processes**

   ◆ **Implement**

   ◆ **Other**

   Note that these are effectively just text labels - it is up to you (or your Administrator) to decide how they will be used, and what type of content you will assign to each Category.

6. If the content object is a simulation project, enter the approximate duration of the simulation (in Demo mode) into the **Duration** field. (I have no idea where this is used, but presumably it is visible to users somewhere in the *Learning Center*.)

7. Check in the content object, and publish it.

Editing SAP-provided content

For some systems (such as SuccessFactors), SAP provides a suite of pre-built training material that you can use via the *Learning Center*. You can also edit this material to customize it to your own requirements. To do this, you need to copy

● Learning App Categories are different from Content Categories.

★ To be able to extend SAP-provided content, the SAP-created Workarea that contains the pre-built content must be linked to the Manager component, and your own Workarea (which is attached to the Web Assistant as the Learning App) must be 'based on' the SAP-created workarea. These are things that your Administrator can do.

the SAP-provided version into your own Workarea, and then change your 'local' copy. In this section, we'll look at how to do this.

Copying SAP-provided content into your Workarea

First, let's suppose that you have accessed the *Learning Center*, and see the following content listed:

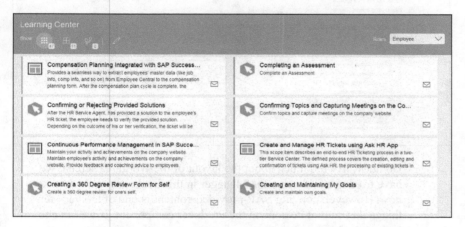

Assume that you identify the *Completing an Assessment* simulation project as content that you want to use, but want to make some changes to it, to tailor it to your company's specific needs. Copy this content into your own Workarea as follows:

1. In the *Learning Center*, click on the **Edit** button to switch into Edit mode. The **Send feedback to author** (envelope) button in the lower-right of the content tile changes to an **Edit** button.

Edit

2. Click on the **Edit** button for the content object you want to change. You are passed into the Manager component of Enable Now, and positioned on the entry for the selected content object.

▲ In this Author's experience, you are not always positioned on the content object. In this case you will need to locate the object yourself. You *could* search for it, but in the search results you do not have the option you need to select in Step 3.

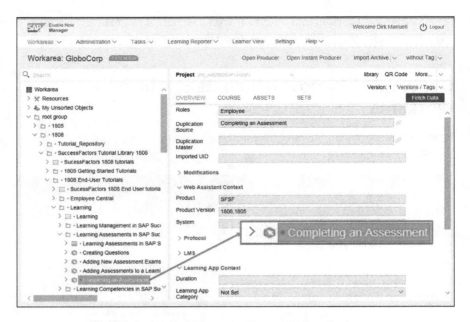

Do not worry too much about the layout of the Workarea screen; we have tried to avoid using the Manager in this book, and we won't start now. However, copying SAP-provided content is one of the very few things that cannot be done in the Producer component. If we *have* to look at the Manager, there are a few things worth noting here. First, note that to the right of the Workarea name at the top of the screen is an orange icon indicating "Extended". This indicates that this Workarea is based on another Workarea (the SAP-provided one). You will also note that some of the content objects listed in the hierarchy on the left have an orange dot to the left of the object name. This indicates that the object exists in the underlying base (SAP-provided) Workarea, and therefore needs to be adopted into your own Workarea before you can change it. This is the case for the *Completing an Assessment* simulation that we have identified in our current example.

3. Make sure that the content object is selected in the hierarchy, and then click on the **Fetch Data** button on the upper-right of the *Object Editor* pane. The content object is copied over into your own Workarea. Now the object no longer has an orange dot next to its name in the hierarchy, and the icon now contains the familiar 'cloud' indicator.

You can now edit the content object, and make any necessary changes. To do this you *could* just close down the Manager component and go back to the Producer to edit the content in a more familiar environment. However, now that we have finally opened a window into the Manager, we may as well look at how you can edit the content object directly from here.

Editing content from within the Manager

To edit a content object from within the Manager, carry out the steps shown below.

1. With the content object selected in the Workarea hierarchy on the left, click on the **Start Editing** button in the upper-right of the *Object Editor* pane (in the place previously occupied by the **Fetch Data** button).

2. Click on the **Edit** link on the toolbar at the top of the *Object Editor* pane. You are passed into the **Web Editor**. You can now edit the content object as required.

    Some basic help on using the *Web Editor* is given in *Editing via the Web Editor* on page 461, although that is more from the perspective of editing standard Web Assistant content. In short, (almost) anything that you can do in the *Project Editor* in Producer you can also do in the *Web Editor* (although some menu options and buttons are in different locations). To save repeating information that is largely the same, you should refer to *The Project Editor* on page 104 and *Working in the Book Page Editor* on page 261, as necessary.

    ➕ There is rumor that the Web Assistant may eventually be the primary editor, even from within Producer, where it would replace both the *Project Editor* and the *Book Page Editor*.

3. Once you have finished editing the content object, save your changes, and then close the **Web Editor**. You are returned to the Manager.

4. Click on the **Finish Editing** button in the upper-right of the *Object Editor* pane. The *Finish Editing* dialog box is displayed.

● The *Finish Editing* dialog box is very similar to the equivalent dialog box in Producer. The instructions provided here are fairly succinct, assuming that you are already familiar with the Producer version. If you are not, refer to *Checking in a content object* on page 36.

Finish Editing	
Assigned to:	⌄
Status:	⌄
Comment:	
Send Mail to Watchers:	☑

Save   Cancel

5. If you want to change the person to whom the object is assigned, then select the required person in the **Assigned to** field.

6. If you want to change the **Status** of the object, then select the required status in the **Change Status** field.

7. Optionally, you can enter a comment—for example, explaining what has changed—in the **Comment** field.

★ Watchers are Enable Now users who should be notified about certain events that take place for objects. Watchers are assigned to content objects in the Manager.

8. If you want Watchers for this object to be notified via (automatic) email that the object has been edited and checked in, then select the **Notify Watchers** checkbox. Otherwise, make sure that this checkbox is not selected.

9. Click **Save**.

10. Back on the Manager main screen, if the object should be published now (so that it is made available to users) click on the **Publish** link on the toolbar at the top of the *Object Editor* pane. Users will not see your changes until you publish the object.

Reverting content

If you subsequently decide that you do not want to keep your changes, and want to revert to the SAP-provided version, you can simply delete the copy that you adopted into your own Workarea (and also delete it from the Trash). The SAP-provided version will then be visible again to users via the Learning Center.

You can now log out from the Manager (click the **Logout** button in the upper-right corner of the window) and return to the *Learning Center*.

Editing via the Web Editor

When editing Web Assistant help, the *Bubble* tabbed page of the **Edit Content** pop-up panel provides basic formatting for the Bubble text, such as font formatting, alignment, and so on. If you need to perform some more advanced editing then you can do this via the *Web Editor*.

Accessing the Web Editor

To access the *Web Editor*, carry out the steps shown below.

1. Make sure you are in Edit mode and positioned within either the screen for which you are editing the Help Tiles, or within the Guided Tour that you are editing. Note that you do not need to select a specific Help Tile, as all Help Tiles on the same screen will be accessible in the *Web Editor* (they are stored within the same project).

2. Click on the **Options** button on the *Carousel*, to display the *Options* pop-up menu.

   Options

3. Select **Edit in Manager** from the *Options* menu. The *Web Editor* is opened in a separate browser tab. The content of the *Web Editor* is explained in *The Web Editor screen* on page 461

   ▪ Don't be fooled by the name; this does not take you into the Manager (or anywhere near it).

4. Edit the Help Tiles or Guided Tour as explained in *Editing Web Assistant content in the Web Editor* on page 463.

The Web Editor screen

The *Web Editor* is similar to the *Project Editor* in Producer, but is a 100% web-based application (it does not even rely on Java the way Producer does). An example of a typical *Web Editor* screen is shown below:

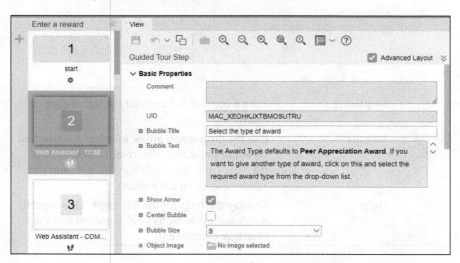

This example screen may not look much like the *Project Editor* screen, but that's only because this example has been changed from the default layout. The *Web Editor* provides the same four main components as the Project Editor, namely the *Editor Toolbar*, the *Step View*, the *WYSIWYG Editor*, and the *Macro Editor*. However, with Web Assistant help content, no screenshots are ever captured, so there is no point in displaying the *WYSIWYG Editor*. So in the example above, we have used the **Divided Layout - 1** view, and then dragged the divider between the *WYSIWYG Editor* and the *Macro Editor* to show only the *Macro Editor*. Let's look at each of the applicable components in slightly more detail.

The Web Editor Toolbar

The *Web Editor Toolbar* provides access to a few of the same features as the *Project Editor Toolbar*, although most of these aren't applicable to Web Assistant content because they relate to the *WYSIWYG Editor* which we're ignoring here. The ones that are useful for editing Web Assistant content are explained in the table below.

Button	Name	Purpose
💾	**Save**	Save your changes.
↩ ⌄	**Multifunction**	The drop-down arrow for this button provides access to several common editing functions. The button itself defaults to the last function used. The full list of options is shown in the following image:
		↩ Undo ↪ Redo ✂ Cut 📋 Copy 📋 Paste 🗑 Delete
🗗	**Duplicate**	Take a copy of the currently-selected Step or macro.
☰ ⌄	**Layout**	Use the drop-down arrow to select the required layout of the screen (the relative positions of the *Step View*, the *WYSIWYG Editor*, and the *Macro Editor* on the screen).
⑦	**Help**	Display the help for the Manager. This is pretty much useless here, as you're not even in the Manager component.

The Step View

For Web Assistant Guided Tours, the **Step View** contains one 'Step' per Tile (regardless of whether this tile is for a Guided Tour Step or a Help Tile). Each Step contains only one macro, and the 'thumbnail' area will be blank as there is no associated screenshot.

For Help Tiles (including Link Tiles) there will be only one 'content' Step, representing the single screen to which the help applies. This will include one macro for each Tile.

Clicking on a Step or a Macro in the Step View will show the properties for that Step or macro in the *Macro Editor* pane.

In addition to these Tile-related Steps, the first Step in the help 'project' is named **Start**, and contains a SETTINGS macro. Although there are properties for each of these (the Step and the macro) that you can display by clicking on them, there are no properties that make a difference to Web Assistant content, so we will not cover them here.

The Macro Editor

The *Macro Editor* within the *Web Editor* works in the same way as the *Macro Editor* in the *Project Editor* within Producer. To avoid repetition, you are referred to *The Macro Editor* on page 107 for basic details of how to use this editor (specifically, the types of fields available, how to activate them, how to change them, and so on). The properties specific to Web Assistant content are described in the next section.

Editing Web Assistant content in the Web Editor

Everything you can do to influence the display of Guided Tours and Help Tiles in the Web Assistant is done through the *Macro Editor*. However, not all of the properties available actually apply to Web Assistant content. The table below lists all of the properties available, and explains their use (or lack of availability) with Web Assistant Tiles.

● The *Web Editor* is also used for simulation projects accessed via Instant Producer, and some properties are included to support that.

Property	Use	Guided Tour	Help Tile	Link Tile
Basic properties				
Comment	Not available for editing; unused.	○	○	○

Property	Use	Guided Tour	Help Tile	Link Tile
UID	Unique identifier of this macro. Cannot be changed.	○	○	○
Tile Title	This is used in the Tile and in the Bubble. You can change it here, if necessary.		●	●
Tile Text	This is the main text used in the Tile itself, and appears immediately below the Tile Title. You can change it here, if necessary, although you can only make simple text changes; there are no formatting options available.		●	●
Link to	For Link Tiles, this specifies the URL of the object to be displayed when the user clicks on the Tile. If you are linking to Enable Now content (in the same Workarea) then you can click on the Link button to the right of the field to navigate to and select the relevant Enable Now content object.			●
Use Click Offset	If selected, the Bubble pointer will be positioned at the exact location within the object on which you clicked during recording.	●		
Object Image	Irrelevant for Web Assistant; ignore.	○		
Hide	Can be used to suppress the visibility of a Tile or Step.	●	●	●
Bubble Title	For Guided Tours only. This is used in the Tile and in the Bubble. You can change it here, if necessary.	●		
Bubble Text	This property contains the full text of the Bubble that is displayed for Help Tiles and Guided Tour steps. Note that all the 'standard' functionality for editing Bubbles is available here, including using styles, and inserting tables, images, placeholders, and so on. Refer to *Adjusting Bubble text* on page 111 for full details.	●	●	
Show Arrow	Determines whether the Bubble includes a pointer, pointing to the Hotspot (or to the Tile, if there is no Hotspot).	●		
Center Bubble	Center the Bubble on the screen.	●		
Bubble Size	The size of the Bubble (**XS**, **S**, **M**, **L**, or **XL**).	○	●	

Property	Use	Guided Tour	Help Tile	Link Tile
Bubble Orientation	Defines the position of the Bubble relative to the object.	●	●	
Bubble Offset	You can use the X,Y values in this field to shift the location of the Bubble reference point (the tip of the pointer) relative to the Hotspot (or Icon).		●	
Hotspot	Technical information identifying the tethered object. Do not change.	○	○	
Hotspot Style	Specifies the visual type of Hotspot displayed for the help tile. This can be one of **Circle**, **Rectangle**, **Underline**, or **Icon**.		●	
Icon Type	**Hotspot Style** of **Icon** only. This field identifies the specific icon that will be displayed.		●	
Icon Position	**Hotspot Style** of **Icon** only. This field identifies the position of the icon relative to the object.		●	
Icon Offset	**Hotspot Style** of **Icon** only. This field specifies the (X,Y) offset of the icon relative to the **Icon Position**.		●	
Change Size	Hotspot Style of Rectangle or Underline only. Pixel increase or decrease of the width and height of the Hotspot.		●	
Hotspot Size	The size of the Hotspot circle overlaid on the tethered screen object (**XS**, **S**, **M**, **L**, or **XL**).		●	
Show in Lightbox	Select if the linked content is to be displayed in a lightbox, over the application screen. Otherwise the content will be displayed in a new browser tab.			●
Lightbox Size	If **Show in Lightbox** is selected then select the portion of the screen in which the lightbox is sized for display. See Step 10 of *Creating a Link Tile* on page 444 for an explanation of the available options.			●
Width, Height	If the **Lightbox Size** is set to **User-Defined** or **User-Defined (Overlay)** then specify the height and width of the lightbox, in pixels.			●

➕ **Hotspot Style** and **Hotspot Type** were introduced in the 1811 release.

Property	Use	Guided Tour	Help Tile	Link Tile
Show as Splash Screen	Select this option if you want the linked object to be opened automatically when the user first access the application screen (with which the Link Tile is associated).			●
Logical Info Object	No idea.	○	○	○
Advanced				
Object Type	Irrelevant for Web Assistant; ignore.	○	○	
Screenshot Position	Irrelevant for Web Assistant; ignore.	○	○	
Action	Irrelevant for Web Assistant; ignore.	○		

● Available and used. ○ Available but not functional.

Make any necessary changes to the help as described in the table above. Note that you are generally limited to editing existing content (created in the application). You can insert a new Step via the **Add** button in the upper left of the *Step View*, but you cannot insert new macros into this. The only way to add a new macro from here would be to **Duplicate** an existing macro in another Step, and then drag that onto your new Step. And even then, you would not be able to assign a Hotspot, so it's really better to just do the whole thing from the application, and then just use the *Web Editor* for some advanced tweaks to the bubble text.

Once you have finished your edits, click on the **Save** button, and then close the *Web Editor* browser tab to return to the application.

Publishing Help Content

Any changes that you make to the Web Assistant help are effectively made in a 'development' version of the help system; they do not become visible to the users until you publish them (although they will be visible to other Authors). This is useful as it allows you to test and review the help before you make it available.

How you publish your Web Assistant help is largely the same, regardless of whether this help is a Guided Tour, a Help Tile, or a Link Tile. To publish help content for a screen, carry out the steps shown below.

1. Make sure that you are in Edit mode (click on the **Edit Mode** button if you are not).

2. Click on the **Options** button on the *Carousel*. The following pop-up menu is displayed:

Options

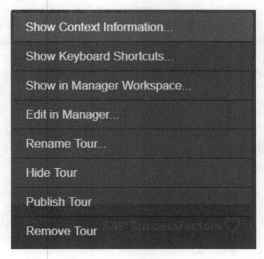

Show Context Information...

Show Keyboard Shortcuts...

Show in Manager Workspace...

Edit in Manager...

Rename Tour...

Hide Tour

Publish Tour

Remove Tour

● This screenshot shows the *Options* menu for a Guided Tour. The options listed on the menu will be different for other help content types.

3. For Guided Tours, select **Publish Tour** from the pop-up menu. For Help Tiles and Link Tiles, the option that you click on is **Publish Help**. A confirmation message similar to the example below is displayed (note that it will refer to "Help" and not "Tour" for Help Tiles and Link Tiles).

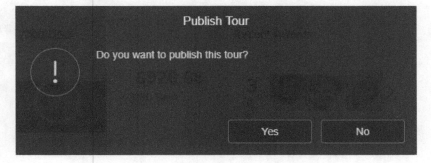

Publish Tour

Do you want to publish this tour?

| Yes | No |

4. Click **Yes**. The help is published, a confirmation message is briefly displayed at the top of the screen, and the **Status** icon changes to green, to indicate that this content has now been published.

**Status
(Published)**

5. Click on the **Edit Mode** button to exit from Edit mode.

Removing Help

If you decide that the help is no longer required, then you can select the relevant **Remove** option from the *Options* pop-up menu. If you want to remove it from view, but not delete it, then you can use the **Hide** option—and then use the **Show** option when you are ready to have it displayed.

Summary

The Web Assistant allows you to provide in-application help for browser-based applications. It natively supports SAP applications using the Fiori interface, but SAP are working to make it available for selected other web-based application. The Web Assistant can provide Guided Tours, Help Tiles, and Link Tiles. You can also provide access to further training material via the Learning tile, by linking to a Learning App, community websites (such as Yammer), and so on.

For some SAP products, such as SuccessFactors, SAP provides pre-built training content that you can use, or even edit. To edit pre-built content, you first need to copy it into your own Workarea (which is a one-click task) and then edit it from there.

12

Working with Documents

Enable Now allows you to create 'printable' versions of simulation projects. This includes Word, PDF, HTML, and PowerPoint formats. This may be useful if you have a requirement to provide printed work instructions or other 'compliance' documents for activities carried out in your systems. Most documents are generated 'per simulation', but you also have the ability to generate a few specialized documents that include multiple simulations.

All of these documents are generated using information contained in the simulation(s) themselves, with the only difference between the various documents being which pieces of information are included or excluded in a given format. There are several items of information that apply solely to documents, but these are also defined within the simulation itself.

Because the document formats only use information that is already contained within the simulation, it is important that your simulations are 'final' before you generate the required document(s). If you subsequently change the simulation, you will need to re-generate the document(s).

Although Enable Now provides the ability to publish a simulation in eleven different document or presentation outputs, you would typically not use all of these. It is recommended that—for delivery to end-users—you choose one document format and use this consistently for all simulations.

In this chapter you will learn:

- What document types are available
- How to generate the various document types
- How to edit simulations to influence the document output

Available document types

The table below lists all of the available document types, and identifies the format(s) in which they can be generated and the bubble text used in the document. The specific icon used to indicate the availability of the document type/format combination is the same icon as is used in Enable Now.

Document Type	Text mode	Word	PDF	HTML	PowerPoint
Audit and Compliance Document	Demo	▣	▣	▣	
BPP Document	Demo	▣	▣	▣	
Hands-On Guide	Demo	▣	▣	▣	
HPQC Guide	Demo	▣			
Job Help	Practice	▣	▣	▣	
PowerPoint Document	Demo				▣
Process Guide	Demo	▣	▣	▣	
Standard Document	Demo	▣	▣	▣	
Test Sheet	Demo	▣	▣	▣	
Training Document	Demo	▣	▣	▣	
Work Document		▣	▣	▣	

Before looking at how to generate these documents, and specific changes that you can make to your simulation to influence them, it is worth looking at an example of each of them, using the default options. This will allow you to better determine which of the available document types you want to use for your project.

Sample output types

This section provides examples of each of the document types that are available, and explains their contents.

These examples have all been generated for the same example simulation project of *Processing a Travel Request*, which was recorded via SAP Fiori. The bubble style is Green Meadow (just for variety) and no documentation fragments have been specified (that is, the documents are as close to 'vanilla' as possible). Documentation Macros have only been used to the extent that they are required (that is, where omitting them would leave blank spaces in the document).

To compress these examples and avoid wasted space, extraneous page breaks have been removed. A blue wavy line indicates the point at which these page breaks would normally be present.

Note that (obviously...) not all pages are shown in these examples—only those with content or layout specific to that document type are shown.

Documents are presented alphabetically, by document type.

★ Documentation fragments can be defined for inclusion in a document type via **Resources | Documentation Settings | *{document type}* | Fragment *x*.**

The Audit and Compliance Document

The *Audit and Compliance Document* is designed to support compliance with certifications and audits, by providing information typically requested when demonstrating such compliance. This information is provided through the use of several documentation macros (see *Audit and Compliance Macros* on page 518), and these can be populated with information specific to your audit requirements.

The first page of this document is in the form of a 'cover page' which provides standard information (provided via documentation macros) for the document.

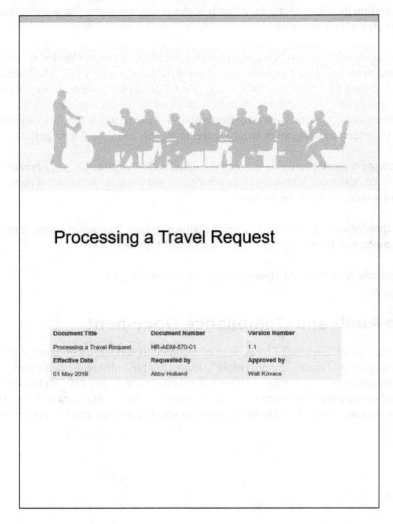

The cover page is followed by one or more pages that provide additional information that is included via the Macro Set for this document type (see *Audit and Compliance Macros* on page 518), but this information can be included or excluded depending upon your specific requirements.

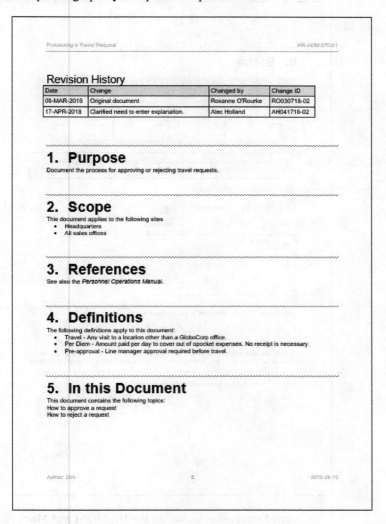

This is followed by the actual 'content' of the simulation, which is provided in a similar format to most document types (of including the cropped screenshots and bubble texts), but here there are no sub-headings per Step.

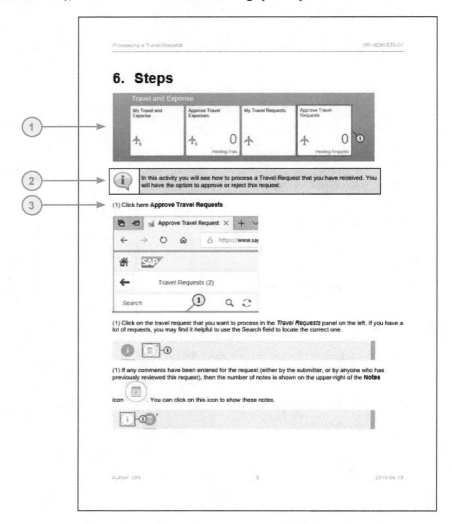

1. Cropped screenshot including the **Highlight** and **Marker**.

2. EXPLANATION macro.

3. Bubble text (one list item per macro; restart numbering per Step).

Note that there is only one header for the entire simulation, and no sub-headings at the Step level.

The BPP Document

BPP stands for **Business Process Procedure**. A BPP document typically describes how to perform a specific business task (a *process*—although the term 'process' is often used to describe a *sequence* of tasks).

The first page of the *BPP Document* is in the form of a 'cover page' which provides standard information (provided via documentation macros) for the document. Note that most 'document-specific' information required for this document type can be provided by the **BPP Marcos** Macro Set (see *BPP Macros* on page 517).

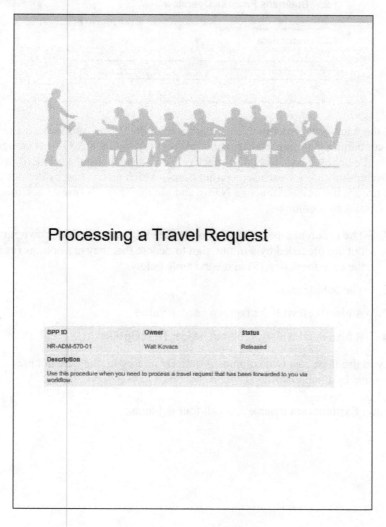

Processing a Travel Request

BPP ID	Owner	Status
HR-ADM-570-01	Walt Kovacs	Released

Description

Use this procedure when you need to process a travel request that has been forwarded to you via workflow.

The next page of content includes several items drawn from the document macros. The most interesting of these is the *Input Data* section, which provides a table of the **Object Name** and **Input Text** properties for every INPUT TEXT macro in the simulation.

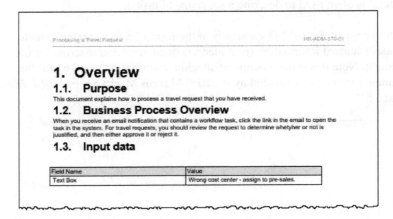

Next, the document provides the simulation content. This is formatted as a single table containing the screenshots and bubble text (including any **Object Image** used in the bubble text). The table effectively contains one row per macro, with a full-width subtitle for each screen (not Step—which means that by default the name used is the SCREEN macro's **Name** and not the Step's **Name**). Each macro row contains four columns:

● The name used for the subtitle is controlled by the **Use Title as Heading** property on the SCREEN macro. By default, this is selected, which means that the **Title** property is used for the subheading. If this option is deselected then the Step's **Title** is used for the subheading.

1. The action number. Note that options in a branch have their own number, but are preceded by a minus sign to denote that they are options (as is the case for action (5) in the example below).

2. The bubble text.

3. A blank cell with the column header **Value**.

4. A blank cell with the column header **Description**.

How you use these last two columns is entirely up to you; they are not predetermined by Enable Now.

Note that **Explanation** macros span all four columns.

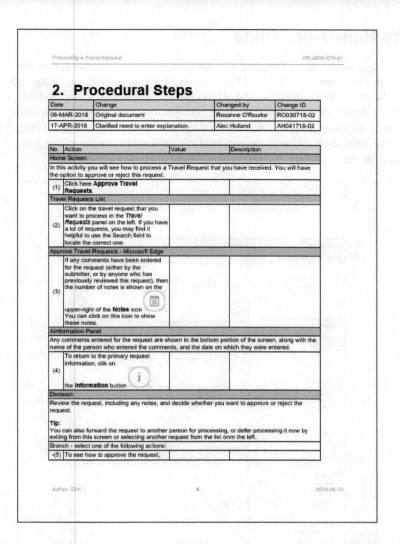

2. Procedural Steps

Date	Change		Changed by	Change ID
08-MAR-2018	Original document		Roxanne O'Rourke	RO030718-02
17-APR-2018	Clarified need to enter explanation.		Alec Holland	AH041718-02

No.	Action	Value	Description
	Home Screen		
	In this activity you will see how to process a Travel Request that you have received. You will have the option to approve or reject this request.		
(1)	Click here **Approve Travel Requests**.		
	Travel Requests List		
(2)	Click on the travel request that you want to process in the *Travel Requests* panel on the left. If you have a lot of requests, you may find it helpful to use the Search field to locate the correct one.		
	Approve Travel Requests - Microsoft Edge		
(3)	If any comments have been entered for the request (either by the submitter, or by anyone who has previously reviewed this request), then the number of notes is shown on the upper-right of the **Notes** icon. You can click on this icon to show these notes.		
	AInformation Panel		
	Any comments entered for the request are shown in the bottom portion of the screen, along with the name of the person who entered the comments, and the date on which they were entered.		
(4)	To return to the primary request information, clik on the **Information** button.		
	Decision		
	Review the request, including any notes, and decide whether you want to approve or reject the request.		
	Tip:		
	You can also forward the request to another person for processing, or defer processing it now by exiting from this screen or selecting another request from the list onm the left.		
	Branch - select one of the following actions:		
-(5)	To see how to approve the request,		

Finally, after the simulation content, the *BPP Document* contains a last page containing a section title of "Results/Related Scenarios", drawn from the documentation macro of the same name.

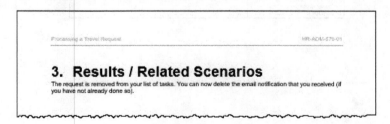

3. Results / Related Scenarios

The request is removed from your list of tasks. You can now delete the email notification that you received (if you have not already done so).

The Hands-on Guide

The *Hands-on Guide* is designed as a companion to a demonstration of the simulation—most likely Guided Presentation mode or Free Presentation mode in a classroom environment—and allows the user (or instructor) to follow along with the demonstration. The document consists of (only) a single table with columns for the bubble text and the cropped screenshot (including the **Highlight** and **Marker**). Subheadings are provided per screen, defaulting to using the screen **Name** for the heading.

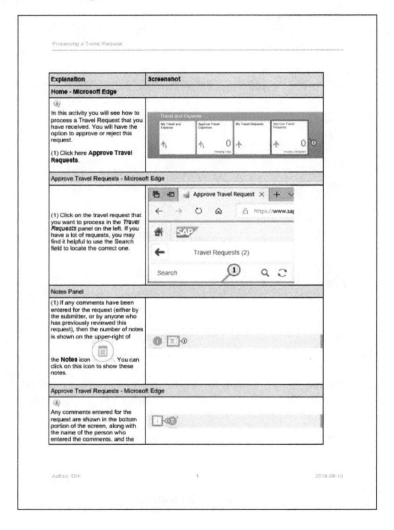

The HPQC Document

The *HPQC Document* is designed to be used in conjunction with HP Quality Center, and generates a testing document that can be loaded into Quality Center. It is expected that the **HPQC Header** document macro is used in conjunction with this document type, as shown in this example. (See *The HPQC Header macro* on page 494.)

Aside from the contents of the **HPQC Header** macro, the *HPQC Document* consists of a single table, with one row per interaction macro (EXPLANATION macros are omitted), and columns for the action number, bubble text, and expected results. This last column is empty, allowing the test results to be entered during testing.

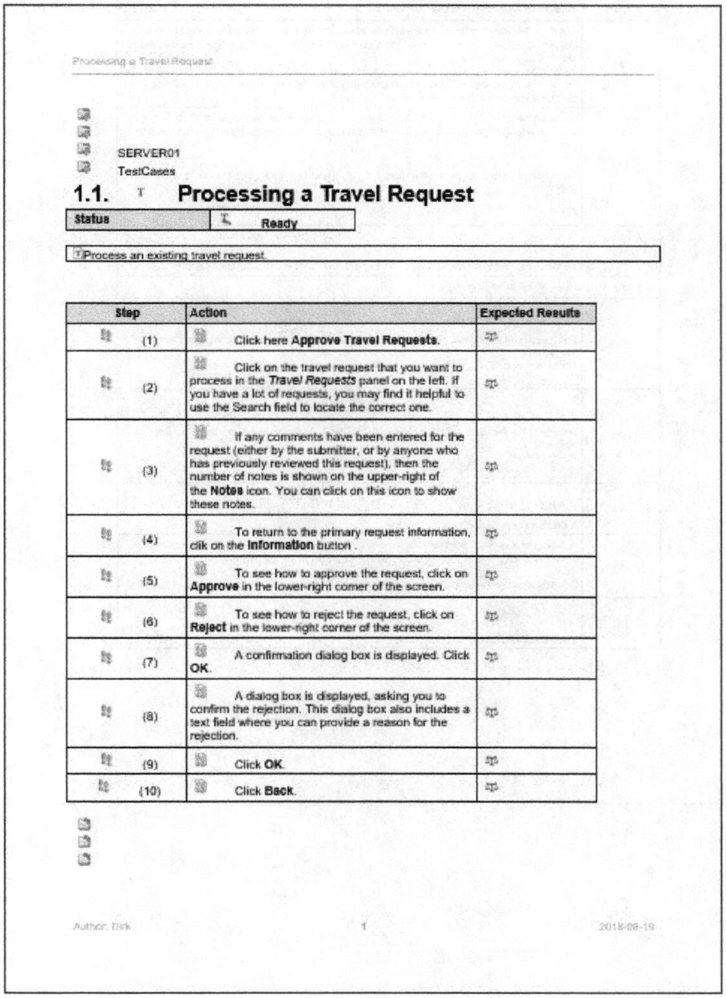

Processing a Travel Request

SERVER01
TestCases

1.1. Processing a Travel Request

Status	Ready

Process an existing travel request.

Step	Action	Expected Results
(1)	Click here **Approve Travel Requests**.	
(2)	Click on the travel request that you want to process in the *Travel Requests* panel on the left. If you have a lot of requests, you may find it helpful to use the Search field to locate the correct one.	
(3)	If any comments have been entered for the request (either by the submitter, or by anyone who has previously reviewed this request), then the number of notes is shown on the upper-right of the **Notes** icon. You can click on this icon to show these notes.	
(4)	To return to the primary request information, clik on the **Information** button .	
(5)	To see how to approve the request, click on **Approve** in the lower-right corner of the screen.	
(6)	To see how to reject the request, click on **Reject** in the lower-right corner of the screen.	
(7)	A confirmation dialog box is displayed. Click **OK**.	
(8)	A dialog box is displayed, asking you to confirm the rejection. This dialog box also includes a text field where you can provide a reason for the rejection.	
(9)	Click **OK**.	
(10)	Click **Back**.	

Author: Dirk 1 2018-09-19

The Job Help document

The *Job Help* document provides a concise version of the simulation steps, presented as a two-column table, with columns for step number and bubble text. Only interaction macros are included, not EXPLANATION macros or any documentation macros. Note that the bubble text used in this document is the Practice mode texts, which is different to most document types.

The PowerPoint Document

The *PowerPoint Document* provides a version of the simulation in the form of a PowerPoint presentation. One slide is generated per Step in the simulation project, which includes the bubble text for all macros in the Step, along with the cropped screenshot.

● The *PowerPoint Document* also includes a 'title slide', but that has not been included here as it's not that interesting, consisting only of the simulation title and a boilerplate graphic.

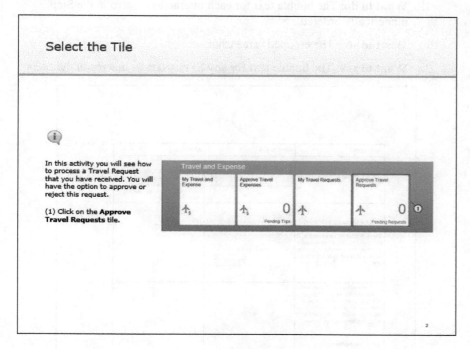

The Process Guide document

The *Process Guide* provides a reasonably-concise summary of the simulation. It contains a single, three-column table with one row per Step (and no subheadings). The columns contain the following information:

1. **What to do**: The bubble text for each interaction macro in the Step, numerically ordered.

2. **What to see**: The cropped screenshot.

3. **What to say**: The bubble text for any EXPLANATION macros in the Step.

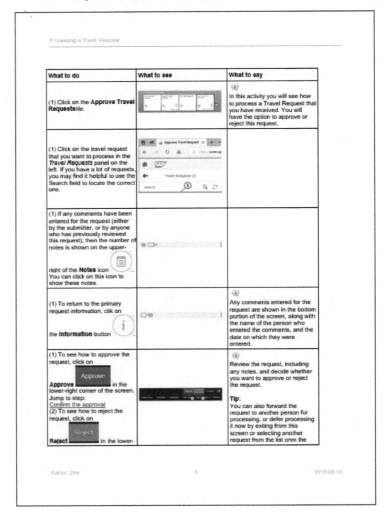

The Standard Document

The *Standard Document* contains the complete content of the simulation project (all Steps, all bubble texts, all cropped screenshots) in a format that is suitable for most purposes.

The simulation **Title** is included as a Level 2 Heading, followed immediately by the simulation **Description**. This is followed by a section for each Step in the simulation. For each Step, the Step **Name** is included as a Level 3 Heading, and this is followed by the cropped screenshot and the bubble text for each (action or Explanation) bubble in the Step. Explanations are shown on their own, in a box (and not numbered).

● It may seem odd that the first heading in the document is a Level 2 Heading, but this is for the benefit of Compound Documents and Master Documents which (can) contain multiple simulations. (See *Generating a Master Document* on page 523 and *Generating a Compound Document* on page 530 for more information on these documents.)

★ The Administrator can configure the heading levels and numbering via **Resources | Documentation Settings | Standard Document | Project Content.**

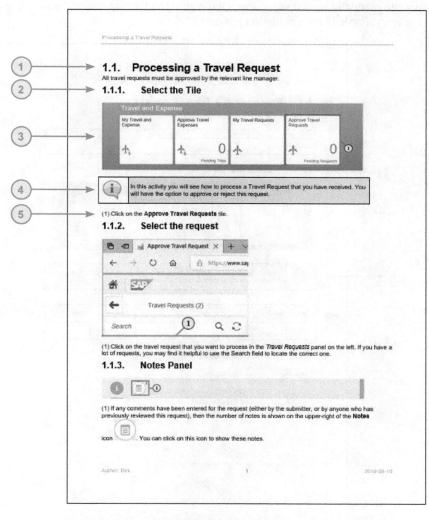

1. Level 2 heading of the simulation **Name**, followed by the simulation **Description**.

2. Level 3 heading per Step, using the Step **Name**.

3. Cropped screenshot including the **Highlight** and **Marker**.

4. EXPLANATION macro.

5. Bubble text (one list item per macro; restart numbering per Step).

The Test Sheet

The *Test Sheet* is designed to be used for manual testing of the application. The key content is a Step/Action table that lists the steps to be carried out, along with space to manually record input, expected results, and actual results (these things are not available in the simulation project).

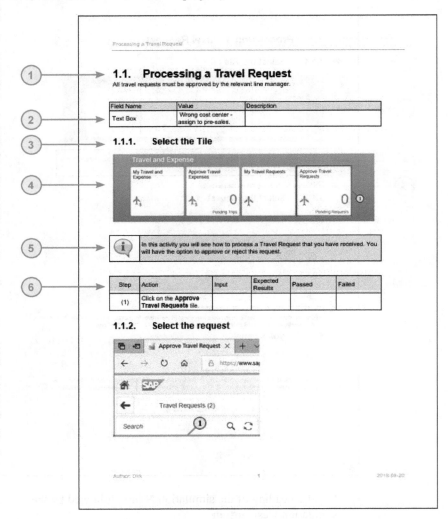

1. Simulation **Name**, followed by the simulation **Description**.

2. Table of the INPUT TEXT macros' **Object Name** and **Input Text** properties. The **Description** column is blank and can be completed by the user.

3. Level 3 heading per Step, using the Step **Name**.

4. Cropped screenshot including the **Highlight** and **Marker**.

5. EXPLANATION macro.

6. Step/Action table showing:

    i. Step number.

    ii. Bubble text.

    iii. Empty column for entering the value to use (if applicable).

    iv. Empty column for entering the expected results.

    v. Empty column for recording the actual results if the step passes.

    vi. Empty column for recording the actual results if the step fails.

The Training Document

The *Training Document* is designed to be a companion document to a training course, and contains the complete content of the simulation project (all Steps, all bubble texts, all cropped screenshots).

The key differentiator between the *Training Document* and the *Standard Document* is that in the Training Document the interaction macro bubble texts are presented in a table instead of as a numbered list. This can make for a cleaner layout (in the *Standard Document* the numbered list does not have a hanging indent, which can make it more difficult to 'scan') but can look incongruous if each Step has only one interaction macro.

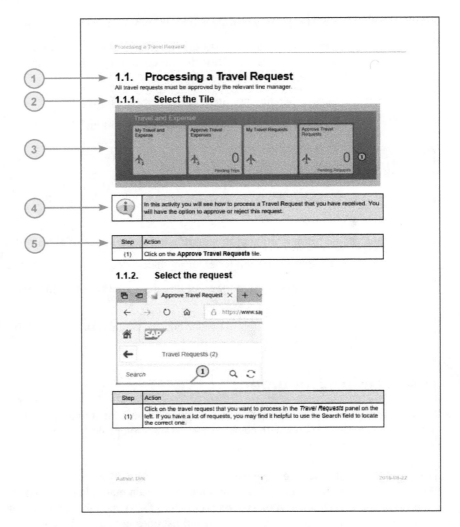

1. Level 2 heading of the simulation **Name**, followed by the simulation **Description**.

2. Level 3 heading per Step, using the Step **Name**.

3. Cropped screenshot including the **Highlight** and **Marker**.

4. EXPLANATION macro.

5. Step/Action table containing one row per interaction macro. Each row contains:

   i. Sequential interaction number (starting at **1** per table).

   ii. Bubble text.

The Work Document

The *Work Document* is an interesting document, containing a few things that appear in some of the other documents, but also containing a few components that are (by default) unique to this document type.

The 'unique selling point' of this *Work Document* is the **Process Flow**, which is a graphical representation of the various screens within the simulation and the flow between them. In addition to this, the Work Document includes a 'table of contents' (to the Step level), Test mode maximum score and required score, and (inexplicably) the project language. Most of this information is shown on the first page.

★ Although the Process Flow is included automatically in only the *Work Document*, the Administrator can add it to any other document type as a **fragment**, via **Resources | Documentation Settings | {document type}**.

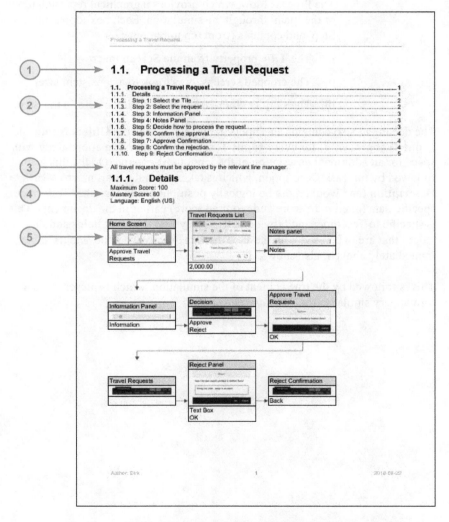

1. Level 2 heading of the simulation **Name**, followed by the simulation **Description**.

2. Table of Contents, using the Step **Name** preceded by "Step x:".

3. The simulation **Description**.

4. A level 3 heading of "Details" (generated by Enable Now—it is not present in the simulation) followed by:

    i. The **Maximum Score** property from the SIMULATION START macro.

    ii. The **Required Score** property from the SIMULATION START macro.

    iii. The **Language** property for the simulation.

5. The Process Flow, which provides a graphical representation of the 'path' through the simulation. Each box represents one Step, and contains (from top to bottom):

    i. The **Title** property from the **Screen** macro.

    ii. The cropped screenshot, shrunk to a consistent size.

    iii. The **Object Name** from every action macro in the Step.

▲ The Process Flow is not a true process flow, in that it simply presents all of the Steps in the order they appear in the simulation. It does not take into account any branches or **Jump to Step** macros.

The document also contains an 'inputs' table, which lists the **Object Name** and **Input Text** properties for every **Input Text** macro in the simulation, along with space for an additional description of the input to be entered. Oddly, this is then followed by the Task Description, which is taken from the Start macro's **Task Description** (and would more be logically positioned with the other Test-mode specific data (maximum score and required score) earlier in the document). This is specific to Test mode, and (by default) simply lists the input fields and the values that are to be used with these—which is exactly what the 'inputs' table immediately above it also shows.

This is followed by the true content of the simulation, which is presented in a format very similar to the *Standard Document*.

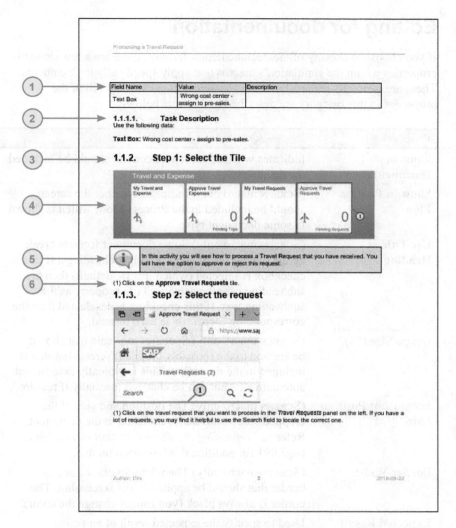

1. Table of all INPUT TEXT macros in the simulation, including columns for the **Object Name** and the **Input Text**, and a blank column for manually entering an explanation of the input.

2. Header 4 of "Task Description" followed by the **Task Description** property from the SIMULATION START macro.

3. Header 3 (repeating per Step) of the Step Title preceded by "Step x:".

4. Cropped screenshot including the **Highlight** and **Marker**.

5. **Explanation** macro.

6. Numbered list of contiguous action macros in the Step (that is, action macros not separated by an EXPLANATION macro or other non-interaction macro).

▲ Unfortunately the numbered list of action macros is not a 'true' numbered list in that it does not have a hanging indent, which makes it a little harder to read.

Editing for documentation

If you choose to use any of the documentation formats, there are a few standard properties within the simulation's macros that apply specifically to documents. These are generally grouped into the *Documentation* category. All of the properties in this category are described in the table below.

Property	Purpose
Show in Documentation	Indicates whether the macro content should be included the document.
Show in Process Flow	(SCREEN macro only) Indicates whether the screen should be included in the Process Flow, which is shown in some document types.
Use Title as Heading	(SCREEN macro only) Some document formats break up the overall list of actions with subheadings. If this checkbox is selected (which it is by default) then the subheading uses the screen's Title property as the subheading text. If this checkbox is deselected then the corresponding Step Title is used instead.
Image Size (%)	(SCREEN macro only) Specifies the scale that should be applied to the (possibly cropped) screenshot that is included in the document. This is typically determined automatically, but can be changed manually if required.
Screenshot Position / Size	(SCREEN macro only) The position and size of the cropped screenshot that is included in the document. Refer to *Controlling the documentation screenshot* on page 491 for additional information on this.
Border Width	(SCREEN macro only) The width, in pixels, of any border that should be applied to the screenshot. The border is always black (you cannot change the color).
Expected Result	Used to specify the expected result of an action. Appears in the *Test Sheet* document and the *HPQC Document*.
ROC	Used to indicate if an input field is **Required, Optional,** or **Conditional**.
Description	Used to provide additional information about an input field.
Screenshot	(INPUT TEXT macro only) Contains a cropped screenshot of the action area after the action has been performed.
Object Image Position	(INPUT TEXT macro only) The (X,Y) position at which the Screenshot should be overlaid onto the screenshot (prior to cropping) in the document (to show the field as filled in). By default this is the same as the Highlight Position.

● For an explanation of how the **Screenshot** and **Object Image Position** properties are used, refer to *Working with the 'after' object image* on page 155 for additional information.

Property	Purpose
Highlight Position / Size	The position and size of the Highlight (the border around the action area) that is to be overlaid on the screenshot in the document. This defaults to the same values as the *Control* **Position and Size**, but can be changed if necessary.
Marker Orientation	Can be used to specify the position of the numbered marker that is placed on the screenshot, relative to the highlight to which it is pointing. Normally you can leave this as **Auto**, and Enable Now will determine the best placement, but there may be circumstances under which you want to explicitly define this yourself (for example, where you have multiple input fields/markers on the same cropped screenshot, and need to make sure that these do not get in the way of each other).

Controlling the documentation screenshot

Many of the documentation types described earlier in this chapter include a cropped version of the screenshot in the SCREEN macro. This cropping is performed automatically, based on settings in **Tools | Settings | Authoring Settings | Auto Crop**, and will include the Highlight area and a specified area around this. The currently-cropped area for a screenshot is only visible in the *Step View*, where it appears as a dark gray rectangle. The following screenshot shows an (enlarged) example of this.

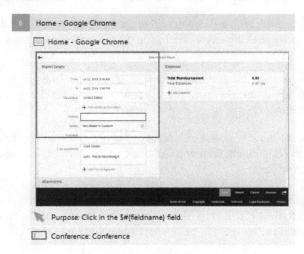

In some circumstances, you may find it useful to specify a different area to use in the documentation—for example, to reduce the overall size of the document.

To re-crop the documentation screenshot, carry out the steps shown below.

1. Make sure that the SCREEN macro is selected in the *Step View*.

2. Click on the **Manual Crop** button at the top of the Macro Editor pane. A new window, titled *Crop Image*, is opened up, showing the full screenshot and with the current crop area delineated by a red bounding box.

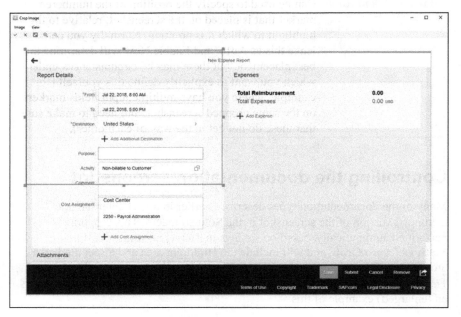

3. Redefine the crop area by dragging the handles on the bounding box, and/or by clicking anywhere inside the current crop area and dragging it to a new location.

4. Once you are done, click on the **Confirm** button (the green check mark) in the upper-left corner of the window to save your changes and return to the *Project Editor*.

If you don't want the screenshot to be cropped at all, and want the full screenshot to be used in the document, then you can click on the **Uncrop** button at the top of the *Macro Editor* panel.

If you subsequently decide that you do not want to keep your crop changes, and want to revert to the default crop for the screenshot, you can click on the **Auto Crop** button, and the image will be re-cropped according to the default settings.

The details of the screenshot crop are also specified in the **Screenshot Position / Size** property for the SCREEN macro, where you can edit them directly, for pixel-perfect positioning. This property, and the other properties that can be used to influence the screenshot in the document, are listed in the table on page 490.

Documentation macros

So far in this book we have looked at interaction macros (such as the MOUSE ACTION macro, the INPUT TEXT macro, and even the SCREEN macro), and special macros (such as the FORM STRUCTURE macro, the BRANCH macro, and so on). There is another category of macro available within the project editor: **Documentation** macros.

Documentation macros typically provide additional information that is used exclusively in the document output formats. Most document macros can be used in any printed document, but some must be present in certain document formats to provide information that is inserted into the document via the predefined document template.

To insert a documentation macro into your simulation, carry out the following steps:

1. Click on the existing macro in the *Thumbnail Pane* after which the documentation macro should be inserted. For most macros this will be the Simulation Start macro.

2. Select menu option **Insert | Insert Documentation macro |** {required macro}.

3. Adjust the macro properties as required.

The available macros and their properties are described separately in the sections below. Examples of the output generated by each macro are also given in these sections. You can use this information to determine whether or not you want to use any of these macros (they are generally optional, although there are two document types—the *BPP Document* and the *Audit and Compliance Document*—in which some macros must be included for the document to be populated with the necessary information.

The HEADER INFORMATION macro

The HEADER INFORMATION macro allows you to provide a brief text segment, and a heading or title for this text. Unfortunately, this heading does not use a specific heading style, and is not numbered, so depending on where you insert it, it may not be logically sized according to its position within other headers (see the example below), although your Administrator can adjust the *Title* style in the document template to adjust this.

The following screenshot shows an example of the properties for this macro.

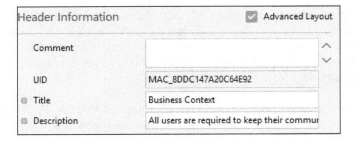

The following table describes the purpose of each of the available properties for this macro.

Property	Purpose
Title	Provide a 'heading' for the information that is provided in the **Description** property.
Description	A sentence or two of information that is to be included in the document.

An example of this macro, as it appears in the *Standard Document*, is shown below. Note that the exact position of this information may be different in different document types, but its formatting will always be as shown here.

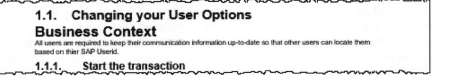

The HPQC HEADER macro

The HPQC HEADER macro is used to specify information that is specific to the *HPQC Document*. The *HPQC Document* is used with HP Quality Center, to record the results of a test case.

The following screenshot shows an example of the properties for this macro.

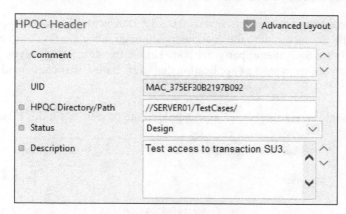

The following table describes the purpose of each of the available properties for this macro.

Property	Purpose
HPQC Directory/ Path	Specify the location of HP Quality Center on your PC.
Status	The current status of the test case. Choices are **Design**, **Imported**, **Ready**, and **Repair**.
Description	A short text description of the test case.

An example of the output generated by this macro, as it appears in the *HPQC Document*, is shown below.

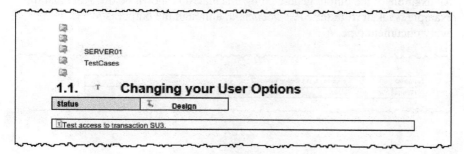

The TRANSACTION CODE macro

The TRANSACTION CODE macro inserts the SAP Transaction Code and Menu Path for the transaction into the document. Although this macro is designed specifically for SAP, the property fields are simple free-text fields, so you can also use it for any other system or application that uses 'transaction codes' and 'menu paths'.

The following screenshot shows an example of the properties for this macro.

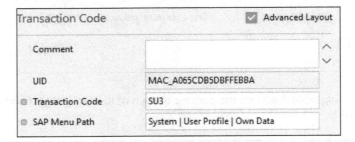

The following table describes the purpose of each of the available properties for this macro.

Property	Purpose
Transaction Code	The SAP Transaction Code or other command.
Menu Path	The full menu path of the transaction. This is free text and can be entered in any format (with any separator).

An example of the output generated by this macro is shown below. Note that this example is taken from the *SPD Document*, although the output is identical in every document type.

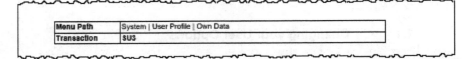

The PARTIAL SCREENSHOT macro

The PARTIAL SCREENSHOT macro allows you to insert an additional—or alternative—screenshot into your document. This macro must be inserted after the SCREEN macro in a Step, and will allow you to select a separate portion of the screen than the area selected by the screenshot crop for the SCREEN macro.

This is useful if, for example, you want to document an additional area of the screen, but do not want to expand the existing crop area as it would make the overall screenshot too large, or it would include too much irrelevant information. Alternatively, you could use this macro when you want to zoom in on a specific area of the screenshot.

The following screenshot shows an example of the properties for this macro.

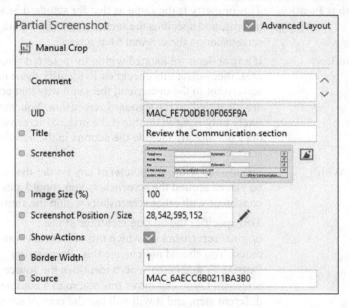

The following table describes the purpose of each of the available properties for this macro.

Property	Purpose
Title	If you want your screenshot to be treated as a Step in your document and have its own header (which is normally taken from the Step's **Name** property), then enter the required header. This will be numbered at the same level (Heading 3), and in sequence with, the Step Title.

Property	Purpose
Screenshot	When you first insert this macro, you are prompted to select the area on the preceding screenshot to use. This property shows a thumbnail image of the selected area (you can click on this to show the image full size). You can re-select this are via the **Manual Crop** action button at the top of the Macro editor. You can also replace this image with another one, via the **Replace Image** button (see *Editing a screenshot image* on page 151).
Image size	Specify the scaling that should be applied to the image. You should try to be consistent with the scaling of other screenshots.
Screenshot Position / Size	This property is the same as that for standard SCREEN macros, and specifies the location and size of the screenshot on the original Step screen.
Show Actions	If any actions are located within the selected screenshot area, then select this checkbox to identify these on the screenshot in the document, the same way that actions are identified on the standard screenshot. You would likely only want to do this if the original screenshot does not already include the actions in the additional screenshot.
Border Width	Specify the width (in pixels) of any border that is to be placed around the screenshot. You should aim to be consistent with other screenshots within the simulation.
Source	This specifies the unique identifier of the original screenshot on which this screenshot was based. You should not change this. Because the PARTIAL SCREENSHOT macro identifies the source screenshot, you can move this macro to a completely different step, and it will still use the correct screenshot (and not the screenshot for the Step it is moved to).

● If there are no actions for this partial screenshot but you want to draw attention to a specific object on or area of the screen, consider using a DOCUMENT HIGHLIGHT macro or a DOCUMENT ARROW macro.

Let's look at a more detailed example of the output generated by this macro. This example is taken from our sample simulation for transaction SU3. Within that simulation, there is already a Step named *Change your Address details*, which has several actions that take place within the *Work Center* section of the screen. We also have an EXPLANATION macro that provides information on the *Communication* section of the screen. We have already cropped the screenshot for the Step to show only the *Work Center* section, and don't want to expand this to also include the **Communication** section, so we will add a PARTIAL SCREENSHOT macro that includes this section. Because the EXPLANATION macro refers to information on this additional screenshot, we need to place our PARTIAL SCREENSHOT macro before the EXPLANATION macro. The *Step View* for this Step, including our PARTIAL SCREENSHOT macro (highlighted) thus appears as follows (you can also see the cropping for the original document screenshot here, too):

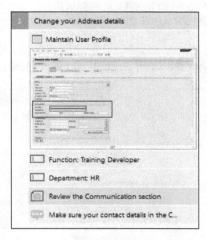

Now let's look at how this manifests itself in the output document. The example below is taken from the *Standard* document, using the property settings shown at the start of this section.

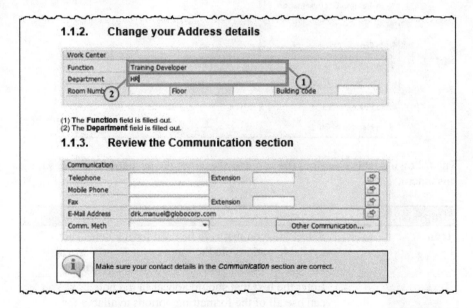

Here, you can see that the **Title** is used as a level-3 heading, and the explanation following the PARTIAL SCREENSHOT macro is indeed shown after the partial screenshot.

The NOTE macro

The NOTE macro allows you to insert a note box that is effectively the same as one produced by the EXPLANATION macro but that appears only in the printed document.

The following screenshot shows an example of the properties for this macro.

The following table describes the purpose of each of the available properties for this macro.

Property	Purpose
Icon	Select the icon that is to be used for the note. The available options are the same as for EXPLANATION macros, being: **Remark**, **Tip**, **Info** and **Warning**.
Text	Enter the text that should appear in the note box. You can use all of the formatting options available for standard bubbles (refer to *Adjusting Bubble text* on page 111 for details).

Property	Purpose
In Standard Documentation	
In Training Documentation	
In Test Sheet	Select the document types in which the Note should appear.
In Process Guide	
In BPP Document	Note that not all document types are available for selection, as this macro is not used in all document types.
In Audit and Compliance Document	
In PowerPoint	
In Hands-On Guide	

An example of the output generated by this macro is shown below. Note that this example is taken from the *Standard* document, although the output is identical in every document type.

 This document is uncontrolled when printed. Always refer to the on-line *GloboCorp Training Repository* for the latest version.

The DESCRIPTION macro

The DESCRIPTION macro allows you to insert a paragraph of text into your document. This appears in the same format as any other macro text, but without any paragraph numbering.

The following screenshot shows an example of the properties for this macro.

The following table describes the purpose of each of the available properties for this macro.

Property	Purpose
Text	Enter the text that should appear in the document. You can use all of the formatting options available for standard bubbles (refer to *Adjusting Bubble text* on page 111 for details).
Reset Global Index Counter	Each interaction macro within a Step is numbered sequentially (starting at **1** with each Step). If you want this numbering to reset to **1** again (for the macro following the DESCRIPTION macro) then select this checkbox.

Property	Purpose
In Standard Documentation	
In Training Documentation	
In Test Sheet	Select the document types in which the Note should appear.
In Process Guide	
In BPP Document	Note that not all document types are available for selection, as this macro is not used in all document types.
In Audit and Compliance Document	
In Hands-On Guide	

An example of the output generated by this macro is shown below. This example is taken from the *Test Case* document type. In this example, there are three fields to be maintained on the screen, and the DESCRIPTION macro is inserted immediately before the third of these, with the **Reset Global Index Counter** checkbox selected, so that the step numbering restarts.

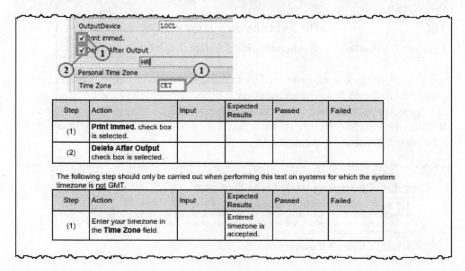

The HEADING Macro

The HEADING macro allows you to insert an additional heading into your document. You can choose the heading level, and it will be formatted and numbered appropriately within the Word document.

When choosing the location and level of the heading, bear in mind that the project **Name** is inserted as a Level 2 heading, and the Step **Name** is inserted as Level 3 headings. (Level 1 is reserved for compound documents).

The following screenshot shows an example of the properties for this macro.

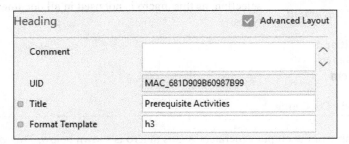

The following table describes the purpose of each of the available properties for this macro.

Property	Purpose
Title	The text to be used as the heading.
Format Template	The heading level to use (h1, h2, h3, etc.).

An example of the output generated by this macro is shown below. This example is taken from the *Standard* document type. In this example, a Level 3 heading (of "Prerequisite Activities") is inserted in the Start Step, and is followed by a DESCRIPTION macro ("Before performing..."). The heading "Start the transaction" is the **Name** property of the next Step.

1.1. Changing your User Options
1.1.1. Prerequisite Activities
Before performing this activity, make sure that you have successfully signed on to the client within which you want to change your user options. Note that you need to perform this activity separately within each SAP client to which you have access.
1.1.2. Start the transaction

The Highlight macro

The Highlight macro allows you to add a highlight (the default red marquee that appears around action areas) to a screenshot (or partial screenshot—see *The Partial Screenshot macro* on page 497). You can specify text to be used with the highlight, in which case this text appears the same way as bubble text for an interaction macro, including having an associated marker.

The following screenshot shows an example of the properties for this macro.

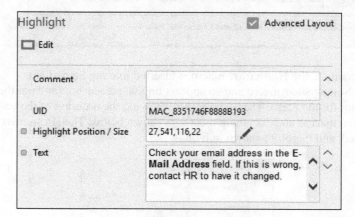

The following table describes the purpose of each of the available properties for this macro.

Property	Purpose
Highlight Position/ Size	When you first insert this macro, you are prompted to select the area on the preceding screenshot to use. This property shows the position and size of the selected area. You can re-select this are via the **Edit** button at the top of the *Macro Editor*.
Text	Any text associated with the highlight. This is optional, and if omitted, the highlight will appear without a marker.

An example of the output generated by this macro (and using the settings shown in the properties above) is shown below.

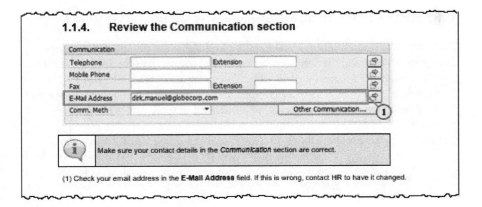

1.1.4. Review the Communication section

Communication			
Telephone		Extension	
Mobile Phone			
Fax		Extension	
E-Mail Address	dirk.manuel@globocorp.com		
Comm. Meth		Other Communication... (1)	

ℹ Make sure your contact details in the *Communication* section are correct.

(1) Check your email address in the **E-Mail Address** field. If this is wrong, contact HR to have it changed.

In this example, the HIGHLIGHT macro is inserted into the Step after a PARTIAL SCREENSHOT macro and so appears on that screenshot (and not the screenshot for the Step). The Step for this, showing the ordering of the various interaction macros and document macros is shown below. The HIGHLIGHT macro is selected, and therefore shown in blue.

The ARROW macro

The ARROW macro allows you to add an arrow to a screenshot (or partial screenshot—see *The Partial Screenshot macro* on page 497). You can specify text to be used with the arrow, in which case this text appears below the screenshot.

The following screenshot shows an example of the properties for this macro.

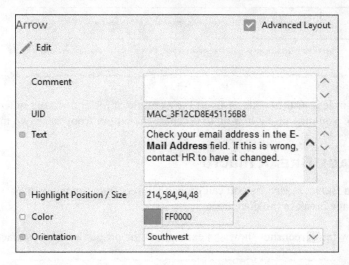

The following table describes the purpose of each of the available properties for this macro.

Property	Purpose
Text	The text to appear below the screenshot (on which the arrow appears).
Highlight Position / Size	When you first insert this macro, you are prompted to position and size the arrow on the screenshot. This property shows the position and size of the selected area. You can re-select this are via the Edit action button at the top of the *Macro Editor*.
Color	The arrow defaults to red, but you can select any other color via this property.
Orientation	Select the direction in which the arrow should point. You can select any of the standard eight compass points.

An example of the output generated by this macro (and using the settings shown in the properties above) is shown below.

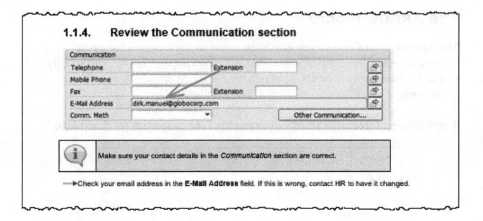

This example uses the same set-up as the example of the HIGHLIGHT macro on page 506. You may find it helpful to compare the output from these two macros.

The PAGE BREAK macro

The PAGE BREAK macro, as you can probably guess from the name, allows you to force a page break in the document.

The following screenshot shows an example of the properties for this macro.

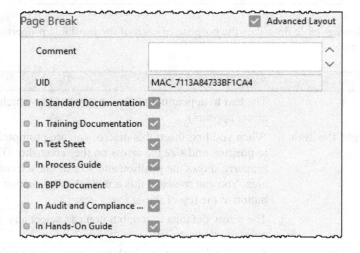

The checkboxes allow you to choose the document formats to which the page break should be applied.

The DOCUMENT PROPERTIES macro

The DOCUMENT PROPERTIES macro provides you with a way of including additional, custom information into the document output types. For example, perhaps you have a requirement to include the name of the person who approved the document for release on the document. To do this, you could include a property of Approver, and then set the value of this property to the name of the approver.

This relies on pre-named properties being defined in the template on which the document type is based, and placeholders being included in the document where the value of these properties should be inserted. This will need to be done by your Administrator, but the *BPP Document* output type and the *Audit and Compliance Document* have properties and placeholders pre-defined, so we will use one of these in the examples below. It also relies on the property name being entered correctly, and a value for this property being specified in the simulation (which requires a certain amount of discipline from Authors).

Note that this macro should be included in the Start step for your simulation, so that the property values are available when the document is generated. If you do have custom properties (and these are defined in the document template) it is strongly suggested that you use a simulation template, and include this macro and have all of the properties (but not their values) specified in it by default.

The following screenshot shows an example of the properties available for the DOCUMENT PROPERTIES macro.

The DOCUMENT PROPERTIES macro effectively consists of six Name/Value property pairs, although if you need to define more than six properties, you can simply include this macro multiple times.

For completeness, here's an explanation of the properties:

Property	Purpose
Name	Specify the exact name of the document property, as it is specified in the Advanced Properties for the Word document template. If your Administrator has defined custom properties, they should provide you with these names.
Value	Enter the text that is to be inserted in the generated document at the position denoted by the document property placeholder.

● If you do not know the exact document property name, generate the document, open it, then go to the document's *Info* page, select **Properties > Advanced Properties**, and you will find them listed on the *Custom* tab (see the example in this section)

The screenshot above shows the document properties that are predefined for the *BPP Document*. The names shown are the actual document property names that are predefined in the output document; the values are unique to the simulation project (in this case, a simulation for *VA01 - Entering a customer order*). To make this connection clear, here's the document property definitions within the Word template on which the *BPP Document* is based:

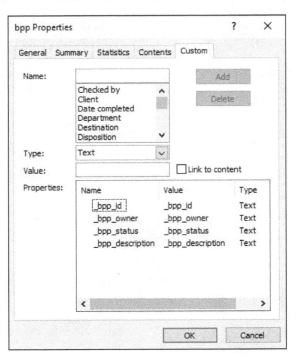

Note that the above example is from the template, *before* the document has been generated. The values (which default to the names of the properties) are replaced with the values specified in the DOCUMENT PROPERTIES macro's properties (see the previous screenshot) when the document is generated.

An example of the *BPP Document* for which the predefined properties have been defined (and their values specified), is shown below. This example uses the settings shown in the screenshot of the *Macro Editor* at the start of this section.

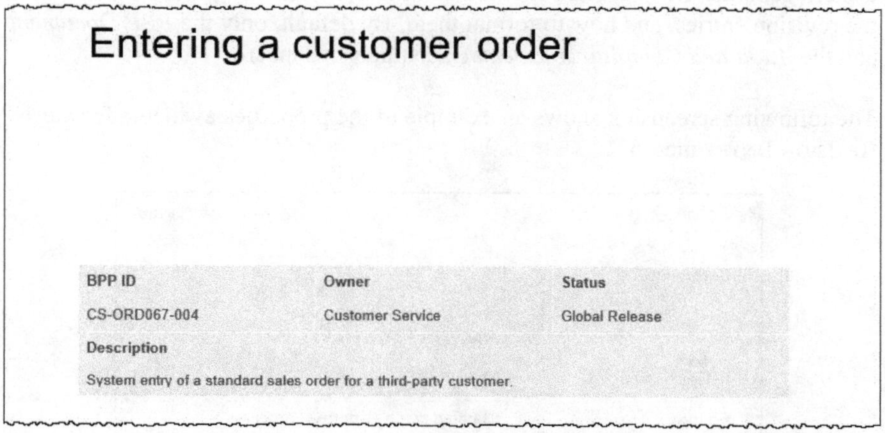

Entering a customer order

BPP ID	Owner	Status
CS-ORD067-004	Customer Service	Global Release
Description		
System entry of a standard sales order for a third-party customer.		

The above screenshot shows page 1 of the *BPP Document* generated for our simulation. The shaded table into which the property values have been inserted exists in the document template itself.

The REVISION ENTRY macro

The REVISION ENTRY macro is used to provide a change log entry for a document—including who made the change and when. If this macro is used, a new instance of the macro would be inserted each time the document is revised. REVISION ENTRY macros require specific placeholders in the document template used to generate the document type, so that Enable Now knows where to insert the revision entries, and how to format them. By default, only the *BPP Document* and the *Audit and Compliance Document* support this macro.

The following screenshot shows an example of the properties available for the REVISION ENTRY macro.

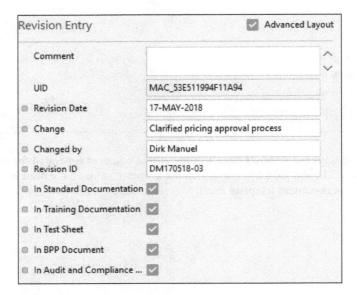

The following table describes the purpose of each of the available properties for this macro.

Property	Purpose
Revision Date	Enter the date on which the revision was made. This is a simple text field, and the date can be entered in any format (just be consistent).
Change	Enter a short text description of the change. This should be sufficient that the reader can easily determine if the change is something they need to be aware of, and locate the details of the change if it is.
Changed by	Enter the name, Userid, or other identifier of the person who made the change. Again, this is a free text field, so you can enter the name in any format. (You could also choose to use a department name or other reference.)

Property	Purpose
Revision ID	Revision identifiers are typically used to group related changes (across multiple documents) together, or to tie the change to an object another system, such as a change request or helpdesk ticket.
In Standard Documentation	
In Training Documentation	Select the document types in which the revision entry should appear.
In Test Sheet	Note that although you can select all of these document types, the revision entries will only appear in the documents that have been specifically configured to display this information. By default this is only the *BPP Document* and the *Audit and Compliance Document*.
In BPP Document	
In Audit and Compliance Document	

An example of the output generated for the REVISION ENTRY macro is shown below. This example is taken from the *BPP Document*, and includes two separate REVISION ENTRY macros.

Date	Change	Changed by	Change ID
06-JAN-2018	Original document	Walt Kovacs	WK060118-01
17-MAY-2018	Clarified pricing approval process	Dirk Manuel	DM170518-03

The INPUT VALUES macro

The INPUT VALUES macro allows you to insert a table of all input fields used in the simulation and the values entered, along with some other field-level data that can be specified (see below).

The following screenshot shows an example of the properties available for the INPUT VALUES macro.

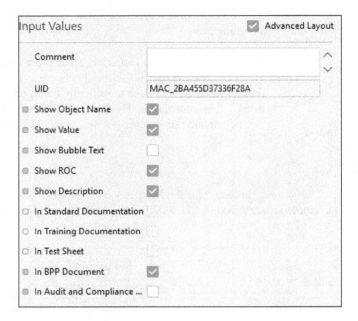

The following table describes the purpose of each of the available properties for this macro.

Property	Purpose
Show Object Name	If selected, include the **Object Name** in the input values table.
Show Value	If selected, include the **Input Text** in the input values table.
Show Bubble Text	If selected, include the bubble text (for the mode from which the document will be generated) in the input values table.
Show ROC	If selected, include the contents of the **ROC** property for the INPUT TEXT macro in the input values table. Values are **Required**, **Optional**, and **Conditional**.
Show Description	If selected, include the contents of the **Description** property for the INPUT TEXT macro in the input values table.

Property	Purpose
In Standard Documentation	
In Training Documentation	Select the document types in which the input values table should appear.
In Test Sheet	Although you can select the *Test Sheet* document type here, do not select it. A table of input fields/values is included in this document type automatically (even if the INPUT VALUES macro is not used). If you then use the INPUT VALUES macro and select this document type for it, the input values table will be inserted twice.
In BPP Document	
In Audit and Compliance Document	

To clarify the source of the data for the columns in the input values table, the following screenshots show the relevant properties for an input field:

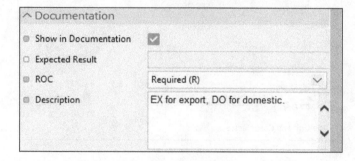

An example of the output generated for the INPUT VALUES macro is shown below. This example is taken from the *BPP Document*, and uses the properties shown in the screenshot shown earlier.

Field Name	Value	ROC	Description
Commmand	va01	R	Transaction code
Order Type	or	R	
Sales Organization	0001	R	Use your own sales organization code.
Distribution Channel	ex	R	EX for export, DO for domestic.
Division	mp	O	Only specify if your sales org. is split by division.
Sales Office	usa	O	Country
Sales Group	ne	C	Department

The LOGON VALUES macro

The LOGON VALUES macro allows you to insert a table that specifies information about the system in which the task (described by the simulation) should be carried out, and the access required to do this. The purpose of this table is to provide the user with enough information to be able to get to the point where the simulation starts. If this information is already provided within the simulation steps, or is obvious to all users, you do not need to include it again via this macro.

The following screenshot shows an example of the properties available for the LOGON VALUES macro.

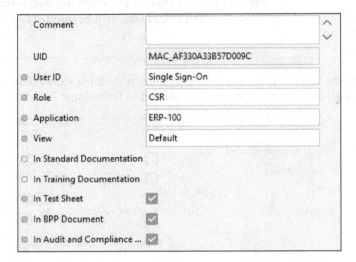

The following table describes the purpose of each of the available properties for this macro.

Property	Purpose
User ID	Specifies the Userid that should be used to log on to the system.
Role	Specifies the role that should be assigned to the user.
Application	Specifies the application that the user should log on to.
View	If applicable, can be used to specify the view or application screen/page that the task starts from.

Property	Purpose
In Standard Documentation	
In Training Documentation	
In Test Sheet	Select the document types in which the logon values table should appear.
In BPP Document	
In Audit and Compliance Document	

An example of the output generated for the LOGON VALUES macro is shown below. This example is taken from the *BPP Document*, but the layout and content is exactly the same for all document types (in which it can be included).

Logon ID/Role	Single Sign-On	CSR
Application/View	ERP-100	Default

Predefined documentation macro sets

Any of the 14 documentation macros described above (see *Documentation macros* on page 493), can technically be included in just about any document type, although in several cases a specific placeholder fieldcode must be present in the document template to receive the generated output if it is provided.

Two document types are pre-built with specific constructs and placeholders that require certain macro content—from multiple document macros—to be provided in order to populate them. To facilitate this, Enable Now provides specific commands to insert all of the required documentation macros for each of these documents. These sets are explained in the sections below.

BPP Macros

To insert all of the documentation macros required for the *BPP Document*, select menu option **Insert | Insert Documentation Macro | Insert BPP Macros**.

This will insert the following macros:

- In the Start Step:

- ♦ DOCUMENT PROPERTIES: All required document properties are predefined

- ♦ REVISION ENTRY: Blank

- ♦ DESCRIPTION: Header 1 text of "Overview"

- ♦ DESCRIPTION: Header 2 text of "Purpose" followed by a boilerplate paragraph

- ♦ DESCRIPTION: Header 2 text of "Business Process Overview" followed by a boilerplate paragraph

- ♦ DESCRIPTION: Header 2 text of "Input Data"

- ♦ INPUT VALUES

- ♦ DESCRIPTION: Header 2 text of "Procedural Steps"

- In the End Step:

  - ♦ DESCRIPTION: Header 1 text of "Results / Related Scenarios" followed by a boilerplate paragraph

The **Comment** property for each macro will start with "BPP" to make them easier to identify if you also have other documentation macros in your project.

For information about the content of each of these macros, refer to *Documentation macros* on page 493.

Audit and Compliance Macros

To insert all of the documentation macros required for the *Audit and Compliance Document*, select menu option **Insert | Insert Documentation Macro | Insert Audit and Compliance Macros**.

This will insert the following Documentation macros:

- In the Start Step:

  - ♦ DOCUMENT PROPERTIES: All required document properties are predefined

  - ♦ REVISION ENTRY: Blank

  - ♦ PAGE BREAK

  - ♦ DESCRIPTION: Header 1 text of "Purpose"

  - ♦ DESCRIPTION: Header 1 text of "Scope" followed by a boilerplate paragraph

  - ♦ DESCRIPTION: Header 1 text of "References" followed by a boilerplate paragraph

- DESCRIPTION: Header 1 text of "Definitions" followed by a boilerplate paragraph and bulleted list
- DESCRIPTION: Header 1 text of "In this Document" followed by a boilerplate paragraph and a bulleted list
- DESCRIPTION: Header 1 text of "Steps"

The **Comment** property for each macro will start with "A&C" to make them easier to identify if you also have other documentation macros in your project.

For information about the content of each of these macros, refer to *Documentation macros* on page 493.

Generating documents

Now that you know what types of document are available, know how to edit simulation content for use in a document, and know what additional information can be included in the various document types through the use of document macros, let's delve into the mechanics of actually generating these documents.

There are principally two ways in which you can generate a document for a simulation: via the *Project Editor*, and via the Workarea. These two methods are described separately in the subsections below. Before we get there, though, there's a few things you need to understand.

Although Enable Now (generally) uses a 'single source' philosophy for the creation of training deliverables—and that single source is the simulation project—when you create a document from a simulation project the document is effectively a snapshot of the contents of the simulation as it existed at the time of document creation. This means that if you subsequently change the simulation project, these changes will not automatically be reflected in the document(s) generated from this simulation project. Therefore, if you update the simulation you need to re-generate the document. For this reason, it is better to leave the creation of the documents late in the simulation development process—ideally, until after the simulation has been finalized.

There is an advantage to this approach, however. Because the document is not auto-re-generated every time you change the source simulation, you can make changes to the document post-generation, and these will not be overwritten. This makes it possible to include additional information in the document (and as you may have noticed, some document types provide space for such information to be entered). Of course the danger then is that if you *do* re-generate the document, you will have to re-do any manual changes that you made.

Generating documents from the Topic Editor

The most common time to generate a document for a simulation is when you are editing it: either during editing to check that your document-specific edits are correct, or once you have finalized the simulation, to generate the distributable version.

To generate a document from a simulation during editing, from the *Project Editor*, carry out the steps shown below.

■ You can also click on the **Documentation** menu, select the document format from the drop-down menu, and then select the document type from the sub-menu.

★ The document type in the upper-left corner is the 'default' document type. The Administrator can change this by selecting the required document type in **Resources | Documentation Settings** and then clicking on the **Set as Default** button at the top of the *Object Editor* pane.

1. Open the simulation project *in edit mode* in the *Project Editor*.

2. On the *Project Editor Toolbar*, click on the button for the appropriate document format (DOC, PDF, HTM, or PPT). A drop-down panel is displayed, showing the document types that can be generated in this format.

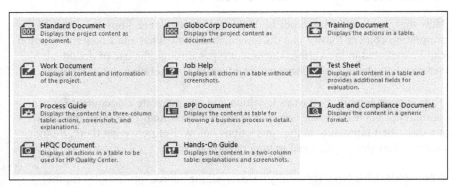

The above example is for Word format documents. Other formats will have different document types listed. Refer to *Available document types* on page 470 for a cross-reference table of types versus formats.

■ If you want to generate multiple document types at the same time, then instead of using the *Toolbar* buttons, select menu option **Documentation | Generate Documentation** to display the *Generate Documentation* panel, and complete this panel as described in *Generating documents from the Workarea* on page 521.

3. Click on the relevant document type in the drop-down panel. A progress panel is displayed.

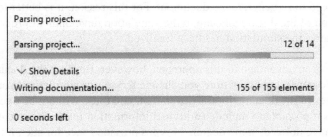

If there are any problems with the generation then you may find it useful to click on the **Show Details** drop-down and review any error messages.

Once generation is complete, the following message is displayed:

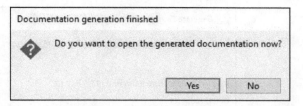

Documentation generation finished

Do you want to open the generated documentation now?

Yes   No

4. If you want to display the document, click on the **Yes** button, and the document will be opened in the relevant application.

   If you don't need to see the document now, then just click on the **No** button to close the dialog box.

5. By default, the name of the generated document will be exactly the same as the documentation type (for example, "Standard Document"). You may find it helpful to rename this—for example, to have the same name as the simulation project.

Generating documents from the Workarea

The main advantage of generating documents from the Workplace is that you can generate (multiple) document types for multiple simulation projects at the same time. This can be a great option if you are leaving document generation to the end of development, or if your document template has changed, or if you just want to make sure that the latest versions of all documents are available.

When you generate a document from the Workarea, you can do so without opening the simulation in the Project Editor. Enable Now will automatically check the simulations out to you, and then check them back in once the documents have been generated.

To generate documents from the Workarea, carry out the following steps:

1. In the *Object Navigation Pane* of the Workarea, click on the simulation project for which you want to generate the document(s), or click on the Group containing the project(s) for which you want to generate the documents. Note that if you select a Group, generation is recursive—that is, documents will be generated for all simulations in the selected group and all sub-groups all the way down to the lowest level.

2. Select menu option **Documentation | Generate Single Documents**. The *Generate Single Documents* dialog box is displayed.

■ Once a document has been generated, you can display it at any time by double-clicking on it in the asset list below the simulation object in the Workarea.

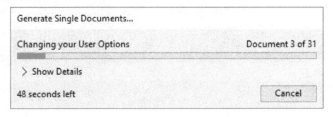

The *Generate Single Document* dialog box contains a matrix of all of the available document types (as rows) and all of the formats in which these documents can be generated (as columns). Again, note that not all document types are available in all formats. Checkboxes are provided for each intersection, and should be selected to generate that document type in that document format. By default, only the types/formats currently generated for the selected project(s) will be selected (if any, and if consistent; otherwise all types/formats will be selected).

3.   Make sure that only the document type / document format combinations that you want to generate are selected.

The top row of checkboxes allows you to quickly select or deselect all document types for a format, and the leftmost column of checkboxes allows you to select or deselect all formats for a specific document type. There is also a button at the bottom to **Select All** combinations, although annoyingly there is no **Deselect All** button (which would invariably be more useful).

4.   Click **Ok**. Enable now will work through the projects, generating the requested documents. During generation, progress is shown in a dialog box, as shown below:

If you expand the **Show Details** section, you can see slightly more information about the progress (such as the number of objects processed), and a scrolling list of projects processed.

5. Once all documents have been generated, the dialog box closes. There is no confirmation message.

Generating a Master Document

Whereas all of the documents discussed so far are generated for a single simulation project, a *Master Document* contains the document output for multiple simulations. This is very useful if, for example, you want to provide a single 'desk reference' (or similar document) for an entire functional area, role, or other grouping.

Note that the actual content of the *Master Document* will be *one* of the document types outlined in *Available document types* on page 470—it will just contain this document type for multiple simulation projects. (Effectively, it provides the same thing as you would get if you merged multiple single-simulation documents into a single file.)

The *Master Document* leverages Microsoft Word's Master Document functionality. This means that it does not create (content for) the individual simulation documents. Instead, it simply collects existing simulation documents and includes these as linked references in a single document (the 'Master Document'). This means that in order to create a *Master Document* you must first create all of the individual simulation-level documents (as explained earlier in this chapter). You may find it useful to use the functionality described in *Generating documents from the Workarea* on page 521 to make sure that all required documents exist, before you create the *Master Document*.

To generate a *Master Document*, carry out the steps shown below:

1. In the Workarea, click on the Group that contains the simulations for which you want to generate the *Master Document*.

2. Click on the **Generate Master Document** button on the *Producer Toolbar*. (You can also select menu option **Documentation | Generate Master Document**.) The *Generate Master Document* dialog box is displayed.

Generate Master Document

■ If you want to create a *Master Document* for simulations that are located across different Groups (for example, your Workarea is structured by *process area*, but you want a *Master Document* for a *role*), you can simply create a separate Group, copy all required simulation projects into that as references, and then generate the *Master Document* for this Group. You can also use a filter in the Workarea to limit the simulations selected.

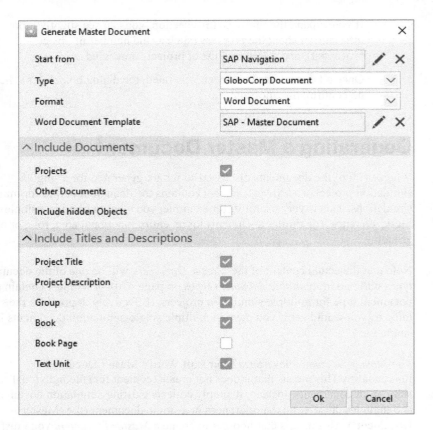

3. The **Start From** field defaults to the Group you selected in Step 1. If necessary, you can use the **Edit** button for this field to navigate to and select another Group.

4. In the **Type** field, select the document type that you want to use for this *Master Document* (see *Available document types* on page 470 for an explanation of the available document types). Individual documents of this type must already exist for each simulation to be included.

5. In the **Format** field, select the document format in which the *Master Document* should be generated. This can be either **Word Document**, **PDF Document**, or **Word and PDF Documents** (which generates both, as separate files). Again, files of these types must already exist for the simulations.

6. If you have a customized template that you want to use for the *Master Document*, then select this in the **Word Document Template** field. Otherwise, you can leave this with the default template.

7. Under **Include Documents**, choose the types of documents that are to be included in the *Master Document*. The following options are available:

   - **Projects**: Include documents for simulation projects (these are the only types of projects that can be included in a *Master Document*.

- **Other Documents**: If you have imported external documents into the selected Group, then select this option to also have these included in the *Master Document*. (See *Importing content files* on page 551 for information on how to import external documents.)

- **Include Hidden Objects**: If any of the documents selected for inclusion have the **Hide** property selected (so that they are not included in the *Trainer*), they will (by default) not be included in the *Master Document*. If you *do* want to include these documents, select this option.

8. In the **Include Titles and Descriptions** section, select whether the simulation **Name** and **Description** properties, and the **Name** property of other included documents should be included in the generated document.

9. Click **Ok**. The *Master Document* is generated. Once generation is complete, the following message is displayed:

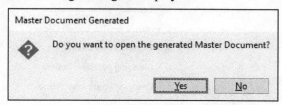

If you want to display the document, click on the **Yes** button, and the document will be opened in the relevant application.

If you don't need to see the document now, then just click on the **No** button to close the dialog box.

10. The generated *Master Document* is stored in the group that you selected in Step 1, and will be given a name of "Master Document {Document Type}". You may want to rename this (for example, to match the Group name, which would really be more logical).

Example of a Master Document

In this section, we'll look at the contents of a sample *Master Document*. The images provided are for our sample *SAP Navigation* course, which consists of a Book and Book Pages, and several simulations. To better understand these examples and what they are showing, it is worth reviewing the contents of the Group from which the *Master Document* was created. This is shown in the image below:

With this in mind, let's look at what was generated for this Group. The first page is a standard cover page. It contains nothing but the Group name, and a boilerplate graphic.

● Note that these examples reflect the Microsoft Word document format; content is slightly different for PDF, as noted below. Note also that blank space has been cropped from these examples, to minimize wasted space in this book.

1. The Group **Name**.

This is followed by a Table of Contents. By default this will include (up to) three levels of heading, although you can change this using standard Word functionality (**References | Table of Contents | Custom Table of Contents | Show Levels**).

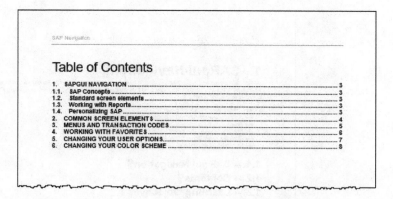

In this example you can see this matches our Group structure, showing our Book (*SAPgui Navigation*) and the Books contained within this, and five simulations.

Following on from the Table of Contents, the document includes the information from our source documents (for the content objects within the selected Group. This is where things get interesting. The following image shows the page for our Book, *SAPgui Navigation*.

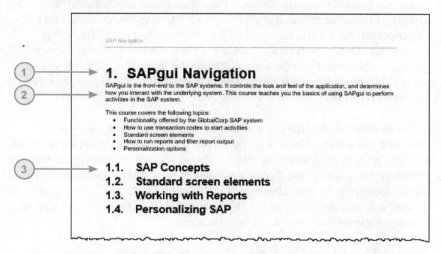

1.   The Book **Name**.

2.   The Book **Description**.

3.   Sub-headings for each Book nested within this book.

There is one thing in particular to note here. Although Books are included (along with their **Descriptions**), any Book Pages within these Books are not. Looking back at the Properties we used to generate the *Master Document* above, you will see that the option **Book Pages** under *Include Titles and Descriptions* is not selected. So maybe this is why we don't see the Book Pages? Well, not exactly. Here is (a portion of) the same page, with that option selected:

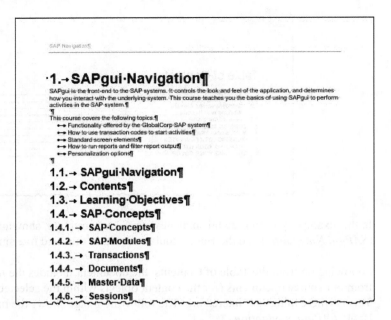

Here, you can see that now the Book Page **Name** now appears (and the **Description** would appear if any of the Book Pages in this example had a Description), but we still do not have the actual content of the Book Pages themselves. This is by design—Book Page content simply does not appear in the *Master Document*. If you do want to include the Book Page content, you need to use a **Compound Document**, explained in *Generating a Compound Document* on page 530, instead.

You may wonder what the point of this is, then, if you don't get the actual content itself. One reason is that you may have information in the **Description** that you want to include in your *Master Document*. Another more compelling reason is that you may use Books to organize your content, and provide links to simulations from the Book Pages within these Books (and not directly from the Trainer outline). By including the Books and their **Descriptions**, you can carry this organization over into the *Master Document*.

So much for Books and Book pages. Let's continue our examination of our example generated *Master Document*. The following image shows the page for one of the simulations in our selected Group.

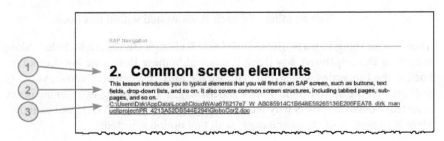

1. Simulation project **Name**.

2. Simulation project **Description**

3. Link to the simulation-level document that is being included in this *Master Document*.

That's it, in its entirety. All you get is a link to the existing document. But this isn't really a 'hyperlink-style' link—it is a Microsoft Word Master Document link. When you *print* this document, the 'linked' documents are automatically expanded, so that the full content of these documents is available in your printed copy.

This emphasizes the importance of making sure that the simulation-level documents already exist before you generate the *Master Document*. If the document doesn't exist, it means that there is nothing to link to, and you end up with a page similar to the following (which is for one of our example simulations for which the document was deliberately not generated):

Common screen elements

3. Menus and Transaction Codes

In this example, the simulation project **Name** is included, there is no **Description** (defined for this simulation), and because the source document does not exist, there is no link, either.

There is a significant advantage in this approach of creating a *Master Document* that only contains links to other documents. If any of the linked (simulation-level) documents change, these changes will automatically be picked up the next time that you open the *Master Document*—you don't have to re-generate the whole thing.

If you want to display the entire content of the *Master Document*, with all of the source documents embedded in it, then you can do so using Word's standard functionality, as follows:

1. On the Word *View* ribbon, click on **Outline** in the *Views* group.

2. On the *Outlining* ribbon, click on the **Expand Subdocuments** button in the *Outline Tools* group.

3. Click on the **Close Outline View** button to return to the previous view.

To go back to showing only the links, repeat these steps, but click on the **Collapse Subdocuments** button in Step 2.

Finally, note that this only applies to Word-format documents. If you generated the *Master Document* in PDF format then all subdocuments are already expanded. (Technically, Enable Now creates the Word-format *Master Document*, and then 'prints' this to PDF, which expands the subdocuments).

Generating a Compound Document

A *Compound Document* is a special type of document that consolidates multiple content objects into a single document. This can include not only simulation projects, but also Books, Book Pages, text units, and even Groups.

To generate a *Compound Document*, carry out the following steps:

■ If you want to create a *Compound Document* for simulations that are located across different Groups (for example, your Workarea is structured by *process area*, but you want a *Compound Document* for a *role*), you can simply create a separate Group, copy all required simulation projects into that as references, and then generate the *Compound Document* for this Group. You can also use a filter in the Workarea to limit the simulations selected.

1. In the Workarea, click on the Group that contains the simulations for which you want to generate the *Compound Document*.

2. Click on the **Generate Compound Document** button on the *Producer Toolbar*. (You can also select menu option **Documentation | Generate Compound Document**.) The *Generate Compound Document* dialog box is displayed.

Generate Compound Document

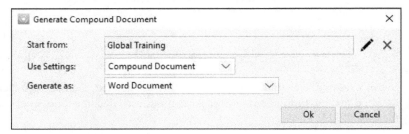

3. The **Start From** field defaults to the Group you selected in Step 1. If necessary, you can use the **Edit** button for this field to navigate to and select another Group.

➕ Administrators can define custom styles for the *Compound Document* in **Resources | Documentation Settings**, in the Workarea. This must have a **Base Type** of **Compound Document**.

4. If you have a custom documentation type that you want to use, then you can select this from the **Use Settings** drop-down list. Otherwise, use the default one.

5. In the **Generate As** field, select the document format in which the *Master Document* should be generated. This can be **Word Document**, **HTML Document**, or **PDF Document**.

6. Click **Ok**. Once generation is complete, the following message is displayed:

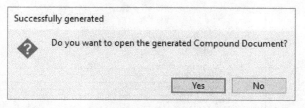

Successfully generated

Do you want to open the generated Compound Document?

| Yes | No |

If you want to display the document, click on the **Yes** button, and the document will be opened in the relevant application.

If you don't need to see the document now, then just click on the **No** button to close the dialog box.

7. The generated *Compound Document* is stored in the group that you selected in Step 1, and will be given a name of "Compound Document". You may want to rename this to something more specific or descriptive.

Example of a Compound Document

In this section, we'll look at the contents of a sample *Compound Document*. As before, the images used here are taken from the *Compound Document* generated for our sample *SAP Navigation* course. The contents of the Group selected for the generation is the same as the one shown on page 526. You may find it useful to compare this Group against the resulting document.

As with the *Master Document*, the first page of the *Compound Document* is a standard cover page. It contains nothing but the Group name, and a boilerplate graphic.

SAP Navigation

Again, the second page contains a Table of Contents. However, this one is slightly fuller than the corresponding one for the *Master Document* because it also includes Book Pages.

● This example emphasizes the need to enter meaningful step names, and not rely on the default settings of using the name of the captured screen..

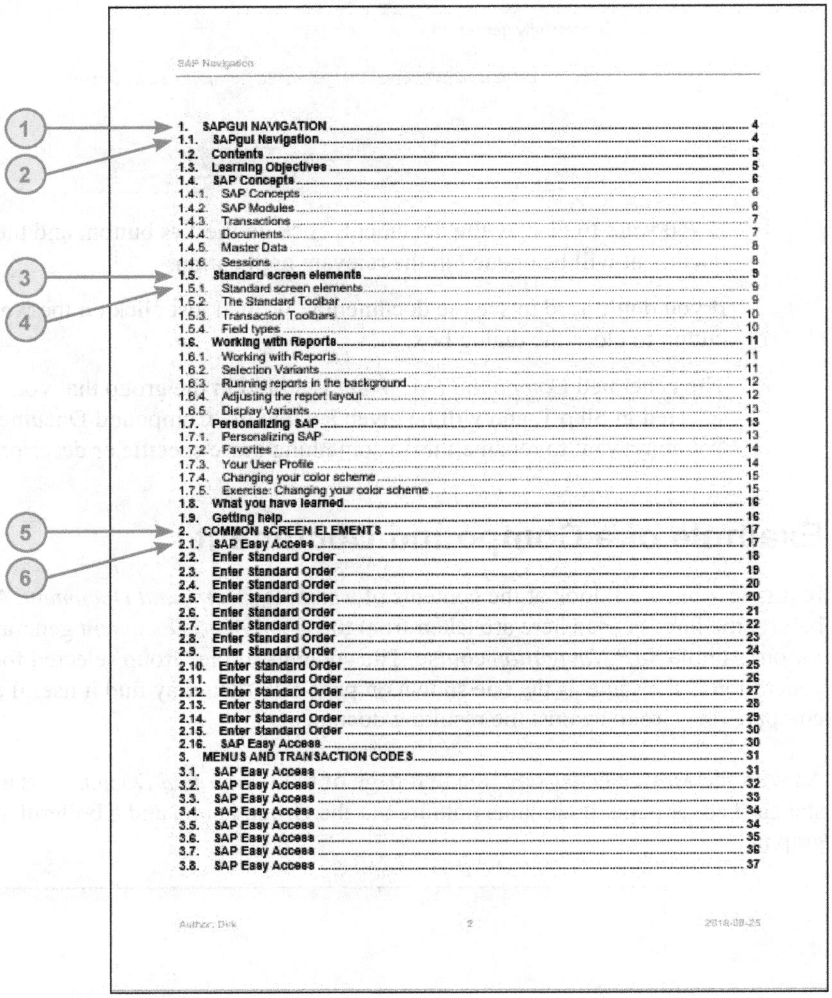
SAP Navigation

Author: Dirk 2 2018-08-25

1. Book.
2. Book Page within the Book.
3. Book nested within the first Book.
4. Book Page within the nested book.
5. Simulation.
6. Step within the simulation.

If you compare the above Table of Contents with the source Group from which it was generated (see the screenshot on page 526) you will see that whereas the Group includes a Book Page called **SAP Navigation_Index**, which appears immediately underneath the **SAP Navigation** Group, this is not listed in the Table of Contents. This is because this particular Book Page is used as the index page for the **SAP Navigation** Group (it specified in the **library Autostart** property for the Group), and therefore has its **Hide** property selected.

Now let's look a bit further into the document, to see how Book Pages appear. The following page is taken from our example Book *Changing Your Color Scheme*, which you may recognize from *Chapter 8, Books and Book Pages*.

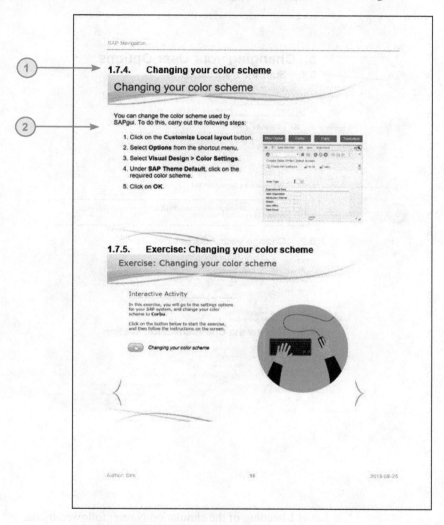

1. Book Page **Name**.

2. Book Page content.

Note that the Book Page content is inserted as a fixed-size, static image. If there is any animation on the page, then the image reflects the state of the Book Page *before* any animation has been triggered, but with all information that is initially hidden and then 'animated in' displayed (otherwise most Book Pages would be blank!). Note that this document type will not automatically add a border to the

Book Pages (which would look nicer here), although you can add one via the Book Page's **Border** property (in the *Design* category).

Finally, let's look at a page from our *Compound Document* that relates to a simulation.

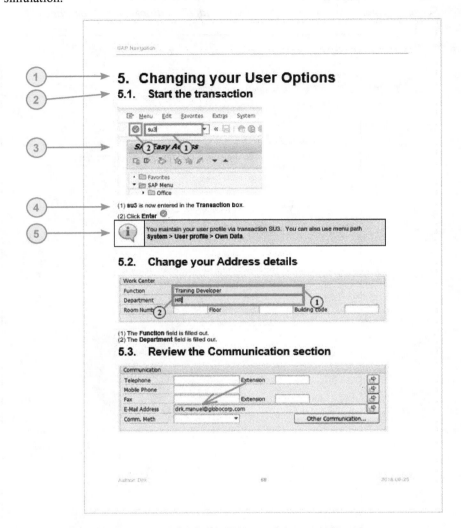

1. Level 1 heading of the simulation **Name**, followed by the simulation **Description** (if defined).

2. Level 2 heading per Step, using the Step **Name**.

3. Cropped screenshot including the **Highlight** and **Marker**.

4. Bubble text (one list item per macro; restart numbering per Step).

5. **Explanation** macro.

You will notice that this is effectively exactly the same format as the *Standard Document* (see *The Standard Document* on page 483), but the simulation starts at Header Level 1 instead of Header Level 2 (which is curious because in the single-simulation *Standard Document* there is no higher heading level than the simulation, whereas here there is).

Summary

SAP Enable Now provides a number of document types that can be generated for a simulation. It also provides a way of including additional information (not directly related to the recording) through the use of documentation macros.

In addition to the documents that can be created per simulation, you can also generate a *Master Document* that consolidates multiple simulation-level documents into a single document, and a *Compound Document*, which can include multiple simulations, along with Books and Book Pages, Text Units, and so on.

13

Additional Workarea Functions

This chapter describes several pieces of Enable Now functionality related to content in the Workarea that you may or may not need to use—but it's useful to know that they exist. Read over the list of topics covered in this chapter (below), and then come back and refer to the relevant section as and when you need it.

This chapter covers the following:

- Creating a Glossary and assigning this to content
- Importing and exporting Enable Now content (.dkp files)
- Importing images and other assets
- Converting PowerPoint presentations into Books and Book Pages
- Importing non-Enable Now content objects
- Integrating 'unsorted' simulations created in Instant Producer
- Maintaining your Workarea structure via Microsoft Excel
- Client-server functionality prior to the 1811 release

Using a Glossary

Enable Now provides a rudimentary glossary function. This allows you to define glossary terms and definitions, and then have all instances of the glossary terms in your content to be turned into 'glossary links' that display the relevant glossary definition in a pop-up box when clicked on. You can also include a glossary in your Trainer, for reference.

Note that you can have multiple Glossaries, but you can only link one Glossary Group to your *Trainer* (although you can nest multiple Glossaries within this one linked Group).

Defining a Glossary

An Enable Now Glossary is effectively comprised of a number of specialized Text Units which have a Document Type of **Glossary**. Each Glossary Text Unit has the glossary term as its **Name**, and the glossary definition is entered into the Text Unit's **Description** property.

All of the Glossary Text Units need to be stored in the same Group—which you might want to call "Glossary" for clarity. You should create sub-Groups by letter ("A", "B", "C", and so on) within this, to keep your glossary entries organized. These will be used as hierarchical groupings in the *Trainer*.

To define a new glossary term, carry out the steps shown below.

1. In the Workarea, click on the Group within which you want to create the Glossary Text Unit. Make sure that you have this checked out for editing.

2. Click on the **New Object** button on the *Producer Toolbar*, and then select **Text Unit** from the drop-down panel. The *New Text Unit* dialog box is displayed.

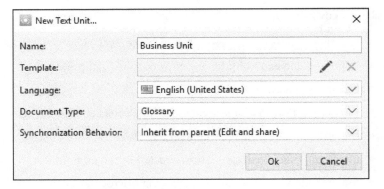

3. Enter the glossary term into the **Name** field. This is not case sensitive.

4. If you have a template that you want to use for glossary entries, then select this in the **Template** field.

5. Select the language for the glossary entry in the **Language** field.

6. Select **Glossary** in the **Document Type** field.

7. Make sure that the **Save to server as** well checkbox is selected.

8. Click on **Ok**. The Text Unit is created.

9. Go to the properties for this new Text Unit, and enter the glossary definition in its **Description** property. Note that you can use all of the standard text formatting options for this text (see *Adjusting Bubble text* on page 111).

Importing a Glossary

As an alternative to manually creating Text Units for all of your glossary entries, you can import them from a .csv file, as follows.

1. Create a text file containing your glossary entries. Enter each glossary term and glossary definition on a separate line, separated by a comma, and save the file with a file type of .csv.

2. Select menu option **Tools | Glossary | Import Glossary**. The *Import Glossary* dialog box is displayed. This is a standard Windows 'Open File' dialog box.

3. Navigate to and select the file created in Step 1, and then click on the **Open** button. The *Import Glossary* dialog box is displayed.

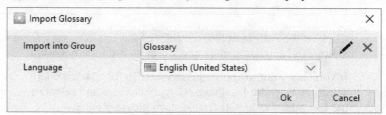

4. Click on the **Edit** button for the **Import into Group** field, and navigate to and select your Glossary Group.

5. Select the language for your glossary entries in the **Language** field.

6. Click **Ok**. The glossary entries are imported.

New Glossary Text units are created for each of the imported glossary term/definition pairs. These will be created within letter-specific sub-groups within the main Glossary Group (these letter Groups will be created for you if they do not already exist).

Applying a Glossary to your content

Once you have created your Glossary, you need to apply it to your content objects. This will turn each of the instances of the glossary term into a hyperlink that displays the glossary definition.

To apply a Glossary to your content, carry out the steps shown below.

1. In the Workarea, click on the content object(s) or Group(s) to which you want to apply the Glossary. You would normally want to select the

▲ This only really works if your glossary definitions are single-paragraph text definitions with no formatting applied to them.

highest-level Group for your content, to apply it to all content below this.

2. Select menu option **Tools | Glossary | Apply Glossary**. The *Apply Glossary* dialog box is displayed.

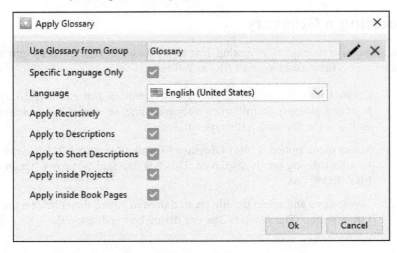

3. Click on the **Edit** button to the right of the **Use Glossary from Group** dialog box, and navigate to and select your Glossary Group.

4. If you only want to apply glossary entries for a specific language, then select the **Specific Language Only** checkbox, and select this language in the **Language** field. Otherwise, each glossary entry will be applied to all content objects of the same language as the entry (this is normally what you would want to do).

5. Select the remaining options as required. These are:

   ♦ **Apply Recursively**: Apply the Glossary to all instances of the glossary term within the text unit (Bubble, Description, and so on). Otherwise, only the first instance is turned into a glossary link.

   ♦ **Apply to Descriptions**: Apply the Glossary to the object's **Description** property.

   ♦ **Apply to Short Descriptions**: Apply the Glossary to the object's **Short Description** property.

   ♦ **Apply inside Projects**: Apply to the project (simulation, Guided Tour, etc.) contents.

   ♦ **Apply inside Book Pages**: Apply to the text on Book Pages.

6. Click **Ok**.

The Glossary will be applied to all of the selected content objects. Any objects updated will be checked out and then checked back in, but no entry will be written to the **History** in the *Protocol* property category for the change.

Here's an example of how a glossary link looks during playback.

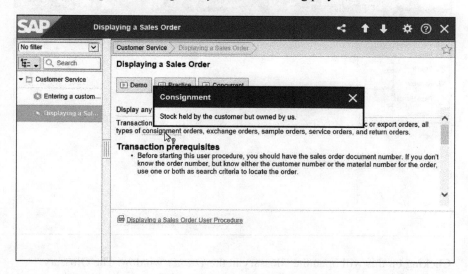

This example shows the index page for a simulation, with the glossary term ("consignment") identified in the **Description** property. Note that the cursor shows a question mark in the lower-right corner when you hover over the glossary link. The dialog box is displayed when the user clicks on the glossary link. This contains the glossary term in the header, and the glossary definition below this.

Including a Glossary in your Trainer

You can include your Glossary in your *Trainer* so that it is available to your users as a reference. To do this, simply select your Glossary group in **Tools | Settings | Playback Settings | Library | Glossary | Glossary Group**. If you only want this Glossary to include entries for the same language as the root group you select for publishing your *Trainer*, then select the **Use library language** option in the same settings category.

Once a Glossary has been defined in the settings, then the *Trainer* will include an additional option on the **Selection** button's drop-down menu, as shown in the example below.

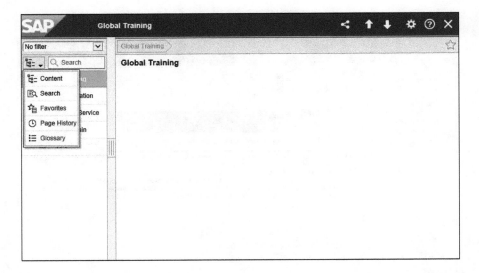

Clicking on this will open the Glossary in the *Trainer* window. The Glossary terms will be shown in the content hierarchy on the left, organized into the same Group structure as used in the Workarea when creating the Glossary. Clicking on any level of the Glossary hierarchy (from the highest-level Group to a single glossary term) will display the glossary entry (or entries, for a Group) in the pane on the right. An example of this, is shown below.

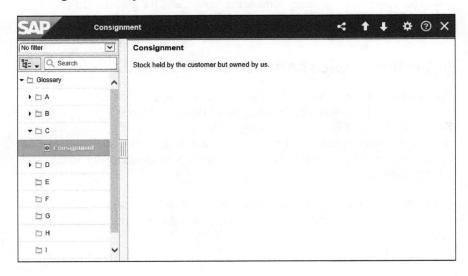

Importing and exporting Enable Now content

Although you typically create and edit all of your content within the same instance of Enable Now, there may be times when you need to copy content objects to or from another instance of Enable Now. Alternatively, if you have multiple Workareas within your own instance of Enable Now, the only way to move (or copy) content from one Workarea to another is to export it from the source Workarea and then import it into the destination Workarea.

Exporting content objects

To export one or more content objects, carry out the following steps:

1. Select menu option **Workarea | Export**. The *Export Archive* dialog box is displayed.

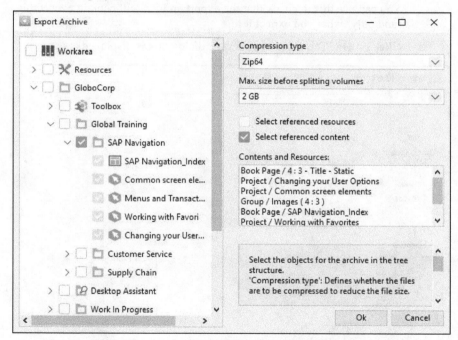

2. By default, all content objects in the Workarea will be selected. Make sure that only the content objects you want to export are selected (selecting/deselecting a Group will select/deselect all Groups and content objects below it).

3. By default, the content objects will be compressed when you export them. This is useful for saving space, but may take slightly longer. If you do not want the content objects to be compressed, select **No Compression** in the **Compression Type** field.

> ■ If you only want to export a single content object (and do not care about any referenced resources or content objects) then you can right-click on the object and select **Export** from the shortcut menu, and continue with Step 9.

4. By default, all selected objects will be saved to a single file. If you need to store the exported file(s) on a media that has a size limit (for example, CD or DVD) then select the maximum size of a single export file in the **Max size before splitting volumes** field. The archive will then be split into multiple files, if necessary, to stay below this limit.

5. If you want to include any resources used by the exported content objects, then select the **Select referenced resources** checkbox. You should normally only need to do this if your content objects use customized resources—the destination Workarea will already contain all standard resources.

6. If you want to include any other referenced content objects (for example, shared images or other assets) then select the **Select referenced content**. This will avoid any cases of broken links or missing content.

7. Any referenced resources or content objects that will be included as a result of selecting the **Select referenced resources** or **Select referenced content** checkboxes will be listed in the **Contents and Resources** box. You can use this to check that the export archive will contain everything (and only) what you expect it to.

8. Click on **Ok**. The *Exporting archive* dialog box is displayed.

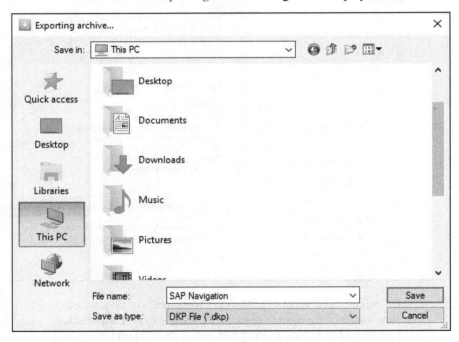

9. Navigate to the location to which you want to save the export file(s), and enter a suitable name for the archive in the **File name** field.

10. The **Save as type** field will always default to **DKP File (*.dkp)**. You cannot change this.

11. Click **Save**.

The export file is created and saved to the selected location. You can now archive, transfer, or otherwise process this file, as necessary. How to import it into another Workarea (or the same Workarea as part of disaster recovery) is explained in the next section.

Importing content objects

To import one or more content objects, carry out the following steps:

1. Select menu option **Workarea | Import Archive**. The *Import Archive* dialog box is displayed.

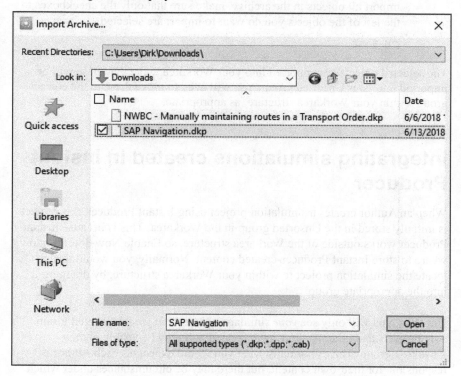

2. Navigate to and select the .dkp file that contains the content objects that you want to import into your Workarea. Note that if the export split the archive into multiple files, you will need to import each file separately.

3. Click **Open**. A list of all importable content within the archive is displayed. This can include content objects, resources, and other asset files.

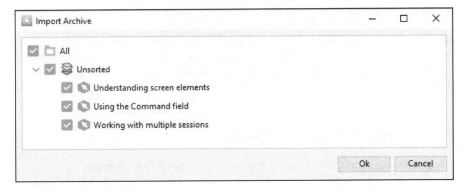

4. By default, all objects will be selected for import. If you do not want to import all objects in the archive, make sure that only the checkboxes to the left of the objects you do want to import are selected.

5. Click **Ok**.

The selected objects are imported into your Workarea. Note that these will be imported into your Unsorted group. You will need to move these to the correct group within your Workarea structure, as appropriate.

Integrating simulations created in Instant Producer

When an Author creates a simulation project using Instant Producer, this project is initially stored in the Unsorted group in the Workarea. This is because Instant Producer works outside of the Workarea structure, so Enable Now doesn't know where to store Instant Producer-created content. Normally, you would then re-locate the simulation project to within your Workarea structure, by dragging it into the appropriate group.

■ In the Manager component of Enable Now you can see *all* 'unsorted' content, but as an Author you probably won't need to use the Manager, so it is not covered in this book.

● Despite the menu name and the dialog box title, you are not actually 'checking out' anything in the traditional sense. All you are doing is moving the content object out of the **Unsorted** group so that it is accessible to all Authors (and, when published, to all Learners).

However, you will only see *your* simulation projects in *your* **Unsorted** group. Any projects that other Authors have created will only be visible in *their* **Unsorted** group. This is normally what you would expect, as each Author is responsible for their own content, but there may be circumstances under which you want to see another Author's 'unsorted' content. For example, you may have Subject Matter Experts recording simulations in Instant Producer, and then you—as the Author—are responsible for editing these simulations. Fortunately, Enable Now provides a way of allowing you to see another Author's Unsorted objects.

To locate an 'unsorted' simulation created by another Author in Instant Producer, and relocate this to the Workarea structure, carry out the following steps:

1. Select menu option **Manager Workarea | Check Out Objects**. The *Checkout* dialog box is displayed. (Alternatively, you can select **Check**

Out Assigned Objects to select only objects that have been assigned to you, and skip the remaining steps.)

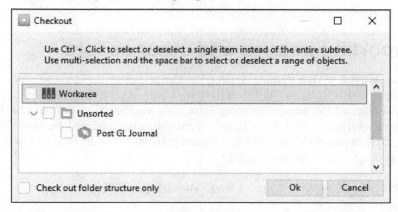

2. Expand the **Unsorted** folder, to see all 'unsorted' simulations.

3. Select the checkbox to the left of the simulation project(s) you want to relocate.

4. If you want to relocate the entire Unsorted Group (which will effectively relocate all of the simulations inside them) then select the **Check out folder structure only** checkbox. This will allow the Author who created the simulations to keep working with them, but when the Author finishes editing the simulations, they will automatically be relocated to the new location of the Group.

5. Click **Ok**.

The selected simulation project is copied into your **Unsorted** folder, as shown below.

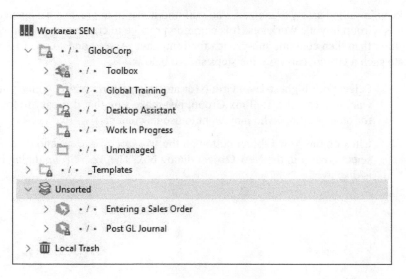

You can now drag this content object to the relevant group in your Workarea structure.

Importing images and other assets

To add interest to your training content, you can add images, videos, and other files to your Book Pages—and even to your simulations. You can import these files as required (for example, during Book Page creation) directly from your PC within the relevant editor, but if there is a possibility that you will use these files in more than one place, you will find it more efficient to import them as assets that you can then re-use as required.

Enable Now allows you to import the following types of files:

- Documents: `.doc, .docx, .ppt, .xls, .xlsx, .pdf, .rtf`
- Pictures: `.gif, .jpg, .jpeg, .png, .bmp`
- Audio: `.wav, .mp3, .wma`
- Video: `.avi, .swf, .mov, .wmv`

Note that although you can import files such as Microsoft Word or PowerPoint, you cannot insert these files into a 'publishable' Group and have them appear in your *Trainer* navigation structure the same way that native Enable Now content objects do; you can only include them within (or link to them from) Enable Now objects.

Creating an Assets group

To keep imported assets organized, you will find it useful to create a designated 'assets' Group in your Workarea. It is common practice to create a Group called **Toolbox** than then contains sub-groups for Templates, Assets, and so on. To create such a Group, carry out the steps shown below:

1. Select your highest-level Group (or any other Group within which you want to create the **Toolbox** Group; just make sure that it is easy to locate for other Authors who may want to use its contents)

2. Click on the **New Object** button on the *Workarea Toolbar*, and then select **Group** in the **New Object** dialog box. The *New Group* dialog box is displayed.

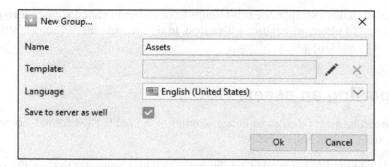

3. Enter a suitable name for the Group (such as **Assets**) in the **Name** field.

4. Make sure that the **Save to server as well** checkbox is selected.

5. Click **Ok**.

6. Click on the new Group in the Workarea hierarchy, to show its properties in the *Object Editor*.

7. In the **Subtype** field, select a suitable Group type. This really just controls the icon used for the Group and nothing else. A Subtype of **Master Data** would be suitable (this uses the icon shown in the example below).

8. If the contents of this Group will be used by other Authors (and especially if it will also contain Templates that should be used), select the **Must have** checkbox. This will ensure that its contents are always downloaded to each Author's local repository, and will therefore always be available.

9. If you have not created this Group in a relatively easy-to-find location, you can select the **Create Shortcut** checkbox to create a shortcut to this Group at the highest level of your Workarea structure.

An example of a suitable structure for an **Assets** Group is shown below:

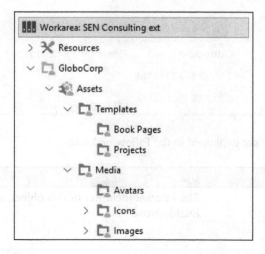

Note that in this example, the sub-Groups have all been created with a **Subtype** property of **Folder**, which uses a blue icon, to differentiate these Groups from content object Groups.

Importing an asset

To import an asset (such as an image or other 'non Enable Now format' content), carry out the steps shown below:

1. In the Workarea, click on the group in which you want to store the asset.

2. Click on the **Insert File** button at the top of the *Object Editor* pane. The *Select external document* dialog box is displayed (this is a standard Windows 'Open' dialog box.)

   Insert File

3. Navigate to and select the file that you want to import.

4. Click **Open**.

The external file is imported. You can now use it as an asset in any content object.

Imported asset properties

As for any other object in Enable Now, a number of properties are maintained for external files that have been imported into Enable Now. These are shown in the partial screenshot below.

These properties are explained in the following table.

Property	Use
File Name	The internal identifier of this object, as used by Enable Now.

Property	Use
Original File Name	The actual filename of the object before it was imported into Enable Now.
Name	The descriptive name of the object. This defaults to the **Original File Name** minus the filetype, but can be changed if necessary. This name is used in the Workarea group, and also in the object list of a Book Page in which the asset is included.
Hide	Select this checkbox to prevent the file being listed in the *Trainer* outline. You would not normally include your Assets Group included in the *Trainer* anyway, so this should be unnecessary.
Preview	This field shows a thumbnail image of the asset. You can click on this to show a full-sized version of the image. This property is only available for image files.
Original Path	The location on your PC from which the asset was uploaded. This is used by the **Update File** action (see below).
Last Import	The date and time at which the asset was imported (or re-imported) into Enable Now
Modified	The time-stamp of the actual file.

At the top of the *Object Editor* pane for external files are object action three buttons. These are:

Button	Name	Purpose
	Open	Open the file in the relevant helper application.
	Replace File	Replace this file with another file on your PC. The object you upload can be entirely different (location, filename, and even file type) but will keep the same **File Name** and **Name** properties as the original object.
	Update File	Re-import the object from the original file (based on the **Original Path** property. This is useful if you have edited the source file outside of Enable Now, and now want to import these changes.

Importing content files

In addition to importing reusable content such as images and other 'assets', you can also import other external files that contain training content (or anything else, really). These files can then be linked to training simulations or Books and Book Pages (or Group texts).

Let's say we have a training simulation for SAP ECC 6.0 transaction VA01 called *Entering a customer order*. Suppose also have a quick reference guide created outside of SAP Enable Now in PDF form, called *Sales Order Type Guidelines*, that explains when to use which order type. We want to make this quick reference available as a part of this simulation. To achieve this, we can import the quick reference as a file, and then attach it to our simulation content object.

To import an external file into your Workarea, carry out the steps shown below.

1. In the Workarea, click on the object to which you want to attach the external file. This can be a simulation project, or a Group.

2. Click on the **Insert File** on the toolbar at the top of the *Object Editor* pane. The *Select external document* dialog box is displayed. This is the standard Windows 'open' dialog box.

Insert File

3. Navigate to and select the file that you want to import, and then click on the **Open** button. The file is inserted in the Workarea, below the selected object.

Content files have the same properties as files imported as assets, and can also be replaced and updated in the same way as described above. (Enable Now treats them exactly the same way—we have just described them separately here to differentiate their uses)

Now let's look at how this appears in the Trainer.

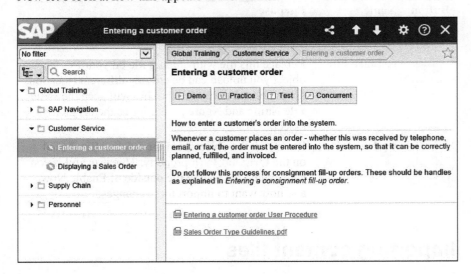

Here, you can see that the external file is linked at the bottom of the index page for the simulation—in exactly the same way as the document output types are. If you had imported the file under a Group, then the file would be linked the same way: at the bottom of the Group's index page and not in the *Trainer* content hierarchy.

If you do not want the file to be listed on the index page for an object, and just want to be able to link to it from somewhere else (maybe from a Book Page) then you can hide it (by selecting its **Hide** property), and then link to it from wherever you need to (via a **Document Link** - see *Inserting links* on page 290).

Importing a PowerPoint file as a Book

Enable Now has excellent functionality for creating presentation content, in Book Pages. Arguably, this functionality is more powerful and effective than PowerPoint (albeit requiring a little more effort), but there may be situations where you have an existing PowerPoint presentation that you want to use within Enable Now.

You *could* import this as a content file and link to it (as explained in *Importing content files* on page 551), but if you want to use the full functionality of Enable Now, you can import it as a Book, with each slide in the presentation being converted into a Book Page.

PowerPoint import limitations

When you import a PowerPoint file into Enable Now, a static image is taken of the entire contents of the slide (and ignoring any animations or action objects), and this image is used for the Book Page. None of the content of the slide is in any way editable.

★ A utility is available to Enable Now implementers that does a better job of importing PowerPoint and converts each slide into editable Book Pages, but as this is not standard, built-in functionality, it is not covered in this book.

To import a PowerPoint presentation and convert it to Enable Now content objects, carry out the steps shown below:

1. In the Workarea Structure, select the Group into which the resulting Book and Book Pages should be stored.

2. Select menu option **Tools | Import | PowerPoint as Book**. The *PowerPoint Import Selection* dialog box is displayed.

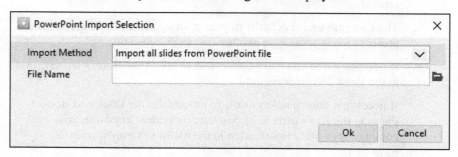

3. If you want to import the entire PowerPoint presentation as a Book, and convert each slide in the presentation into a Book Page, select **Import all slides from PowerPoint** in the **Import Method** field, and then navigate to and select the PowerPoint file that you want to import in the **File Name** field.

   If you want to import only selected slides within the PowerPoint presentation, then select **Import selected slides from PowerPoint** file in the **Import Method** field. Then open the presentation in Microsoft PowerPoint and select the individual slides that you want to import, before returning to Enable Now Producer.

4. Click on **OK**. The **PowerPoint Import** dialog box is displayed.

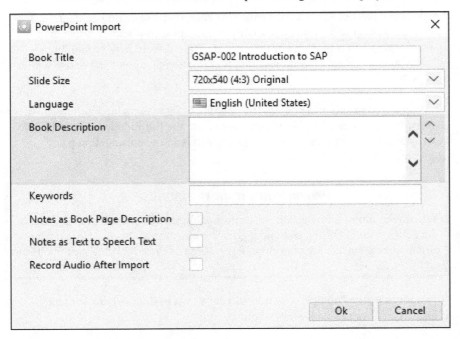

5. The **Book Title** is taken directly from the PowerPoint presentation. You can over-type this with a new name, if necessary.

6. In the **Slide Size** field, select the size of the Book Pages that are to be created.

7. The **Language** field defaults to your primary authoring language. If the presentation is actually in another language, select this.

8. If necessary, you can enter a short text to use as the Book's **Description**, in the **Book Description** field.

9. If necessary, enter any keywords to be used for the Book and Book Pages in the **Keywords** field. Separate individual keywords with commas. (For more information in the use of keywords, refer to page 69.)

10. If any Slide Notes in the presentation are to be used as the **Description** for the respective Book Pages, then select the **Notes as Book Page Description** checkbox.

11. If you want the Slide Notes (if any) to be used as the basis for audio for the respective Book Pages, then select the **Notes as Text to Speech Text** checkbox. (For more information on using audio, refer to *Chapter 14, Adding Audio to Your Content*.)

12. If you want to immediately record audio for the Book Pages after the import has completed, select the **Record Audio After Import** checkbox.

13. Click **Ok**. Each slide is converted to its own Book Page, and (if you selected an **Import Method** of **Import all slides from PowerPoint**) a Book is created to hold these Book Pages.

14. If you selected the **Record Audio After Import** checkbox, then the *Record Audio* dialog box is displayed. Record the audio as explained in *Chapter 14, Adding Audio to Your Content*, and then close this dialog box to continue with Step 15.

15. You are passed into the *Book Page Editor*. Edit the Book and/or Book Pages as explained in *Chapter 8, Books and Book Pages*. Once you have finished, close the *Book Page Editor*.

Maintaining the Workarea structure externally

As explained in *Chapter 2, Navigating in Producer*, you build a Workarea structure through the use of Groups. It may be that you need to reorganize the Workarea structure after this initial creation—perhaps because of organizational changes, or maybe when your project moves from development mode to production support.

To reorganize your Workarea, you *can* just drag and drop your Groups into the required structure. However, with extremely large structures, this can be cumbersome—even using the *Double Tree View* (see *Workarea Views* on page 61). For these situations, Enable Now provides the ability to export your Workarea structure to a Microsoft Excel worksheet, so that you can reorganize it there, and then load this reorganized structure back into Enable Now.

Before you adjust your Workarea by using this method, you should make sure that your Workarea is up-to-date, and nothing is checked out. You should also ensure that no changes are made in the Workarea between the download of the current version, and the upload of the reorganized version.

Exporting your Workarea structure

To export your Workarea, carry out the steps shown below.

1. Click on the highest-level Group that you want to reorganize, to select it. (Note that you can reorganize the Workarea at any level—from any Group down.)

2. Select menu option **Tools | Workarea Structure | Export Structure**.

3. In the dialog box that is displayed (which is a standard Windows 'Save' dialog box), navigate to the folder into which you want to save your Workarea structure, enter a suitable filename, and click **Save**.

4. Once the Workarea has been downloaded, a confirmation message is displayed, asking *Do you want to open the selected file?*. Click **Yes** to open it, or **No** to edit the file later.

The Workarea structure is downloaded as a `.csv` (Comma Separated Values) file. This format of file can be opened in any spreadsheet program.

Editing your Workarea structure

Once you have downloaded your Workarea structure, open the downloaded file in your preferred spreadsheet program. The following screenshot shows a downloaded structure file opened in Microsoft Excel.

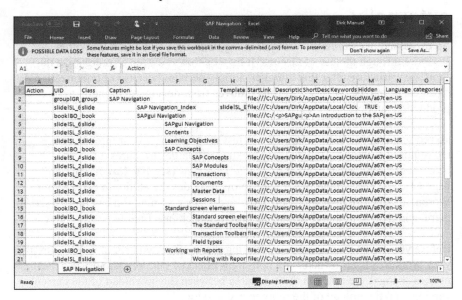

The file contains a header row, followed by one row for each object in the downloaded structure. Note that if an object is linked into your Workarea outline multiple times, it will be included in this spreadsheet multiple times—once for each reference.

The table below identifies the contents of the columns (from left to right):

Column	Content
Action	You must flag any changes that you make to objects in this column, by entering one of the following values: • **Update**: You have changed one or more of the object's properties, or changed its position within the Workarea structure. • **Add**: You want to create a new object in the Workarea. You would typically only do this to create new Groups for organizing your content, but you can also use this for creating placeholder simulation projects that will be recorded later. • **Delete**: You want the object to be deleted from the Workarea.
UID	The unique identifier of the object. Do not change this.
Class	The object type. This will typically be one of: • **Group** • **Project** • **Book** • **Slide** (actually a Book Page) This should not be changed.
Caption	These columns define the hierarchical structure of the Workarea, with each level of nesting being reflected by a shift one column to the right. Only one **Caption** column per row will contain a value, which is the **Name** property of the object. There will be as many of these columns as there are levels in your hierarchy. Be very careful when moving rows (objects) to make sure that the grouping/indentation is correctly reflected, and you have not introduced empty nesting levels.
Template	The UID of any template used to create the object.
StartLink	The full path to the object in your local repository.
Description	The object's **Description** property (see *Description* on page 51).
ShortDesc	The object's **Short Description** property (see *Short Description* on page 51).
Keywords	The object's **Keywords** property (see *Keywords* on page 52).

▲ It is worth re-emphasizing here that if you move an object within the Workarea hierarchy, you should use **Update**. Do not use **Delete** to remove it from its current place, and **Add** to insert it in a new position, as this will delete the current object and create a new, empty one.

Column	Content
Hidden	The object's **Hide** property (see *Hide* on page 51). Note this is not the **Hide in Table of Content** property, which is not downloaded.
Language	The object's **Language** property.
Categories	The object's **Tags** property (see *Tags* on page 51).
Content_categories	The object's **Content Categories** property (see *Content Categories* on page 52).
Roles	The object's **Roles** property (see *Roles* on page 52).
modification_time	**Modification Time** property. Do not change.
creation_time	**Creation Time** property. Do not change.
sub_type	**Subtype** property (used for Groups and Projects only). See *Subtype* on page 52.
macroset	For projects, indicates the project type as one of **Desktop Assistant, Web Assistant**, or **Standard** (simulation).
doc_type	For Text Units, specifies the object subtype.
h4_product	The object's *Web Assistant Context* **Product Name** property.
h4_product version	The object's *Web Assistant Context* **Product Version** property.
h4_system	The object's *Web Assistant Context* **System** property.
da_start_link	The object's **Start Link: Desktop Assistant** property.
sm_*	These columns are all used for synchronization with Solution Manager and should not be changed.

To change your Workarea structure you can move objects around in the Group hierarchy by cutting the row(s) for the object(s) and inserting them in another position (use **Insert Cut Cells**). If you do this, make sure that the Groups are specified correctly in the **Caption** columns, and that you specify an action of **Update**.

You can also update any of the downloaded properties in the table, except where noted above, by over-typing the relevant cell with the new value.

Once you have made all necessary changes, save the file. It is strongly recommended that you save this under a new name (and do not overwrite the downloaded file) in case something goes wrong and you need to revert to the original structure.

Importing your Workarea structure

To import your changes to the Workarea structure, carry out the steps shown below.

1. Select menu option **Tools | Workarea Structure | Import Structure**.

2. In the dialog box that is displayed (which is a standard Windows 'Open' dialog box), navigate to and select the file containing your reworked Workarea structure, and then click **Open**. The structure is analyzed, and a summary of the changes that will be made is displayed in the *Import Structure* dialog box, similar to the example shown below.

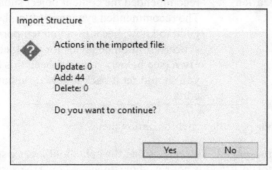

3. Review the information and make sure that this is what you expect, and then click on **Yes**.

4. The structure is updated as per the changes made in file. Make sure that you check in all objects that were checked out to you as part of the change.

▲ In this author's experience this isn't entirely working in that it always seems to want to **Add** all the objects in the upload file. It doesn't—it will only make the changes indicated in the file (but it *will* check out everything).

■ You can check in all objects by selecting the highest-level Group that you reorganized, and then click on the **Show Tree Operations** button and select **Finish Editing All Objects** from the drop-down menu.

Client-server functionality prior to the 1811 release

In the 1811 release of Enable Now, the client-server functionality was significantly reworked. The pre- and post-1811 approaches are so radically different that I do not want to assume that a reader still on the 1808 (or earlier) version can just read the information provided for 1811 in this book and somehow work out the equivalent functionality in their version. So for the sake of backwards-compatibility, this section provides a brief explanation of client-server functionality in versions of Enable Now prior to the 1811 release.

Synchronization with the server

Prior to the 1811 release, synchronization (or not) of content objects between your local repository and the server was performed based on the **synchronization behavior** assigned to the individual objects. For each object, two additional properties are available in the *Basic Properties* category. These are explained in the table below.

Property	Purpose
Synchronization Behavior	This shows the synchronization behavior of the object. This can be set for all objects in the Workarea via menu option **Manager Workarea	Manage	Set Synchronization Behavior for All Objects**, but can also be set individually for an object via this field.
Recommended Synchronization Behavior	This is the synchronization behavior that it is recommended the content object should have. The recommended synchronization behavior is good to know, because if you temporarily set the synchronization behavior for an object to **Edit and Own** (see below) you can check this field to see what you should set it back to once you have finished your edits.

There are four possible synchronization behaviors:

- **Unmanaged**: This means that the content object exists only in your local repository, and is not saved to ('managed on') the server. Because if this, there is no Write Token associated with the content object, which means that it cannot be shared with other Authors. Unmanaged objects can only be seen by you; they will never be visible to users, or even to other Authors.

- **Read-only**: Authors will be able to open the content object for reading, but will not be able to edit it (the **Start Editing** button [explained below] is not displayed). Note that this does not really 'lock' the object for editing, as an Author can just change the synchronization to one of the 'edit' options and then open it for editing, but it does put another hurdle in their way, and prevent Authors from accidentally checking out objects they don't need to.

- **Edit and Share**: When you click on the **Start Editing** button for an object (or double-click on the object to open it for editing), the object is checked out to you and you are granted the Write Token. When you click **Finish Editing**, the object is checked back in, and the Write Token is returned.

- **Edit and Own:** When you set the synchronization behavior of an object to **Edit and Own** the object is immediately checked out (the Write Token is assigned to you), and the object will remain checked out to you. You can edit the object, but you will not be able to check it in and return the Write Token (the **Finish Editing** button is not available) until you change the synchronization behavior (back) to **Edit and Share**.

There is another important consideration when choosing between **Edit and Share** and **Edit and Own**. When you close the Producer, you are prompted to synchronize your local repository to the server, or just shut down without synchronizing. If you choose to synchronize, then Enable Now will check in all objects that you have checked out, and return all of the Write Tokens—with the exception of all objects for which you have set the synchronization behavior to **Edit and Own**. These *will* be saved to the server (as a new version), but you will retain the Write Token(s) and the object(s) will still appear as checked out to you, the next time you access Producer. This option (**Edit and Own**) is therefore very useful when you are still working on an object, and do not want anyone else obtaining the Write Token when you exit from Producer.

Setting synchronization behavior

You are prompted to set the synchronization behavior for an object when you create it. For example, here is the *New Project* dialog box for pre-1811 releases:

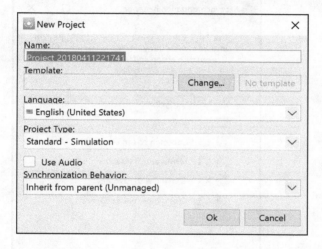

The synchronization behavior is selected in the **Synchronization Behavior** field, but you can change it at any time, by carrying out the steps shown below:

1. Right-click on the content object for which you want to change the Synchronization Behavior, and select **More | Set Synchronization Behavior** from the shortcut menu. (You can also select **Manager Workarea | Manage | Set Synchronization Behavior** from the main menu.) The *Set Synchronization Behavior* dialog box is displayed.

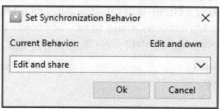

2. The **Current Behavior** field shows the current synchronization behavior for the selected object, for your reference.

3. Use the drop-down field to select the required synchronization behavior.

4. Click **Ok**.

You can also set the synchronization behavior for multiple objects at the same time. This is useful if you have been working on a set of content objects in the Unmanaged Group, and now want to move them to the server. To do this, carry out the steps shown below:

1. Right-click on the Group that contains the content objects for which you want to change the Synchronization Behavior, and select **More | Set Synchronization Behavior for All Objects** from the shortcut menu. (You can also select **Manager Workarea | Manage | Set Synchronization Behavior for All Objects** from the main menu.) The *Set Synchronization Behavior* (object selection) dialog box is displayed.

2. Make sure that the checkbox is selected only for the objects for which you want to change the synchronization behavior. Selecting or deselecting a Group will select or deselect all of the objects in it; you may need to expand Groups to see the objects in them, if you want to select individual content objects.

3. Click **Ok**. The *Set Synchronization Behavior* (set behavior) dialog box is displayed.

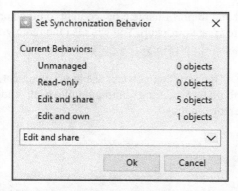

4. The **Current Behaviors** fields show how many objects in your selection are currently set to the various synchronization behaviors, for your reference. Use this to make sure you are not accidentally setting behaviors for objects that you don't mean to.

5. Use the drop-down list to select the required synchronization behavior. All of the selected objects will be set to this same, single behavior.

6. Click **Ok**.

Understanding Write Tokens

The pre-1811 release of Enable Now uses the concept of Write Tokens to control write access to objects on the server. A Write Token is effectively a key that unlocks a content object so that it can be edited. If you want to edit an object, you must first obtain the Write Token from the server. As long as you have the Write Token, no-one else can edit the content object—although anyone can read it (or at least the last version of the content object on the server). When you have finished editing an object, you save it to the server, and then return the Write Token, so that it is available to other Authors.

Enable Now still technically uses Write Tokens in the 1811 release, but the term is no longer visible in the Producer. As soon as you open a content object for editing (either by double-clicking on it in the Workarea, or by selecting it and clicking on the **Edit** button or the **Start Editing** button), you are effectively assigned the Write Token. As soon as you finish editing the content object (by clicking on the **Finish Editing** button), the Write Token is returned.

Summary

Enable Now allows you to import non-Enable Now content into your Workarea. This includes re-usable assets, such as images, as well as PowerPoint presentations (which you can convert to Books and Book pages), and other reference documents.

You can export and import Enable Now content to move or copy it between Workareas, or to create a backup. You can also maintain your Workarea structure in Microsoft Excel, if necessary.

You can create a Glossary that you can use in your content. This Glossary can be used to highlight terms during simulation playback, and can also be used as a standalone reference in the *Trainer*.

14

Adding Audio to Your Content

In this chapter we will look at how to add audio to your training content. This includes adding audio to both simulations and Book Pages.

In this chapter, you will learn:

- How to capture audio at the time of recording
- How to record or import your own audio
- How to use Text-to-Speech

Enable Now provides audio support at two levels. Firstly, it allows audio to be captured during simulation recording. This level of audio is not necessarily expected to be made available to users, but is more a way for the recorder (typically a Subject Matter Expert) to provide additional information about what they are doing—or, more importantly, *why* they are doing it—to the Author who will edit this recording. The second level of audio is what is best thought of as 'published audio'. This is audio that is included in the published training content, to provide trainees with a 'voiceover' of what they are seeing on the screen.

Should you provide audio?

Although Enable Now *provides* audio functionality, should you even *use* it? There is a school of thought that argues that 'auditory learners' retain more information they hear than information they read, but this theory has largely been debunked in recent years. The most common argument for audio is that it makes training "more professional", but this is highly subjective, and it is difficult to quantify the cost/benefit of this. That aside, it is possible to concede that audio does add some degree of nebulous 'value' to training (or, conversely, it is difficult to argue that providing audio is *detrimental* to the 'learning experience'). But how much of an increase in value does it provide? Does it take a course that is 95% effective to a course that is 98% effective? And what is the cost (both initial and maintenance) of providing this marginal increase in the 'feel good factor'?

Typically, providing audio requires the development of a script of what will be said (*never* just ad-lib on the fly, no matter how good or experienced a trainer you think you are!), procuring a 'voice talent' to record this (never underestimate the degree to which users will object to even the slightest whiff of a regional accent!), and then importing all of these audio files into the correct place in your training content. And then if anything changes, it's necessary to either find the same voice talent, or re-record everything (at least within the learning unit—simulation or Book, in Enable Now) so that it all matches. And then multiply this by the number of languages in which you provide your training material. It's costly, time-consuming, and is of little provable value. For these reasons and more, this author advises against using audio at all.

That said, there are always clients who *insist* on having audio in their training material. In these cases, consider using Enable Now's Text-to-Speech functionality. This uses the text that already exists in the training content object, and converts this to audio via Windows' built-in Narrator functionality. No, it's not *perfect*, but voice synthesis has come a long way since the days of SAP Tutor's Wizard, and is perfectly *adequate* (and cost-effective) for those who feel that audio is "essential".

Tips for audio recording

Assuming that you want to record 'live' audio, as opposed to using Text-to-Speech, here are some very basic tips for recording audio for your training content. Typically this will be narrative (voiceover) sound.

- Always have a script of what you want the audio to say. Write this out in full (so you can read it directly), using a conversational voice. This is especially important if you will have someone else record the audio.

- Record in as quiet an environment as possible (check if your organization has a sound-proofed room available to you—large organizations often do, for corporate communications). If you do not have a dedicated recording studio, find a small room, with lots of soft furnishings, to reduce echo (personally, I have found a walk-in closet works well!).

- Remove as many sources of ambient noise as you can (such as ticking clocks, and even air conditioning. Set your phone to silent and disable all alerts on your PC.

- Use a decent quality microphone. Do not rely on your laptop's built-in microphone, or a telephone headset. Reasonable-quality USB microphones are relatively cheap, and make a significant difference.

- Practice your script, in full, several times, before you record it. This will give you the opportunity to adjust the overall flow of the narrative (and update the script if necessary), as well as work out which words to emphasize, and where to pause.

- When recording, try to add more cadence (variation in pitch) than you would normally use in face-to-face speech, to avoid talking in a monotone. You may also find the recording sounds more natural if you talk at a slightly higher pitch than normal. Read *slightly* slower and more purposefully than you normally talk, and enunciate clearly, without it sounding forced.

- If you make a mistake recording a short audio clip, just delete it and re-record it. If you stumble during a longer audio clip, return to the start of the last sentence and continue, without pausing recording— you can edit out the mistakes after you have finished.

- If you need to re-record anything after the initial recording session (for example, after you have incorporated the audio into your training deliverable, and the content changes) try to record the replacement audio in exactly the same environment as the initial recordings, so that everything sounds consistent.

Using audio with simulations

It is important to note that audio is only available in Demo mode. It is not available in Practice mode, Concurrent mode, or any other mode. It is also not available in the Desktop Assistant or in Web Assistant.

Creating a project as an audio project

To include audio in a simulation project - regardless of whether you (or the SME) will capture this audio at the time of recording or whether you will include 'published' audio, you need to explicitly identify the project as an 'audio project'. Typically, you would do this when you create the project, but it is also possible to 'convert' a simulation to being an audio project at any time during editing, as explained in *Converting an existing project to an audio project* on page 569.

To designate a project as an audio project at the time of creation, you simply select the **Use Audio** option in the *New Project* dialog box (see *Chapter 3, Recording a Simulation*). As soon as you select this checkbox, the *New Project* dialog box is updated to include two additional fields, as shown in the example below.

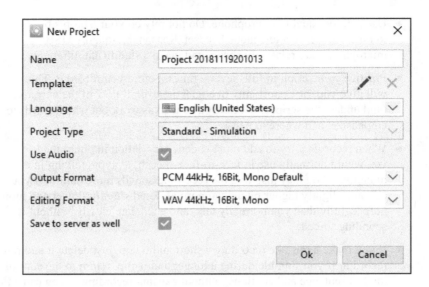

These two (audio) fields, and their use, are shown in the table below:

Name	Purpose
Output Format	Select the format of the final audio that will be played to the user. This is usually a variation of PCM (Pulse Code Modulation), but you have the option to choose the quality (frequency) of this, and whether the sound is in stereo or mono.
Editing Format	Select the format in which sound will be edited during content creation. This is usually a variation of WAV, but you have the option to choose the quality of this, and whether the sound is in stereo or mono.

Once you have selected the required audio settings, you can record your simulation as usual (again, see *Chapter 3, Recording a Simulation* for full instructions). Note, however, that simply selecting the **Use Audio** option will not automatically create Text-to-Speech audio for you; it will simply enable the **Audio** menu option in the *Project Editor*. You will still need to create the audio yourself, as explained in *Recording audio during recording* on page 568, or *Adding audio during editing* on page 570.

Recording audio during recording

Assuming that you have defined your project as an audio project, there is one more setting that you have to make, to be able to capture audio during recording. This is the **Record Audio** option, which is shown in *Step 1. Select Window and Profile*.

Just select this option, and then as soon as you start recording, audio will automatically be captured via the default microphone. An 'audio level' indicator, similar to the one shown below, will be included in the *Recording Bar* to confirm that this is being done.

Once you finish recording, the audio will be available for review and/or editing in the project, as explained in *Editing audio* on page 589.

Converting an existing project to an audio project

If you have an existing simulation project that you did not initially define as an audio project, you can still turn it into an audio project after it has been created (and at any stage of the development process).

To convert a project to an audio project, carry out the following steps.

1. Open the project in the *Project Editor*.

2. Select menu option **Project | Convert to Audio Project**. The *Select Audio Project* dialog box is displayed.

■ Note that this is a one-way conversion. Once a project has been identified as an audio project, you cannot go back to it being a 'non-audio' project. However, deleting or disabling all audio for the project will effectively do this.

3. In the **Output Format** field, select the format of the final audio that will be played to the user. This is usually a variation of PCM (Pulse Code Modulation), but you have the option to choose the quality (frequency) of this, and whether the sound is in stereo or mono.

4. In the **Editing Format** field, select the format in which sound will be edited during content creation. This is usually a variation of WAV, but you have the option to choose the quality of this, and whether the sound is in stereo or mono.

5. Click **Ok**.

The project is converted to an audio project. You can confirm this by checking that the **Audio** menu is now available on the menu bar. You can now record your audio, as explained in *Adding audio during editing* on page 570.

Adding audio during editing

If your simulation project has been designated an 'audio project' (either at the time of recording, or post-recording), you can record audio at any time during editing. If audio already exists (for example, if it was captured by the SME during recording) then this will be replaced by whatever you record during editing.

Audio is provided (recorded and played back) at the Step level—and for all macros within the Step at the same time.

To record an audio clip for a Step in a simulation project, carry out the steps shown below:

1. In the *Project Editor*, click on the Step for which you want to record audio, to select it.

2. Select menu option **Audio | Record Audio**. (If you do not see the *Audio* menu then your project has not been designated an audio project. Refer to *Converting an existing project to an audio project* on page 569.) The *Record Audio* dialog box is displayed.

3. Click on the **Start Recording** button, and start speaking into the microphone. The level meter will light up to indicate that you are recording. Try to keep the volume in the 'green' section.

4. When you have finished your narrative, click on the **End Recording** button.

5. Click on the **Ok** button to close the *Record Audio* dialog box.

The audio has now been created, and an 'audio' icon is shown on the right of the Step bar, to indicate this.

You can click on this icon to play the audio (and click on this icon again, if you want to stop the audio while it is playing).

If you want to edit the audio, you can do so as explained in *Editing audio* on page 589. If you subsequently decide that you do not like the audio and want to remove it, just select the Step and then select menu option **Audio | Delete Audio**.

Importing audio

As an alternative to recording audio directly in the *Project Editor*, you can create your audio files outside of Enable Now, and then import them. This is a good option if you have professional recording facilities available to you, and/or are using a separate person for recording the audio.

To import an audio file for use as narrative for an Enable Now Step, carry out the following steps:

1. In the *Project Editor*, click on the Step to which you want add audio.

2. Select menu option *Audio | Import Audio File*.

3. In the *Import Audio File* dialog box (which is a standard Windows 'Open File' dialog box), navigate to and select the audio file, then click **Open**.

Normalizing your Audio

After recording (or importing) all of your audio, you may find it useful to 'normalize' all of the audio in the simulation. This will set it all to a consistent, optimal volume. To normalize your audio, select menu option **Audio | Normalize All Audio Files**.

Using Text-to-Speech in a simulation

As an alternative to providing your own audio narrative for a simulation, you can use Enable Now's built-in Text-to-Speech function.

In order to use Text-to-Speech for a simulation, the simulation must already be identified as an 'audio project'. Refer to *Creating a project as an audio project* on page 567 or *Converting an existing project to an audio project* on page 569, as appropriate.

Defining the Text-to-Speech Options

The default settings for Text-to-Speech are defined in **Tools | Settings | Authoring Settings | Audio**. These settings are Workarea-wide and will apply to all simulations created or edited in the Workarea. However, some of these settings can be overridden in the simulation project itself, at the Step level.

To define simulation-specific Text-to-Speech options, carry out the following steps.

■ It actually doesn't matter which Step you select when adding the Text-To-Speech Options macro; it will always be added to the Start step, and apply to all Steps in the simulation.

1. In the *Step View*, click on the Start Step, to select it.

2. Select menu option **Insert | Insert Special Macro | Text-To-Speech Options**.

3. A Text-To-Speech Options macro is added to the Start Step. Click on this to display its details in the *Macro Editor* pane.

Text-To-Speech Options	☑ Advanced Layout
Comment	
UID	MAC_2CA4B0899E4FAE9E
▢ Voice for Text to S...	
▢ Speed	0 ⌄
▢ Volume (%)	90 ⌄
▢ Silence	200
▢ Use Demo Text	

■ Where the default Windows system voice is defined will depend upon your version of Windows. As an example, for Windows 10 it can be found in the *Control Panel* under **Ease of Access Center | Use the computer without a display | Set up Text To Speech | Voice Selection**.

4. If you want to use a specific voice for the Text-to-Speech audio, then select this in the **Voice for text to Speech** property. This will default to **Default Windows system voice**, but if you have other voice options available (for example, Google Voice), you can select one of those.

5. If you want to speed up or slow down the audio then select the appropriate value for the **Speed** property. You can select a value in the range +9 to -9. This is not an exact measurement of anything (for example x times faster or slower); it is more of an overall indicator from slowest (-9) to fastest (+9).

6. By default, the audio will be played at 90% of the recorded volume. If you want to change the volume, update the **Volume (%)** property accordingly.

7. By default, Enable Now will wait for 0.2 seconds after loading the screen before starting the audio (which is usually enough to allow for any network lag). If you want to use a different period of silence, then enter the number of *milli*seconds Enable Now should wait before starting the audio in the **Silence** field. Note that this default can be overridden at the Step level in a TEXT-TO-SPEECH OVERRIDE macro.

8. The **Use Demo Text** property is an interesting one. In theory you can select this option to have Text-to-Speech use the Demo mode text as the source for the audio instead of the Practice mode text, but there is already a Workarea-level setting of **Bubble Text for text To Speech** that lets you choose either **Text from Demo Bubble** (which is the default) or **Text from Practice Bubble**. Perhaps this option simply lets you change it back to using Demo mode text for ts specific simulation if the Workarea-level setting was changed to use Practice mode.

★ The Workarea-level text selection setting is defined in **Tools | Settings | Authoring Settings | Audio | Bubble Text for Text To Speech**.

Creating Text-to-Speech Audio

It is important to note that Text-to-Speech applies at the Step level, and not the individual macro or Bubble level. This means that if you have a Step that contains a number of interaction macros and several Explanation macros, the Text-to-Speech functionality will read out each of these, one after the other (in the sequence in which they appear within the Step).

Let's look at this by way of example. We will use our example *Processing a Travel Request* simulation for this. The first Step in this simulation contains an EXPLANATION macro that contains introductory text, followed by our first interaction, which is to click on the **Approve Travel Requests** tile. This appears in the *Step View* as follows:

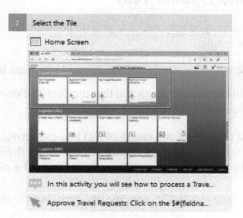

To create Text-to-Speech audio for a Step, follow the steps shown below:

1. Click on the Step header (the blue bar, in the example above) for the Step for which you want to create audio, to select it. You can select

multiple steps if you want to generate audio for multiple steps at the same time (audio will still be created per step).

2. Select menu option **Audio | Convert Text to Speech**. (Alternatively, you can right-click on a Step and select **Convert Text to Speech** from the shortcut menu.)

The Text-to-Speech audio has now been created, and an 'audio' icon is shown on the right of the Step bar, to indicate this.

You can click on this icon to play the audio (and click on this icon again, if you want to stop the audio while it is playing). For our example above, you will hear the audio for the EXPLANATION macro ("In this activity you will...") followed immediately by the audio for the Mouse Action macro ("Click on the...").

The Text-to-Speech audio is created using the Bubble text as it exists at the time you perform the conversion. This means that if the bubble text (in any of the macros within the Step) changes, the audio will not automatically reflect these changes. It is therefore important that you re-generate the Text-to-Speech audio every time you change the bubble text. This is a good argument for leaving the creation of the audio until the end of simulation creation and editing. Note that you don't need to delete any existing Text-to-Speech audio—you can just re-convert and this will replace any existing audio. However, if you have recorded or imported your own audio for a Step, you will need to delete this before generating the Text-to-Speech audio, as recorded audio always takes priority.

Overriding the Bubble Text

In some circumstances, you may find that you do not want to use the Bubble text exactly as-is. For example:

- The Step contains a number of macros and you want to summarize these
- The Bubble text contains a word that the Text-to-Speech function is mispronouncing

In these cases (and any others you can think of) you can provide your own text that will be used for Text-to-Speech, in place of the actual Bubble text. Note that this will not affect the Bubble text, which will continue to be displayed as-is.

To override the Bubble text for Text-to-Speech, carry out the steps shown below.

1. In the *Step View*, select the Step for which you want to override the Bubble text.

2. Select menu option **Insert | Insert Special Macro | Text-to-Speech Override**.

3. A TEXT-TO-SPEECH OVERRIDE macro is added to the Step. Click on this to display its details in the *Macro Editor* pane.

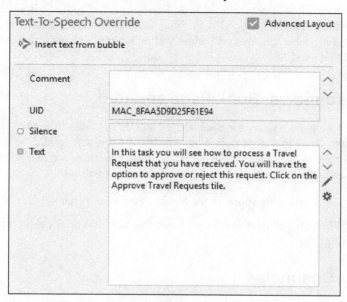

4. If you want a period of silence before the audio starts, then enter the number of *milli*seconds Enable Now should wait before starting the audio in the **Silence** field.

5. The text from all of the Bubbles for the step is automatically inserted into the **Text** field. Adjust this so that it contains the text that you do want to use for Text-to-Speech.

   Tip:
   If you subsequently decide to scrap your changes and start again, you can delete all of the existing text in this field, and then click the **Insert text from bubble** button at the top of the *Macro Editor* pane to re-insert the bubble text.

6. With the Step still selected in the *Step View*, select menu option **Audio | Convert Text to Speech**, to generate the new audio using the edited text.

Audio for Books and Book Pages

Enable Now effectively provides the ability to include two types of sound for your Book Pages. The first of these is best thought of as 'narrative' sound, and typically includes the 'voiceover' of the text on a Book Page. The second type of sound is 'supplemental' sound, and includes such things as background music, sound effects, and so on. This distinction is not black and white, as supplemental sound can also include narration and sound effects can be added to the Page sound, but for simplicity we will discuss these two types of sound separately.

Book Page Audio Concepts

Before delving into the actual creation and assignment of audio, it is necessary to understand the way in which Enable Now handles sound for Book Pages. Understanding these concepts will allow you to better plan your sound and decide how it will be used.

Book sound vs. Book Page sound

Book are simply containers for Book Pages, and do not include any actual content of their own. They therefore cannot have audio of their own - audio must be defined for the Book Pages within the Book. That said, there are two points at which sound should be considered for the Book as a whole:

- When assigning sound to the Book Sound sound channel (see below)
- When recording sound for all Book Pages within the Book at the same time

Sound Channels

Enable Now allows multiple sound elements to be played at the same time, as long as each of them is played in a separate *sound channel*. As soon as one sound element is played in a channel, it will replace all other audio in that channel, but sound in all other channels will still be heard. Having multiple channels allows you to effectively 'layer' sound—for example, having background music playing throughout a Book, an audio narrative (voiceover) playing on each individual Book Page, and then sound effects playing when they are triggered by certain events on the Book Page (for example, playing a 'click' sound when the user clicks on an object on the page.

Enable Now provides the following five Sound Channels:

- **Book Sound**: Audio files assigned to this channel are played regardless of which Book Page is currently displayed on the screen (whereas all other categories apply only to the page on which the audio objects are placed). It is therefore suitable for background music.

  Note that you still assign Book Sound audio to a Book Page, and not to a Book. If it truly should be heard throughout the entire period the Book is displayed, you should attach the include it via the *first* Book Page in the Book.

- **Page Sound**: This channel is the primary channel for Book Pages. If you provide narrative audio via the **Page Sound** property (described above) then it will be assigned to this layer. Although you can assign supplemental audio to this channel, any narrative audio provided via the **Page Sound** property will take precedence and any supplemental audio on the channel will be ignored.

- **Explanations**: This channel should be used for additional—possibly optional—narrative that is not included in the main Page Sound. A typical use case would be narrative that is only played in response to a user action (for example, providing additional explanation when the user hovers over an object on the screen).

- **Effects**: This channel should be used for 'sound effects'.

- **Others**: This channel can be used for anything not covered by the previous categories.

When deciding which channels to use for what purpose, you may find it useful to consider the controls available to the user for controlling sound levels in the Book Reader. Refer to *Sound in the Book Reader* on page 577 for more information on this.

Volume settings

You can define the volume settings for each sound object (treating Page Sound as a single object) independently. Default volumes are defined centrally for the Workarea, under **Tools | Settings | Playback Settings | book reader | Audio**. These will likely be set once by your Administrator, but it is worth knowing what each setting controls, especially in relation to the individual sound channels. The table below lists the settings that are available, and the channels they impact.

Setting	Use
General	Defines the default volume for audio on the **Others** sound channel.
Narrative	Defines the default volume for audio on the **Page Sound** and **Explanation** sound channels.
Book Sound	Defines the default volume for audio on the **Book Sound** sound channel.
Effects	Defines the default volume for audio on the **Effects** sound channel.

Sound in the Book Reader

Over and above the volume settings defined centrally and the volume setting for each audio object, users can also control the volume of playback in the *Book Reader*.

Confusingly, the *Book Reader* only allows the user to independently control the volume of **three** categories of sound, even though there are **four** audio level settings at the Workarea level, and **five** channels for a Book Page.

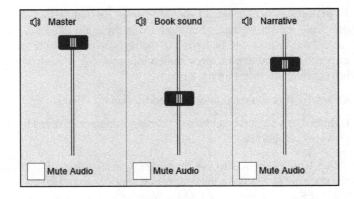

These options control the various channels as follows:

Control	Channels				
	Book Sound	Page Sound	Explanations	Effects	Others
Master	✓	✓	✓	✓	✓
Narrative		✓	✓		
Book Sound	✓				

Providing 'narrative' sound

The most common type of sound to provide for a Book Page is narrative—effectively a spoken 'voiceover'. Let's look at how to provide this.

There are two ways of providing narrative audio: by recording or importing your own audio, and by using Text-to-Speech. Both of these options are considered below (Text-to-speech for Book Pages is different enough from the same functionality for simulations that it warrants its own discussion here.)

Recording your own narrative

Narrative audio is provided via the **Page Sound** property of the Book Page. You do not need to select the **Page** object before recording the sound; it will automatically be added to this property, regardless.

To record **Page Sound** audio, carry out the steps shown below.

1. Within the *Book Page Editor*, make sure the page for which you want to record audio is displayed (and selected

Add Audio

in the *Book Explorer*) and then click on the **Add Audio** button on the *Toolbar*. (You can also select menu option **Book Page | Add Audio**.)

2. The *Add Audio* dialog box is displayed.

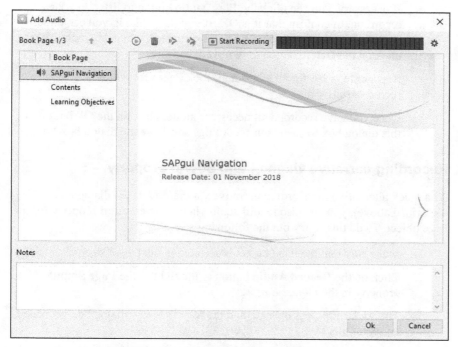

The selected Book Page is listed in the navigation pane on the left. If there are additional Book Pages in the same Book, then these will also be listed. This is useful as it allows you to record audio for multiple Book Pages in quick succession from the same dialog box.

● Only Book Pages that you currently have checked out will be listed. In the example above, there are actually five Book Pages in the same Book, but we only have three of these pages checked out for editing.

The selected Book Page is displayed on the rightmost side of the dialog box. Although it is always recommended that you have a script to work from, it is also useful to have the Book Page visible while you are recording the narrative. If you do have a script, you may find it useful to place this text in the **Notes** field at the bottom of the dialog box, so you can read it from there. These notes will be stored in the **Text to Speech Text** property for the Page (even if you are not using the Text-to-Speech function).

3. Make sure that the Book Page for which you want to record the narrative is selected in the navigation pane. You can use the **Next Book Page** and **Previous Book Page** buttons on the dialog box's Toolbar to navigate between multiple pages in the same Book, or just click on the required Book Page to select it.

4. Click on the **Start Recording** button, and start speaking into the microphone. The level meter will light up to indicate that you are recording. Try to keep the volume in the 'green' section.

● If necessary, you can use the **Audio Settings** button located on the right of the level meter to choose the recording device or adjust the recording settings.

5. When you have finished your narrative, click on the **End Recording** button. An 'audio' icon is shown to the left of the Book Page name in the navigation pane to indicate that audio now exists for this page.

6. If necessary, you can click the **Play Audio** button to listen to your recording, to confirm that it is OK. If you don't like it, you can either re-record it (any new recording will overwrite the existing recording) or click on the **Delete** button to remove it entirely.

7. Repeat Steps 3-6 for all additional Book Pages for which you want to record narrative audio.

8. Once you have recorded all necessary audio, click on the **Ok** button in this dialog box to save your recordings and close the dialog box.

Recording narrative via the Page Sound property

As a quick alternative to recording narrative via the *Add Audio* dialog box (described above), you can also record audio via the **Page Sound** property for the Page object. To do this, carry out the following steps:

1. Make sure that the Page object is selected in the *Objects* pane.

2. Click on the **Record Audio** button to the right of the **Page Sound** property in the *Object Editor*.

3. The *Audio Editor* is opened, and the *Record Audio* dialog box is opened on top of this.

4. Make any necessary adjustments to the recording settings in the **Recording Device, Output Format,** and **Editing Format** fields (click on **Show Settings** if these are not visible).

5. Click on the **Start Recording** button, and start speaking into the microphone. The level meter will light up to indicate that you are

recording. Try to keep the volume in the 'green' section. As you record, you will see the audio sound-wave scroll across the *Audio Editor* screen, behind the *Record Audio* dialog box.

6. When you have finished your narrative, click on the **End Recording** button.

7. Click on the **Ok** button to close the *Record Audio* dialog box. You are passed in to the *Audio Editor*, where the recording sound-wave is still displayed. If necessary, you can adjust your recording as explained in *Editing audio* on page 589.

8. Once you are happy with your audio, click on **Save and Close** in the lower-right corner of the *Audio Editor*.

Using Text-to-Speech narration

As an alternative to providing your own narration, you can use Enable Now's built-in Text-to-Speech functionality to provide narration. Unlike Text-to-Speech for simulations, Enable Now does not use existing text in the book Page as the source for this—which means that you always need to enter the text yourself. This may seem like duplicate effort—especially if you want your narration to basically be a reading of the text on the screen—but with the huge amount of flexibility Book Pages provide in terms of page objects and possible animation of these, it would be just about impossible for Enable Now to work out what text you wanted narrated, and in what order.

To provide Text-to-Speech narration for a Book Page, carry out the following steps.

1. Within the *Book Page Editor*, make sure the page for which you want to record audio is displayed.

2. Make sure that the Page object is selected in the *Objects* pane.

3. Click on the **Edit Text to Speech** button to the right of the **Page Sound** property in the *Object Editor*. The *Edit Text to Speech* dialog box is displayed.

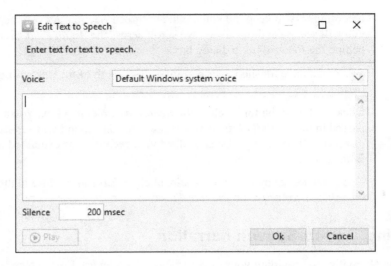

4. Enter the text that you want to be converted to speech into the large text area in the middle of the dialog box.

5. If you want to use a specific voice for the Text-to-Speech audio, then select this in the **Voice** field.

6. By default, Enable Now will wait for 200 milliseconds (0.2 seconds) after loading the screen before starting the audio (which is usually enough to allow for any network lag). If you want to use a different period of silence, then enter the number of *milli*seconds Enable Now should wait before starting the audio in the **Silence** field.

7. If necessary, you can click on the **Play** button to hear how your audio sounds. Make any necessary adjustments (for example, typing words phonetically if the pronunciation is incorrect—such as typing "essay pea" in place of "SAP") before continuing.

8. Once you are happy with your narration, click on **Ok** to close the *Edit to Text Speech* dialog box.

Your Text-to-Speech audio has now been created. It is not necessary to click a Generate Text-to-Speech button like you have to for simulations.

Editing Page Sound

Every Book Page has a **Page Sound** property, which can be used to capture or edit audio for the Book Page. This 'property' consists of a number of buttons that are used to access the various audio-related functions for the Book Page. These buttons, and their purpose, are shown in the table below.

Button	Name	Purpose
📁	Import Audio	Navigate to and select an existing audio file for use as the page sound.
⏺	Record Audio	Record new narrative audio. Refer to *Recording narrative via the Page Sound property* on page 580.
⟨⟩	Edit Text to Speech	Click on this button to display a dialog box into which you can enter the text to be used as the basis for Text-to-Speech. Refer to *Using Text-to-Speech narration* on page 581.
✎	Edit Audio	If Page Sound has been defined for the Page (either recorded, imported, or defined via Text-to-Speech), then this button will be available. Click on it to open the *Audio Editor*, in which you can edit the audio. Refer to *Editing audio* on page 589 for details.
⇄	Change Audio Format	If you want to change the format in which the audio is edited and/or played back, click on this button to display the *Convert Audio Format* dialog box, and then change the **Output Format** and/or **Editing Format** fields as required.

Convert Audio Format ✕

Output Format:

PCM 16kHz, 16Bit, Mono Current ⌄

Editing Format:

WAV 16kHz, 16Bit, Mono Current ⌄

Ok   Cancel

Button	Name	Purpose
🗑	Delete Audio	Click on this button to delete any Page Sound audio currently created for the Page.
▶	Play Audio	Play the currently-defined Page Sound audio.
■	Stop Audio	Stop the playback of the Page Sound audio.

Page Sound Information

You may have noticed that there is a category of properties named *Page Sound Information* in the *Object Editor* pane.

Page Sound Information

Text to Speech Text	This course includes the following topics: 1. Accessing the Fiori System 2. Structure of Fiori screens 3. Tile basics 4. Input fields 5. Searches 6. Personalizing your Fiori experience 7. Getting help
Text to Speech Voice	audio_tts_system_voice_key
Editing Format	PCM 22 kHz, 16 Bit, Mono
Output Format	PCM 44 kHz, 16 Bit, Mono

These properties provide basic information about the **Page Sound**, including any Text-to-Speech text, the voice to use, and the editing and output formats for the sound. None of these can be edited via these properties—they are shown here purely for convenience. If you need to change them, you can do so via the buttons available for the **Page Sound** property.

Providing supplemental sound

Supplemental sound (basically everything except Page Sound audio) is provided via audio objects. You cannot record this audio within the Book Page editor; it must always be provided by a sound file (whether this is an existing 'asset' in your Workarea, or is a file on your PC that you are going to import). Let's look at how to import a sound file, and then we'll look at a couple of different ways of applying this audio to our Book Pages.

Inserting audio files into a Book Page

It is important to understand that audio files are imported as objects into Book Pages (and not Books). If you intend on using the same audio files on multiple Book Pages, you should import the file(s) into the **Resources** group in your Workarea, and the insert them into your Book Pages from there. In fact, unless you know for certain that the audio file will only ever be used on a single Book Page, you should probably always import it into your Workarea, just in case you (or another Author) end up re-using it later anyway.

To insert an audio file into a Book Page, carry out the following steps.

1. Make sure you have the Book Page open in Edit mode in the *Book Page Editor*, and that the Book Page is displayed in the *WYSIWYG Editor*.

2. On the *Book Editor Toolbar*, click on the **Insert Media Object** button to display the drop-down panel of possible media object types.

Insert
Media
Object

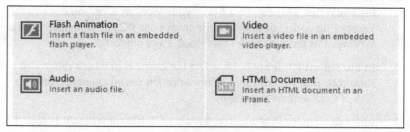

| <image> | Flash Animation
Insert a flash file in an embedded flash player. | <image> | Video
Insert a video file in an embedded video player. |
| Audio
Insert an audio file. | | HTML Document
Insert an HTML document in an iFrame. |

3. Click on the **Audio** option. An **Audio Object** placeholder is added to the Book Page. This is represented by an Audio icon on the outside upper-left of the visible Book Page, as shown below:

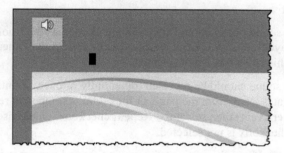

Make sure that this Audio icon is selected (it will have a red dashed border if it is selected, as shown in the example above), and you will see the properties related to this object in the *Object Editor* pane.

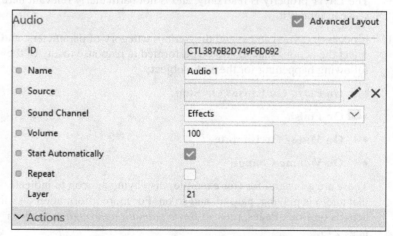

Audio	☑ Advanced Layout
ID	CTL3876B2D749F6D692
☐ Name	Audio 1
☐ Source	✎ ✕
☐ Sound Channel	Effects ∨
☐ Volume	100
☐ Start Automatically	☑
☐ Repeat	☐
Layer	21
∨ Actions	

4. Enter a suitable name for your audio object in the **Name** field. You will see this name in pick-lists for actions on other objects, so it is important to choose a meaningful name, and not just accept the default name.

5. Click on the **Edit** button for the **Source** field, and navigate to and select the audio file. This can be a file in your Workarea, or you can use the **Insert File** option to upload a file from your PC (it will appear in the Workarea as an asset under this Book Page object).

6. In the **Sound Channel** field, select the channel in which this audio should be played. For more information on sound channels, refer to *Sound Channels* on page 576.

7. Enter the required volume (on a scale of 0-100) at which this sound should be played into the **Volume** field. You should consider this sound in relation to all other audio objects that could be played—especially if these may be played at the same time. For example, you may choose to use a level of 10 for background sound, 75 for 'effects' and 100 for narrative.

8. If the sound object should start playing as soon as the Book Page is displayed, select the **Start Automatically** checkbox. Otherwise, make sure this checkbox is not selected.

9. If the sound should be repeated (potentially forever, or until the user navigates away from the page, or the audio is stopped in response to another event) then select the **Repeat** checkbox. Otherwise, make sure this checkbox is not selected.

   You should use this option with caution (sound can get very annoying very quickly!). An exception would be background sound, where the audio file has been specifically built for looping.

10. The **Layer** property is read only, and is not particularly relevant here; you can ignore it.

11. If necessary, you can expand the *Actions* category of parameters, and select the actions that should be performed in response to any of the following happening for the audio object:

    ♦ **On Play / On Pause / On Stop**

    ♦ **On Finish**

    ♦ **On Mute / On Unmute**

    ♦ **On Volume Change**

    These are all useful for (for example) displaying an icon to indicate that audio is playing, paused, and so on. For more information on using actions on Book Pages, refer to *Basic animation through Actions* on page 275.

You now have an audio object available to your Book Page. However, unless you have the **Start Automatically** option selected, this sound will never be played; you need to manually trigger it. Let's look at a few ways of doing this.

Adding sound to Book Page objects

A commonly-used method of playing audio on a Book Page is to have the audio played in response to something happening to an object on the screen. For example, you may want to provide a number of audio clips for a user to listen to, and want each of these to be played when the user clicks on a play button. Alternatively, you may want a confirmation sound to be played when a user clicks on a button, or want a specific sound to be played when an object appears on the screen.

In *Chapter 8, Books and Book Pages*, we built an example Book Page that allowed users to see how four different color schemes would look in SAPgui. An example of this page is shown below.

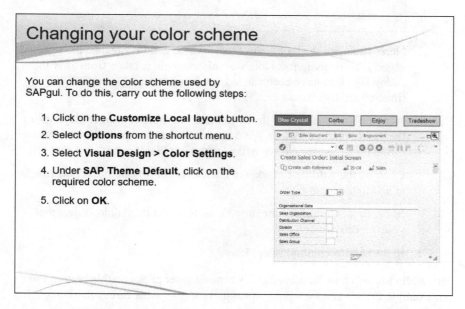

Let's add a sound effect to each of the buttons (above the image), to provide auditory confirmation to the user that they have clicked on a button. (For simplicity we'll use the same sound file for each button, but you could just as easily use a separate sound for each one.)

To add a sound effect to an object on the Book Page, carry out the steps shown below. Note that this assumes that you have already imported the audio into your Book Page as an Audio Object (see *Inserting audio files into a Book Page* on page 584 for instructions if necessary).

● This means that if you want to use the same audio effect on multiple pages, you need to attach it to multiple pages.

1. In the *Book Page Editor*, navigate to the Book Page that contains the object to which you want to assign a sound effect. The Audio Object should also be present on this same page.

2. Select the object for which the audio should be played in the *WYSIWYG Editor* (it will have a red bounding box around it when it is selected).

3. In the *Object Editor*, locate the *Actions* category of properties. An example of this is shown below:

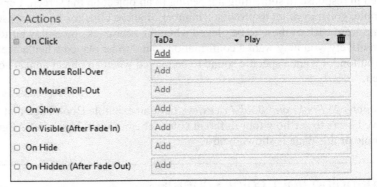

Here, you can see all of the events to which actions (against the selected object) can be assigned. Note that this example is taken from after the following steps have been carried out, just so you can see what the finished product would look like.

4. Activate the property for the action that you want to trigger playback of the audio. In our example, we want the sound to be placed when the user clicks on the button, so we will use the **On Click** action.

5. Click on the **Add** link inside the input field for this action. A new row is added to the input field.

6. In the first column, use the drop-down to select the Audio Object that you want to be played.

7. In the second column, select **Play**.

● If you need to apply the same action (in this case playing a specific audio file) then you can first select all of the objects, and then change their properties collectively.

This audio file will now be played every time the user clicks on this button. For our example Book Page we would repeat these steps for the three remaining color scheme buttons.

Adding background sound to a Book

Although we noted earlier that audio is applied to a Book Page and not to a Book, the Book Sound channel allows you to define audio that will keep playing as long as the Book is open—even when you switch between pages.

There are a couple of things to bear in mind when using Book sound. Firstly, you should (obviously) put this audio on the first Book Page in the book. Secondly, if you have nested Books (for example, to organize your Book content into chapters or sections) then the Book Sound will only keep playing for as long as the user is in the Book to which the audio is attached—if they open a page in a nested book, the audio will stop.

To add background sound to a Book, carry out the following steps. Note that this assumes that you have already included the audio into your Book Page as an Audio Object (see *Inserting audio files into a Book Page* on page 584 for instructions if necessary).

1. In the *Book Page Editor*, navigate to the Book Page that contains the Audio Object (this should be the first Book Page in the Book).

2. Select the Audio Object, and make sure that the **Sound Channel** property is set to **Book Sound**.

3. If necessary (especially for shorter audio clips) select the **Repeat** checkbox.

You could just make sure that the **Start Automatically** property for the Audio Object is selected, but let's look at a slightly more interesting (albeit more complicated) way of doing the same thing, just for the sake of learning something new. Continue as follows.

4. Select the Page object for the Book Page, in the *Object Overview* pane.

5. In the *Object Editor* pane, navigate to the *Actions* category.

6. Activate the **On Page Loaded** property, and click on the **Add** link inside the input field. A new row is added to the input field.

7. In the first column, use the drop-down to select the Audio Object that you want to be played.

8. In the second column, select **Play**.

Your audio will now be played as soon as the Book Page is visible on the user's screen, and will keep playing as long as the user remains in the same Book.

■ For more information on using actions as triggers, and other fun things you can do with Book Pages, refer to *Chapter 8, Books and Book Pages*.

Editing audio

You can edit any audio that you have created within Enable Now, via the *Audio Editor*. This includes audio captured during recording of a simulation, any audio captured during editing of a simulation or a Book Page, and even any audio generated via Text-to-Speech. You cannot edit audio files that you insert into Book Pages as Audio Objects, but you probably wouldn't need to, as they will presumably have been created and edited via a separate application already. If you do need to edit imported audio files, edit them outside of Enable Now (for example, using Audacity) and then re-import them.

Opening the Audio Editor

To open the *Audio Editor* from the *Project Editor*, select menu option **View |
Components | Audio Editor**.

To open the *Audio Editor* from the *Book Page Editor*, select the page object in
the *Objects* list, then click on the **Edit** button alongside the **Page Sound** property.
Note that this button will only be present if audio already exists for the page
(either by being manually recorded or generated via Text-to-Speech).

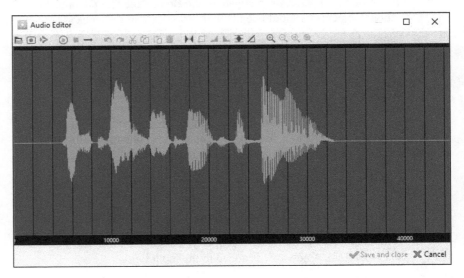

Editing an audio clip

All editing that you can do to the audio is done via the toolbar at the top of the
Audio Editor dialog box. The table below identifies the buttons on this toolbar,
and explains what you would use them for.

● Using any of **Import**,
Record, or **Text-to-
Speech** will replace any
existing audio (recorded
or otherwise) for the Book
Page or simulation Step.

Button	Name	Purpose
	Import	Navigate to and select an existing audio file for use as the page sound.
	Record	Record new narrative audio. Refer to *Recording narrative via the Page Sound property* on page 580.
	Text-to-Speech	Click on this button to display the *Edit Text to Speech* dialog box. You can then enter or change the text to be used as the source of Text-to-Speech. See *Using Text-to-Speech narration* on page 581 for details of how to do this.
	Play	Play the currently-selected section of the audio (or the entire thing, if nothing is selected).

Button	Name	Purpose
❚❚	Pause	Pause the audio playback.
■	Stop	Stop the audio playback.
→	Repeat	Select a portion of audio and then click on this button to mark the section for repetition. When you subsequently click on the Play button, this portion will be played back in a repeating loop, until you click on Stop or Pause. Note that this only applies to playback in the editor; it will not apply to your published audio.
↻	Cancel Repeat	Cancel the previously-selected repeating section.
↺	Undo	Undo the last change that you made.
↷	Redo	Re-do the last change that you undid.
✂	Cut	Cut the selected portion of the audio to the clipboard. The audio timeline will be closed up (that is, no gap will be left where the audio was removed).
⧉	Copy	Copy the selected portion of the audio to the clipboard.
⧉	Paste	Paste the audio currently on the clipboard into the audio timeline at the position of the play head. The existing audio on the timeline will be shifted to accommodate this (that is, it will not be overwritten).
🗑	Delete	Delete the selected portion of the audio. The audio timeline will be closed up (that is, no gap will be left where the audio was deleted).

Button	Name	Purpose
![Insert Silence icon]	Insert Silence	Insert a period of silence into the audio. Position the play head at the point at which you want to insert the silence, and click on this button to display the *Insert Silence* dialog box.

Enter the length of the silence (in milliseconds) in the input field, and click Ok to insert it. Existing audio will be shifted to accommodate this.

Button	Name	Purpose
![Trim icon]	Trim	Select the section of audio that you want to keep and click on this button to trim the audio to retain only the selected section (and delete all of the other audio).
![Fade In icon]	Fade In	Fade in the current audio selection from silence to the audio level at the end of the selection.
![Fade Out icon]	Fade Out	Fade out the current audio selection to silence at the end of the selection.
![Normalize icon]	Normalize	Click on this button to change the volume of the audio to the 'optimal' level. This is useful if you have a number of audio recordings that were possibly recorded at different times and in different environments, and want to set them all to a consistent volume level. You should not need to do this if you are using Text-to-Speech, as this should be generated at the optimal volume, anyway.
![Change Dynamics icon]	Change Dynamics	Fine-tune the audio, See *Changing audio dynamics* on page 593.
![Zoom In icon]	Zoom In	Zoom in the audio display.
![Zoom Out icon]	Zoom Out	Zoom out the audio display.
![Zoom To Fit icon]	Zoom To Fit	Zoom the audio display (in or out, as necessary) to show the entire recording.
![Zoom to Selection icon]	Zoom to Selection	Zoom the audio display to show just the selected portion.

Once you have made any necessary adjustments to the audio, click on **Save and close** to save your changes and return to either the *Project Editor* or *Book Page Editor*, depending on where you were before you opened the *Audio Editor*.

Changing audio dynamics

If you click on the **Change Dynamics** button on the *Audio Editor* toolbar, you are passed into the *Change audio dynamics* dialog box. An example of this is shown below.

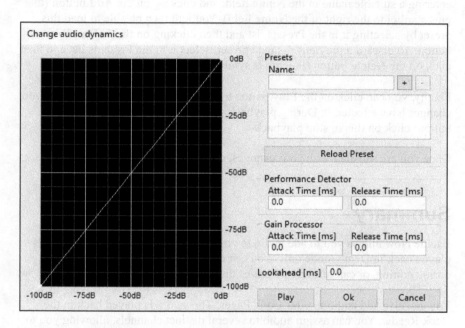

The *Change audio dynamics* dialog box allows you to fine-tune your audio. Honestly, this is probably overkill for most corporate training needs, but in case you're a bit of an audiophile, some (very) basic information on using this is provided below.

The graph on the left of the dialog box shows the audio input level along the bottom (horizontal axis) and the output level scale on the right (vertical axis). Initially, this shows a straight line, showing that audio is output at the same volume as it is input (that is, originally recorded). You can adjust this—for example, to play back quieter sounds louder—by clicking on the yellow line, and dragging the line point to a new location. You can make multiple adjustments by clicking on different points on the line and dragging them to new positions. If you subsequently want to remove an adjusted point, then right-click on it.

Under **Performance Detector** are two fields that allow you to specify how long (in milliseconds) it should take to apply the adjustment to the output sound levels identified in the graph. **Attack Time** specifies how long it should take to apply the effect, and **Release Time** specifies how long it should take to remove this effect afterwards. The two fields under **Gain Processor** provide the same function but for the input sound levels. In general, these fields will 'smooth out' any change in volume.

The **Lookahead** field specifies how many milliseconds ahead in the audio clip the sound processor should 'look' before determining whether it needs to make the adjustments. Normally this should be at least as long as any attack or release time.

Once you have made any adjustments, you can save these settings as a preset, by entering a suitable name in the **Name** field, and clicking on the **Add** button (the plus symbol to the right of the **Name** field). You will then be able to load this preset by selecting it in the Presets list and then clicking on the **Reload Presets** button. To discard a previously-saved preset, select it in the Presents list and then click on the **Delete** button (the minus symbol to the right of the **Name** field).

Finally, you can click on the **Play** button to play the audio back and see how your changes have affected it. During playback, the **Play** button changes to a **Stop** button; click on this to stop playback.

Once you are satisfied with your changes, click **Ok** to return to the *Audio Editor*.

Summary

Enable Now allows you to add audio to your simulation projects. This audio is played back in Demo mode only. You can capture this audio during recording, during editing, or can import audio files that were created outside of Enable Now.

You can also add audio to your Book Pages. This audio is played back in the Book Reader. You can assign audio to several distinct channels, allowing you to provide (for example) narrative, background music, and sound effects. Sound can be played automatically, or in response to actions associated with objects on the Book Page.

In addition to recorded or imported narrative audio, you can also use Enable Now's Text-to-Speech function to generate spoken word narrative from your bubble text, or other entered text. This can be spoken using any system voice available on your PC (the sound will be embedded into the content object, so the same voice does not need to be available on the user's device for playback).

15

Localizing Your Content

Often, you will find that your users are located in multiple countries, and speak various languages. You may want to provide these users with training in their own language—or you may have a legal requirement to do so. Enable Now makes this relatively easy to do.

In this chapter, you will learn:

- How to 'automatically' translate template text for simulations.
- How to export custom simulation text and Book Page content for submission to a translator, and how to import the translated content.
- How to replace application screenshots with local-language versions.

Decide what to translate

You can effectively translate any content objects for which you have entered any form of text. This includes:

- Simulations—Texts and optionally screenshots, plus properties
- Books and Book Pages—Text content and properties
- Groups—Names and their properties
- Glossaries—Terms and definitions
- Text units

Make sure you include all applicable content when planning your localization.

Localizing a simulation

Localizing a simulation is effectively a three-step process:

1. Translate the template text
2. Translate the custom text
3. Replace the application screenshots, if necessary

Each of these steps is explained separately, below.

Preparing for localization

Before you localize your simulation, there are a few things that you should do, to make the localization process easier.

Firstly, make sure that the primary language version is finished. Do not try to translate too soon. It is tempting to try to get a head start on the translation as soon as possible, but if you start the translation process and then the original version changes, you will lose too much time re-doing the translation, or trying to maintain copies in two (or more) languages.

Secondly, if you will be localizing the application screens, merge your screens as far as possible before generating your localized simulation (see *Working with the 'after' object image* on page 155). This will leave you with less screens to recapture.

Finally, if you have a Glossary attached to your simulations, make sure that you remove this from the localized version (before extracting the custom text), via menu option **Tools | Glossary | Remove Glossary**. You can then translate your Glossary separately, and then apply the translated Glossary to your localized content objects once all text has been translated. Refer to *Using a Glossary* on page 537 for more information on using a Glossary.

Translating the template text

The first step in creating a localized version of a simulation project is to take a copy of the current original-language version. This will create a brand new simulation in the library that contains all of the content.

By way of example, we will take our *Changing your User Options* simulation for SAP ECC 6.0, which we created in English, and will translate this into German. Assume for this simulation we left most of the bubble texts as the default values, and only entered our own texts for a single step.

To create a local-language copy of a simulation, carry out the following steps:

1. In the Workarea, right-click on the original-language version of the simulation, to select it.

2. Select menu option **Tools | Localization | Automated Translation All**. The *Translate Content* dialog box is displayed.

3. Click on the target language in the list, and then click **Ok**. A copy of the simulation selected in Step 1 is created, in the language selected in Step 2 (this will be reflected in the **Language** property of the new simulation).

All of the default (Recording Dictionary derived) text in the simulation will be automatically translated into the target language—including the object name! For example, here's a partial screenshot of the first action step in our simulation:

■ Check any translated object names against the system, and make sure that these are correct. Note that if you will also be replacing the screens, then the correct object names should be captured during the re-recording, anyway.

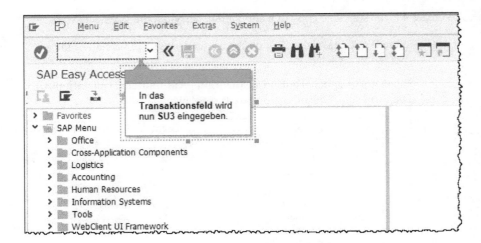

However, this (automated translation) will only apply to default 'template' text—text that was automatically generated during recording, and has not been changed in any way during editing. As soon as you make *any* changes to bubble text, the link to the Recording Dictionary breaks, and it is considered 'custom' text. Such text will not be automatically translated into the target language.

● The **Translate Manually** property is just a regular checkbox property, and you can change it if necessary. However, you would not normally need to, and even if you deselect it for a custom text bubble, the custom text will not miraculously be translated automatically.

Handily, there is a property that effectively indicates whether a text is template text or custom text. This is the **Translate Manually** property, and can be found separately in both the *Demo Bubble* category and the *Practice Bubble* category. By default (for example, immediately after recording), the checkbox for this property is not selected, which means that the text has not been changed from the Recording Dictionary default text, which in turn means that it can be translated 'automatically', as explained above. As soon as you edit a Bubble's text, this checkbox is automatically selected, which means that the text is (now) 'custom' text and needs to be translated manually.

In our sample exercise, we entered our own text into the Bubble for one of the STRING INPUT macros. Even after performing the automatic translation, this still appears as follows:

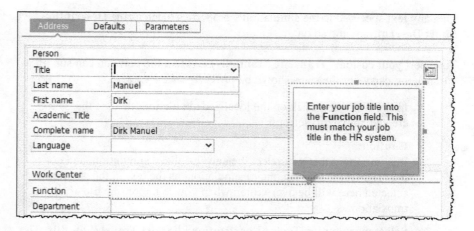

Note that whereas the field name is also translated for template text, this is not the case for untranslated custom text - even though in both cases the field name is inserted into the bubble text by way of a placeholder variable. If you will be recapturing your application screens then the object names will be recaptured at that time, anyway. Otherwise, you may need to select the **Include Control Names** option when you export the custom text for translation, or manually adjust them yourself.

So let's look at how to translate our custom texts. We'll do this in the next section.

Translating custom text

There are effectively two ways of translating custom text. The first of these is to simply go into the simulation in the *Topic Editor* and over-type all of the custom text with the local language text. If you are bilingual, this is by far the easiest (and cheapest) option. However, most of us are rarely so fortunate. This leaves us with the second option, which is to have someone else translate the text for us. Most commonly this will be a translation service, but could just as easily be another person in your organization. In either case, it is unlikely that the translator has access to Enable Now (or the skills to use it), so translation will involve extracting the text from Enable Now, passing this to a translator to be translated, and then importing the translated text back into Enable Now. So let's look at how to do this.

Exporting the custom text

The first step is to export the text from your simulation. Fortunately, Enable Now is smart enough to know what text is 'template text' and is translated already, and what text is 'custom text' and does need to be translated. Enable Now will then only export for translation the custom text—effectively, any Bubble text for a bubble for which the **Translate Manually** property is selected (see above), along with any text specified in the simulation's properties (such as the **Description**, **Short Description**, and so on).

To export your custom (**Translate Manually**) text to a file that you can submit to a translator, carry out the steps shown below.

● You can select multiple simulations or Groups at the same time, if necessary. All localized text for all of the selected content objects will be included in the translation file.

1. In the Workarea, click on the localized simulation (the one that you created above), to select it.

    Caution:
    It is important that you select the new, localized simulation, and not the original (source-language) simulation, as the text in the simulation selected here will be overwritten when you re-import the file after translation.

2. Select menu option **Tools | Localization | Export Translation File**. The *Export Translation File* dialog box is displayed.

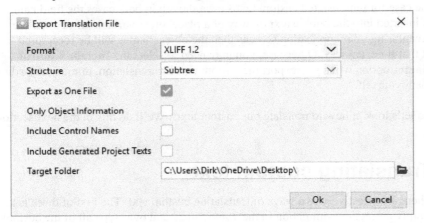

3. In the **Format** field, select the format in which you want the export file to be generated. The following options are available:

    ♦ **Microsoft Word**: The text is exported to a Microsoft Word document that can be manually edited by the translator.

    ♦ **XLIFF 1.2**: XLIFF is a specialized XML format that is designed to be imported into a specialized translation software program—typically for initial machine translation, followed by manual adjustments.

    If you are not sure which option to use, check with your translator.

4. In the **Structure** field, select whether you want to export only the currently-selected object(s), all of the objects in your Workarea, or all objects below the selected Group.

5. If your selection includes multiple objects and you want the text for all objects to be included in a single export file, then make sure that the **Export as One File** option is selected (this is the default). Otherwise,

make sure that this option is not selected, and a separate file will be created for each content object. Generating multiple files is useful if you will divide the translation work between multiple translators.

6. If you only want to translate the content object's **Name**, **Description**, and **Short Description** properties, then select the **Only Object Information** checkbox.

7. By default, **Object Name** properties (typically, field and button names) will not be included in the exported file. This is because normally either the interface stays the same, or they will be recaptured via rerecording anyway. However, if you want the object names to be translated by your translator, then select the **Include Control Names** checkbox.

8. By default, template texts (generated from the Recording Dictionary) will not be included in the translation file. If you do want to include these texts, select the **Include Generated Project Texts** checkbox. You may want to do this if you are translating into a language that is not natively supported by Enable Now, and for which there is no Recording Dictionary that can be used to automatically translate these texts.

● If you have followed the steps above to create the localized content object, all of the template texts will already be translated into the local language, and will therefore appear already-translated in the translation file.

9. Use the button to the right of the **Target Folder** field, navigate to and select the folder into which the exported file should be saved.

10. Click **Ok**. The texts are exported. Once this has completed, a confirmation dialog box is displayed, giving you the option of opening the exported file, opening the folder it is in, or just closing the dialog box.

You can now pass this file to your translator for translation. Once you receive it back, continue with *Importing the custom text* on page 604.

Example of an exported Word document

An example of the Word document generated for the export of your custom text is shown below:

● In this example, most of the sections are blank. This is because they only contain template text, which is automatically translated and therefore does not need to be included in the translation file.

```
project|PR_36CE3941B8C10493:.caption_pt:TEXT
```
Changing your user options

```
project|PR_36CE3941B8C10493:.shortdesc_rt:html
```

```
project|PR_36CE3941B8C10493:.description_rt:html
```

```
project|PR_36CE3941B8C10493:.keywords_pt:TEXT
```

```
project|PR_36CE3941B8C10493:macro|MAC_F8HNH5LBAXBZ18SY:.explanation_d_rt:html
```
Enter your job title into the [PH type="#" name="fieldname"/] field. This must match your job title in the HR system.

```
project|PR_36CE3941B8C10493:macro|MAC_FXZA04B3398DB686:.end_caption_pt:TEXT
```

```
project|PR_36CE3941B8C10493:macro|MAC_FXZA04B3398DB686:.end_caption_p_pt:TEXT
```

```
project|PR_36CE3941B8C10493:macro|MAC_FXZA04B3398DB686:.end_caption_t_pt:TEXT
```

```
project|PR_36CE3941B8C10493:macro|MAC_FXZA04B3398DB686:.end_text_rt:html
```

```
project|PR_36CE3941B8C10493:macro|MAC_FXZA04B3398DB686:.end_text_p_rt:html
```

```
project|PR_36CE3941B8C10493:macro|MAC_FXZA04B3398DB686:.end_text_t_passed_rt:html
```

```
project|PR_36CE3941B8C10493:macro|MAC_FXZA04B3398DB686:.end_text_t_failed_rt:html
```

Your instructions to the translator should be to "Overtype any text that follows a 'project' statement with the translated text". Be sure to tell them that they must not change anything else in the file—including any placeholder text (denoted as **[PH.../]**).

Example of an exported XLIFF file

An example of an XLIFF file generated for localization is shown below.

```xml
<?xml version="1.0" encoding="UTF-8"?>

<xliff xmlns="urn:oasis:names:tc:xliff:document:1.2"
xmlns:xsi="http://www.w3.org/2001/XMLSchema-instance"
xsi:schemaLocation="urn:oasis:names:tc:xliff:document:1.2 xliff-
core-1.2-transitional.xsd" xmlns:htm="urn:datango:xsd:xliff:htm"
xmlns:dgo="urn:datango:xsd:xliff:dgo" version="1.2">
<file original="project!PR_B6CE394198C10493" datatype="x-datango-tour-
project" tool-id="SAP Enable Now Producer" product-name="SAP project"
product-version="10.2.4" source-language="en-US">
<header>
  <tool tool-id="SAP Enable Now Producer" tool-name="SAP Enable Now
Producer" tool-version="10.2.4" tool-company="SAP"/>
</header>
<body>
  <trans-unit id="project!PR_B6CE394198C10493:.caption"
datatype="plaintext" restype="x-dgo-TEXT" maxwidth="511" size-unit="char">
    <source>Changing your user options</source>
    <target>Changing your user options</target>
  </trans-unit>
  <trans-unit id="project!PR_B6CE394198C10493:.keywords"
datatype="plaintext" restype="x-dgo-TEXT">
    <source></source>
    <target></target>
  </trans-unit>
  <group id="MAC_988BE919AEB2188F">
    <trans-unit id="project!PR_
B6CE394198C10493:macro!MAC_988BE919AEB2188F:.explanation_d"
datatype="htmlbody" restype="x-dgo-HTML">
      <source><g ctype="x-html-p" id="1" dgo:tag_name="p">Enter your job
title into the <g ctype="x-html-span" id="2" htm:font-weight="bold" dgo:tag_
name="span" dgo:span_type="0"><ph dgo:ph_type="#" dgo:ph_name="fieldname"
ctype="x-dgo-ph" id="3"/></g> field. This must match your job title in the HR
system.</g></source>
      <target><g ctype="x-html-p" id="1" dgo:tag_name="p">Enter your job
title into the <g ctype="x-html-span" id="2" htm:font-weight="bold" dgo:tag_
name="span" dgo:span_type="0"><ph dgo:ph_type="#" dgo:ph_name="fieldname"
ctype="x-dgo-ph" id="3"/></g> field. This must match your job title in the HR
system.</g></target>
    </trans-unit>
  </group>
  <group id="MAC_FE2A04B3399DB6B6">
    <trans-unit id="project!PR_B6CE394198C10493:macro!MAC_
FE2A04B3399DB6B6:.end_caption" datatype="plaintext" restype="x-dgo-TEXT">
      <source></source>
      <target></target>
    </trans-unit>
    <trans-unit id="project!PR_B6CE394198C10493:macro!MAC_
FE2A04B3399DB6B6:.end_caption_p" datatype="plaintext" restype="x-dgo-TEXT">
      <source></source>
      <target></target>
    </trans-unit>
    <trans-unit id="project!PR_B6CE394198C10493:macro!MAC_
FE2A04B3399DB6B6:.end_caption_t" datatype="plaintext" restype="x-dgo-TEXT">
      <source></source>
      <target></target>
    </trans-unit>
  </group>
</body>
</file>
</xliff>
```

● For ease of reference, in this example the source text that is to be translated is shown in green. The translation application will replace the text in red with the translated version.

Importing the custom text

Once you receive the file containing the translated texts back from the translator, you can load this file back into Enable Now. Because the project and macro identifiers are encoded into the file, Enable Now will automatically know where to place these texts.

To import a translated file, carry out the steps shown below.

1. Select menu option **Tools | Localization | Import Translation File**. The *Import Translation File* dialog box is displayed.

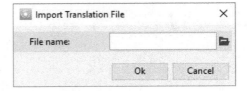

2. Use the button to the left of the **File name** field to navigate to and select the file that contains the translated texts.

3. Click **Ok**. The text is imported, and the text in the source language is overwritten with the new, translated text. Note that there is no confirmation message that this has been done, but you should see the object names change to the local language in the Workarea.

If we now look at our Step with custom text, it shows the local-language text, as shown in the example below (compare this with the pre-translation example on page 599).

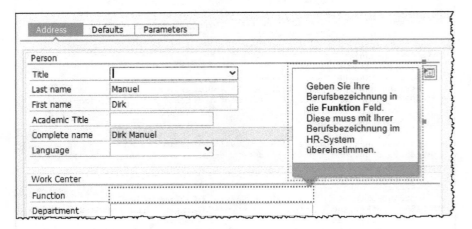

Of course, the actual application screens are still in the original language. If your users (of this translated content) will also use the application in another language, you will also want to replace all of the screens with translated ones. How to do this is explained in the next section.

Recapturing the screens

To recapture the screens in your localized simulation, you just need to use the re-recording function explained in *Re-recording a simulation* on page 92. In most cases you should be able to use fully-automatic re-recording, or simply press ENTER for each control to confirm the capture.

As an alternative to re-recording, you can manually swap out the screens as explained in *Replacing a screenshot* on page 152.

Once the screens have been replaced, you will have a fully-functioning, completely localized version of your simulation. The following partial screenshot shows how this looks for our example exercise.

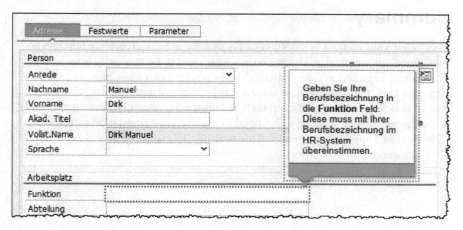

Localizing Book Pages

You can localize Book Pages in much the same way as you localize simulations. However, there is no Recording Dictionary equivalent for Book Pages, so there is no 'automatic' translation feature available. There are also no screenshots, so there is no need to use the re-record function. The process for localizing Book Pages is therefore simplified to:

- Export all of the source text
- Import the translated text

You do this in exactly the same way as for simulations, which is explained in *Exporting the custom text* on page 599 and *Importing the custom text* on page 604.

Given that this includes effectively *all* of the text in the Book Pages, you may wonder what the advantage of using the 'localization' functionality of Enable Now is, versus just getting someone to over-type the text in the Book Pages themselves. The primary benefit in using it is that Enable Now will extract all (and only) the *text*—regardless of where this appears on the Book Page (which could be hidden, or layered, or otherwise difficult to locate, depending on your animation), and then import the translated text into exactly the same place.

I would offer the caveat, however, that you need to pay attention to the size of the text boxes or other objects in which the text is located. Many languages result in different length texts (versus English). In particular, Chinese and Japanese tend to result in much shorter texts, and German typically results in longer texts. You should therefore go through the translated versions and make sure that your text containers are appropriately sized.

Summary

Localizing your content is extremely easy in Enable Now. Template text can be 'translated' automatically, leaving only custom text to be manually translated. This can be exported in a format suitable for sending to a translator, and then imported back into Enable Now once it has been translated. Enable Now takes care of making sure the translated texts are inserted to the correct content objects in the correct places. You may also need to replace your simulation screenshots with localized application screens. This is easily done through the use of Enable Now's re-record functionality.

Index